UNDERSTANDING NORTH EAST INDIA
Cultural Diversities, Insurgency and Identities

UNDERSTANDING NORTH EAST INDIA

Cultural Diversities, Insurgency and Identities

MADHU RAJPUT

MANAK
PUBLICATIONS PVT. LTD

First Edition 2011

Published by

MANAK
PUBLICATIONS PVT. LTD
B-7, Saraswati Complex, Subhash Chowk,
Laxmi Nagar, New Delhi 110092 INDIA
Phone: 22453894, 22042529
E-mail : manak_publications@hotmail.com

USA Office
8145 KOLB AVE, ALLEN PARK, M.I. 48101 USA
E-mail: rahul_upma@yahoo.com

ISBN 978-81-7831-239-2

Layout by
KHUSHNUMA

Laser Typeset by
T. ALI, Hamdard Nagar, New Delhi

Printed in India by
Nice Printing Press, New Delhi

CONTENTS

PURNO A. SANGMA
Former Speaker, Lok Sabha

34, Aurangzeb Road
New Delhi-110011
Tele: 23010123
Telefax: 23794263

FOREWORD

Madhu Rajput has done a very useful service to the society as a whole by publishing the collection of articles from renowned and eminent scholars and brought it in the form of a book "Understanding North East India." In fact, the book highlights various aspects which are not known to most of the people in the rest of the country. Any reader will easily get enlightened about the various aspects of different states, different tribes, their history, their origin, of the North Eastern region of our country.

The author has very skillfully divided the book into three Sections viz. History of North East, Insurgency and Society, Culture and Economy of North East India. Each Section deals extensively with the topics. For instance the Section dealing with History contains eight important articles such as Assimilation and Alienation of North East Indian States in Historical Perspective and Contemporary Situation, a Recent Perspective on the Prehistoric Cultures of North East India, Sino Indian Conflict of 1962 & Nehru, Arunachal Pradesh: A Matter of Dispute between India and China. Section II deals with

Insurgency in the North East. This Section is very important as the articles contained in this Section analyses the reasons for Insurgency, the mindset of the people of the North East, their alienation from the rest of the country, external influences on them, more importantly Inter Tribal conflicts in the North East India and the Problem of Social Exclusion. Understanding their ethnicity, identity crisis and the Ethnic Resurgence will help in finding a lasting solution to the insurgency prone North East. The third Section deals with the societies prevailing in the North East, their culture and their economy. The articles contained in this Section deal with the economic problems, cultural conflicts, the different tribes, their rich heritage, their pride etc.

I hail from the Garo Hills of Meghalaya and also belong to the Garo Tribe. The article Garos: A Study of Struggle and Accomplishments in this Section throws light about the topography, about the inhabitants, the history of Garos, social and religious institutions developed by the Garos, their matriarchal form of inheritance, about their customs, their beliefs, the efforts being made for bringing about the much needed transformation, with references from the books published by renowned authors viz. Tarunchandra Sinha's *Anthropological Survey of India* and Prof. B.B. Dutta's *Modernization of a Tradition the Garo Dimension,* Jhum A.G. *Khan's Cultivation and Societal Status*: An Enquiry of Garo Tribe Women in Meghalaya and Khan Ali Morshed's *Cheated out of their Own Land*.

I congratulate the author for the painstaking efforts she has made to throw light on the various issues confronting the people of North East such as alienation and the need to take effective steps to bring about national integration. It is a useful work which will help to understand North East from within.

(Purno A. Sangma)

PREFACE

In 1947, with independence a dream was born of a peaceful, self reliant India and later in 1950 when we adopted our constitution, it marked the dawn of a new era where we set the goal of making our mark in this world, not to repeat our past mistakes and become a global force to reckon with but today sixty two years later, it seems something has not gone according to the plan. There are still problems and discontent that threatens the integrity of the nation. To reach our full potential and implement the plans of the freedom fighters whom we owe our freedom to, we need to revise our strategy and remodel our act to get back on track to becoming a peaceful, prosperous, progressive India.

In our quest for harmony in a diverse nation we are still searching the answers to many questions, of which North East is one. North East is geographically bounded together except Sikkim; a region which shares a 2000 km long border with Bhutan, China, Myanmar and Bangladesh and is connected to the rest of India by a narrow corridor 20 km wide. Except the two valleys the Brahmaputra and the Barak where the bulk of the population lives, the rest is dotted with hills of various heights.

North East comprises of seven sisters and Sikkim has been added recently as the eighth state. The division of the country in 1947 followed by the great earthquake in 1950 and the Chinese invasion in 1962, and Naga, Mizo, Bodo, Manipuri, ULFA and other movements and insurgencies, some still ongoing, had an adverse effect on the development of the North East region.

The exquisite charm and mystic splendour of North Eastern region of India has beholden many hearts since time immemorial. Rich in cultural heritage and home to variegated flaura and fauna, it is none less than a paradise on earth. No human being with a sensitive heart can remain untouched by ineffable aura and appeal that the region emits. However this region is known for its ethnic diversity and conflicts which is a challenge for policy makers and administrators alike.

North East is rich in resources but is sadly neglected. The problems that plague the region did not occur overnight; they built up for more than half a century. This kind of damage does not heal overnight it requires time and patience and most importantly a sincere effort. Before we figure out the effort we need to analyze and identify the problems first.

The people of North East have lived with terrorism whether domestic or external, since independence. Insurgency paralyses the government machinery and halts the progress of the state in general as funds, resources and efforts are redirected to counter the graver problem in hand and even the important issues like education, employment industries, food and environment take a back seat in the presence of this dark omen.

There are no winners in this war, sides are predestined to loose from the beginning and that is the people of the state. Both the government and the insurgents, who claim to have welfare of the people as agenda, fail to meet their goal in reality. Infact the insurgent groups have no moral code to follow now; they have degenerated into money minting machines and don't hesitate to target even women and children.

To put a full stop on this proxy war, people have to be included in the effort.

We need to open a dialogue among the government, insurgents and the people. The grievances of the people must be heard and redressed. Then only we can hope to solve this problem.

We should keep in mind that India has always been a nation of "Unity in diversity". Even the insurgents are our people and their discontent-ful actions are a sure sign of a bigger problem lurking around the corner. Maybe we are missing the big picture here, it's just not domestic terrorism like everybody seems to label it and may be some new approach is needed, to bring the reform. We need a fresh perspective which identifies the problems and suggest better solutions for peace. And once we achieve peace all the rest we so desperately strive for, will follow.

Dreams have to be changed in realties and people of North East who are tired of stagnation and aspire to see their region emerge peaceful, strong and marching on path of economic, social and cultural progress will have to develop a proper strategy somewhat like their neighbour Bhutan has found in their theory of Gross National Happiness. Good governance, preservation of culture and heritage, economic development and environmental protection may be the answer to the manifold problems inflicting this area.

This seminar on "Assimilation and Alienation of North East Indian States in Historical Perspective and Contemporary Situation", conducted by Department of Western History, University of Lucknow (U.P.), India, on 20-21 Nov 09 was one such gesture to identify and discuss the past, present and future of North East region. It was great encouragement for us that several scholars working at this region participated in this seminar. The deliberations in the two day seminar focused on the history, society, culture, economy and issue of insurgency in this region. It was discussed whether the North East Vision 2020 which is an effort to dream, think and plan for the future of this region is an answer to the problems facing the North East region.

The seminar was significant in building up a consensus on the issues concerning North East as the saying goes "Remember it is drops that fill up the ocean". No deed is small, and when every body chips in his share, I am more than sure that North East will soar to new heights, it so rightfully deserve.

The proceedings of the two day seminar are now being published as a book which can be a useful as a research document. I hope that it will deepen the understanding of the region, so intricately a part of India. As the title suggests the book explores the process of assimilation of North East India, its journey towards development and the sense of alienation etched somewhere in the pshyce that gives birth to turbulence that the region is subjected to.

Regrettably not all the papers presented could be published. We trust that their authors will understand the constraint of space under which we are working. The fact that they could not be published does not diminish in any way their importance or their contribution made in the seminar.

I hope that the formal papers and discussions that took place served the purpose of understanding the North East better; however some of the most valuable discussions took place outside formal sessions. These were not recorded but were a one to one dialogue with the scholars who had taken the pains to come from all over India sparing their precious time for us. The discussions have contributed in no small way to the success of seminar and to the development of close affinity.

The acceptance of my seminar proposal by ICSSR, New Delhi was not only a great encouragement but also opened a new learning chapter for me. I would like to express my deepest appreciation for aid and support given by ICSSR, New Delhi and North East Council, Shillong, Meghalaya.

Our Chief Guest His Excellency Shri Ranjit Shekhar Mooshahary not only took pains of coming all the way from Shillong but his presence was an inspiration for all those present. I would also like to thank the honorable Vice Chancellor of Lucknow University Prof. M. K. Mishra for agreeing to preside over the inaugural session and for the support and cooperation he gave us throughout the seminar. The guidance given by the head of the department Prof. P. K. Srivastava who was also the convener of the seminar and the team effort of the members of the organizing committee saw to the smooth conduct of the seminar. Space does not permit me to name all the individuals who had played a vital role in the preparation and had so actively participated in the seminar. We trust that they know who they are and I look forward to working with them in the years to come.

I would only like to add that only awareness and discussion of any problem and a fresher perspective to the grievances of the people can bring about a solution and restore peace and development so that North East can rise to its optimum ability and pay its maximum contribution to the progress of nation.

This seminar would not have been possible without financial support of ICSSR, New Delhi, North East Hill Council, Shillong, State Bank of India and UCO Bank, Lucknow. I would also like to thank Mr. Afzal Ahmad advocate for his firing efforts during the Seminar and helping out to publish this work.

Finally I express my sincere gratitude to my publisher Shri M.P. Yadav for published this book in shortest possible time.

Dr. Madhu Rajput

LIST OF CONTRIBUTORS

1. Niru Hazarika, Professor, Deptt. of Political Science, Gauhati University, Assam. This paper was presented as the Keynote Address on the occasion of National Seminar on North East on 20-21st November 2009, conducted by Deptt. of Western History, University of Lucknow, Lucknow (U.P.).
2. Manjil Hazarika, Ph. D Research Scholar, Faculty of Arts, Leiden University, The Netherlands.
3. Dr. Salem Irene, Reader, Deptt. of History, Manipur University, Manipur.
4. Ranjana Mishra, Reader, Deptt. of History, University of Mumbai, Mumbai.
5. Professor Satyadeo Poddar, Head, Deptt. of History, Tripura University, Tripura.
6. Ajai Kumar Misra, Research Scholar, Deptt. of Western History, University of Lucknow, Lucknow (U.P.).
7. Amit Kumar Pandey, Research Scholar, Department of Western History, University of Lucknow, Lucknow (U.P).
8. Dr. B.B. Kumar, Former Principal, Science College, Kohima; former member, Executive Council, Academic Council and University Court, North Eastern Hill

University, Shillong; is the editor of Quarterlies, *Dialogue* and *Chintan Srijan*, Delhi. He has authored over 100 books.

9. Dr. Rajib Handique, Reader, Department of History, University of Dibrugarh.
10. Dr. Bhawani Singh Shekhawat, Professor and Head (Retd.), Department of Political Science, University of Rajasthan, Jaipur.
11. Rakhee Bhattacharya, Fellow (Reader), Maulana Abul Kalam Azad Institute of Asian Studies, Kolkata.
12. Anand Kumar, Associate Fellow, Institute for Defence Studies & Analyses, New Delhi.
13. K.N. Jena, Associate Professor & Head, Dept. of Pol. Sc., Tripura University.
14. Bindu Ranjan Chakama, Assistant Professor, Netaji Subhash Maha Vidyalaya, Udaipur Tripura.
15. C.D. Amar, Deptt. of Political Science, B.R. Ambedkar, University, Muzaffarpur (Bihar).
16. Swati Thakur, Research Scholar, Deptt. of History, University of Lucknow, Lucknow (U.P.).
17. Kumkum Singh, Head, Deptt of Psychology, R.G. (PG) College, Meerut (U.P.).
18. Anju Rawat, Research Scholar, Deptt. of Western History, University of Lucknow.
19. Th. Hethang (George) Haokip, Reaserch Scholar, Manipur University, Manipur.
20. Amita Sonker, Assistant Professor, Deptt. of Western History, University of Lucknow, Lucknow (U.P.).
21. Shalini Gupta, Associate, Professor, Deptt. of Commerce, MPG College, Mosssouri.
22. Dr. Gulshan Sachdeva, Associate Professor, School of International Studies, Jawaharlal Nehru University, New Delhi.
23. Deepak K. Mishra, Associate Professor, Centre for the Study of Regional Development, School of Social Sciences, Jawaharlal Nehru University, New Delhi.
24. Amar Yumnam, Associate Professor, Deptt. of Economic, University of Manipur, Manipur.
25. Achla Sonker, Senior Lecturer, Deptt of History, Dayanad

Girls (P.G.) College, Kanpur (U.P.).

26. Dr. Shubhra Rajput, Senior Lecturer, Deptt of English, Dayanand Girls (P.G.) College, Kanpur (U.P.).
27. Dileep Medhi, Professor and Head of Deptt. of Anthropology, University of Gauhati, Guwahati, Assam
28. Dr. Alka Chadha, Asst. Prof., Deptt. of Drawing & Painting, R.G. (P.G). College Meerut (U.P.).
29. Manjari Mehrotra, Research Scholar, Calcutta University, Kolkata.
30. Shilpi Singh, Research Scholar, Deptt. of Western History, University of Lucknow, Lucknow (U.P.).
31. Sakshi Roy, Research Scholar, Deptt. of Medieval and Modern Indian History, Lucknow University, Lucknow, (U.P.).
32. Dr. Pankaj Sharma, Lecturer, N.A.S. College, Meerut, (U.P.).
33. Dr. Rashmi Nirwal, Lecturer, R.G. (P.G.) College, Meerut, (U.P.).
34. Dr. Madhu Rajput, Associate Professor, Deptt. of Western History, University of Lucknow, (U.P.).

INTRODUCTION

*Shri Ranjit Shekhar Mooshahari**
Governor of Meghalaya

Let me first make it very sure that I am here as a man from the North East, as a state owner in the development of North East and its integrity with the rest of India. What I am going to say does not reflect the views either of my government or my official capacity in any way. This is the view of an individual who has worked all over India but who was born and brought up and educated in the North East and who has tried to combine the best of the culture that is there in this plural society of a big country.

I am sure that many of you have gone to the North East and seen the places, people and the lifestyle but there are many of you who may not have seen or visited but heard from the people about this region.

Many times I ask the young people competing in

---

* Inaugural Speech as delivered on 20th November 2009 in Malviya Hall, University of Lucknow (U.P.), India, on the occasion of National Seminar on North East.

examinations like CAT to tell me the capital of North Eastern states but they don't know. This absence of knowledge is a contributory factor to the distance that exists between the mainland and the North East. But if you look at the history of the North East particularly in ancient Indian history you can see the gigantic civilization, in particular in the valley. Let me narrate the North East in three chapters—the ancient, the medieval and the modern. In ancient times the North East was known as Kamarupa. Most of you may know why the name Kamarupa came. This is a part of the great Indian story that when Sati, the consort of Lord Shiva died due to vexation of her father Daksha, Lord Shiva was so angry and unhappy that he carried the dead body of Sati on his head and wandered about the world. Lord Vishnu followed him and chopped the dead body of Sati with a discus into fifty one pieces which fell all over the places. Most important parts fell in the North East. That is why the place came to be known as Kamakhya and Sati came to be known as goddess Kamakhya; the goddess of desire. But lord Shiva did not stop his penance and continued to wander about. The other gods feared that Lord Shiva may get the universal power so they decided to divert his attention, to dilute his concentration and they sent the Indian cupid Kamadeva to make Lord Shiva fall in love with it. Kamadeva succeeded but so enraged was lord Shiva after knowing the truth that he ruined his dreams into ashes with his third eye, the eye between his two eyes. That is why Kamadeva was reduced to ashes and thus the place was known as Kamarupa. Incidentally Kamadeva was restored to life. It is a story which indicates the spiritual and mythological integration of North East with the rest of India.

If you read Mahabharata there are number of references to the North East in it. It is said that Lord Krishna was so struck by the beauty of Kamarupa princess Rukmini that he married her much against the wishes of her father. Her father wanted her to marry someone from Kamarupa itself. So Krishna lifted her, brought her along and married her. Not only this, his grandson Aniruddha was also mesmerized by the beauty of the princess of Tezpur Usha. She was also forcefully married by Aniruddha. Aniruddha was captured by Usha's father and lord Krishna had to go to rescue him and bring him back along with Usha. So this shows the irresistible beauty of the women of the North East.

Even when Arjuna and Bhima were wandering during vanvasa Arjuna fell in love with the princess of Manipur Chitrangada and married her. Their son became the ruler of Manipur for a long time. Bhima, the mighty Bhima of Mahabharata met princess Hidimba, when he was in the hills of Assam and married her. Their son Ghatotkatch fought in the war of Mahabharta and caused a lot of destruction in Kaurava's forces. These are the stories that we have. But despite all these, in modern times people tend to know less and less about the North East. They are busy more with their technological development and political factors. Once there was a debate about Mizoram. Someone said that Mizoram must be father of Jagjivanram. This is the extent of ignorance that can prevail in the matters of North East.

Why is it that it is the most volatile territory on the earth? It is not only in India that North East is volatile; it is volatile through out the globe. Let me tell you a small story again why it is so. When god created India he had four boxes with him. There were people from North, South, West and North East. God said that there are four boxes, you can take any of them, open them and see what is there inside and you are going to be that. North Indians, as they are very smart people, got up first and picked up a box. They opened it, it was written- Beauty. That's why north Indians are so good looking. People from south opened another box and it was written-brain. People from west opened the third box, it was written-wealth. Then the people of North East picked up the last box. Inside was written-emotions. Without emotions you can not enjoy beauty, brain or wealth. You need emotion to enjoy life. That is why people of North East enjoy life despite all the devastations. And people are very emotional that is why they are volatile. Where people are emotional it is bound to be volatile. So this is the story that narrates, to an extent, the characteristics of people of North East.

It is a recorded history that Hiuen-Tsang visited

Kamakhya in 7th century. He was the contemporary of Harshavardhana in 606-648. While Hiuen-Tsang came to his kingdom, Harshavardhana was in Bengal. He received the pilgrim in Bengal and he was very impressed. From Bengal Hiuen-Tsang went to Kamarupa. Harshavardhana invited him to come to Kannauj for a religious discourse. At that time Hiuen-Tsang was with Bhaskara Varman in Kamarupa—Pragjyotishpur, the ancient name of Guwahati. After receiving invitation from Harshavardhana, Bhaskara Varman decided to march to Kannauj. It is said that Harshavardhana marched on the southern bank of the Ganges from Bengal and Bhaskara Varmana and Hiuen-Tsang marched on northern bank. Bhaskara Varman had 500 elephants in armor accompanying him. After ninety days of journey they reached Kannauj. There was a huge gathering of religious and spiritual people. That was the integration of the people of that period recorded by Hiuen-Tsang and in the books of history of Assam. So this is very surprising as to why the question of alienation has come now when there has been so much of integration and assimilation of people of two territories?

The next important period in the history of Kamarupa was the advent of warriors from Siam. Those days Thialand was known as Siam. Some tribes and a prince came in early 13th century. His force consisted of eight officers, 1800 foot soldiers, 300 cavalries and two elephants. They came, conquered, established themselves and ruled Assam for six hundred years till it became a part of the East India Company. They were probably Buddhist when they came but in over the years they became Hindus. The conquerors were overpowered by the absorbent nature of Hinduism. Hinduism had established deep rootes in that period. Later on they came to be known as Ahoms. The name came because the rulers had moved in from the land of Siam. Ha-Sam: Ha means land and Sam means Siam. That was the original Ha Sam which later on became Assam.

Ahoms had an advance sense of history. They kept a record of everything. So from the 13th century the history of Assam is recorded in a very thorough manner. In their six hundred years of rule many things happened but the most important was the influence of Hinduism on the royal family. The royal family and their subjects converted to Hinduism. But it did not extend to the hill areas of North East. Meghalaya, Mizoram, Arunachal Pradesh and Nagaland were free from this development because these were very inaccessible areas and Hindu Brahmins did not feel safe to go to these places and take Hinduism to these areas.

Hindus worship Shakti. Even now there are sacrifices, much against the spirit of rational religion. In many parts of North East animal sacrifices take place. It is time now that we try to stop it.

Assam became a part of East India Company in early 19th century, precisely in 1826 but ten years down the century there was a decline of Ahom's rule in Assam. For ten years there was Burmese occupation and this was the one of the darkest period in the history of Assam. There was untold devastation and misery of the people because of perpetuation of cruelty and injustice in general. With the British came the exploitation of oil, tea and forest products. English literature and Christianity spread. They built rail which we still use in North East. With independence someone has remarked that the partition of Bengal made North East even more remote. Earlier the farthest capital of North East was Agartala and it was linked to Kolkata by road which was 300 km long. After the partition the distance became 1,700 km. North East became surrounded by five neighboring countries. India has international boundaries with six nations out of which five bound North Eastern territory while it is connected with only 10 per cent of the land of India. This is what partition did to North East and problem came after that.

After independence the hill areas realized that they were too remote to be part of India. First it was the Naga insurgents who said that they wanted independence. It was followed by Mizoram. When these insurgents manifested in very violent form, Indian forces had to take action against them and the alienation started from that point. At that time some people in India thought that insurgents in Nagaland were influenced by Christian missionaries as they were all Christians. Subsequently insurgency sprouted in Manipur and Assam but who were the leaders of insurgents in Manipur and Assam? They were Hindus. They were as much Hindu as people in Lucknow or Mathura. Most of the insurgents in United Liberation Front of Ulfa and the other groups are Hindu exploiters.

These are contributory factors but the basic thing was that they wanted to preserve the identity of people. They wanted peace but not by assimilation with the bigger culture of India. Another factor that gave identity was a huge migration of people from across the border. They followed the theory of "Move to Open Space" since there are open spaces in Assam, Tripura and other North Eastern states. From across huge number of people came and displaced the local people. The difference between the displacement on the western border and that on the eastern border is that on the western border partition brought a war of displacement. Those who were Hindu and Sikhs came to India and those who were in minority religion groups went to Pakistan. It was a turn of a kind that was soon over. But in North East it continued for decades. It started in early 20th century and went on and brought about a great demographic distortion. People saw what happened to Tripura.

In Tripura people migrated in large numbers displacing the tribes who were majority at that time but are minority now. They are 32 per cent or even less than that. So people have become very sensitive to migration issue. The All Assam Student Union and the tribes feel that if this migration goes on, they will not be able to survive. So this was one of the factors that caused insurgency along with the discontent towards the government and outrage among the people. It went out of control and manifested in violence, destruction of the innocent people.

It has also been mentioned by the previous speakers that the treatment meted out to the North Eastern people when they are in other states, also breeds a sense of separation among them. Unfortunately it did not happen in the 18th century, it is happening just now. Once when I told my name to someone, he immediately connected it to Japan, then China and later to Thailand. When I told him that I was from Bodoland he did not know where Bodoland was. This is what happens and if it can happen to me I can understand what the poor students must be feeling because it is not a compliment, it makes you feel a sense of not belonging. So we have to be sensitive in these matters at least those who are educated. But I am sure many of you also do not know where Bodoland is. It is a territory under the VIth Schedule of the constitution of India in Assam.

Assam has a number of administrative and autonomous units under the State Act under the VIth schedule of the constitution. In order to give expression to the aspirations of the people the government created a number of units so that they can prosper according to their own genius.

Insurgency groups today have no ideology. They have degenerated into money collecting groups without accountability. They no more enjoy any popular support and right now all the states in North East except Manipur and parts of Assam are very peaceful. The example that Mizoram and Meghalaya have set is that an insurgency inflicted territory can also become peaceful. Mizoram had the worst insurgency and Meghalaya had insurgency for ten years but today things have changed for better.

There are facilitators of integration. One of these facilitators is the mobility. Large number of people, particularly the young people is going out of North East in search of education and employment. Likewise large number of people from rest of India is visiting North East for industry, business and tourism. So improving communication is important. While this communication improvement is going on, I am sure that the governance improvement is a matter of time. Positively we will have better governance in North Eastern states.

Let's come to assimilation and alienation. We have seen the history of Assam from ancient times. I think in democracy assimilation is not the right thing, it is accommodation. The right word for integration is accommodation. We have to learn to accommodate unity in diversity. Unity in diversity does not mean uniformity in diversity, it means that the diversity must be protected; diversity must be united as it is. It is not that red color will overtake the black color and black will overtake other colors. All colors must constitute the mosaic of diversity.

We are carrying the burden of the past mistakes. Let us not repeat those mistakes and carry forward that burden into the future for every language and culture is drawn from various angles of this heart. As we have tested the drowning swim of civil war and segregation, let us now emerge from that dark chapter.

Section I
History

1

ASSIMILATION AND ALIENATION OF NORTH EAST INDIAN STATES IN HISTORICAL PERSPECTIVE AND CONTEMPORARY SITUATION

Niru Hazarika

North East India comprises of eight states—Assam, Arunachal Pradesh, Manipur, Meghalaya, Mizoram, Nagaland, Sikkim and Tripura. At the time of independence of India the existing Manipur, Tripura and Sikkim were separate entities. Sikkim abolished its monarchy and became the 22nd Indian State on 16th May 1975. The rest of North East was Assam as one state. The northern and eastern boundaries of the region are natural barriers represented by Himalayan Mountains and Patkai hill ranges respectively. The Arakan Yoma of Myanmar and Chittagong and Tippera hills and Surma plains of Bangladesh lie in the south of the region. To the west of it lies West Bengal and Bangladesh. The notable point is that the major part of the region is surrounded by four foreign countries viz., China, Myanmar, Bangladesh and Bhutan. Therefore, the region assumes a great strategic importance.

Pre-British Period: Bishnuram Medhi, a prominent political leader and Chief Minister of Assam in his foreword on the book 'Discovery of Assam' gave an account of stages of growth and process of assimilation in this region. The Bodos, Kacharis and the Ahoms exercised sovereignty in Assam at different times under different names before the British. In those days people of the hill areas used to come down and carry on trade by establishing contact with the plains people and friendly relationship was maintained with them. One important factor should always be borne in mind that Assam was the meeting place of the Indo-Mongoloid and Indo-Aryan people in India. It is a fact that Assam was ruled for a long time by the Indo-Mongoloid or Mongoloid people most of whom are known to-day as plains tribal and that, as a result of a long contact of the Mongoloid people with Indo-Aryan, there grew up a peculiar blended culture and civilization in Assam which was adopted by the tribal people in the plains. Since then a process of mutual assimilation was being maintained here in Assam between the plains tribal people and other non-tribal indigenous Assamese people. Besides them a large number of Garos, Mikirs (Karbi) Rabhas, Miri (Mising), Lalungs (Tiwa) and other hill tribals who were already settled in the plains of Assam served as link between the hills and the plains.

Past history indicates a continuous attempt to harness the cooperation of the tribals in all enterprises whether of war or of peace or of economic development of the country. The tribals have freely adopted whatever they found good in our way of life, our language and culture. In the same way we have adopted many of their customs, institutions and practices. The Assamese people are composed of tribals and non-tribals and the Assamese language is a composite structure of words borrowed from Sanskrit, Persian and tribal languages. The tribals who lived in the plains maintained close friendship with the rest of the population. Even the Nagas were living in perfect harmony with the people of the plains. One may come to this conclusion from the following statement of Robinson, the author of the *Descriptive Account of Assam* (one of the earliest records in English):

> "The circumstances of the Assam Government having always raised a revenue from the imported salt of the hills, and the dependence of the Nagas on the Assam markets for the exchange of salt for grain or other articles, has contributed to a mutual good understanding between the two peoples. The Naga hills have in consequence been always accessible to the people of the plains; whilst the Nagas have on their part been always permitted access to the markets on the frontier."

"In the Naga Hills there exist different sub-tribes speaking different dialects, and one sub-tribe cannot understand the dialect of the other sub-tribe. The Assamese language serves as a *lingua franca* in the entire autonomous Naga Hills and the people living therein exchange their ideas through the irregularly spoken Assamese language or broken Assamese language adopted by them.

Similar contacts were established by the Assamese with the Khasis, Garos, Bhutias Nishis, Mishis etc. and maintained until introduction of British rule." (*Medhi: 1964*) In this context mention may be made of Saint Sankaradeva, a religious leader and social reformer who accepted disciples from amongst the tribesmen and Muslims and placed them on equal footing. For example, Chandsai, a Muslim, Govinda, a Garo, Paramanand, a Mising, a Kaibartta were his disciples.

Now coming to the political background of the region one finds that pre-historic and proto-historic period of Assam is shrouded in mystery and very little is known about it. Assam was known as Pragjyotisha in ancient times and as Kamrupa in the early medieval times. Modern Assam was a part of the ancient land Pragjyotisha. While the first epigraphic reference to Kamrupa is given in the Allahabad Pillar Inscription of Samudragupta, an authentic account of the land is to be found in the accounts of Chinese pilgrim Hiuen-Tsang. He visited Kamrupa when it was a strong and prosperous Kingdom ruled by a Hindu King Bhaskara Varman.

The political history of Pragjyotisha-Kamrupa may be said to have begun with the foundation of Varman dynasty which ruled from the middle of the fourth to the middle of the seventh century A.D. The Salastanbha dynasty which supplanted the

Varman dynasty ruled from the middle of the seventh to the end of the tenth century A.D. The Pala dynasty ruled for about 150 years. In the thirteenth century a new Kingdom—Kamatapura Kingdom came into existence comprising a portion of the existing Kingdom. Besides these two Kingdoms, there were 12 Bhyuans who divided the remaining portion of the Brahmaputra Valley among themselves. In the meanwhile Ahoms penetrated into Assam. A new dynasty of Koch was established by Biswa Singha.

The Kochs waged relentless war against the Ahoms for territorial expansion. The invasion of Assam by the Ahoms is a decisive factor in its history. The Ahoms, a Shan tribe wandered into the Brahmaputra Valley from Burma about the year 1226 and established themselves firmly in Upper Assam. Thereafter they began the policy of conquest and annexation. By 1700 they conquered the territories once included in the Kingdom of Kamrupa.

But the decline of the Ahoms began with the Moamaria rising in 1769. The three successive rebellions of the Moamarias shook the foundation of the Ahom Kingdom. The Burmese for the first time interfered in the internal affairs of the Ahoms at the insistence of Chandrakanta who was at the logger heads with Purnanada Buragohain. Purnanada Buragohain did not forgive Chandrakanta for his traitorship. He deposed Chandrakanta and placed Purandar Singha on the throne. Chandrakanta did not keep quiet. He sought the help of the Burmese. The Burmese invaded Assam for the second time and restored the throne of Chandrakanta. But the Burmese suspected the loyalty of Chandrakanta and therefore invaded Assam for the third time. Chandrakanta fled to Goalpara and sought the help of the British. The British declared war against the Burmese and annexed the entire Brahmaputra Valley including Sadiya Frontier Tract.

British Period: On 24 February 1826 the Treaty of Yandaboo was concluded. By this Treaty the British acquired the control of whole of the Brahmaputra Valley. Thus Assam came under the control of the British. From 1826 to 1874 Assam was a Commissioner's Division under the Bengal Government. But it was found that with so much diversity Assam occupied a geopolitically important position and possessed unexplored potentialities; therefore it should not be an appendage of Bengal. Sir John Lawrence therefore suggested that Assam should be constituted into a Chief Commissioner's Province. Sir John Campbell, the Lt. Governor of Bengal did not agree with the proposal. He tried to keep Bengal intact and at the same time desired to constitute Assam into a special Commissionership. He wrote, "When the strength and directness of power are required in any subordinate administration, it is best to place that administration under the supreme Government, so that it may, as directly as possible, enjoy the support and carry authority of the Governor General-in-Council. Assam and eastern districts seem to be eminently a case requiring such administration." The territories proposed to be included in the new administrative unit were the five districts of Assam, Kamrup, Nowgong, Darrang, Sibsagar and Lakhimpur, the Naga Hills, the Khasi and Jaintia Hills, the Garo Hills, Goalpara of Koch Behar Division and Cachar and Sylhet of the Decca Division with a total area of 54,000 sq. miles.

The people of Sylhet submitted a memorandum to the Governor General against the transfer of the district to Assam on the ground that they would be deprived of the Calcutta High Court and the rule by a Lt. Governor. However, on the assurance of the Government of India and the Bengal Government the Secretary of State for India agreed and allowed inclusion of Sylhet into Assam on 12 September 1874. (Rao & Hazarika: 1983)

Referring to the British administration in the region it may be noted that some of the British policies also caused adverse affect on the social life in the region. For example, the British introduced "Inner Line system." The Inner Line may be considered as one of the sources of tension in the region. It was a source of tension between the administration and the people and between the hills and the plains. The Inner Line Regulation was created by the British under certain specific circumstances. In 1872-73 it was found that there was an urgent need and absolute necessity for bringing under more stringent control, the commercial relations of the British subjects with the Frontier

Tribes. In Lakhimpur, specially the activities of the speculators in unvolcanized rubber had led to serious complications. Therefore, the Government came to the conclusion that it was necessary to take special powers and lay down rules for regulating the relationship between the plains and hills. Accordingly, a Regulation was framed by the Governor General -in-Council to give effect to this policy. This Regulation gave power to the Lt. Governor of Bengal to prescribe the line to be drawn. This line was called Inner Line in the tribal areas. Beyond this line no British subject and certain classes of foreigners could enter without a pass. The Pass might impose such conditions or limitations as might be necessary, upon the person to whom it was issued Beyond this line the tribals were left to manage their own affairs with only such interference on the part of the Frontier Officers in the political capacity, as might be considered advisable.

The people of the plains were not happy with this act of the British and complained that it was a device adopted by the British to alienate the tribals from the people of the plains and thereby promote their Imperial policies. In fact, the Inner Line aimed at two things—to protect the people of the plains from the raid and plunder of the tribals and in the same way to protect innocent tribals from the exploitation by the plains. Further, Inner Line was not established in all the hill areas. For example, it was established in Mizo and Naga hills not in the Khasi hills. Whatever may be the intention of the British it is found that the Inner Line Regulation generated separatist tendency in the tribals.

Another source of tension was formation of the "Line System" in the plains—rather the control of immigration. The main immigrants were tea garden laborers, Nepali graziers and settlers from East Bengal. In the beginning the immigrants from East Bengal were confined to the border district of Goalpara. They were concerned with the Char areas in the district. Later on, the immigrants sought land in other places in the Valley. Nowgong and Kamrup districts were the main areas for settlement of the immigrants. Gradually Darrang and North Lakhimpur sub-divisions were also under the wave of immigration. By 1916 the problem of immigration became serious. Therefore, the district officers drew Lines in Barpeta and Nowgong. Thus the Lines were drawn at the discretion of the district officers. The Government did not interfere with the discretion of the Deputy Commissioners. A colonization officer was also appointed in Nowgong to regulate the immigrants. (*White Paper on Constitutional Reforms, Dec. 1931, proposal 61, see also JPC report 1933-34,* p. 16).

At the beginning there was plenty of land for settlement. But as this was gradually absorbed by the immigrants, the new immigrants started buying land from the Assamese people by offering tempting prices. Further, the immigrants were industrious and magnificent cultivators. They had succeeded in bringing under cultivation the land which the Assamese world did not look at. The Line system restricted the settlement of the immigrants in certain areas. The main intention of the Line system was to protect the indigenous Assamese and prevent conflict between the Mymensingias and the poor indigenous people like Kacharis and Tiwas.

Dismemberment of Assam: The year 1947 is the watershed in the political history of Assam. When India was in the threshold of Independence some areas demanded cessation from Assam. One of them was Sylhet. Since 1874 Sylhet wanted to be separated from Assam and join Bengal. On 3 June 1947 Mountbatten announced that Sylhet should be amalgamated with the Muslim part of Bengal as it was a Muslim dominated area after a referendum (Shiva Rao: 1967). Accordingly a referendum was held and Sylhet joined East Pakistan. With the departure of Sylhet, Assam lost a substantial portion of its territory.

Almost immediately after the loss of Sylhet another piece of territory was taken away by Bhutan. It may be remembered that in 1866 after the conclusion of Bhutan war, the British annexed the Eastern Duars and attached it to Goalpara in the Cooch Behar Division of Bengal. In 1874 Goalpara and Eastern Duars were transferred to the Chief Commissionership of Assam. After India became Independent, the Bhutan Government demanded return of the duars to its sovereignty as they were essentially Bhutanese areas. The Assam Legislative Assembly and Parliament transferred these duars. (ALAP 1951)

In 1954 there were various demands for reorganization of Assam. The APCC, the CPI, the Tripura State Congress Committee and the Government of Assam were broadly in favor of status quo. The Government of Assam would, however, welcome the merger if possible of Cooch Behar, Manipur and Tripura and closer connection with NEFA which was constitutionally a part of Assam. The hill districts of Assam demanded a Hill State. This demand contemplated the unification of all the hill districts mentioned in 'Part A' of the Sixth Schedule including the Naga Hill district. The NNC sought independence from India and to remain aloof from the proposed Hill State. Then there was a demand for the formation of Kamatapur State, consisting of Goalpara, Garo Hills, Cooch Behar, Darjeeling and Jalpaiguri. The next demand was Purbachal State consisting of the area round Cachar.

The State Reorganization Commission did not accept any of these demands (*Report of the SRC 1955, para 679-723*). Ultimately, the recommendations of the SRC did not affect Assam. There was no addition or subtraction of its territory. But the recommendations of the SRC were not acceptable to the hill people. The Nagas continued to demand for independence from India. The other hill areas also continued to press for separation from Assam. The moderates among Nagas gave up the demand for independence but wanted amalgamation of all the areas inhabited by the Nagas, contiguous to one another and to constitute one political unit. In partial fulfillment of the demand, the Tuensang Frontier Division of NEFA was added to the Naga Hills district on 1 December 1957.

On 1 August 1960 Prime Minister of India announced in the Parliament that the Government of India has decided to make Nagaland a State, 16th State of India. During that time the language controversy in Assam drew the attention of almost all the sections of the people in the State.

Meanwhile the Government of Assam passed the Official Language Act announcing Assamese as the official language which aggravated the situation in Assam. In 1962, the State of Nagaland Act was passed by the Parliament and the State was inaugurated by the President of India on 01 December 1963. The people of other hill districts were encouraged by it and continued their agitation for Autonomy and ultimately the States of Meghalaya, Mizoram and Arunachal Pradesh were created by dismantling the State of Assam.

Illegal Immigration: The illegal immigration took a serious turn in 1979. The Charan Singh Ministry rocked by defections resigned and recommended the dissolution of Lok Sabha and midterm elections to Lok Sabha. Election was to be held in January 1980. The All Assam Students' Union and All Assam Gana Sangram Parishad demanded the postponement of election in Assam. The demand was made on the ground that the electoral rolls contained a large number of foreign nationals and it would affect the political world of the state. The All Assam Students' Union also expressed the fear of losing the identity of the people of Assam. The illegal immigration poses a serious threat to the security of the country. The AASU launched a movement against illegal foreign nationals for about six years. It received unprecedented support from all sections of the people of Assam. This movement caused a turning point to the political history of the State. For the first time in the history of Assam a regional political party, Asom Gana Parishad came to power and majority of the members of the Cabinet were ex-AASU leaders. But this change of political scenario also could not solve the problem of immigration into Assam.

Lt. General (Retd) S.K.Sinha, Governor of Assam studied the problem very deeply and submitted a report on illegal migration into Assam to the President of India, K.R. Narayan. In his letter addressed to the President of India the Governor says,

> "Large scale illegal migration from East Bengal/Bangladesh over several decades has been altering the demographic complexion of this State. It poses a grave threat both for the identity of the Assamese people and to our national security. Successive Governments at the Centre and in the State have not adequately met this challenge.

> As Governor of Assam, I felt it is my duty, both to the nation and the State I have sworn to serve, to place before you this report on the dangers arising from the continuing silent demographic invasion. I have also formulated my recommendations for dealing with this issue of vital importance. I earnestly hope that this matter will receive due consideration and suitable action taken to avert the grave danger that has been building up for some time."

Sinha's request to the President of India through the report was the outcome of wide discussion on the issue with almost all shades of opinion in the State which included politicians, leaders of the minority community, journalists, lawyers, government officials, both serving and retired, social workers and so on. He also discussed the issue with the Indian High Commissioner at Dhaka. His extensive tour to the border areas of Assam with Bangladesh and visits to Border Security Force and study on literature and statistics on the issue also helped to submit the report. He indicated the dangerous consequences of illegal migration as, "The dangerous consequences of large scale illegal migration from Bangladesh, both for the people of Assam and more for the nation as a whole, need to be emphatically stressed. No misconceived and mistaken notion of secularism should be allowed to come in the way of doing so. As a result of population movement from Bangladesh, the specter looms large of the indigenous people of Assam being reduced to a minority in their home State. Their cultural survival will be in jeopardy, their political control will be weakened and their employment opportunities will be undermined......"

IMDT Act: At the height of the movement against illegal immigration into Assam and immediately after the massacre in Nelie and large scale violence during movement in the perspective elections to be held in 1983 the Parliament passed the Illegal Migrants (Determination by Tribunals) Act 1983 (IMDT Act) on 25th December, 1983. It was an Act to provide for the establishment of Tribunals for the determination of, in a fair manner, of the question whether a person is an illegal migrant, to enable the Central Government to expel illegal migrants from India. But the Act invited conflicting viewpoints.

Some sections of the people, particularly minorities belied that most of the so called illegal migrants were Bengali speaking Muslims and the issue was unnecessarily blown out of proportion. They fear that in the garb of deporting foreigners, the Indian Muslims would be harassed. Thus they were against the continuation of the IMDT Act. On the other hand majority community of Assam and some political parties were gravely concerned about the large influx of illegal migrants and want their ingress stopped. They also wanted that the highly discriminated IMDT Act should be repealed. Ultimately, the Act was repealed by the Supreme Court of India. In this context what is desirable is that the policy of the Government, on any such sensitive and conflicting issues, must be above controversy and mutually acceptable solution to such burning problems. (Sinha : 1998)

Ethnic Pluralism

Assam

The total population of Assam in 2001 Census has been 26,655,528 out of them 3,308,570 persons are Scheduled Tribes (STs), constituting 12.4 percent of the total population of the State. Among STs Bodo represents nearly half of the total ST population of the State (40.9 percent), Mising (17.8 percent), Karbi (10.7 percent), Rabha (8.4 percent), Kachari (7.1 percent), Tiwa (5.2 percent) are the other major STs. Besides them, Dimasa constitutes 3.4 percent and Deori 1.2 percent of the total ST population of the State. The ST population in Assam is predominantly rural with 95.3 percent rural and 4.7 percent urban population. North Cachar Hills and Karbi Anglong Hill districts of Assam are predominantly tribal housing two important STs of the State—the Dimasa and the Karbi. As per 2001 Census, the North Cachar Hills has got the highest 68.3 percent ST population, followed by Karbi Anglong (55.7 percent). (http;/ / en.wikipedia.org/wiki/Assam) The State of Assam shelters sixteen Scheduled Castes and in the

Autonomous districts there are fourteen main Scheduled Tribes and thirty seven sub-tribes. In the rest of Assam excluding the autonomous districts there exist nine Scheduled Tribes. *(The Scheduled Castes and Scheduled Tribes Orders (Amendment) Act, 1976 (No. 109 of 1976, dated 18th September 1887)*

Arunachal Pradesh

Arunachal Pradesh can roughly be divided into several semi distinct cultural areas on the basis of identity, language, religion and material culture—the Tibetic area bordering Bhutan in the west, the Tani area at the centre of the State, the Mishimi area to the east of that, the Tai/ Singpho/Tangsa area to the far west and the "Naga"—like area to the immediate south. In between there are a few transition zones, such as the Aka/ Hrsuo/ Miji/ Sherdukpen area which provides a "buffer" of sorts between the Tibetic Buddhist tribes and animist, hill-tribal Tani.

Within each of these cultural spheres one finds populations of related tribes speaking related languages and sharing similar traditions. In the Tibetic area one finds large number of Monpa people with several sub-tribes speaking closely related languages, and also large number of Tibetan refugees. The Tani area shelters Nishi tribe, which has recently come to be used by the people to encompass Bangni, Tangin and even Hill Miri. Apatanis also live with the Nishis maintaining separate identity of its own. The central area accommodates Galo with major sub-tribes Lare and Pugo. In the east one finds Adi with many sub-tribes including Padam, Pasi, Minyong and Bokar. Milang, while falling within the general Adi sphere, are also in many ways distinct. In the east Idu, Miju and Digaru constitute the Mishimi cultural-linguistic area. The south/east is inhabited by the Tai Khamti and they exhibit considerable convergence with the Singpho and Tangsa tribes of the same area. Interestingly all these groups are also found in Burma. The Nocte and Wancho exhibit cultural and possibly also linguistic affinities to the tribes in Nagaland, which they border, in addition to a large number of migrants from different parts of India and Bangladesh. *http;//en.wikipedia.org/wiki/Arunchal*

Pradesh. Arunachal Pradesh shelters 16 Scheduled Castes and 12 Scheduled Tribes. *The Scheduled Castes and Scheduled Tribes Orders (Amendment) Act, 1976 (No. 109 of 1976, dated 18th September 1987).*

Manipur

Manipur accommodates 7 Scheduled Castes (Dhupi, Dhobi, Lois, Muchi, Ravidas, Namasudra, Patni, Sutradhar, Yaithibi) and 29 Scheduled Tribes (Aimol, Anal, Angami, Chiru, Chothe, Gangte, Hmar, Kabui, Kacha Naga, Koirao, Koireng, Kom, Lamgang, Mao, Maram, Maring, Mizo, Monsang, Moyon, Paite, Purum, Ralte, Sema, Simte, Sahte, Tangkhul, Thadon, Vaidon, Zou). The hills are mainly inhabited by Nagas, Kukis and small tribal communities and the valley mainly by the Meities and Bhamons. The Scheduled Castes and Scheduled Tribes Orders (Amendment) Act, 1976 (No.108 of 1976, dated 18th September 1976).

Meghalaya

The strength of population in Meghalaya according to 2001 Census is 2,175,000. The tribal people constitute the majority of Mghalaya's population. The Khasis are the largest group, followed by the Garos. Other groups include Koch and Hajong, Dimasa, Hmar, Kuki, Lakhar, Karbi, Rabha and Nepali.

Khasi is one of the chief languages of Meghalaya. Many words in the Khasi language are supposed to have been borrowed from Indo-Aryan languages such as Bengali and Assamese. Garo language has close affinity with the Bodo Language. (*http;//en.wikipedia.org/wiki/Meghalaya*) The State shelters 16 Scheduled Castes (Bansphor, Bhuinmali, Brital Bania, Dhupi, Dugla, Dholi, Hira, Jalkeot, Jhalo, Malo, Jhaomalo, Kaibartta, Jaliya, Lalbegi, Mahara, Mehta Bhaangi, Much, Rishi, Namasudra, Patni, Sutradhar) and 14 Scheduled Tribes (Chakma, Ddimasa, Kachari, Garo, Hajong, Hmar, Khasi, Jaintia, Synteg, Pnar, War, Bhoi, Lyngngam, Kuki, Lakher, Man, Mizo, Mikir, Naga, Pawi, Synteg), with 37 sub-Tribes. (*The Scheduled Castes and Scheduled Tribes Orders (Amendment) Act, 1976 (No.108 of 1976, dated 18th September 1976)*

Mizoram

Mizoram became the 23rd State of India on 20 February 1987. Its population at the 2001 Census stood as 888,573. Mizos are divided into numerous tribes, the largest of which possibly be Lushais and it comprises 2/3rd of the State's population. Other Mizo tribes include Hmar, Mara, Paite, Lai and Ralte. The Riang, a sub tribe of Tripura and the Chakma of Arakanese origin, are a non-Mizo tribe living in Mizoram. (*The Scheduled Castes and Scheduled Tribes Orders (Amendment) Act, 1976 (No. 109 of 1976, dated 18th September 1887)*

The Mizo community is an amalgam of several indigenous tribes who had their own unique lifestyle and distinctive dialects. The Duhlian dialect, also known as Lusei among the local people was the most popular language in Mizoram. This traditional Lusei language was interspersed with traces of other dialects like Mara, Lai and Hmar and their collective medley led to the formation of Mizo language. Subsequently the Christian missionaries developed the Mizo script. This was a significant milestone that marked the development of a colloquial dialect to a formal script. *(http;en.wikipedia.org/wiki Mizoram).*

Nagaland

Nagaland is one of the smallest state with a population of nearly two million. The tribes of Nagaland are Angami, Ao, Chang, Khiamniungan, Konyak, Lotha, Phom, Pochury, Rengma, Sangtam, Sumi, Yimchungru and Zeliang of which the Konyaks, Angamis, Aos, Lothas and Sumis are the largest Naga tribe.

Almost all the tribes of Nagaland have their own language. Nagas speak 60 different dialects belonging to the Sino-Tibetan family of languages. The traditional languages do not have script of their own. The Christian missionaries used Roman script for these languages. Nagamese, a creole language form of Indo-Aryan Assamese and local dialects is the most widely spoken market language. Every tribe has its own mother tongue but communicates with other tribes in Nagamese. http;//

en.wikipedia.org/wiki/Nagaland. In Nagaland 5 Scheduled Tribes live with several sub-tribes of Naga.

Sikkim

Sikkim is the least populous State in India with a population of 540,493 and second smallest area after Goa covering only 7,096 kilometers. Majority of Sikkim's residents are of Nepali ethnic national origin that arrived in the 19th century. The native Sikkimese consists of the Bhutias, who migrated from the Khan District of Tibet in the 14th century and the Lepcha who are believed to have migrated from the East.

Nepali is the lingua franca of Sikkim. Bhutia and Lepcha are also common. English and Hindi are also spoken and understood in the State. Other languages include Dzongkha, Groma, Gurung, Limbu, Magar, Majhi, Majhwar, Nepal Bhasa, Rai, Sikkimese, Sherpa, Sunuwar, Tamang, Thulung, Tibetan and Yakha. *(http;//en.wikipedia.org/wiki/Sikkim)*

Tripura

In Tripura 32 Scheduled Castes (Bagdi, Bhuimali, Bhunar, Muchi, Dandasi, Dhenuar, Dhoba, Dum, Ghasi, Gour, Gur, Jalia Kaibarta; Kahar, Kalindi, Kan, Kan, Kanda, Kanugh, Keot, Khadit, Kharia, Koch, Koir, Kol, Kotal, Mahisyadas, Mali Mehtor, Musahar, Namasudra, Patni) and 19 Scheduled Tribes (Bhil, Bhutia,, Chamal, Chakma, Garoo, Halam, Jamatia, Khasia, Kuki, Lepcha, Lushai, Mag, Munda, Noatia, Orang, Riang, Santal, Tripuri, Uchai), including 17 sub-tribes live. *(The Scheduled Castes and Scheduled Tribes Orders (Amendment) Act, 1976 (No. 109 of 1976, dated 18th September 1887)*

The discord among different groups defined by their ethnic identity or race claiming redrawing of the politico-administrative map of the region is a very sensitive question particularly in today's Assam. The socio-cultural pluralism is manifested in the existing society prominently. Disappearance of the British rule from North East India on 15th August 1947 could not make the nation out of danger caused by the socio-cultural pluralism. This question on North East India appeared very significantly in the Constituent Assembly Debates leading to the formation of a sub-Committee under the chairmanship of Gopinath Bordoloi on 27th February 1947. On its recommendation the Sixth Schedule was incorporated into the Constitution of India which provided mainly administrative autonomy to the hill people of the region to preserve their unique culture or to maintain the multi-color culture of the nation as a whole. Most probably it was the best politico-administrative strategy to be adopted by the country searching for "unity in diversity" without destroying the multi-color culture of the nation. Interestingly enough within sixty years of independence of India different social groups have started searching for "Diversity in Unity."

Gopinath Bordoloi occupies a special place in the heart of the people and the political history of Assam. He laid the foundation of the new Assam (undivided Assam). The concept of new Assam was an integrated state comprising all the hills districts in which all sections of the colorful population irrespective of religion, language, ethnicity, hills and plains would live in harmony and peace. With this idea in view, he initiated a move for bringing the tribals, both of plains and hills to the main stream of national life.

Immediately after the creation of Nagaland as State of India, Prime Minister Indira Gandhi made an announcement on 13th January 1967 that Assam would be further reorganized on the basis of federal structure. It encouraged even the plains tribals of Assam to conceive the idea of a separate State for them.

The All Bodo Students' Union was founded on 15th February 1967 at Kokrajhar. On 27th in the same month the tribal leaders from all corners of Kokrajhar met at Edinbari under the chairmanship of Modaram Brahma, an eminent educationist and a social worker. All the grievances of the tribals were discussed thoroughly in the meeting. The Bodos compared their position as regards the constitutional safeguard with that of the Scheduled Tribes in the hills of Assam and the Scheduled Tribes living in other parts of the country and found that the plains tribals of Assam enjoy minimum constitutional safeguard in comparison to Scheduled Tribes in other States of India, who enjoy the benefits of Fifth Schedule. They demanded a separate State of Bodoland in the north bank of the river Brahmaputra.

Bodoland Autonomous Council was created under the Bodoland Autonomous Council Act of Assam 1993. But the Bodos were not satisfied with terms and conditions of the Act and started agitation for creation of a Council under the Sixth Schedule to the Constitution of India. Ultimately, the Bodoland Territorial Council was created on the basis of a Memorandum of Settlement, signed on 10th February 2003 at New Delhi, by Hgrama Mahilary, Chairman of the Bodo Liberation Tigers on behalf of BLT and other Government officials in the presence of L.K. Advani, Deputy Prime Minister of India and Tarun Gogoi, Chief Minister of Assam.

The State of Assam faced another challenge when the Backward Classes started demanding ST status to them. During the rule of Congress Ministry under the leadership of Hiteswar Saikia as Chief Minister the process of granting ST status to them began. Just before the election to Parliament the President of India promulgated an Ordinance on 27th January 1996 for granting the ST status to the Koch Rajbanshi Community. In the Monsoon session in 1996 a Bill was introduced in Parliament to replace the Ordinance. But it faced a strong resistance from a section of MPs. Ultimately, the Bill was sent to a Select Committee headed by Amar Roy Pradhan. In Assam the tribal communities with unprecedented solidarity opposed the Bill. With the pressure of the Government of Assam and political parties Select Committee granted the ST status not only to the Koch Rajbanshi but also to Other Backward Classes (OBC) people in Assam viz, Tai Ahoms, Chutias, Morans, Motok, Tea and ex-tea Garden labor. While the matter was under consideration the Government of Assam provided the benefit to the Koch Rajbanshis. The Tribal Students' Federation of Assam filed a PIL in the Gauhati High Court challenging the Ordinance.

In this connection we may go back to the dawn of independence of India and find that the tribals in Assam were divided in two categories—Scheduled Tribes (Plains) and Scheduled Tribes (Hills). Geographical consideration was the basic factor for this division. With this division the problem was not ended, because the Khasi, Naga, Mizo, Karbi, Garo, Dimasa etc are found in the hills as well as in the plains of Assam. Similarly, Tiwa, Bodo, Deori, Sonowal, Kachari etc are available in the hills also, though they are the Plains tribals. While categorizing the Khasi, Karbi, Naga, Garo, Dimasa etc living in the hills as the ST (Hills) and the Bodo, Rabha, Deori, Sonowal etc as plains tribals, their counterparts living in the plains and the hills are excluded from the process of scheduling. What would be their status? The Government is silent in this regard. The administration might have thought the process of assimilation would be an answer to this question. But it did not happen. Though the process of assimilation began, it took a reverse turn with the political development of the region.

Reference may also be made to the Select Committee of MPs to make recommendations on the salient features of the law to extend the provisions of the Part IX of the Constitution to the Fifth Scheduled areas which held its first meeting on 15th July 1994. In the meeting it constituted a sub-Committee consisting of K. Pradhani, MP, M. Kamson, MP, Bandi Oran, Vice-Chairman of SC/ST Commission, Dr. Bhupimder Singh, Expert, Dr. B.D. Sharma, Expert, Sushma Singh, Joint Secretary in the Ministry of Rural Development, Convener, Daleep Singh Bhuria, Chairman. After investigating the problem, the Committee expressed its views on the problem as, "The Constitution presently provides Fifth Schedule for all over the country and Sixth Schedule for some tribal areas of the States of Assam, Meghalaya, Mizoram and Tripura in he North East region. The major features of the Fifth Schedule are a Tribes Advisory Council, Governor's power to adapt laws passed by Parliament and State Legislatures and making regulations for the Scheduled Areas having force of law and extension of the executive power of the Union Government to the giving directions to a State for administration of Scheduled Areas. The Sixth Schedule deals with constitution of autonomous district council and autonomous regions specifying for them legislative, judicial, executive, developmental and financial powers and functions....... It is noteworthy that some tribal areas in the country are covered neither by the Fifth Schedule nor by the Sixth Schedule to the Constitution. For instance the hill areas of Manipur comprising of 90 per cent of the total geographical area of the State is predominantly tribal in demographic character. In Assam the tribal areas have been left out of Fifth and Sixth Schedules to the Constitution. The tribals of the north plains of Brahmaputra have been unable to take the advantage of either the Fifth Schedule or the Sixth Schedule....." (Committee of MPs and Experts: 1995)

One important factor to be taken into account, in the case of Assam is that almost each village has its uniqueness. For instance, there exist forest village inhabiting mainly the tribal population, ex-tea garden villages in which people having roots in Orissa, Bihar, Chennai, Uttar Pradesh etc.

Another concept of administration tagged with the ethnic based Autonomous Councils created to Bodo, Rabha, Tiwa, Mising, Deorietc is "Satellite Area" Under this concept an Autonomous Council will consist of Satellite Areas of the Village Councils. It will be created in a village having more than fifty percent tribal population in the concerned tribal dominated area with a population of 6000 to 8000.

The background in which the "Satellite Area" concept originated was the demographic pattern of the State of Assam. The tribal population is scattered throughout Assam. For instance, Bodos are found in Kokrajhar, Dhubri, Goalpara, Barpeta, Nalbari, Darrang, Sonitpur, Kamrup, Nagaon, Morigaon, Dibrugarh, Karbi Angling etc. Similar is the case with all the plains tribals. Under this situation the concept of "Satellite Area" may face challenges. The conflict may arise between the Core Area and the Satellite Area relationship. When the demands come from all the Satellite areas for representation in the Apex Body, will it be able to satisfy all the areas? Further the members of the same community living in different areas may face different problems which can best be solved locally with the cooperation of the neighbors. One has to realize that these problems may be solved locally irrespective of the demographic pattern of the area.

Closely connected to the ethnic pluralism is the Sixth

Schedule to the Constitution of India. It has become a source of tension in the State of Assam today. In the Constituent Assembly the members who wanted to uplift the nation on modern foundation of law, individual's merit, secular education etc could not ignore the question of socio-cultural pluralism in North East India. Even the British rulers had to give special attention to this question. As one of the architects of the Constitution, Dr. B.R. Ambedkar said, "As far as the ultimate goal is concerned, I think none of us need have any apprehension. None of us need have any doubt. Our difficulty is not with regard to the ultimate, our difficulty is how to make heterogeneous mass that we have today to take the decisions in common and march on the way which leads us to unity." Any effort toward analysis of the situation in North East cannot be divorced from this explicit expression of Dr. Ambedkar (Shiv Rao: 1967)

Now let us look back to the Constituent Assembly Debates leading to the formation of the sub-Committee. The Cabinet Mission in its statement of 16th May 1946 stressed that the tribal and Excluded areas required a special care of the Constituent Assembly. The Constituent Assembly also realized that the Advisory Committee should be requested to appoint a sub-Committee to study the problems of those areas. Accordingly a sub-Committee was constituted on North East Frontier (Assam) Tribal and Excluded Areas with Gopinath Bordoloi as its Chairman. The other members were J.J.M. Nichols Roy, Rupnath Brahma and A.V. Thakkar. Later on Aliba Imti was co-opted as member to the sub-Committee.

The members of the sub-Committee visited all the district headquarters of the hills and interacted with the officials, village headmen, influential personalities, organizations etc to understand the situation in the hills of the region. They found that the concept of autonomy was expressed by different people differently living in different hills or in the same hill by different groups. For example the District Conference of Lushai hills (Now Mizoram) meant full autonomy leaving the issue of defense to the Government of India. The Naga National Council suggested that they would remain under the guardianship of the Government of India for a period of ten years and after that they would decide their own faith. The Khasi and Garo communities wanted to stay with Assam for the administration of those subjects for which they did not have competence and for the rest they demanded financial and administrative autonomy.

The sub-Committee placed its report before the Constituent Assembly and on the floor of the House a threadbare discussion took place on the Sixth Schedule which was recommended by the sub-Committee. The hill leaders were given an opportunity to participate in the discussion both from within and outside the Constituent Assembly. Everybody felt the need of making India a comfortable home for each and every social group for which each one would contribute to their capacity for the progress of the country. Thus the autonomy, integration and development may be considered as the basic philosophy behind the creation of the Sixth Schedule to the Constitution of India. (Shiva Rao: 1967).

But just at the last part of the 20th century the Sixth Schedule has become a source of tension in the region. The plains tribals of Assam started demanding ethnic autonomy within the framework of the Sixth Schedule. It has already been granted to the Bodos. The problem has not yet been solved.

Insurgency

Insurgency issue occupies a prominent place in the socio-political history of the North East States. At least 18 separate Islamist militant groups, besides ULFA and NDFB, have so far been identified by security agencies in the State of Assam. The Muslim United Liberation Front of Assam (MULFA), Muslim Liberation Tigers of Assam (MULTA), Peoples United Liberation Front (PULF), Students' Islamic Movement of India (SIMI), Adam Sena, Jehad Council etc are significant. The Muslim United Liberation Front of Assam is an umbrella organization floated by a number of separate outfits to carry out their activities in a concerted manner. Most of these groups are based in Dhubri, Goalpara, Barpeta districts of Lower Assam, Nagaon, Morigaon districts of Central Assam and

Cachar, Karimganj and Hailakandi districts of Barak valley, besides the Char areas in the Brahmaputra River.

Similarly in Manipur also a rebellion has been raging since 1964, although the violent phase of movement markedly increased in 1978. They demanded a separate sovereign state. The main factors for this demand were lack of development of the region, plundering of local resources etc. The Rebels also complained that they had the feeling of alienation from the Indian society. There are presently 34 groups including non-violent ones that demanded independence from India In 1999, many of these groups coalesced into an alliance organization called, "Manipur People's Liberation Front." Of these three most prominent are United National Liberation Front (UNLF), Peoples Revolutionary Party of Kangleipak (PREPAK) and People's Liberation Army (PLA). The Indian News Organization, Rediff contends: "as of today Manipur is the worst case scenario in the North East as far as militancy is concerned. Apart from the fact that there are more militant groups in the state than anywhere else- at least seven prominent groups operate in Manipur" *(http;//en.wikipedia.org/wiki/Manipu).*

Siliguri in North Bengal, the gateway of the North East state, is fast becoming a heaven for ISI agents. It shares borders with three countries—Bangladesh, Bhutan and Nepal. Its cosmopolitan culture has created a congenial environment for the people with different culture to stay comfortably. The arrest of thirteen persons suspected to be on the ISI payrolls for quite sometime, reveals how the subversive organization has hatched a plan for spreading its network in the North Eastern states to carry out their activities. *(Deccan Herald 3 January 1999)*

India shares 1,525 km land border and maritime border of 200 km long with Myanmar. The people living at the Indo-Myanmar border have a strong socio-cultural affinity, which is the legacy of the historical process of intermingling among the people of the border area. The ULFA cadres are reportedly involved in drug trafficking and they are using the sale proceeds for purchase of arms and ammunition. The Kachin Independent Army (KIA) and Burmese Communist Party (BCP), the Arakan Liberation Party (ALP) and other such attempts have all developed nexus with NSCN and ULFA for drug trafficking across the border.

While looking to the involvement of the foreign countries it must be admitted that insurgency activities depend to a great extent on the foreign help and guidance mainly for two reasons—training and organization of Camps. Further transfer of arms and light weapons and other relevant materials for carrying out their activities the militants depend on the foreign countries.

The Sixth National level meeting between the officials of (Ministry of Home Affairs) India and Myanmar devoted much of its time discussing cross-border terrorism in the North East. Apart from the question of promoting of border trade, they also agreed to check movement of militants and the narcotic smuggling across the Indo-Myanmar border. The two sides also discussed the possibility of exploring the ways of joint operations against the militants operating out of Myanmar resulting "Operation Golden" and it affected ULFA to a great extent. *(The Assam Tribune*, 29 Sept. 1999).

According to a report of the Home Ministry of India on insurgents in the North East India, Thailand has a flourishing clandestine arms bazaar located in the Pagoda Pass area opposite Karen state in Myanmar, and along the Ranong coast adjoining Tenasserim division along the country's coastline.

While unfolding the genesis of North East insurgents' relations with Thailand's arms dealers the report says that the NSCN was the first group from the region to establish its presence in the country in 1987. Several ULFA activists are also known to have visited Thailand for negotiating the purchase of arms and communication equipment. According to an official source, it was ironic that due to lack of good weapons and sophisticated communication aids with Government agencies, the militants were being able to smuggle their deadly arsenal into India. *(The Assam Tribune*, 4 July 1999).

The movement of arms to the region from different foreign countries must be controlled. Most of the arms used by the militants are foreign made arms. Here mention may be made of the recent efforts made by UNO through Arms Trade Treaty

(ATT). The summary may be quoted as, 'on 6 December 2006, 153 member States of the UN General Assembly reached a landmark decision, voting overwhelmingly in favor of taking first step towards a legally-binding Arms Trade Treaty to ensure comprehensive and effective regulation of international transfer of conventional arms.'

While looking to the sustenance of insurgency in the region it may be said that in addition to the economic problems, the success stories of independent and small kingdoms during pre-British period and heroic deeds of Maniram Dewan, Pioli Phukan, Lachit Borphukan, Kanaklata Baruah and several others including the contributions of Bal Gangadhar Tilak, Subhash Chandra Bose etc may also work as the spurce of inspiration to the insurgents because different people may justify this kind of activities or deeds differently. Further there may be misconception or misinterpretation of these deeds. The nexus between the political leaders and the militants, high militarization, certain laws like Armed Forces Special Power Act 1958, the Assam Disturbed Act 1955, the Nagaland Security Act 1962 etc, provocative remarks of the political leaders, killing and harassment of the family members of the insurgents, use of SULA as the source of information and also as means of counter-insurgency operation etc. may be considered as the contributory factors to it. It is also noticed that wrong handling of the problem of insurgency by the administration leads to sustenance of the problem. In most cases the problem manifested in the surface is the main determinant for the nature of counter insurgency strategy which is based on incomplete picture and inadequate information. Experience shows that every problem gets complicated with the inclusion of other related issues like ethnicity, language and political and money power.

As regards the impact of Counter Insurgency operation one cannot deny its positive impact. It has caused destruction of insurgent camps both within and outside the region. It has also made neighboring countries aware of the consequences of the problem. Several hard core militants have surrendered and engaged in self-employment schemes.

Is democracy a solution to the problem of insurgency in North East India? When army operation fails one has to think of adopting democratic or humane oriented device to solve the problem. Nobody can deny that the ingredients of democracy are fundamental variables to cure this ailment in the society. The democracy is by the people and it is also for the people. Abraham Lincoln had great faith on this philosophy of democracy. Today also we have realized that "Rule by the people" concept cannot be divorced from the concept of "Rule for the people." Closely related to it is another fact that progress of the human civilization depends on creative quality of men which flourishes in a democratic environment. This environment should not be allowed to be affected by the progress of science and technology or the process of modernization. In democracy the use of coercion should always be the last resort in settling disputes of any problem. Without public support or involvement it is not possible. Here one must know how to make distinction between forced support, spontaneous support and manipulative support. Democracy cannot exist on unexplained tradition. It survives in the free and fair thought and expression of views. (Mayo; 1960)

Conclusion

Socio-cultural diversity may favor division leading to the emergence of the problem of assimilation and alienation. Assimilation depends on persuasion, not on coercion because persuasion is based on convincingness. It has permanent value in the human society. Interestingly, India is well known for its humanism oriented culture throughout the world, but it is degenerating fast. Let us make our own people belonging to different professions, communities or otherwise aware of the significance of it. It is urgently needed in the global village.

The concepts of Decentralization, Autonomy and Responsibility require a fresh look in the contemporary situation. With the emergence of administrative State the question of decentralization in administration has become a very significant issue specially in India. Though the principle of democratic decentralization was insisted upon at the initial stage of India's administration immediately after independence based on Gandhi's idea of "Village Swaraj" it was the most neglected sector till Rajiv Gandhi, then Prime Minister of India made an effort on this line. He realized the importance of it. The centre should make effort to acquire from the grass root level democracy, while giving emphasis on the centralization in administration. The Bhuria Committee, 1995 also stated that there has to be substantial and meaningful decentralization. On account of absence of effective democratic decentralization to even the district levels, demands and agitations for separate States in the country have taken root in Jharkhand, Bodoland, Uttarakhand etc. Iniquitous policies and actions and economic imbalances have led to resentments among the deprived regions. (Committee of MPs: 1995).

Autonomy without responsibility and Responsibility without Autonomy has no meaning. Recent tendency of most of institutions is to divorce responsibility while insisting on autonomy. This is noticed in the case of Assam very prominently. While granting autonomy to the grass root level institutions due care has to be taken in this area.

The politics of modern State is heavily constrained by money power. North East India is also not an exception. Public decisions and behavior are controlled by money power. The youths must be motivated through education or other socializing processes to acquire intellectual power also. We may think of Territorial Autonomy instead of Ethnic Autonomy because Ethnic Autonomy is an unending process.

North East occupies a unique position as regards social culture. It is not only a very rich social resource but also a strong integrating force. Each community can enjoy, preserve and demonstrate its culture without affecting the culture of other communities. On the other hand it provides scope to other communities to learn and enjoy the culture of others. This is how assimilation may take place.

As regards the feeling of alienation administration must initiate the process of removing the feeling. The efficient and committed service of the civil servants is appreciated and needed by all sections of the people. Human Rights education in the educational institutions is also the need of the hour.

Further the concept of democracy does not confine to the election process only. It is a very wide concept giving stress on human values and dignity. The Preamble to the Constitution of India always reminds us of these values. It is for the leaders of the country to contribute whole heartedly to construct a path on which all of us can walk comfortably to the destination of the nation so that India becomes strong.

References

Constituent Assembly Debates.

Mayo, H.B., (1960): *An Introduction to Democratic Theory;* Delhi: Sterling Publishers (P) Ltd.

Medhi, Bishnuram, (1964): "Foreword," *Book Discovery of Assam,* Satis Chandra, (ed.) *Kakati,* Bholanath Hazra, Calcutta.

Shiva Rao, B., (ed.), (1967): *Framing of India's Constitution.*

Rao, V. Venkata & Niru Hazarika, (1983): *A Century of Government and Politics in North East India,* Vol. 1, "Assam," New Delhi: S.Chand and Co., pp. 1- 14.

Sarin, V.I.K., (1980), *India's North East in Flames,* New Delhi: Vikas Publishing House, p. 11.

Shiva Rao, B., (ed.), (1967): *Framing of India's Constitutions.*

Sinha, S.K., (1998): *Report on Illegal Migration into Assam* submitted to the President of India by the Governor of Assam on 8 November 1998: DO NO GSAG<3/98.

Report of the Committee of members of Parliament and Experts constituted to make recommendations on law concerning extension of provisions of the Constitution (Seventy-Third Amendment) Act 1992 to Scheduled Areas: Ministry of Rural development, Government of India; January 1995.

White Paper on Constitutional Reforms, Dec. 1931, proposal 61; see also JPC Report 1933-34, p. 16.

2

A RECENT PERSPECTIVE ON THE PREHISTORIC CULTURES OF NORTH EAST INDIA

Manjil Hazarika

Introduction

North East India is one of the most ethnically and culturally diverse areas of Asia. It includes the present states of Assam, Arunachal Pradesh, Nagaland, Manipur, Meghalaya, Mizoram, Tripura, and Sikkim. This area is strategically located at the junction of South, East and Southeast Asia which interconnects these three broad regions naturally and culturally. Due to prehistoric and proto-historic movements of people to this region from mainland India, South China and Southeast Asia, Medhi[1] referred to the territory as the Great Indian Corridor. Chatterji[2] believes that North East India is destined to play the most crucial role in shaping the Indian nation in the eastern part of the country.

As early as 1867, just after 4 years of the well-known first discoveries of prehistoric tools in Pallavaram, Madras in India by Robert Bruce Foote in 1863 and in France by Boucher de

Perthes in 1863, Sir John Lubbock[3] reported for the first time the evidence of prehistoric archaeological record from North East India in Atheneaume of London. Since then, several British administrators have contributed in a great extent into the research in archaeology in the pre-independence era. In the beginning, great amount of archaeological material, especially neolithic stone artefacts were collected by the British administrators during their administrative explorations. These findings were published in national and international journals and periodicals which proved the antiquity of prehistoric man in this part of the country. Mills[4] was one of the first who understood the necessity of archaeological research in this area and pointed out the importance of 'the spade, the chief tool of archaeologists' to be used in the research in Assam. But, a detailed review[5] of the research into the prehistoric archaeology of this region shows that the research is confined to basically surface sites and rarely excavated sites of Neolithic cultural period and it is true for even historical sites. So, this part of India still suffers from insufficient data for reconstructing the past cultures though it has long history of more than 140 years of archaeological research. The present status of archaeological research is surprisingly poor and it can still be considered as *terra incognita* compared to other parts of India. Here we shall try to bring out the current status of the prehistoric cultures of North East India.

Paddayya[6] aptly highlights the archaeological potentiality of this region in his discussion on the status of archaeological research in India. To express in his own words, "North East India, which has in recent years yielded pre-Neolithic cultural assemblages, offer excellent scope for investing diversity in human diversity in human adaptations. Forming as it does a halfway house between the Indian mainland and Southeast Asia, this area probably enabled early societies to develop individual identities of their own."

However, these are several factors which limit problem-oriented research with large-scale archaeological explorations and excavations in this region. Hazarika[7] has recently pointed out certain physical problems in archaeological research which are related to the problems of flood in the river Brahmaputra and its tributaries and huge deposits of sediments, extensive covers of thick vegetation, long duration of rainy climate, insurgency problem, surface soil-cover disturbance due to slash and burn cultivation in the hills resulting displacement of the context of the archaeological material, high levels of groundwater, poor preservation condition of the archaeological material in this region. Moreover, there are several drawbacks of archaeological research such as less academic departments dealing with archaeological research, relying on traditional approach; and lack of adequate technical knowledge, multidisciplinary approach, infrastructure and general interests in archaeology in North East India.

Palaeolithic Cultures

One of the major focuses of attention among the present Palaeo-anthropologists and Prehistoric Archaeologist is at establishing the earliest human occupation in various areas. Moreover, emphasis is given towards understanding the early human dispersal in the old world from Africa, the cradle of humankind. This issue emerged as the 'out of Africa' model implying early Homo species stepping outside Africa and dispersing to different parts of the old world. The formulation of this popularly known model is based on the recent evidence of early human presence in the form of hominid remain itself or the traces of their cultural activities in different sites. Recent data with absolute dates authenticates human presence in the Early Pleistocene time or even in the Late Pliocene outside Africa in Atapuerca[8] in Spain, Pirro Nord in Italy,[9] Dmanisi in Georgia,[10] Ubeidiya[11] in Israel, Riwat, Pabbi Hills[12] in Pakistan, Isampur[13] in India, Java[14] in Indonesia, and Longuppo Cave[15] in China. But, few attempts have been made to establish the earliest human occupation in North East India. Recently on the basis of circumstantial evidence, Hazarika[16] argues, "North East India as it connects Indian Subcontinent with East and Southeast Asian landmass may have acted as a possible mid-way from Africa to Southeast Asia through South Asia for the eastward dispersal of early hominids. Many early Palaeolithic sites are found in neighbouring southern China dated to early Pleistocene geological period." If North East India has acted as a corridor for these dispersals, great possibilities occur to have many unexplored sites dated to the early Pleistocene age.

However, presence of early Palaeolithic cultural material in North East India has remained as a debated issue in Indian Prehistory.[17] On the basis of tool typology, several assemblages have been placed within the context of 'Palaeolithic' in this region. One of the important areas which have yielded large number of prehistoric artefacts is the Garo Hills of Meghalaya and they occur in relatively younger deposits and mostly in the surface with Neolithic stone tools and potteries. Garo Hills in Meghalaya provide the largest amount of Palaeolithic stone tools, but the chrono-stratigraphic context of the material is still not well- understood. Here we shall discuss some important sites of Garo Hills of Meghalaya.

Sharma[18] in his field explorations in Rongram and Simsang river valleys of Garo Hills, Meghalaya located several Stone Age sites at Rongram Alagiri, Chitra Abri, Selbalgiri, Michimagiri, Watri Abri, Waramgiri, Chibragiri and Rombhagiri in an undulating area of 1500 to 2500 feet altitudes. A trial trench at the site of Selbalgiri, located at the terrace of the Rongram River yielded ground and polished stone axes and pottery in the upper 60 cm deposit and till the natural soil, Microliths were found. Typologically the artefacts are categorized into four distinct industries, (i) a flake and blade industry, (ii) a microlithic industry, (iii) a chipped stone axe industry, and (iv) a ground and polished stone industry associated with a crude handmade pottery. Moreover, he observed some roughly flaked discoid tools and stone axes "showing Lower Palaeolithic tool tradition." The site of Waramgiri has well exposed dolerite dykes which were utilised as raw material for making artefacts from "Lower Palaeolithic" to end of Neolithic period. The artefacts occur in the eroded surface and as well in the mint condition of the yellowish silt layer. A few handaxes and scrapers and points showing Mousterian character, were dug from the silt layer. No ground and polished stone and pottery were found at the site of

Waramgiri. Flake and blade industries are found at the sites of Michimagiri and Watri Abri, where frequency of blades is more in the Watri Abri site.

Sharma[19] narrates his observations on the Garo Hills industries as:

1. Both pebble tool and chopper element in association with the handaxe facies of crudely flakes Abbevillian and late Acheulian types present in this industry.
2. Elements of Levalloisian-Mousterian tradition present in the flake tools. The tools include usual types of scrapers and points and even tanged point of Aterian type and Mousterian types of flakes with thick blunt back.
3. Blade industry also shows well development.
4. Less development of the Microliths is attributed to unsuitability of dolerite as raw material for the preparation of Microliths.
5. Another significant observation is the presence of the element of Hoabinhian cultures, a stone axe industry dominantly found in Southeast Asia, based on the production of unifacially flaked axes from flattish oval pebbles.

Sharma[20] brings out the archaeological remains of Meghalaya and mentions about the Neolithic and Palaeolithic periods. He divides the entire prehistoric period into four series such as:

Series I: It includes artefact types such as Handaxe, cleavers, choppers, chopping tools, discoids, pointed tools etc. found at the prehistoric sites of Garo Hills. These artefacts are found associated with cemented coarse gravel in in-situ position or rested directly over the bedrock of sandstone and shale at Rongram, Rombhagiri and Chibragiri.

Series II: This series is characterised by the flake tools and majority of these flakes shows the prepared multifaceted striking platform with a prominent bulb of percussion. Regular tool types are scrapers, points and borers.

Series III: Blades and blade tools such as scrapers, points, blades and burins are the main components of this series. These artefacts come from erosional surface of the river terraces, hence the stratigraphic position is not understood.

Series IV: It is represented by microliths such as points, scrapers, borers, blades, bladelets and arrowheads made on fine grained dolerite.

According to Sharma[21] the Stone Age artefacts has similarities with the Early, Middle and Late stone age complexes of India. Moreover, the handaxe tradition of Garo Hills has close parallel with Padjitanian of Java, Southeast Asia. He argues for developmental stages within the artefacts from Early Palaeolithic to Neolithic cultural stages.

Excavations[22] conducted during March 1976 at the site of Michimagiri (25o33′ N and 90o17′ E), Garo Hills, Meghalaya, reveals that surface as well as the artefacts recovered during the excavation which shows homogeneity in nature and both belong to the same industrial tradition. The raw material is fine grained blackish dolerite which is heavily weathered with a patina of reddish brown sandstone like colour. Besides the prepared core technique as a dominant technique, hinged fracture technique was also used for preparation of the artefacts. Typologically, the artefacts reveal at least three industrial tradition; Levallois flake tradition as the dominant one, blade production and Acheulian tradition. The artefacts tools includes side scraper, end-scraper, borers, and utilised Levallois flakes, points, blades, micro lunates and leaf shaped points. The excavators concluded with an argument that in the absence of similar assemblage in Southeast Asia and as the Garo Hills material does not differ significantly from those found in Mainland Indian sites, an Indian origin of the Michimagiri artefacts can be postulated.

Sharma and Roy[23] discovered Stone Age artefacts in-situ at two sites (NBG-A and NBG-B) at Nangwalbibra at the confluence of the Simsang and Rongu rivers during 1977 and 1978. The site of NBG-A has yielded choppers, chopping tools and flakes of dolerite in a cemented gravel deposit. The site of NBG-B produced scrapers, points, flakes and cores of chert, without pebble tools and except the chert artefacts, other material are found in stratified context. Some of their significant observations are:

(i) The handaxe-cleaver tradition is not present at the site of Nangwalbibra by which it differs with other sites of central Garo hills.
(ii) The possibilities of typological and technological similarities between Nangwalbibra pebble tools and those of Sohanian of Northwestern India can not be denied.
(iii) Since the chert tools are recorded for the first time in Garo Hills, attempts should be made to place them in chrono-stratigraphic position.

The site of Michimagiri (III)[24] of Central Garo Hills within 25°30′ and 25°45′ N and 90°15′ and 90°30′ E at an elevation of 2500 ft above MSL has yielded "huge quantity of finished tool, waste flakes and cores indicating characters of an extensive factory site." A small trench at the site reveals one cultural layer of 01 meter thickness. The artefacts are mainly made on flakes and blades representing Mousterian, Levalloisian and blade techniques. Acheulian types of tools are smaller in size. Cleavers are made on flakes. They divided the industry into (a) flake industry and (b) blade industry comparable to the Middle and Upper Palaeolithic industries of India.

In 1969, Sankalia[25] visited Garo Hills and observed that the Palaeolithic elements might be present in the area. Later, Ghosh[26] strongly contradicted the occurrence of Palaeolithic artefacts in Garo Hills and he referred to the artefacts as "Neolithic debitage." Since then, controversy has been going on regarding the presence of Palaeolithic cultures in this region. Medhi[27] interprets the Garo Hills situation on the basis of his field work in the context of Palaeo-ecology of the area. The artefacts which are not typical Neoliths, have been grouped by him "under 'pre-Neolithic' with a clarification that the term is provisional and may be accepted for the time being as equivalent to 'Palaeolithic' elsewhere in India." Further, he prefers to assign "the pebble choppers and Microliths (?) found at Nangalbibra of Garo Hills to Neolithic origin." Medhi[28] surveys the state of research into the prehistory of Assam including the other states of North East India separately. He mentions his study undertaken during 1982 and 1984 in the Garo Hills and states that the tools in Garo Hills are not found in a stratified context and the ground and chipped tools are found together. Further, he comments on the 'Neolithic Debitage' problem initiated by Ghosh[29] that the chipped stone tools are not simply debitage, but purposefully knapped artefacts. Recently, Medhi[30] has claimed some Palaeolithic artefacts from Mizoram which need serious attention from the scientific community.

Similar claims (for a review see Sharma[31]) has been made in other areas too in different sites, but failed so far in establishing an undisputed chronology for the prehistoric cultures prior to the Neolithic. Due to absence of established context, these evidences of Palaeolithic cultural material are always neglected and generally not considered in the discussions on Indian Palaeolithic. Moreover, North East India is referred to be an inaccessible region during the Palaeolithic due to dense forests, hilly terrains and climatic conditions and interpreted as a geographical barrier for early hominid migrations and dispersals and unfavourable for their adaptations.

There is no concrete chronology for the prehistoric cultures of North East India because it has no C14 date from any other site except the sites of Tripura. Ramesh[32] proposed a chronological scheme for prehistoric cultures of Tripura on the basis of available stratigraphic data and typo-technological evidences, corroborated by radiocarbon dates as follows:

Holocene-Evolved Tripurian =Upper Palaeolithic-Early Neolithic	3450 + 110 B.P.
Late Pleistocene- Late Tripurian = Late Middle Palaeolithic	35690 +3050 B.P.

It is clear from the above discussions that the earliest evidence of the presence of man and the context of Palaeolithic in North East India is not understood with undisputed chronometric data.

Sharma[33] brings out another interesting evidences of a

group of artefacts separated from the collections from the collections now housed in Pit Rivers Museum of Oxford University and Ethnographic Museum of Gauhati University, which are made "either wholly by flaking or by flaking all over and grinding at the cutting edge." Excavations during 1977-78 at the Rongram terrace site with an altitude of about 490 m above MSL yielded artefacts bearing horizons. On the basic of the stratigraphic position and typology of the stone artefacts, Sharma assigns the cultural material to late Pleistocene and early Holocene period. Typo-technologically, these chipped pebble tools can be compared with the Hoabinhian culture of Southeast Asia and some influence of Southeast Asian culture over North East India during early Holocene period are suggested.

Ramesh[34] brought to light some artefacts made on silicified fossil wood from number of sites like Teliamura, Sonai Bazar area, Mohanpur, Sonaram area etc. in west Tripura. The assemblage is comprised of pecked and ground axes, adzes, grinding stones, points etc. The use of silicified fossil wood as a raw material for making artefacts were recorded by Goswami and Sharma[35] in Daojali Hading of North Cachar Hills, and recently there are many sites yielding fossil wood artefacts in Lalmai Hills and Chaklapunji area of Bangladesh[36] which may be considered as a sign for cultural links of this region to the prehistoric cultures of Burma, and Bangladesh. In fact, this entire region might have undergone similar cultural developments in the late Pleistocene and early Holocene period.

Another interesting feature of the Holocene period is the discovery of Hoabinhian artefacts, which may again imply connections with the Southeast Asian Holocene cultures. The excavator[37] at the site of Nongpok Keithelmanbi of Manipur observes a Hoabinhian stratum below the Cord-impressed ware layer. Again, some artifacts similar to Hoabinhian artifacts are found in Garo Hills of Meghalaya.[38] The Hoabinhian techno-complex[39] is defined purely on the basis of tool categories comprising pebble tools, utilised flakes, and a small proportion of edge-ground tools and bone tools, and in the later period pottery and fully ground axes and adzes also occur. The Hoabinhian sites are spread over a broad region from Southern

China, North Vietnam, Malaya, Thailand, Laos, Cambodia, Sumatra, Taiwan and North East India.[40]

Neolithic Food Producing Cultures

During the 1960s and 1970s, three important excavations were carried out, one in the North Cachar Hills (1961-1963) and two in the districts of Kamrup (1972-1974). These excavations authenticated the Neolithic assignments of ground stone tools and pottery. In 1963, Goswami and Sharma[41] carried out Excavations at Daojali Hading which have given for the first time stratigraphical occurrence of ground or polished axes and also pottery. These were so mixed up that a cultural division between using and non-pottery using period is not possible.[42,43] Sixty fives Stone implements were recovered from the excavations, sixty from the road cutting and seventy seven from the surface. The sixty five excavated ones comprises of thirty two edged tool; out of which fourteen are complete and are broken, twenty two grinding stones, four querns, six mullers, eleven quartzite pebbles and fossil wood. The raw materials used was shale, sandstone, quartzite and fossil wood. Shale was used for making edged tools and so also fossil wood; sandstone for grinding stones whetstones, querns etc. which are locally available. Out of over 600 potsherds, 595 were of Cord-impressed variety, 19 of Stamped Dull Red variety, and 11 of Brick Red variety. The majority of the potsherds are heavily weathered, and those few that were well backed are relatively in good condition. Shapes and forms of vessels are difficult to make out, as the potsherds were in small fragments.[44]

Rao[45] conducted excavations at the Neolithic site called Sarutaru in Kamrup district, Assam during 1967-73. Sarutaru lies on the top of a small hillock about 125 meters high from the foot-hill, situated at 25 km. southeast of Guwahati. The cultural contents recovered from the excavations include nine ground stone celts and potsherds. The celts are made on slate of grey to black colour sandstone of cream to buff colour and are manufactured in two stages: chipping and grinding. The stone tools are classified into two types: (a) Shouldered celts and (b) Round-butted axes. Several potsherds were recovered in association with the stone axes which does not have complete shape. The Pottery is hand made and made of clay mixed with quartz particles. The three ceramic types on the basis of colour are: Brown, Buff and Grey. The ceramics are sometimes decorated with cord-impressions or basket-impressions in the form of either parallel or criss-cross lines with paddle which is wrapped in cord or matting. The neck or rim portion is plain without any sort of decoration. The ceramic tradition is similar to the ceramics of Daojali hading of North Cachar Hills, Assam. Marakdola,[46] another excavated site at a distance of one kilometer from the Neolithic site of Sarutaru reveal wheel turned pottery of fine kaolin clay and a shouldered celt. Comparing both the sites of Sarutaru and Marakdola, another excavated site with a single cultural stratum of one meter thickness from which recovered a shouldered celt and wheel turned pottery of fine kaolin clay, Rao[47] argues for a provisional date about the beginning of Christian era for the Neolithic Sarutaru. Besides these excavated sites, there are many surface sites in different parts of North East India which have yielded a great amount of stone artifacts and pottery now housed at various museums and departments.

Compared to the vast antiquity of the Neolithic period, very little is known so far about the origin and developmental stages. The three characteristic features of the Neolithic culture in North East India viz. celt making traditions, Cord-impressed pottery, and rice agriculture, are more or less similar to the Neolithic cultures of East Asia and Southeast Asia. Dani[48] has demonstrated the stone tools of various regions from North East India with various parts of Southeast Asia and East Asia.

The Neolithic culture of North East India is distinguished by the predominance of shouldered celts and the characteristic Cord-marked pottery. The shouldered tool type has a sporadic distribution in the adjacent states of eastern India. Yet, as far as Neolithic period is concerned, there appears to be no doubt about the relationship between North Eastern India and the countries of South-East Asia.

From the above table, it is clear that the Cord-impressed pottery is the predominant ceramic ware of these sites. These

Table 1

NEOLITHIC TOOLS OF NORTH EAST INDIA AND ITS RELATION WITH EAST AND SOUTH-EAST ASIAN COUNTRIES (SOURCE: DANI 1960)

Zone of North East India	*Related Zone in East and South-East Asia*
Cachar Hills Zone	Upper Burma, communication through Manipur
Sadiya Frontier Zone	Yunan of Southeast China
Naga Hiils Zone	Burma, Malaya, Siam, Laos, Yunan and Cambodia
Khasi Hills Zone	Cachar Hills
Garo Hills zone	Cachar Hills
Brahmaputra Valley Zone	Shantung province, Hong Kong, Naga Hills, Cachar Hills and Garo Hills

excavated sites have yielded numerous potsherds, basically the

Table 2

CERAMIC WARES OF SOME IMPORTANT NEOLITHIC SITES OF NORTH EAST INDIA

Name of site	*Ceramic wares*	*Reference*
Daojali Hading of Assam	Cord-marked pottery Incised pottery Stamped pottery Plain Fine Red ware	Sharma[49]
Selbalgiri 2 of Meghalaya	Handmade, coarse and gritty in fabric and grey, grey-brown and dull brown in colour without Cord-impression	IAR[50]
Chungliyimati of Nagaland	Crude, hand made, Thick Grey and Red ware occasionally with cord-marked impressions and incised designs	Nienu[51]
Sarutaru of Assam	Brown, Buff and Grey in Colour with cord-impressions or basket-impressions	Rao[52]

Name of site	*Ceramic wares*	*Reference*
Marakdola of Assam	Kaolin Pottery Cord Impressed pottery	Do
Kamla valley of Arunachal Pradesh	Plain coarse ware Cord-impressed Coarse Red ware Stamped Coarse Brown / Red ware Stamped (square grid) Buff ware Grooved Coarse / Fine Buff ware Plain Brown ware	Ashraf[53]
Taba of Arunachal Pradesh	Plain (thick and coarse) ware Stamped (grid pattern) ware Irregular Corded ware	Do
Pynthorlangtein of Meghalaya	Handmade, Coarse Red ware pottery with cord impression	IAR[54]
Phunan Hills of Manipur	Plain wares Stamped wares Incised wares Cord-marked wares wares with circular spots and Appliqué wares.	Singh[55]
Napachik of Manipur	Plain ware Cord-marked ware Ring Footed ware Tripod Legs ware Spindle Whorl of pottery	Do
Nongpok Keithelmandi of Manipur	Plain ware Cord-marked ware	Do

Cord-impressed and other hand made wares. The earliest evidence of pottery in China and Japan goes back to 21,000-18,000 cal. Yrs. B.P. The early evidence of rice cultivation[56] comes from the recent discoveries at sites like Yuchanyan, Hunan Province and Xianrendong and Diaotonghhuan, and Jiangxi Province which date the origins of rice agriculture to more than 10,000 years ago. Thus the origins of pottery and agriculture can not be presumed to have evolved simultaneously. The origin of pottery is much older than the origin of Agriculture in East and Southeast Asia. The pottery of the cultures of East Asia and Southeast Asia is remarkably alike, and includes simple forms of cord-marked, combed, fingertip-impressed or incised vessels, often on tripods and pedestals. The overall homogeneity of the makes it easy to visualize a common ancestral culture, located quite close in time, from which all the descendent cultures of the Yellow river basin originated.[57] It is most likely that being the nearest area to China and the Southeast Asian countries, North East India was under the strong influence of these cultures during this period.

Table 3

DATE OF THE EARLIEST POTTERY IN VARIOUS REGIONS OF EAST, SOUTHEAST AND SOUTH ASIA

Name of the site or area	*Date of the pottery / site*	*Reference*
Yuchanyan site of China	14,810 + 230 14C Yrs.B.P.	Yasuda[58]
Miaoyan site of China	15,660 + 260 14C Yrs.B.P.	Do
Linzhou Dalongtan Liyuzui site of China	21,025 + 450 14C Yrs.B.P.	Do
Bashidang site of China	7540 + 80 14C Yrs. B.P	Do
Pentoushan site of China	9785 + 180 14C Yrs. B.P	Do
Xianrendong site of China	19780 + 360 14C Yrs. B.P	Do
Hemudu site of China	6310 + 100 14C Yrs. B.P	Do
Shimomouchi site of Japan	16,250 + 180 14C Yrs.B.P.	Do
Houtouliang site of China	13080 + 120 14C Yrs. B.P	Do
Nongpok Keithelmanbi of Manipur	4460 + 120 Yrs. B.P	Singh[59]
Koldihawa of Vindhyas	6570+210 B.C.	Pal[60]
Mahagara of India	5540 + 240 B.C.	Sharma[61]
Khas-Kalyanput of Tripura	3450 + 150 14C Yrs. B.P	Sharma[62]
Phung Ngugen site of Vietnam	3000 to 1500 B.C.	Do

Name of the site or area	*Date of the pottery / site*	*Reference*
Goa Cha of Malaysia	3020 B.C.	Do
Khok Phanom Di of Cambodia	7000 B.C.	Do
Kak Paam Dih of Thailand	4800 B.C. to 1500 B.C.	Do
Sai Yok of Thailand	4000 B.C. to 2000 B.C.	Do
Spirit cave of Thailand	6600 B.C.	Gorman[63]
Laang Spean of Cambodia	5000 B.C.	Gorman[64]
Non Nok Tha of Thailand	4000 B.C.	Bayord[65]

In the Eastern and Central Indian Neolithic scenario, domesticated rice and hand made pottery occurred at Koldihawa and Mahagara at the Neolithic levels.[66] The radio carbon dates from Koldihawa give a time bracket of ca. 9000-8000 yrs. BP and a C14 date for the pre-Neolithic Mahagarha[67] is 8080 + 115 BC. The occurrence of rice paddy field diatoms in the Lahuradewa[68] lacustrine sediments thus indicate that rice cultivation must have been actively followed in this region since 7,000 yrs BP. Presence of charcoal throughout the succession is indicative of slash and burn cultivation in the area since the last 10,000 years. There is direct evidence of human activity at the habitational site of Lahuradewa for the last 7,000 years. Phytolith evidence and Cerelia pollens in lake sediments also indicate rice cultivation and agricultural activity in Lahuradewa in the form of the slash and burn cultivation beginning in latest Pleistocene earliest Holocene, and well developed agricultural practices became prevalent around 7,000 yrs BP. Sanai Tal deposits (Rai Bareli district) give evidence of slash and burn cultivation and Cerelia pollens since about 15,000 yrs BP.[69]

The present day shifting cultivation in North East India, (see Roy,[70] Medhi,[71] Sharma[72]), often related to the Neolithic agricultural system, may be an adaptation strategy of the Neolithic people of this area. Roy[73] did an elaborate study on the types of artifact from both prehistoric and modern day slash and burn cultivation. He studied the agricultural implements from the Neolithic sites of the Garo hills, and the tools of ethnographic contexts. According to him, the tools form the Neolithic sites and the ethnographic situation at Garo Hills reveals homogeneity in function. Looking at the tools, it can be presumed that they were used for primitive type of agricultural practice resembling the present day shifting cultivation among the tribal populations. This kind of agriculture is insufficient for subsistence as we have noticed among the shifting cultivators. So, the exploitation of the locally available flora and fauna might be very important for purpose of consumption. The collection of various wild plants and both small and big game hunting and fishing (which is very common among the shifting cultivators), might have been the subsidiary subsistence activities of the Neolithic inhabitants of North East India. The future research in this aspect of shifting cultivation will be very useful for understanding the relationship between man and environment during the Neolithic period in this region.

There seems to be no agreement amongst experts as to whether rice was first a dry land crop, which was then adapted to wet conditions or vice-versa. This same problem remains in order to identify the earliest cultivation of rice in North East India. Most of the Neolithic sites of this region are located near the hilly areas, which are generally away from the big rivers like Brahmaputra and its tributaries; this may indirectly indicate that during the Neolithic time, rice was the dry land crop. However, it does not necessarily imply that the Neolithic people of North East India did not occupy the river valley. Due to the unsystematic research strategy and various disturbance processes like flood activity, we have no significant archaeological data from these river basins till date. Bellwood[74] discusses the uncertainty concerning the issues of variation within Oryza sativa. He made the significant observations about the domestication of japonica and indica species of rice and identified different areas like somewhere to the South, North--Eastern India or perhaps Thailand. Or was japonica rice domesticated along the Huai and indica along the Yangtze? Many possibilities suggest that domesticated Asian rice has more than one homeland. He specifically mentions that the probable domestication of native indica rice may have taken place in North East India.

Domestication generally occurs in a region where the wild species are found. For the understanding of domestication process of plants and animals, it is very important to recognise their wild progenitor species, and identify their natural habitat. Wild progenitor of some major crops has been identified through morphological, biochemical and genetic studies.[75] North East India is a part of the Vavilovian centre of biodiversity and origin of many important cultivated plant species and some domesticated animals.[76] Wild counterparts of many species of domestic plants and animals are to be found in this region. Hazarika[77] has recorded several plants and animals which are very likely to be domesticated in this part of Indian subcontinent, viz. plants like rice, citrus, banana, mango, yams and taro etc. and animals like cattle species, elephants, pigs, silkworms etc.

Botanists base their evidence of the origin of rice, a food crop of immense importance, largely on the habitats of the wild species; it is because of the presumption that the cultivated species have developed from certain types of wild rice.[78] There are various species of wild rice in North East India, such as Oryza rufipogon, Oryza officinnalis, Oryza perennis, Oryza meyeriana, Oryza granulata, Oryza nivara,[79] which are found in different ecological habitats like swamps, marshes, open ditches, rivers, swampy grassland, and rice fields. It is estimated that at least 10,000 indigenous rice cultivars are found in this region.[80] In this regard, Glover[81] writes, "India is the centre of greatest diversity of domesticated rice with over 20,000 (over of 50,000) identified species and North East India is the most favourable single area of the origin of domesticated rice." Intermediate forms such as Tulsibaon, Bogibaon and Kekuabaon are also observed in case of deep-water and waterlogged rice ecosystem. Considering the great varieties of wild, intermediate and domesticated rice found in this region, Hazarika,[82] argues for an early domestication process of rice in this area. The different methods of rice cultivation in the lowland areas of the Brahmaputra valley over different seasons of the same year further shows a very strategic year-round cultivation process in the flood zone. He[83] further claims that this region might have been an area of great importance for the emergence and developments of early farming communities based on rice agriculture. So far we don't have direct palaeo-botanical remains of cultivated plants in this part of India till date, but there is ample evidence of Neolithic ground and polished stone artefacts found in entire region in varied frequency confirms a full-fledged food producing culture.

Cord-marked hand made pottery traditions that can be seen among the present day potter communities of North East India. Cord-marked pottery making tradition is a living tradition among the Oinam, a Mao Naga tribe in the Senapati district of Manipur. They are still in a very primitive technological stage. They make pottery with a very crude technique of moulding and hand-beater methods.[84] The Cord-marked pottery from the archaeological sites of Manipur can not be compared with those of the modern day pottery, except in certain processes of making technology. The Nagas make earthen pottery by hand alone without the use of a wheel. Pots are produced by a few villages notably Viswema and Khuzama of Angami tribe; Thenyezuma, Runguzuoma and Kholazumi of Chakhesang tribe; Tseminyu village of Rengma tribe; Peron and Puilua villages of Zeliang; Changki, Japo and Longsemdang villages of Ao tribe; Tokikehimi and a few other villages of Sema tribe; Wokha and several other villages of Lotha tribe; Kongsang, Yali and Nakshao villages of Chang tribe; Wakching, Shiyong, Leangha, Chui, Choshachinguyu, Longkai, Sheanga and Tangjen of Konyak tribe; Nguro and Lungmutra of Sangtam tribe; Noklu, and Sao villages of Khemungam tribe, and a considerable number of villages in Phom area.[85] The study of handmade simple pottery among these communities can reveal behavioural aspects of the Neolithic culture.

Rao[86] discusses the ethnographic context of the area inhabited by the Khasis and the Mikirs. He describes the agricultural practices, living practice of megalithism etc. and brings out their importance in the archaeological context. This interesting cultural phenomenon of our early ancestors is the tradition of erecting stone (also of wood) megaliths is another focus of attention of prehistoric Archaeologists. The megalithic tradition[87] have persisted in the manner of disposal of the dead in certain old customs and beliefs till today. After cremating the dead, the ashes and the uncalcified bones are deposited in a stone chamber and a memorial stone is erected in many parts of North East India. Interestingly, this is a still living practice among many communities and closely associated with their social-cultural and religious life. Bezbaruah[88] has extensively studied the living practice of erecting megaliths among the Karbis as a post-cremation rite and drawn parallels for the prehistoric megalithic remains of Karbi-Anglong in Assam.

Emerging Issues

Due to the strategic geographical location of North East India which connects the East, Southeast and South Asian regions, cultural affinities can be observed in the material remains since prehistoric times. If North East India has acted as a corridor for the early human dispersals from Africa through South Asia to Island Southeast Asia then great possibilities occur to have many unexplored sites dated to the early Pleistocene age in this region.

On the basis of the use of fossil wood as raw material for making implements in a large area covering Burma, Southern areas of North East India, Bangladesh, with technological and typological similarities in considerably high frequency throughout, suggests an emergence of an identical regional prehistoric cultural tradition within these regions. Moreover, the discovery of Hoabinhian cultural material in this region also can be considered as another sign for cultural links with the prehistoric cultures of South-East Asia. In fact, this entire region might have undergone similar cultural developments in the late Pleistocene and early Holocene period.

These cultural affinities during the Neolithic period in North East India are basically based on the celt making tradition, Cord-impressed pottery making tradition, and rice cultivation. These characteristic features of Neolithic culture of North East India connect its counterparts in China and Southeast Asia.

Also, we find some similarities of these features with the Neolithic cultures of Eastern and Central India to some extent. The strong influence of the Neolithic culture of China and Southeast Asia is one of the prominent factors in the origin and development of the Neolithic culture of North East India, especially for the origins of pottery and agriculture.

The rich diversity of various plants and animals is one of the reasons for which North East India can be considered as an important zone for early domestication process. The domestic plants and animals and their wild counterparts requires more attention in archaeological research to understand the neolithic origin and development of early farming communities in this region. There is an urgent need for undertaking archaeological investigation involving specialist of other disciplines such as archaeo-botany, archaeo-zoology and geo-archaeology in the near future.

Notes

1. D.K. Medhi, (2003): "Potters and Pottery of the Assam Region," in *Earthenware of Southeast Asia* John Miksic (ed.), Singapore: University Press.
2. S.K. Chatterjii, (1970): *The Place of Assam in the History and Civilization of India*, Guwahati: Gauhati University.
3. J. Lubbock, (1867): "The Stone Age Stone Tools in Upper Assam," *Athenaeum*, June 22, pp. 822.
4. J.P. Mills, (1933): "Assam as a Field of Research," *Journal of Assam Research Society*, 1(1), pp. 3-6.
5. H.C. Sharma, (2003): "Prehistoric Archaeology of the Northeast," in *The Anthropology of Northeast India*, in T.B. Subba and G.C. Ghosh (eds.), New Delhi: Orient Longman.
6. K. Paddayya, (2002-03): "The Expanding Horizons of Indian Archaeology," *Bulletin of Deccan College Post-Graduate and Research Institute*, 62-63, pp. 291-309.
7. M. Hazarika, (2008): "Archaeological Research in Northeast India: A Critical Review," *Journal Historical Research*, Annual Publications of the Department of History, Dibrugarh University: Dibrugarh, pp. 1-14.
8. E. Carbonell, J.M. Bermudez de Castro, J. L. Arsuaga, E. Allue,

M. Benito, A. Bastir, I. Caceres, T. Canals, J.C. Diez, van der Made, J., Mosquera, M., Olle, A., Perez-Gonzalez, A., Rodriguez, J., Rodriguez, X. P., Rosas, A. Rosell, J., Sala, R., Vallverdu, J., Verges, J.M. "An Early Pleistocene Hominin Mandible from Atapuerca-TD6," Spain, Proceedings of the National Academy of Science 102, 2005, pp. 5674-5678.

9. M. Arzarello, F. Marcolini, G. Pavia, M. Pavia, C. Petronio, M. Petrucci, L. Rook & Sardella, R., (2007): "Evidence of earliest human occurrence in Europe: the site of Pirro Nord (Southern Italy)," *Naturwissenschaften*, 94: 2007, pp. 107-112.
10. D. Lordkipanidze, T. Jashashvili, A. Vekua, M.S. Ponce de Leo´ n, C.E. Zollikofer, G.P. Rightmire, H. Pontzer, R. Ferring, O. Oms, M. Tappen, M. Bukhsianidze, J. Agusti, R. Kahlke, G. Kiladze, B. Martinez-Navarro, A. Mouskhelishvili, M. Nioradze, L. Rook, (2007), "Postcranial evidence from early Homo from Dmanisi," *Georgia. Nature* 449, 2007, pp. 305-310.
11. E. Tchernov, (1995): "The earliest hominids in the southern Levant," in Gibert, J., Sanchez, F., Gibert, L. and F. Ribot (eds.) *The Hominids and their Environment during the Lower and Middle Pleistocene of Eurasia: Proceedings of the International Conference of Human Palaeontology, Orce,* Orce: Musee Prehistoriay Paleontologia 1995.
12. R.W. Dennell, H. Rendell and E. Hailwood, (1988), "Early Tool Making in Asia: Two Million Year Old Artefacts in Pakistan," Antiquity 62, pp. 98-106.
13. K. Paddayya, B.A.B. Blackwell, R. Jhaldiyal, M.D. Petraglia, S. Fevrier, D.A. Chaderton II, J.I.B. Blickstein and A.R. Skinner, (2002): "Recent findings on the Acheulian of the Hunsgi and Baichbal Valleys, Karnataka with Special Reference to the Isampur Excavation and its Dating," *Current Science* 83(5), pp. 641-647.
14. Sémah, F., Saleki, H., Falguères, C., Féraud, G., Djubiantono, T., "Did Early Man reach Java during the Late Pliocene?" *Journal of Archaeological Science*, 27, 2000, pp. 763-769.
15. H. Wanpo, R. Ciochon, G. Yumin, R. Larick, F. Qiren, H. Schwarcz, C. Yonge, J. de Vos and W. Rink, (1995): "Early Homo and associated artefacts from China," *Nature*, 378, pp. 275- 278.
16. M. Hazarika, (2008): "Archaeological Research in Northeast India: A Critical Review," *Journal Historical Research,* Annual Publications of the Department of History, Dibrugarh University: Dibrugarh, pp. 1-14.
17. M. Hazarika, (2008): "Palaeolithic Cultural Evidences in

Northeast India: A Survey," paper presented at the International Workshop on Plio-Pleistocene Environments and Hominin Adaptations in India, Bhopal, 1st to 5th December, 2008, Stone Age Institute, USA and Panjab University, India.

18. T.C. Sharma, (1975-76): "Recent Archaeological Discoveries in Northeastern India," *Puratattva*, 7, pp. 17-19.
19. Ibid.
20. H.C. Sharma, "Archaeological Findings in Meghalaya," *Bulletin of Assam State Museum*, 1, 1975.
21. Ibid.
22. H.C. Sharma and S.K. Roy , (1985): "On the Discovery of a Pebble-Tool Industry in the Garo Hills, Meghalaya," in V.N. Misra and P. Bellwood (eds.), *Recent Advances in Indo-Pacific Prehistory*, New Delhi: Oxford and IBH Publishing Co.
23. Ibid.
24. M. Sonowal and T.C. Sharma, (1974): "On the Evidence of Flake and Blade Industries in the Michimagiri (III) area of the Central Garo Hills, Meghalaya," Proceedings of the Annual Conference of the ISPQS and IAS, P. Shingh and Tandon O.P. (eds.), Bharat Kala Bhavan, BHU, 1986.
25. H.D. Sankalia, (1974): *Prehistory and Protohistory of India and Pakistan*, Pune: Deccan College, 1974.
26. A.K. Ghosh, (1978): "What Happens When Cultural and Biological Adaptability of Man Fails etc.," in *Cultural and Biological Adaptability of Man with Special Reference of Northeast India*, Dibrugarh: Dibrugarh University.
27. D.K. Medhi, (1989): "Palaeolithic Remains in the Garo Hills, Meghalaya," in *History and Archaeology*, B. Chatterjee (ed.), Ramanand Vidya Bhawan.
28. D.K. Medhi, (1990): "Prehistory of Assam," *Asian Perspective*, 29(1): pp. 37-44.
29. A.K. Ghosh, (1978): "What Happens When Cultural and Biological Adaptability of Man Fails etc.," in *Cultural and Biological Adaptability of Man with Special Reference of Northeast India*, Dibrugarh: Dibrugarh University.
30. D.K. Medhi, (2006): Boichhingpuii and P. Sarma "Palaeolithic Cultural Evidence in Mizoram, India," paper presented at the 18th Indo-Pacific Prehistory Association Congress, 20-26 March 2006.
31. H.C. Sharma, "Prehistoric Archaeology of the Northeast," in *The Anthropology of Northeast India*, T.B. Subba and G.C. Ghosh, (eds.), New Delhi: Orient Longman. 2003.

32. N.R. Ramesh, (1989): *A Study on Geomorphology, Quaternary Geology and Associated Cultural Remains of West Tripura District,* Unpublished Ph.D. Thesis, Guwahati: Gauhati University.
33. T.C. Sharma, (1988): "Discovery of Hoabinhian Cultural Relics in Northeast India," *Adaptation and Other Essays,* in N. C. Ghosh and S. Chakraborty (eds.), Visva Bharati, Santiniketan, pp. 136-139.
34. N.R. Ramesh, (1989): *A Study on Geomorphology, Quaternary Geology and Associated Cultural Remains of West Tripura District,* Unpublished Ph.D. Thesis, Guwahati: Gauhati University.
35. M.C. Goswami and T.C. Sharma, (1963): "A Brief Report on the Investigation into Prehistoric Archaeology in the N.C. Hills," *Journal of the Gauhati University,* 13(2), 1963, pp. 63-66.
36. J.S. Roy and S.M.K. Ahsan, (2007): "Raw Material and Technology of Stone Age Artefacts from Lalmai Hills and Chaklapunji Area," *Pratnatattva* 13, 2007, pp. 49-56.
37. O.K. Singh, (1993): *Stone Age Culture of Manipur,* Unpublished Ph.D. Thesis, Manipur: University of Manipur.
38. IAR: *Indian Archaeology: A Review—1965-66.* Annual Bulletin of Archaeological Survey of India, New Delhi.
39. P. Bellwood, (1978): *Man's Conquest in the Pacific: The Prehistory of Southeast Asia and Oceania,* Auckland: William Collins Publishers Ltd.
40. T.C. Sharma, (1988): "Discovery of Hoabinhian Cultural Relics in Northeast India," in *Adaptation and Other Essays, Proceedings of the Archaeological Conference,* in N.C. Ghosh and S. Chakrabarty, (eds.), Research Publications, Vishwa Bharati, Shantiniketan.
41. M.C. Goswami and T.C. Sharma, (1963): "A Brief Report on the Investigation into Prehistoric Archaeology in the N.C. Hills," *Journal of the Gauhati University,* 13(2), pp. 63-66.
42. IAR, "Indian Archaeology: A Review—1962-63," *Annual Bulletin of Archaeological Survey of India,* New Delhi.
43. T.C. Sharma, (1967): "A Note of the Neolithic Pottery of Assam," *Man,* 2(1), pp. 126-128.
44. Ibid.
45. S.N. Rao, (1973): "The Neolithic Culture of Sarutaru, Assam," *Bulletin of the Department of Anthropology,* Dibrugarh University, 2, pp. 1-9.
46. S.N. Rao, (1977): "Excavation at Sarutaru: A Neolithic Site in Assam," *Man and Environment,* 1: pp. 39-42.
47. Ibid.
48. A.H. Dani, (1960): *Prehistory and Protohistory of Eastern India,*

Calcutta: Firma L. Mukhopadhyay.

49. Sharma, T.C., (1967): "A Note of the Neolithic Pottery of Assam," *Man*, 2(1), pp. 126-128.
50. IAR, *Indian Archaeology: A Review—1967-68*, Annual Bulletin of Archaeological Survey of India, New Delhi.
51. V. Nienu, (1974): "Recent Prehistoric Discoveries in Nagaland—a Survey," *Highlander*, Research Bulletin of Dept. of Art and Culture, Govt. of Nagaland, Vol. II, No. 1.
52. S.N. Rao, (1977): "Excavation at Sarutaru: A Neolithic Site in Assam," *Man and Environment*, 1: pp. 39-42.
53. Ashraf, A.A., (1990): *Prehistoric Arunachal: A Study on Prehistory and Ethnoarchaeology of Kamla Valley*, Itanagar: Directorate of Research, Government of Arunachal Pradesh.
54. IAR, *Indian Archaeology: A Review—1992-93*, Annual Bulletin of Archaeological Survey of India, New Delhi.
55. O.K. Singh, (1993): *Stone Age Culture of Manipur*, Unpublished Ph.D. Thesis, Manipur: University of Manipur.
56. Y. Yasuda, (2002): "Origins of Pottery and Agriculture in East Asia," in *The Origins of Pottery and Agriculture*, Y. Yasuda (ed.), Japan: International Research Center for Japanese Studies.
57. P. Bellwood, (2005): *First Farmers: The Origins of Agricultural Societies*, UK: Blackwell Publishing.
58. Y. Yasuda, "Origins of Pottery and Agriculture in East Asia," in *The Origins of Pottery and Agriculture*, Y. Yasuda (ed.), Japan: International Research Center for Japanese Studies.
59. O.K. Singh, (1983): *Archaeology in Manipur, Naba Chik: A Stone Age Site in the Manipur Valley*, Imphal: State Archaeology, Government of Manipur, 1983.
60. J.N. Pal, (1987): "Neolithic Cord-impressed Ware of the Vindhyas," *Man and Environment*, XI: pp. 61-65.
61. G.R. Sharma, V.D. Misra, D. Mandal, B.B. Misra and J.N. Pal, (1980): *Beginnings of Agriculture*, Allahabad: Abhinav Prakashan.
62. D.P. Sharma, (2004): "Prehistoric Cultures of Northeast India and Southeast Asia: A Comparative Study," in *Indian Prehistory and Protohistory: Recent Studies* (Proceeding of R.B. Foote Memorial National Seminar (1995) Directorate of Archaeology and Museum, Andhra Pradesh.
63. C. Gorman, (1970): "Excavations at Spirit Cave, North Thailand: Some Interim Interpretations," *Asian Perspectives*, 13, pp. 79-108.
64. C. Gorman, (1971): "The Hoabinhian and After: Subsistence Pattern in Southeast Asia During the Late Pleistocene and Early Recent Periods," *World Archaeology* II(3), pp. 300-320.

65. D. Bayard, (1970): "Excavation at Non Nok Tha, Northeast Thailand," *Asian Perspective* XIII.
66. D.P. Agrawal, (2002): "The Earliest Agriculture and Pottery in South Asia," in *The Origins of Pottery and Agriculture*, Y. Yasuda (ed.), Japan: International Research Center for Japanese Studies.
67. G.R. Sharma, V.D. Misra, D. Mandal, B.B. Misra and J.N. Pal, (1980): *Beginnings of Agriculture*, Allahabad: Abhinav Prakashan.
68. V. Prasad, M. Sharma, A. Saxena, I.B. Singh, (2004): *Fossil Diatom Assemblages from Lahuradewa Lacustrine Sediments as Clues for Human Activity*, (Abstract) Paper Presented in the Joint Annual Conferences of IAS, ISPQS and IHCS and National Seminar on the Archaeology of the Ganga Plain, 28-31 December.
69. Ibid.
70. S.K. Roy, (1981): "Aspect of Neolithic Agriculture and Shifting Cultivation, Garo Hills, Meghalaya," *Asian Perspective*, 14(2): pp. 193-219.
71. D.K. Medhi, (1998): "The Garo and Their Material Culture: A study Based on Ethnoarchaeological Approach," *Man and Environment*, 7: pp. 70-77.
72. T.C. Sharma, (1990): "The Prehistoric Background of Shifting Cultivation," In *Shifting Cultivation in Northeast India*, D.N. Majumdar (ed.), Guwahati: Osmos Publications.
73. S.K. Roy, (1981): "Aspect of Neolithic Agriculture and Shifting Cultivation, Garo Hills, Meghalaya," *Asian Perspective*, 14(2): pp. 193-219.
74. P. Bellwood, (2005): *First Farmers: The Origins of Agricultural Societies*, UK: Blackwell Publishing.
75. E.D. Buckler, J.M. Thornsberry, and S. Kresovich, (2001): "Molecular Diversity, Structure and Domestication of Grasses," *Genetic Resources*, Vol. 77, pp. 213-218.
76. K.C. Agarwal, (1996): *Biodiversity*, Agr: Agra Botanical Publishers, India.
77. M. Hazarika, *Northeast India: A Potential Zone for Early Domestication of Plants and Animals*, paper presented at the 6th World Archaeological Congress (WAC-6), during 29th June to 4th July, 2008 at the University College Dublin, Ireland.
78. D.H. Grist, (1975): *Rice*, Longman, New York.
79. D. Bakalial, (2004): "Banaria Dhan" (in Assamese), *Prantik* 23(11), 1-15 May.
80. D.K. Hore, (2005): "Rice Diversity Collection, Conservation and Management in North Eastern India," *Genetic Resources and Crop Evolution*, Vol. 52, pp. 1129-1140.

81. Ian C. Glover, (1985): "Some Problem Relating to the Domestication of Rice in Asia," in *Recent Advances in Indo-Pacific Prehistory* (V.N. Misra and P. Bellwood (eds.), New Delhi, pp. 265-74.
82. M. Hazarika, (2006): "Understanding the Process of Plants and Animal Domestication in Northeast India: A Hypothetical Approach," *Asian Agri-History*, 10, pp. 203-212.
83. M. Hazarika, (2006): "Neolithic Culture of Northeast India: A Recent Perspective on the Origins of Pottery and Agriculture," *Ancient Asia*, 1, International Journal of the Society of South Asian Archaeology, pp. 25-43.
84. O.K. Singh, (1998-99): "Cord-marked Pottery Making Tradition in Manipur," *Puratattva* 29: 60-61.
85. M. Alemchiba, (1967): *The Arts and Crafts of Nagaland*, Kohima: Naga Institute of Culture, Govt. of Nagaland.
86. S.N. Rao, (1979): "Survival and Continuity of Neolithic Traditions of North Eastern India," *Asian Perspective*, 20 (2).
87. S.N. Rao, (1991): "Megalithic Practices among Khasis and Nagas of North Eastern India," in *Archaeology of Northeastern India* (J.P. Singh and G. Sengupta (eds.), New Delhi: Vikas Publishing House.
88. D. Bezbaruah, (2003): *Megalithic Ruins in Karbi Anglong District of Assam: A Study in the Context of Karbi Culture*, Unpublished Ph.D. Thesis, Guwahati: Gauhati University.

3

MANIPUR
Land, People, Demography and Historiography

Salem Irene

Contemporary North East India is a product of British Imperialism and early National Formation of Modern India. It is necessary to know how the British empire of the nineteenth century impacted upon the subject people of the North East. The Historical experiences of the indigenous peoples therefore, are attempts to respond to two major influences in history: 1. The structural transformation in society and polity in the wake of imperialism and colonialism, and 2. The response to the relationship in the context of the modern Indian state.[1]

It is purely by an accident in history that North East formed a part of India. The social formation in mainland India and North East must first of all be explained from historical prospective of three definable phases of periods: pre–colonial, colonial and post colonial periods. Among societies in mainland India, social organisation took the form of a caste structure and this continues to be so, even to the present day. In this way they had been linked up with one another culturally and politically as a part of a chain. With the exception of the Meities in Imphal Valley and the Assamese in Brahmaputra Valley, the hill people remained essentially outside the orbit of the Hindu influence and caste-based societal formation, while mainland Indian society could evolve pan-Indian homogeneities and Hindu ethos in social formation all through the historical period, the hill people in North East with their diverse social alignments and group identities, produced a high degree of fluidity and flexibility in their socio-cultured arenas. Mainland India was unified culturally and politically even before the coming of the British in India. This unity was further strengthened by colonization. This made the people of mainland India to see Indian history as their common past, their subordination to the colonial rule as their common lot, and its final overthrow as their common destination. The colonial secluded policy towards North East retarded the smooth penetration of Indian nationalism among the marginal and peripheral communities.[2]

Even when the nationalist freedom struggle reached its climax under the leadership of Mahatma Gandhi, the waves of Indian nationalism never crossed beyond the Bramaputra Valley. H.K. Sareen rightly observed; 'Those in the leadership of the national movement paid scant attention to the masses of the people in the hills and valleys of the North East India. That is why they did not, or could not devise any ethos of breaking the barrier created by the imperialist rulers and drawing the masses into the struggle for independence. This remained one of the weaknesses of our national movement."[3]

Another factor, perhaps more crucial, was the uneven development of the colonial economy which greatly retarded the uniform growth and maturity of the Indian nationalism among the different ethnic groups of the country. Due to this unequal economic development, national consciousness also developed unevenly. This is so, because the entry of British capitalism in colonial form took place at different times in different regions with varying intensity producing dissimilar effects. Since the port cities of Calcutta, Bombay and Madras Presidencies were the foremost British business centres, and the centre of the capital investment infrastructural development took place faster in these areas. Thus, colonial India experienced two streams of coeval processes as far as its nationality formation was concerned. The first was based on its pan-Indian identity and the second one on its regional ethnic identity. What had actually emerged in course of time were two types of nationalities—Consolidated nationalities and Marginal nationalities. The transformation of these consolidated nationalities into the core nationalism (Indian nationalism) was automatic and spontaneous. On the otherhand, the integration of marginal nationalities including Manipuri, with the Indian state structure took place only at the end of colonial rule.[4]

Manipur is one of the smallest of North Eastern states of India with a population of 23.9 lakhs. It is bounded by Nagaland on the north, Mizoram on the south, Myanmar on the east and Assam on the west. The long international border of Manipur with Myanmar is porous and allows trade and movement of people between India and Myanmar. Manipuris can travel up to Mandalay without a passport by the land route. The centrally located amphitheatre like Imphal Valley with 700 square mile area is predominantly inhabited by the Hindu and Muslim Meitei communities, totaling 16,74,821 population, and the entire hill areas of 7000 square miles that surround the former, are abodes of highly heterogeneous 33 tribal ethnic groups with a population of 7,13,813[5] this geographic division is a determinant factor in the socio-political, historical development of the land.[6] In fact, if the current ethnicity of Manipur valley population could be broad banded by the two majority groups viz. the Muslims and Meiteis (composite of the Hindus and the Sanamahis), then that of the Manipur hills could likewise be overreached by another two: the Nagas and the Kukis. The only two discernible differences being: first, that the valley society long since evolved a pluralistic society, and apparently passed through a detribalization process onto modernization, and second, that two-thirds of the state humans cape congregate in the valley measuring 700 sq. miles or 2,238 kms, while the balance one—third spread out over the remaining 8000 sq. miles or 20,089 kms. hill areas of the state.[7] Aproximately, 76 per cent of the population density live in the rural areas. This results in a population density of 107 persons per sq.km. There are 978 females to every 1000 males, a ratio higher than national statistic 1933 females per 1000 males. There are nine districts, namely, Imphal East, Imphal West, Bishnupur, Thoubal, Chandel, Ukhrul, Senapati, Tamenglong and Churachandpur. Four of these Districts are in the valley where 80 per cent of the population lives. The division of Manipur's population into scheduled tribes and other categories helps reinforce the 'Tribal identity' among the tribes, which is further aggravated by their settlement places in remote areas. Separate reserved political seats also sharpen the sense of difference.[8]

Manipur was an ancient kingdom, a cradle of human civilization and creativity, which has come under the influence of many cultures of different ethnic groups who came at different times, and contributed to the growth of the civilization of Manipur. Manipur, being a gateway of India to Southeast Asia, was influenced by her geographic situation and ecology, in the shaping of her history and cultural development.

Manipur literally means 'The Land of Gems.' According to Sanamahi Laikan (a Manipuri historical work), the name 'Manipur' was first officially introduced in the early eighteenth century during the reign of Hinduised Fasib-niwaza (1709-1748). In the legendary or proto-historical period, the principality which centred at Kangla, the capital of the later Meitei kingdom was known by several names.

As to the common ancestry of three autochthon groups viz. the Meiteis, Nagas and Kukis (excluding the Muslims who were allowed to settle down in the valley only during and after Manipur king Khagemba's reign: 1597-1652 A.D.) The British ethnologist, T.C. Hodson pronounced: "Tradition affords link which makes the Nagas, the Kukis and the Manipuris descent from a common ancestor, who had three sons who became the progenitor of those tribes, the tradition, which is widely spread, agrees in its many versions in assigning the primacy of the descent to the Kukis, the next place being given to the Nagas, while the Manipuris are said to be the children of the youngest of the three brothers.

As regards linguistic affinity "The researches of the

Linguistic Survey of India enable to take place a comprehensive view of the relationship of the Meitei language to the languages spoken by the hill tribes, both in the state and beyond it. Dr. Grierson gives it place in the Tibeto- Burman group to which it belongs, in the following words: "The Kuki-Chin languages are closely connected with all the surrounding groups of the TIbeto-Burman family, the Bodo and Naga languages to the north, Kachin to the east, and the Burmese to the east and south. More particularly, they form a link which connects Burmese with the Bodo and Naga languages, having especially in the north, many relations with the Kachin dialects which in turn, form another chain between Tibetan and the Burmese."[9]

Manipur has been a home to several ethnic communities, found all over the state. Various ethnic groups belonging to the southern Mongoloid group; the Tibeto-Burmans, the Indo-Aryans, and a sizable section of the Tai (Shans) come to Manipur from pre-historic times down to the present day. The present ethnic groups of Manipur viz. the Meiteis, the Naga tribes, the Kuki-Chin tribes, and other Indians communities are the descendents of those migrating people.[10] The valley of Manipur has now assumed a cosmopolitan character through the Meiteis and Muslims are numerically preponderant. Non-Manipuri Indians and Nepalis have also settled here. The hills are the exclusive domain of the tribes, as the states land law does not allow the Meitei and those non-tribals to buy lands in the hills and settle. In Manipur there are twenty-nine Scheduled Tribes—Aimol, Anal, Chiru, Chothe, Gangte, Hmar, Kabui, (i) Puimei an (ii) Rongmei, Kacha Naga-(i) Zemei (ii) Liangmei, Koirao, Koireng, Kom, Lamkang, Mao, Maram, Maring, Mizo (Lushai) tribes, Monsang, Moyon, Paite, Purum, Ralte, Sema, Simte, Suhte, Tangkhul, Thadou, Vaiphei and Zou.[11] 'Nongchup Haram' is the term used for those groups of people who came to Manipur from Tripura, Sylhet, Cachar, Assam and adjoining areas as war captive, part of the dowry of a princess (Chingurembi) who married Meitei prince (Kwakpa Thawanthaba), as learned persons employed by the king's court. Muslims came in King Khagemba's reign (1596-1652) and continued up to King Gambhir Singh's reign (1826-1834). They were known as the Meitei-Pangal (Pangal-a corrupt form of Bangal-Bengal) and married local Meitei woman, and were assigned sagies (clans). Brahmins came from different parts of India from King Kiyamba's reign (1467-1508) up to king Charairengba's reign. They were assigned 'Yumnaks' (Subclans). The Chakpas of Manipur were supposedly not original inhabitants but migrated from Yunam.[12]

In pre-colonial Manipur, under a feudal dynastic system of authority relations, ethnic categories subsisted with frequent interactions which could be economic interdependence, barter of essential goods and supplies, participation in community rituals and of course, fierce protection of collectivities, village and clan settlements from external threat. Primitive subsistence economy, sexual division of labour, ritual participation in hunt and war, and subservience to supra-village political organizations, but very little interventions in the internal lived experience and culture, and general mutual trust for peace keeping were the norms. Mutual trust was founded on the system of reciprocity. Social universe was founded on the village systems, with local authority relations based on lineage or clan leadership, with elders of the clan community maintaining the peace and equilibrium of the population through customs and tradition, and wisdom and grace were mainsprings of community life. The discovery of the pony, and the development of iron technology help integrate the clan and lineage households, and the utilization of communal energy to harness the excess waters, the new system of irrigation led to the development of a native elite, and an indigenous bureaucratic system to devise the forms of a developing or evolving ethno state, which became a reality in the 16th and 17th centuries. The distinctive difference in the undifferentiated social categories where frequent interactions, assimilations, formation of new professional lineages and clans took place, was however, the changes in the social organization of these societies, when the Meiteis in the plains had experience of change and development leading into nationhood, through the state formation exercises. Confrontation with external enemies like the Myanmarese through history, the battles with other states and nations helped develop a sense of identity unique in the North East.[13]

One of the theories of the Meitei origin is Aryan, this Aryan connection was an outcome of the adoption of the Hinduism by the royal family and the valley people in the eighteenth century, and resultant claim of the descent of the ruling dynasty, from Babhruvahana, a scion of the Pandava hero, Arjun of the Mahabharata. The fact is that they are neither of Aryan stock or Indo-Aryan, although they absorbed some Aryan elements from Aryan colonizers, adventurers and immigrants. The representatives of Aryan element are Manipuri Brahmins and the Nongchup Haram. When the Meiteis became the followers of Vaishnavism, a framework of pollution-purity relationship, alienated the non-Hindu tribes. The tribes who have embraced Christianity also have alienated themselves from the Meiteis. This social gap resulted from the mutual alienation, it became wider and wider, with the metamorphosis of the colonial subjects into free citizens of independent India, because political democratization stimulated primordial sentiments.[14]

Another theory is the Moi-Tai origin of the Meiteis. All archaeological and historical evidences point to the relationship of ancient Meiteis with the Mon Khmer and Tai people, but not of Mon Khmer Tai origin of the people. G.A. Grierson in 'Linguistic Survey of India' has grouped the Meitei in the Kuki-Chin sub-family of Tibeto-Burman languages. He is generally right in presuming that the ancestors of the Meiteis were among the Tibeto-Burman speakers in south west china, Eastern Tibet and upper Burma. Ch. Budhi Singh asserted Meitei or Timei, is an outcome of the ethnic blending of people of Mei and Ti tribes of ancient China. Before the coming of the Tibeto-Burman speaking proto-Meitei tribes, there were Mon Khmer speaking austroloid mongoloid people, later absorbed by the Tibeto-Burmans. Indo-Aryans and Tais were also absorbed. Ethnologically and linguistically, the Meiteis are the Tibeto-Burman of the Southern Mongoloid with Austroloid, Aryan and Tai admixtures.

It is not clear how the name 'Naga' originated. It is an old name, popularized by the Ahoms and the British. The latter gave the generic name to the present Nagas of the Nagaland, Assam and Manipur. In Manipur, people are known by their tribe name. Naga legend tells of their migration and settlement in Manipur. It is reliably believed that these tribes were in occupation of the present habitat in the early centuries of the Christian era or even before that. Naga tribes of Manipur are Tangkhul, Zemi, Liangmei, Rongmei (Zeliangrong) including Pumei, Mao, Maram, Anal, Moyon, Monsang, Lamgang, Chothe, Thangal, Koireng, Chiru, who are all Tibeto-Burman speakers.

Some Kuki tribes migrated to Manipur hills in pre-historic times but greater migration occurred in the eighteenth century. The Kuki-Chin tribes are Thadou, Paite, Hmar, Vaiphei, Gangte, Simte, Zou, Biate and Mizo.[15] Their origin used to be shrouded in myths and mythologies, although one such traditional account handed down through generations is that the Kukis came out of the bowel of the earth or a cave called Chinlung, Sinlung or Khul, whose location was believed to be somewhere in China, although others claimed its origin in Tibet.[16]

About the Nagas, T.S. Gangte writes: "Naga life way even in the nineteenth century was best summed up by R.B. Mc Cabe: Grouped in small communities of from 100 to 3,000 persons, the Nagas have remained isolated on their hill-tops, only deigning to visit their immediate neighbours when a longing for the possession of their heads become too strong to be resisted." Even so, the Nagas claim in no ambiguous terms that from time immemorial they had been independent, without however specifying whether they had a monarchy, democracy etc. and what was the territorial boundary of the polity. But in the post-independence era the Tangkhuls (of Manipur) started calling themselves Nagas and took up frontal roles in the Naga political leadership. They felt the need of a common identity with a broad-based foundation in a democratic set-up of government. The great awakening among the Tangkhuls had its impetus in arousing spontaneous response from yet other tribes in Manipur to accept the term Naga as their identity.[17]

Till the time of the 1961 Census, Manipur was a Union territory. In the 1951 Census Manipur remained as a part "C"

State administered by the Central Government. In 1969 the whole State was divided into five districts and twenty-five sub-divisions. In the 1981 Census, there were a total of six districts, in 1991, eight districts and thirty sub-divisions; in 2001- nine districts and thirty-eight sub-divisions. The decadal growth rate of population in the State decreases from 35.04 percent in 1951 to 30.02 in 2001.[18]

Table

MANIPUR—DECADAL VARIATION IN POPULATION SINCE 1951

State/ Districts	*Year*	*Persons*	*Decade Variations*	*Percentage Decade Variations*
Manipur	1951	577,635	—	—
	1961	780,037	202,402	35.04
	1971	1,072,753	292,716	37.53
	1981	1,420,953	348,200	32.46
	1991	1,837,149	416,196	29.29
	2001	2,388,634	551,485	30.02
1.Senapati District	1951	46,608	—	—
	1961	70,792	24,184	51.89
	1971	102,291	31,499	44.50
	1981	153,091	50,800	49.66
	1991	208,406	55,315	36.13
	2001	379,214	170,808	81.96
2.Tamenglong District	1951	33,519	—	—
	1961	37,667	4,148	12.38
	1971	46,034	8,367	22.21
	1981	62,289	16,225	35.31
	1991	86,278	23,989	38.51
	2001	111,493	25,215	29.23
3.Churachandpur District	1951	44,496	—	—
	1961	66,304	21,808	49.01
	1971	100,418	34,114	51.45
	1981	134,494	34,076	33.93
	1991	176,184	41,690	31.00
	2001	228,707	52,523	29.81
4. Chandel District	1951	24,049	—	—

	1961	27,679	3,630	15.09
	1971	38,723	11,044	39.90
	1981	56,444	17,721	45.76
	1991	71,014	14,570	25.81
	2001	122,714	51,700	72.80
5.Thoubal District	1951	99,631	—	—
	1961	135,462	35,831	35.96
	1971	182,500	47,038	34.72
	1981	232,675	50,175	27.49
	1991	293,958	61,283	26.34
	2001	366,341	72,383	24.62
6.Bishnupur District	1951	57,340	—	—
	1961	79,005	21,665	37.78
	1971	108,785	29,780	37.69
	1981	141,760	32,975	30.31
	1991	180,773	39,013	27.52
	2001	205,907	25,134	13.90
7.Imphal District	1951	230,810	—	—
	1961	314.538	83,728	36.28
	1971	431,773	117,235	37.27
	1981	557,254	125,481	29.06
	1991	711,261	154,007	27.64
	2001	833,312	122,051	17.16
8.Ukhru District	1951	41,182	—	—
	1961	48,590	7,408	17.99
	1971	62,229	13,639	28.07
	1981	82,946	20,717	33.29
	1991	109,275	26,329	31.74
	2001	140,946	31,671	28.98

During 1991-2001, the valley districts experienced a sharp decline in the decadal population growth rate. It decreased from 27.29 percent in 1981-91, to 18.51 percent in 1991-2001. Though the decadal growth rate in the hill districts declined from 39.91 percent during 1971-81 to 33.09 percent in 1981-91, it increased to 50.97 in 1991-2001. The decadal growth rate of the hill districts was influenced by the abnormal population growth in the two districts of Senapati and Chandel. (The government decided to "Maintain status quo" until the exact figure was ascertained).

The lone hill district with numerically dominant Kuki-Chin population i.e. Churachandpur has experienced a decline in its decadal growth rate from 31 percent in 1981-91 to 29.81 percent in 1991-2001, whereas the decadal growth rate in the hill districts with numerically dominant Naga population experienced a sharp increase.[19]

Manipur has a tradition of recorded history in the form of royal and family chronicles. In fact, royal chronicles or chronicles of the clans, with or without chronology from the core of historical literature. The "Cheithard Kumbaba" deals with the history of Manipur as an independent, monarchical kingdom. While the act of writing developed at a very early stage of the Meitei civilization, the record keeping or chronicle keeping was started in the fifteenth century. But there are literary texts dealing with historical events which were written in the early period, around the beginning of the Christian era. Education and scholarship were controlled by the royalty and nobility. The king- controlled writing was reflected in chronicle-keeping. The Meitei view of the past (or history) was holistic approach; naturally it was difficult to separate what was historical from what was myth, legends and tradition, and from religion and theology. The classic example is 'Leithak Leikharon' an eighteenth century text, which was a compendium of cosmology, genealogy myth and legends, culture and religion, statecraft and history. Records chronicles, or puyas, were not only 'Historical pieces', but they were used as manuals for administration. The tribals in the hills were also greatly concerned with their past preserved through oral tradition, genealogy and folklore. The tribal account of their past, narrated or preserved in mythical form, are believed to be authentic by themselves. The Nagas have their history in folklore, hymns and songs and migration accounts. The Kuki tribes keep their authentic genealogy for generations and centuries as thorough as possible. The genealogical trees or accounts are the backbone of their past.[20]

The 'Consciousness' of history became very much pronounced in Manipur with the sanskritization of the Meitei royalty and popular in the eighteenth century. The writing of history, keeping of chronicles, use of eras and calendars, origin of the ruling dynasty, the people and country were sankritized. Religious conversion and resultant perception of the Hinduised or Aryan identity had influenced history writing in Manipur since the Hinduization of Manipur. But modern history writing as such was a contribution of the colonial ethnographers and administrators who were posted in Manipur.

King Garibaniwaz, the great Hinduised ruler of the Manipur caused a history of Manipur called 'Vijay Panchali' to be written in 1730 A.D. based on a sanskritized royal genealogy of the Ningthouja dynasty. There are references to Manipur in the writing of the British officers in the eighteenth century and early nineteenth century.[21]

Although Manipur scholars claim that Manipur has a tradition of recorded history, it is only in recent years that scholars have begun to make wide use of them. The first published works in English began with the writings of the British, like T.C. Hodson, 'The Meiteis' first published in 1908. A Manipuri scholar (Noarem Sanajoba) laments that "Till date, historians had not given a serious thought to the history of Manipur. The same scholar makes a very vital point about historiography in Manipur when he writes that the tradition of glorifying the past of the Manipur had greatly influenced the historians. Generally, therefore one can conclude that either we have dynastic recordings and nationalistic glorification or ethnographic studies of the tribes. Although E. Nilakanta Singh writes that the "Research into the past of Manipur is at the moment largely confined to oral traditions and written records including the Puranas (called Puyas in Manipuri), which are plenty.[22]

J.P. Wade mentions the Mughal or Mussalman connection with Manipur in his 'Account of Assam.' Francis Hamilton in his 'Account of Assam' (1808) devotes a section to Manipur. R.B. Pemberton's 'Report on the North Eastern Frontier of British India' was published in 1835 with a major portion devoted to Manipur. Pemberton's 'Report', as it came to be popularly known, has been a reference work not only on Manipur, but on all adjoining areas of India and Burma including the kingdom of Pong. W. Mc Culloch published his 'Account of the valley of Manipur and surrounding hill tribes' in 1859. His observation on ethnography, economy and culture are highly accurate and the work remains for many decades, a chief authority on the subject. Mc Culloch was succeeded by R. Brown who published 'Statistical Account of Manipur' in 1874.[23] While most of these works have turned out to be valuable sources of information, one must keep in mind the fact that these writings developed ideas, which reflected consciously or not, the political and ideological interests of the British.[24]

But the history of Manipur in the proper sense was not attempted till Alexander Mackienzie's celebrated 'History of the Relation of the Government with hill tribes of the North East Frontier of British Bengal' which was published in 1884. This book represents the official views of historical events and is regarded as 'Authentic' history based on official records of the Government of India. E.W. Dun's "Gazetteer of Manipur" 1886 and its abridged edition 1891 were published. In 1890, rejecting Manipur's Aryan origin, the first history of Manipur in Manipuri was published by Haodeijamba Cheitanya. His 'Manipur Itihas' gives the dynastic history of Manipur based on the chronicles written after Hinduisation. The British conquest of Manipur in 1891 created fresh interest on Manipur.

"My Three Years in Manipur" by Mrs. Ethel Grimwood 1891 gave a personal account of these events. The Indian view was presented in R.G. Bask's 'Manipur Prahalika' 1891 in Bengali and Manmohan Gosh's "Did the Manipuri Princess get a Fair Trial?" 1891, containing legal documents. James Johnstone's "My Experience in Manipur and Naga Hills", 1896, gives interesting information on the character of the people and some historical accounts. B.C. Allen's *Gazetteer of Naga Hills and Manipur*, 1904 was a remarkable work followed by T.C. Hodson's Magnum Opus "The Meiteis", in 1908. This is the best full scale study of the Meiteis, their society, polity, religion, and culture based on ethnological and historical evidences. His *Naga Tribes of Manipur*, 1911 is the first comprehensive work on the Nagas of Manipur. John Shakespeare contributed well written papers on religious beliefs of the Meiteis. G.A. Grierson's monumental work *Linguistic Survey of India*, Vol. III, Parts II and III deal with the languages and dialects of different tribes and communities of Manipur. William Pettigrews *Tangkhul Grammar*, is a first authentic study on the Tangkhuls. G.R. Gerini's *Research on Ptolomy's Geography* 1909, refers to the existence of a Hindu kingdom in Manipur in the 6th century BC. *Manipur Purabritta*, the second work on history of Manipur by a local writer P. Parijat was published in 1917.

Sanskrit and English educated scholars of Manipur had started writing on history of Manipur. Among them, Panditraj Atombapu Sharma (representing the literary school) and W. Yumjao Singh (representing the historical school) were the foremost. The first wrote more than one hundred papers and books. The Latter's 'Report on the Archeological Studies' in Bulletin No. 1. 1935 is a landmark in the historical studies in the state.

Robert Reid devoted a chapter to Manipur in *History of Areas bordering Assam* 1942, and R.K. Sanahal Singh wrote *Manipur Itihas* a short, well-documented work in 1947. Other writers viz. A.C. Bannerjee, R.M. Lahiri, S.K. Bhuyan, S.K. Chatterjee made references to Manipur in their works. J. Roy's *A History of Manipur* 1958 in English is factual and refreshing. R.C. Majumdar's *War Against Manipur* 1955, H. Bijoy Singh's *Meitrabakki Wari*, Nandalal Sharma's *Meitrabak* (1960), L.M. Iboongohal Singh's *An Introduction of Manipur* (1960 and 1963) came out. R.K. Jhalajit Singh's *A Short History of Manipur* 1965, is a history of the Ningthorya dynasty of Manipur based on indigenous sources. The *Cheitharol Kumbaba* was edited by L.M. Iboongohal Singh and N. Khelchandra Singh in 1967. O. Bhogeswar Singh published *Ningthourol Lambuba* in 1968. Many old historical works in Manipur were published like *Leithak Leikharon, Chada Laihui* etc. Many cultural and ethnographic studies were published like M. Horam's *Naga Polity and Socio-cultural Life of the Nagas* (Tangkhul), Sanajaoba Naorem edited *Manipur: Past and Present*, an excellent compendium on various aspects of history, society, polity, and culture of Manipur. Gangmumei Kabui's' *History of Manipur in the pre- colonial period (1991)*, is a definitive history of ancient and medieval Manipur.

The Host Kingdom, an English translation of the *Cheitharol Kumbaba* was located by L. Joychandra Singh. Contemporary historical research was focused on the Merger of Manipur into India (1949) and the revolt of Hijam Irabot Singh 1948-1951, for example, H. Bhubhan Singh's *Merger of Manipur* and *Annexation of Manipur*, and K. Manimohan Singh's, *H. Irabot Singh and his political movement.*[25]

While trying to arrive at some conclusion about historiographical aspects of the writings on North- East India, the writings on Christianity Stand out as a very important component. The importance of the rule that Christianity played in the historical developments in many of the societies of North East India can never be denied. Considering the number of works which are there on the subject of Christianity in North-East India, it is unfortunate that there has been very little historiographical assessment done of these works. In the writings on Christianity in North East India, no definite conceptual trend has developed, because the majority of the historians, who are Christian by faith, have not addressed themselves to the philosophies of Christian historiography.[26]

A look into the works done on Manipur and Tripura reveals a very strong tendency to emphasise on the political history rather than trying to integrate social and economic developments with the game of power. One of the main reasons for this may be the overdependence on chronicles like the 'Cheitharol Kumbaba' and Ningthoural Lambuba' and the 'Rajmala.'[27] Yet, the celebrated 'Cheitharol Kumbaba' is the most important royal chronicle of Manipur which records the historical events of nearly two thousands years, covering the reign of 78 Kings from Nongda Lairen Pakhangba (33-154 A.D.) to Bodh Chandra Singh (1941-55). The unique chronicle written in Meitei script is kept in the royal palace and the entry to this state diary is made by the learned royal scribes. Even now, this tradition of history-keeping is still continued by the Pandit Loisang, the college of priests in the royal palace of Manipur. This chronicle was written out in Bengali script and edited by Pandit Thongan Madhob Singh and published by Visvabharati Mandir. Then with the permission granted by Maharaja

Churachand Singh, the chronicle was edited by the L.M. Iboongohal Singh and N. Khelchandra Singh and published by the Manipur Sahitya Parishad in 1967.[28] A more recent English version of it with original text, translation and notes was produced by Saroj Nalini Arambam Parratt in 2005. It will be worthwhile to recall what the pioneer historians said about the 'Cheitharol Kumbaba.' L.M. Iboongohal describes it as the most authoritative diary and history of Manipur and most authentic manuscript. W. Yumjao Singh writes: "Cheitharol Kumbaba" a royal chronicle would have been the most valuable work for historical investigation, but these is a passage which clearly says that in the year 1780 A.D. by order of Jai Singh, this book was rewritten as the former copy was not available. But the important nobles and scholars used to keep private copies of the diary in their private collection, and King Jai Singh's scribes might have copied from them.[39]

The 'Cheitharol Kumbaba' provides information that is useful in reconstructing Manipur's early history, but the earlier part of the chronicle is problematic, both as regards dating and historicity. It reflects the Meetei viewpoint over against that of the other Yeks or clan groups, as well as of other peoples. The earlier part of the book is essentially the story of the expansion of the Meeteis across the valley and hills of Manipur, and of the gradual assimilation of the Yeks (clan groups) and tribes into their kingdom. It is therefore, like most royal chronicles, selective in the events it records, focusing especially on the birth and death of kings, and on their major exploits which contributed to the development of the state.[30] The chronicle reflects the royalty's view of people and events. But it is a very useful and important document.

After the establishment of Manipur University in 1980, academicians and scholars have produced a number of works on history, culture, society, polity, economy, etc. of Manipur, focusing on the life and culture of the different communities in the state.

Notes

1. Lokendra Arambam, (2005): *Ethnicity and Politics of Identity: The Manipur Experience.*
2. Lal Dena Schizophrenic, (2005): *Alienation of North East India: Its Historical Roots*, p. 1.
3. Ibid., p. 3.
4. Ibid., p. 4.
5. T.S. Gangte, (2005): *Land Problem and Ethnic Tension in North East India with special reference to Manipur.*
6. Gangmumei Kabui, *History of Manipur*, Vol. 1, *Pre-colonial Period*, p. 8.
7. T.S. Gangte, *Kuki Naga Ethnicity in Current Manipur Polity.*
8. Mohd Shakil Ahmed, *Identity Construction and its Territorial Dimension—The Naga Experience.*
9. T.S. Gangte, *op. cit.*
10. Gangmumei Kabui, *op. cit.*, p. 15-23.
11. Aheibam Koireng Singh, *Some Reflections on Land Questions and Ethnic Crisis in Manipur.*
12. N. Debendra Singh, *Identities of the Migrated People in Manipur.*
13. Lokendra Arabam, *op. cit.*
14. W. Nabakumar, *Communalism and Ethnic Divide: Anathema to Secular Society.*
15. Gangmumei Kamei, *op. cit.*
16. T.S. Gangte, (1973): *Kuki-Naga Ethnicity, op. cit.*, Ginzatuang, p. 5.
17. Ibid., p. 672.
18. Konjengbam Meghachandra Singh, *Ethnic and Territorial Dimensions of Demograhpic Change in Manipur: Issues and Policy Implications.*
19. Ibid.
20. Gangmumei Kabui, *On History and Historiography of Manipur*, pp. 111-112.
21. Ibid., p. 113.
22. Manorama Sharma, *History and History Writing in North East India*, pp. 79-80.
23. Gangmumei Kabui, *op. cit.*, p. 114.
24. Manorama Sharma, *op. cit.*, p. 63.
25. Gangmumei Kabui, *op. cit.*, pp. 115-122.
26. Manorama Sharma, *op. cit.*, pp. 36-39.
27. Ibid., p. 90.
28. Gangmumei Kabui, *op. cit.*, p. 123.
29. Ibid., p. 127.
30. Sarojini Nalini Arambam Parratt, *The Court Chronicle of the Kings of Manipur: The Cheitharom Kumpapa*, p. 3.

4

WOMEN FREEDOM FIGHTERS IN ASSAM
Negotiating A Historical Disconnect

Ranjana Mishra

> "When the history of India's fight for Independence comes to be written, the sacrifice made by the women of India will occupy the foremost place."
>
> — *Mahatma Gandhi*

The history of India's freedom movement in the remote areas of North East has not been adequately reflected in empirical research. It has either been inadequately mentioned or deliberately ignored. As a result, sixty two years after independence, several pages of history of India's freedom movement have remained unwritten. The contributions of many sections of the Indian society still remain unaccounted for due to lack of proper study and evidence. How freedom movement underwent metamorphosis in the remote areas of India, particularly in the North East, has remained largely in the domain of oblivion. What concerns the role of students, women, workers, farmers, businessmen, tribal communities and so on are all least researched topics. Women's participation in the mainstream freedom movement has never seemed to be a bottom-to-top approach because the contribution of women to the freedom struggle remains grossly understudied. A fair deal to fair sex has remained as much nightmarish as a daydream in all societies, including in India.

Three factors are responsible for this lurking apathy in narrative history. Firstly, an endocentric approach is predominant in history writing, while a gyaenocentric analysis is largely absent. Secondly, focus of history writing has not blended well with the wealth of oral history from across the country in general and from North Eastern India in particular. Thirdly, the urban centric focus on history of freedom movement has effectively filtered out the genuine role of various segments of society, including that of women. This paper tries to fill up a small gap by adding women's participation in Assam's freedom struggle. Based on empirical data collected in Assam by the author through interviews with women participants of the freedom struggle, the paper dwells on the seminal expressions of those who really participated, spearheaded and led the movement to a crowning glory. However, unfortunately, in annals of a patriarchal Indian society, one discovers a vast contour of endocentric activities, where voices of women are largely ignored. The role of gender, particularly of women within the household, the division of labour in the production spheres of activities, and in other political and cultural arenas often reinforces two aspects.[1]

(1) Women are made to confine themselves to the household and remain busy in child bearing, offspring rearing and nursing. The maximum they could stretch is unto the realm of music, dance and literature; thus uplifting the cultural level of the family and the society at large.

(2) Their role in the realm of politics and economy is normally perceived through the prism of men, who act as assessor and appraiser of the role played by women. This asymmetric, gender based perception has been defined through the heroic deeds of few valorous women, whose contribution to the freedom struggle

of India in the remote parts of North East remains indelible.

The role of these women at the micro level has not been studied properly. Although some efforts at assessing the feminine role have been made at macro level, a lot more remains to be done, particularly when it comes to undertaking an in-depth study of women freedom fighters at the provincial level and down below with special reference to their role in the rear of the movement. This article makes an attempt to highlight the role of few women freedom fighters of Assam[2]—then a unified territory of which half a dozen states have been carved out in independent India. Bordering with one of the pioneering states of the Indian national liberation movement like undivided Bengal and motivated by the inherent inclination of patriotism, these women had fought for women empowerment, gender equality and human rights in patriarchal India to free it from the shackles of age-old bondage.

Brief Literature Review

Despite our homage and deep admiration for the womanhood of Assam, it is unfortunate that these women, who in the hours of need for the motherland, had forsaken the shelter of their homes and with unfailing courage and endurance stood shoulder to shoulder with their men in the frontline of Assam's freedom struggle to share with them the sacrifices and triumphs of the struggle in reality, remained marginalized after independence. The existing research on women and Indian nationalism can therefore be described as incomprehensive history and generally a "history from above." Anita Singh in an article entitled "Gender Sensitization of Grassroots" published in 1998, argues that women have not only been a victim of the age old social and cultural limitations; but also of the discriminatory competitive market forces. Bibekanand Das and L.N. Das in the book "The Feminine Gender" write that taking a worldwide view one can accept, without controversy, the proposition that women enjoy a lower status compared to men.[3] In order to bridge this gap, gender equality ought to be ensured and more rights should be given to women. For instance, women's economic and political rights, their social development, mitigation and elimination of gender based discrepancies should forthwith be encouraged.

From a feminine perspective, the patriarchal set-up compels women to subordination, subservience and dependence on men. It locks her in daughter-wife-mother triangle without providing her access to any socially acceptable alternatives as an independent individual and treats her primarily as an instrument of male sexual enjoyment by assigning her the task of continuing his species. As a result, women have little control over economic resources and are reduced not only to economic dependence, but also to resultant social and legal deprivations of status in a male dominated world.[4]

In the midst of all the scholastic generalization, what sets Assam apart is the uniqueness of the position of woman in the Assamese society. Evidences from the Gazetteer of Assam and "History of Assam" by Edward Gait suggest that in comparative terms, Assamese women were socially better off than women in other parts of India.[5] For example, a young woman in the Garo society had the privilege of choosing her husband. The children took the clan name of the mother instead of the father. Consensual divorce was allowed on the grounds of infidelity, adultery and barrenness.[6] But, despite living free from what is known as a rigid patriarchy, one could find Assamese women to be victims of gender discrimination. Though the rural women form the backbone of Assam's subsistence agricultural economy as tea plantation workers, they live in constant inequality. In a research conducted by Guwahati University's Centre for economic development and administration in 1998, on the "Status of Women in Assam"[7] it was estimated that an average woman worked 10.81 hours each day compared to 7.51 hours put in by men. 88 per cent of all domestic activities, 69 per cent of village work and 63 per cent of agricultural activities were done by women. However, of all the earnings outside the home, 69 per cent was earned by men. Men take most of the decisions on how the money is to be spent. Property transactions, sale of animals or major household loans primarily remain a men's prerogative. Thus, outside earning capacity along with access to the market places put men into the job of bargaining and selling and consequently in an advantageous position. They gained confidence in decision making; while women were relegated to the household to take care of the family. The entire history of the freedom movement is replete with the saga of bravery, sacrifice and political sagacity of great men and a few famous women.

In retrospect, we see that women of Assam have rendered yeomen's service to their state in the political, social and economic spheres.[8] Why then in the country's freedom movement, their names have remained obscure? While their male counterparts have been mentioned in all the Government Gazetteers and have a place in all the books written on the freedom struggle, most of the literature purposely ignored women freedom fighters. Thus literature on the freedom movement remains largely endocentric; although a few important names of women freedom fighters have appeared off and on, here and there. The approach in these cases was laudatory and enumerative rather than analytical. Oral histories and reminiscences of women in the national movement are available on tape in some archives. Much more needs to be done in this respect.

A recent book by Dipti Sharma and Anuradha Dutta[9] has highlighted the role of women in the freedom struggle movement. However, their painstaking study does not include women freedom fighters from lower Assam valley, thus ignoring a large segment of participants. Assam was one of the last victims of British imperialism in India; losing her independence after signing the treaty of Yandaboo in 1926. Yet Assam was one of the earliest to rise in revolt against the shackles of foreign rule, when it joined the mainstream of the country's struggle for freedom.[10] Far too long have Assamese women been accustomed to value the freedom of their motherland better than their lives. The glorious tradition of Ramani Gabharu and Mula Gabharu, who had taken up arms to safeguard the honour of the throne, had continued to inspire

Assamese women. That tradition was further enriched by the heroic sacrifices of young women such as Rangili and Padumi.[11] However, when the dream of Assamese women for a united and free India did not materialize even after innumerable sacrifices, they had to wait until the advent of a man like Mahantma Gandhi whose magic call had aroused the entire nation. At the grassroots level, aflame with enthusiasm and throwing their fate into the mainstream of public awakening and cutting across caste-creed barriers of a largely rural India, these women had come out from the mediaeval bondage with courage to fight out the British rulers from their native Indian soil. It is the history of these women that tells us sagacious details of our freedom struggle.[12]

From 1915 onwards, the women of Assam began to organize themselves. The women of Dibrugarh were the first to organize a Samiti of their own.[13] By 1926 their organizational network had spread to the provincial level. They contributed tremendously to the freedom movement either individually or through their local associations. In all the three major national movements in 1921, 1930 and 1942, quite a few women like Nalinibala Devi, Malati Phookan, Sumita Bhattacharya, Snehlata Barua, Chandraprabha Saikiani, Shrijuta Rajbala Das, Suwaranlata Barua, Rohini Gohain, Basantlata Hazarika, Sarhi Prabha Hazarika, Muktabala Baishnavi, Mohini Gohain, Dariki Kachari, Mangri, Smt. Swaranlata Barua, Amol Prova Das, Kanaklata Phuleshwari Devi, Bhogeswari Phukanani and many others had participated in the freedom struggle. These women had contributed through various acts like picketing in front of wine and opium shops, forming barricade in front of government institutions, setting up squads and the ilk; they struck terror into the hearts of the British imperialist rulers.[14] Despite warning, threats, fines, lathi charges, firing, short or long terms of imprisonment etc. their spirit of revolt did not die down; instead their participation increased.

There were many illiterate or semi-literate women from rural areas imprisoned during the freedom struggle movement. Their role was either totally neglected or ignored. This paper is an attempt at corroborating these neglected aspects by taking up a few case studies of still living women freedom fighters, who had participated actively during 1940s in individual Satyagraha and Quit India movement. However, a patriarchal set up has put their names in the backburner of obscurity.

Case Studies

Swaranlata Mohanto,[15] a social worker turned freedom fighter in the district of Sonitpur, joined the civil disobedience movement at the tender age of seven along with her mother and maternal uncle. She took active part in the singing squad to collect funds for the Congress Party. She learnt spinning and wove khadi caps from hand-spun yarn for freedom fighters. Between1937-41, she single-handedly did the work for Parbatia Swadeshi Mahila Samiti. Suspended from her school for a month and deprived of her scholarship for protesting against the orders of anti-national government along with another freedom fighter, Nirmala Das at Barbakari, Swarnalata was defiant despite all her vicissitudes. In 1942, she pledged not to marry. Her marriage was scheduled to be held in August 1942, a time when Quit India movement had begun. Keeping in tune with the true devotion of a nationalist to a cause more sublime than marital bliss, Swarnalata preferred the life of freedom fighter to that of a housewife.

In 1942, as per the directions from the Congress, the Sootea Congress Mahila Sabha under her aegis opened a total of 62 branches across Sonitpur district. She organized various strikes, processions, and meetings and formed the women's Nursing Squad and later the Death Squad. She hoisted the national flag atop the Sootea police station for which she underwent imprisonment along with three of her women compatriots of Sootea Mahila Sabha. Subsequently, she was directed to work underground. She did this job with missionary zeal. Along with Pramila Barua, she met late Gahan Goswami, the then in charge of the underground section of District Congress Committee and discussed with him the action plan for future activities. Against tight governmental security, she was able to pass on the "documents" and papers of revolutionary activities to late Padma Bhushan, Bijay Bhagwati's sister without being caught and flawlessly fled underground in the midst of neck-high paddy fields and jungles. Finally, she was arrested and put into Tezpur jail for three months. After Gandhi's arrest in 1942, she prepared 2,000 women volunteers under the scorching sun to oppose the atrocities inflicted by the police on common people. The police chased them half a mile up the road with rifle; lathis (canes) and steel tipped clubs. The volunteers wildly cheered when she shook off the arm of the British police officer who came to arrest her and marched proudly to the barbed wire stockade where she was interned before being imprisoned.

In 1947, she attended the meeting of Gandhiji at Guwahati. Inspired by his exhortations, she spearheaded the women Seva Dal to organise talks on untouchability across the districts of lower Assam. This enabled her to persuade the untouchables to enter the Hazo temple in 1948, thus demolishing a taboo that Harijans are forbidden to enter the temple. She had a brief stint at Wardha between 1949-50. She got the offer for the post of headmistress from a Guwahati school, but on the advice of late Bijay Bhagwati, she declined that offer and instead took up a job of school teacher at Sootea. Her selfless devotion to the cause of society continued uninterrupted through teaching and social upliftment.

Well into the sixties, the revolutionary spirit continued to enthuse her. During 1962 Chinese aggression, she organised villagers and gave them military training. Besides, she collected gold and clothes from the villagers and sent them to government as financial and material help. She opened six branches of the Mahila Samiti that ran regular activities like weaving, spinning, knitting and sericulture. She also set up Balwadi and study circles. The Balwadi at north Sootea and the sericulture farm at east Sootea are living embodiment of her institutions still functioning.

With the burning desire to serve the nation, she contested the election, won it with a thumping majority and became a Minister of State in 1972. Unfortunately, she had to resign on 8th February 1976 to make way for a male aspirant. Politics took its ugly turn on a women freedom fighter. A revolutionary woman of her calibre, who opened 14 sericulture farms, introduced Tassar weaving in N.C. Hills and opened G.P. cooperatives remained unsung and unhonoured.

Poor health had driven Swarnlata Mohanto weak. Living in a dilapidated home sans luxury without any means of constructing a modern house and refusing to go in for medical treatment, her condition remained pathetic. Despite her intense desire to be a part of present day politics, she was effectively sidetracked from active politics by her male counterparts. This struggle of a solitary woman freedom fighter speaks loud for the gender bias at the micro level in our country.

Another woman of valour, whose contribution to Assam's freedom struggle was immense, was Pushpalata Das. Pushpalata Das,[16] at the age of six, distributed leaflets, containing Gandhiji's message. She joined "Banar Sena" to popularise Khadi among the people and organised "Charkha Sangh." Even her father, a government employee, was compelled by his little daughter to wear only Khadi. Inspired by her mother, she took the pledge for freedom and never looked back. By coming into contact with several frontline leaders of India's freedom movement, she converted herself to a pure Gandhian. She was selected by Gandhiji for individual *Satyagraha* and remained in jail for two and half months as an under trial. She was suspended from school for taking part in individual *Satyagraha*. During Quit India movement, she was arrested and jailed for three years. Due to illness, the government was forced to release her on parole. However, her refusal to be released earned her accolades from Gandhiji. She had organised death squads (Mrityu Vahini) in which 15 martyrs faced the bullets and Assam's heroic Kanaklata was one of them.

She became a member of the Rajya Sabha between 1950 to 1960 and significantly contributed to the debate in the upper house of Indian parliament. The Parliamentary proceedings are eloquent evidence of her activities as a politician. At the time of voting, she once opposed Jawaharlal Nehru's resolution of the working committee; and that was an apparent signal of her political death. She continued to be the president of Kasturba Memorial Trust. Involved in many social activities, a tireless fighter for social justice, she had been partially successful in putting an end to the North East insurgencies by persuading quite a few terrorists to surrender. When offered "Tamra Patra" by the Government, she refused to accept and wrote to the then chief minister of Assam Sarat Chandra Sinha: "with all my profound sense of gratitude to the well wishes of the Government, I would like to say humbly that I did not take part in the freedom movement with an intention to get anything in return. That was complete by itself with joy, so I could not like to accept your honour... Let the beauty of service remain animated." These words, perhaps, rightly reflected her feelings and thoughts of sacrifice. She had donated her entire Padma Bhushan award money for betterment of the downtrodden. Her services to the nation, especially her humanitarian approach to solve problems will long be remembered. Living in a small two-room house in the twilight of life, a valiant soldier remained extraordinarily optimistic. An in-depth analysis of her views reveals that half of the insurgencies in the North East could be resolved by persuasion, if these humble women visionaries are given a say in the present political scenario. What prohibits them from doing their duty for the nation is the domination of male over women in the given political set up and the apathetic attitude of the government to those who really deserve.

Similarly, Pramila Barua's[17] contribution to the Assamese freedom struggle may appear modest, but the spirit and devotion behind her sacrifice makes it all the more significant and memorable. Born on 15 December 1928 in Tezpur, she jumped into the freedom struggle in 1942. Like many others, the Quit India events of 1942 had sparked anti-British ideas in the minds of Barua. She gathered 100 volunteers during individual *Satyagraha* form a Mahila Sevika Dal to work at night to disseminate secret news to underground freedom fighters. This group used to organise rallies, where inspiring patriotic couplets were sung of which just one is reproduced below:

Vishwa vijayi Nawjawan	World conqueror youth, be
Taikariba lagiba Agnisaman	like fire, lightning and
Ulkpath Bajrapat, Hoshiyar, Hoshiyar	thunder, remain alert, alert

In 1942, during the Quit India movement, she was arrested but due to overcrowding of the jail she was released. She was an active member of the Tezpur Mahila Samiti, which was established in 1928 in Assam. In 1947, the Tezpur Mahila Samiti extended its organisational activities by federating a large number of primary, village Mahila Samitis into it. Barua was, however, never offered a rank in politics. After independence, she took up the job of a teacher and continued her social work. She motivated women to join cooperative societies and persuaded them to be self reliant. She kept organising plays to infuse confidence in women to her ripe age. Many of her plays were staged in Assam. Some of her famous popular plays are Karangar, Ligari, Bandini, Kalyani, Jay Mati and Dhatte Panna. She was not happy about the present day circumstances in the country in general and Assam in particular. Her heart bled whenever she saw divisive politics that bred fear that threw the gauntlet of insurgencies in the North- East. She pinned her hopes on the teachers to mould the young generation in such a way that they would feel proud of their nation and devote themselves to its service in the right earnest and promote gender equality.

Hema Kakoti[18] is another woman of Assam who actively participated in the freedom struggle. An octogenarian, Kakoti got inspired to work for the nation through her father late Durganand Kakoti and her grandmother, Sunder Bor Kakoti. Her father used her as an agent to pass on information to revolutionaries, and being young, she was never suspected by the police. In 1942, the police ransacked her house, and arrested both her father and grandmother. However, because of her tender age, she was left alone at home. She later on became the president of Sivasagar District Congress. In 1948 she went to Wardha for training. After that she came in contact with Binoba Bhave. She toured with him on foot, propagating Khadi and Bhoodan. Subsequently, she joined Kasturba Gandhi Memorial Trust and has been working there ever since as a Trust member. She has been working with Shakuntala Chaudhary for the empowerment of women, eradication of social evils and prohibitions. The contribution of these humble women folk speaks volumes of the abilities they possess to build a balanced and harmonious society as dreamt by Gandhiji. It is these women who could help in building up a positive attitude among the youth.

Hema Bharali[19] was yet another woman, whose name should be inscribed in red letter in the freedom history of Assam. She was born on 19 February 1919 at Lakhimpur. Like all great Assamese freedom fighters, Hema Bharali understood best her country and the world. A name synonymous with nationalistic pursuits, she was a great Assamese of whom every Indian can justifiably feel proud of. She dedicated herself to social work and never bothered about popularity, power and fame. Though coming from a very protective family, the parents especially mother wanted her to get married and lead a secured life. But like her brothers she rather gave preference to her social duties. She averred that if the foundation of society will be weak, it would be difficult to achieve national freedom. After her matriculation she joined the freedom movement. For pursuing her education and simultaneously participating in the freedom struggle, Hema Bharali joined Mahila Ashram in Wardha. Wardha was then a focal point of attraction for many prominent national leaders and freedom fighters all of whom inspired her a lot. She fought many odds on her way to free her motherland from foreign yoke. She organised various processions and rallies against British. She felt that the youth should have missionary zeal to work in villages.

Silent Motivators

Behind the story of these active women revolutionaries lies a small but tragic episode of the wives and mothers of some veteran freedom fighters. Jawaharlal Nehru had remarked: "when most of the men-folk were in prison then a remarkable thing happened. Our women came forward and took charge of the struggle." The thousands of housewives, mostly mothers and wives, who provided indirect support from the rear by shouldering family responsibilities when their men went to jail or got killed, should not be forgotten. These women had always been there, but in 20th century there was an avalanche of them, which took not only the British Government but their own men folk by surprise. Women like Mina Agrawala,[20] Surya Bala

Bardoloi[21] and Jayanti Gogoi[22] virtually lived through hell, while supporting their revolutionary husbands. They pledged *Swadeshi*, faced police raids and formed women groups to collect money to help the families of arrested freedom fighters. In order to have more precise information about these women freedom fighters, this author wished to obtain the opinion of their male counterparts. Sincere and arduous efforts helped me to meet a few great surviving male freedom fighters.

With inquisitiveness to find out answers to few searching questions like: "how did they feel about their fellow fighters draped in saree? How did they rate them? Did they find their contribution essential for achieving freedom?" the freedom fighters this author met were Satish Chandra Kakoti, (23rd October 1914) Madhu Das (16th November 1917), Pravin Kumar Sharma, Sarat Chandra Sinha, Gauri Bhattacharjee (10th December 1914) Bipin Pal Das, Rabindra Nath Sarma, Lakshydhar Choudhuri (Assam in 1915) and Navdwip Ranjan Patgiri. All these octogenarians cherished the memory of the freedom struggle movement in a very interesting and enthusiastic manner. All of them reminisced about their rigorous imprisonment by defying the Cunningham Circular of the Government of Assam in 1930s. All of them, at some point or the other, were expelled from their respective schools. All of them actively participated in the Civil Disobedience movement and picketed before the foreign cloth shops in Guwahati and discouraged the people from buying them.

The burning desire of serving the nation compelled all of them to organize movements at their own level. Majority of them realized importance of the pen and felt that a large member of students could be drawn into the movement through transformation of the mindset. During 1942 Quit India Movement, they stuck to writing and circulating pamphlets, revolutionary messages and wrote provoking articles. After independence, all of them served the government selflessly but all of them had one point of view of feeling frustrated at social political and economic policies of post independence India. All optimist octogenarian opined on the same line that the existing insurgencies would not last as these types of activities needed public support. All of them aver that only value based education can solve the problems and the existing nasty political situation has been exacerbating the situation. They talked very vehemently against gender bias. They assertively reiterated that quite a few women participated in the movement and the roles of Kanakalata, Chandraprabha, Saikiani, Amol Prabha Das, Pushpalata Das, Hema Kakoti Suwarnalata Mohanto, Hemlata Bharali and many others could not be neglected, ignored or forgotten. Their heart bleeds in pain when they talk about martyr Kanakalata, who at the age of sixteen sacrificed her life while hoisting the tri-colour flag at Dhekiajuli police station. They all felt that as Florence Nightingale was appreciated everywhere, their women freedom fighters, too deserve to be appreciated and applauded. They had a common complaint against the male dominant politics, which did not give them their due importance. They spoke very strongly about western countries and quoted them liberally that showed to some extent; if not entirely, how these foreign countries recognised the potential of women and gave them due position in public life. On the contrary in India what to speak of 33 per cent reservation for women! The male leaders are not ready to share their limited rights with them. They themselves felt sad that they never included women in their own respective movements. Because of the socialisation they always felt that they should contribute indirectly by taking care of children. But majority is in oblivion. They agreed that despite their capabilities and potentialities, men folk were not letting women come to the forefront, and whosoever came amidst all oppositions, remained unsung and unheard. They all lamented that even 33 per cent representation is not sufficient as regard to their services since women constitute 50% of the population. They strongly felt bad about the neglected position of women after independence. With regard to the position of women in Assam, there was unanimity of opinion that although women in Assam were better off than their counterparts in rest of the country, the patriarchy within the existing political system did not allow them to get their genuine share. They remembered the time, when Anwara Taimur was appointed education minister and how quite a few people had opposed her holding a high position. A few Maulavis of madrassa refused to attend her meeting. They all despised the attitude of male dominated cabinet, which used women at the time of movement as they required female members and dropped them when it came to power sharing. All condemned the existing religious system and claimed that the ethos of religion had to be changed and then only women would get fairness and justice not only in politics, but in all spheres of life. They said that women become so indifferent to their humiliation that they ignore their subservient position. Regarding women all agreed collectively that they have a long way to go. In the patriarchal society they should fight their own battle to assert their rights and carve their own niche in the men's world. They have to wage a relentless struggle to secure a due place in the society. They have to fight as they are the masters of their fate. I felt solace after talking to their male counterparts and felt that at least their partners of freedom struggle empathized with them and wanted them to have their dues and still remember them even if their names were missing from the history books of Assam.

Conclusion

The case study of all these women fighters reveals that they got into the freedom struggle at very tender age, largely because of the influence of the society. The society was then in ferment in a patriotic fervor. And when they came off age, they realized the pressing need of the hour for independence and decided to choose celibacy rejecting the comforts and the security of a married life, plunged headlong into working towards the welfare of the mankind, society and nation. All these panegyrics, however, do not mitigate the pathos they had passed through. Research findings largely keep silent and thus speak volume about the neglect we have meted out to women's participation in the freedom struggle in the patriarchal society of India. The women want to contribute effectively in the progress of nation, but a gender biased society and its restrictions do not permit them to utilize their potential to the optimum.

The history of evolution of the Indian society does not recognize the efforts put in by women folk, yet much can be said about the crucial role played by women during the most significant chapter in Indian history. During the freedom struggle, when there was need of too many people, the patriarchal society included women in order to swell the rank, but forgot to record their role, thus relegating them to the background. Violence, criminalisation and character assassination—all outcomes of gender bias, curtailed their participation in all spheres of activities in the freedom struggle. This is why we are compelled to say that sixty two years after independence, we have failed in redressing inequalities in education, labour, legal rights, art and literature. Generation to come will have to work hard in establishing a genuinely equitable society. The imperative task in front of the nation is to promote and ensure equitable gender relations.

History has always been written from endocentric point of view, focusing on male and their role in building and moulding the society. This lop sided focus needs to strike a balance with gaenocentric analysis, or rather provide its due place to the deserving females, whose role history preserves as memorabilia. An equitable approach to analysis of events of bygone years is what we actually need in rewriting history: not endocentric or gaenocentric, but men and women, shouldering equal responsibility must get equal weightage for their part played in history. Perhaps then into the next millennium India's freedom will have really a different meaning for the citizens regardless of their gender. Gandhi squarely summed up the strength of womanhood in his tribute to the gender by asking a volley of pertinent questions and by saying: "to call woman the weaker sex is a libel; it is man's injustice to women. If by strength is meant moral power then woman is immeasurably man's superior. Has she not got greater intuition? Is she not more self sacrificing? Has she not greater power of endurance? Has she not got greater courage? Will she not be without her man? If non-violence is the law of our being, the future is woman. I have nursed this thought now for years." And the future has to follow this.

Notes

1. Anil Dutta Mishra, (1998): *Gender Perspective*, New Delhi: Radha Publication, p. 5.
2. The author worked in the Northeast between 2000-02 during the summer and autumn breaks to collect data on women freedom fighters of the region. This article is based on observation and interviews.
3. Bibekanand Das and L.N. Das, (1995): *The Feminine Gender*, New Delhi: Manak Publications, p. 138.
4. Meera Koshambi, (ed.), (1994): *Women Oppression in the Public Gaze*, RCWS, SNDT University, p. 3.
5. *History of Freedom Movement papers*, R.I. File No. 39/3, National Archives of India.
6. Satish Chandra Kakati, (1954): *Discovery of Assam*, Guwahati, pp. 23-25.
7. Extracted from *Guwahati University Journal*, 1988, pp. 1-3.
8. Manmohan Kaur, (1998): *Women in India's Freedom Struggle*, Guwahati: Champavati Publication, pp. 14-19.
9. Dipti Sharma and Anuradha Dutta, (1998): *Women's Role in Freedom Struggle in Assam*, Guwahati.
10. P.L. Barua, (1978): *Assam District Gazetteers*, Guwahati.
11. Dr. H.K. Borpujari, (ed.), (1999): *Political History of Assam*, Govt. of Assam, Vols. I, II, III, Guwahati, pp. 39-56.
12. B.N. Dutta and K.N. Baroah, (1969): *Landmarks of the Freedom Struggle in Assam*, Guwahati, pp. 56-78.
13. C.A. Bhuyan, (1970): *Political History of Assam*, Vol. 2, Guwahati, pp. 23-45.
14. *History sheet of T.R. Phookan*, Home Pool, Confidential File No. 66, 1924—K.W.X. NAI.
15. Interview with Swarana Lata Mohanto Baido at her friend's residence at Pan Bazaar, June, 2001. Her contribution to the freedom struggle was referred to by Satish Chandra Kakoti, an eminent freedom fighter during his interview on 28 May, 2001 at his residence at Basistha Chairali, Guwahati, Assam. See Gopinath Bardoloi Committee Report.
16. Interview with Puspalata Das Baido at her residence at Kala Pahar, on 10 June 2001.1) See O.K. Das, Jivansmriti, Guwahati, 1938, p. 179. Also see Puspalata Das, Asohajog Andolanat Narir Abadan.
17. Interview with Pramila Barua on 18 June, 2000 at her residence

at Tejpur near Tejpur Mahila Samiti, in Sonitpur district of Assam.

18. Interview with Hema Kakoti on 25 June, 2000 at her residence in Kasturba Gandhi Memorial Trust at Guwahati, Assam.
19. Interview with Hema Bharali on 26 June, 2000 at her residence in Pub Saraniya at Guwahati, Assam.
20. Interview with Mina Agrawala on 18 June, 2000 at her residence at Tejpur in Sonitpur district of Assam.
21. Interview with Suryabala Bardoloi on 25 June, 2000 at her residence at Rehabari in Guwahati.
22. Interview with Jayanti Gogoi on 26 June, 2000 at her residence at Bamani Press Road, Guwahati.

5

TREND OF HISTORICAL RESEARCH IN TRIPURA
A Survey

Satyadeo Poddar

In consonance with the trend of history writing of India, the North East India and Tripura in particular has seen a glorious tradition of historiography. In Assam, during 13th century, there emerged a class of chronicles called the buranjis in both Tai and Assamese language and in Tripura during 15th century, 'the Rajmala.' The Buranjis in Assam and Rajmala in Tripura are considered a valuable source of information in medieval Indian history of the region. The Buranjis occupied the same place as the "bakhar" and the khayats do in the Maharashtra and Rajasthan respectively.[1] Tripura Buranji written by Surya Kumar Bhuyan (in English and Assamese), Department of Historical and Antiquarian Studies, Gauhati, 1983 is a chronicle of Tipperah in Bengal, which has been reproduced from an old manuscript in the British Museum, London, a photostat copy of which was obtained in January 1936 through the courtesy of Dr. Lionel D. Barnett, the then keeper of Oriental Books and Manuscripts. The manuscript was purchased by the authorities of the British Museum from one J. Rodd on January 8, 1842.[2]

The title of the book, inscribed on the cover of the original manuscript is "Tripura Deser Kathar Lekha" or an account of the country of Tripura, which is amplified in explanatory sub-heading as a description of the friendly missions sent by Maharaja Rudra Singha to Ratna Manikya, Raja of Tripura. The chronicle Tripura Buranji derives its importance principally from the circumstances in which it was compiled, the revelations which it contains of the "international" or Pan-Indian interests of the Assamese monarch Swargadeo Rudra Singha (1696-1714), and the mass of information which it presents about the history, topography, resources and customs of Tripura, and about the revolution at the Tripura capital enacted before the eyes of the narrators. The chronicle was written in 1724 A.D. by Ratna Kandali Sarma and Arjun Das Bairagi who had visited the court as agents of King Rudra Singha on different occasions between the years 1709 and 1715. The Ahom Government had hitherto held no communication with the Tripura Court, though in ancient times the kingdom of Kamrupa and Tripura had intimate political relations. The object of Rudra Singha's embassies was to establish relations with Tripura in furtherance of his aim to organize a confederacy of the Hindu rulers against the Moghuls.[3]

The trend of history writing in North East India in general and Tripura in particular in the 19th and 20th century is influenced by the prevailing approaches of history writing during colonial and post colonial period. All the philosophical and ideological developments of the 18th and 19th centuries had succeeded in dividing the world of social science research (of which historical research is an important element) into two major steps—the Liberal positivist and Historical Materialists or popularly known as the Marxists. Just as the entire Indian history writing developments till 1947 were always a step behind the developments taking place in England, because of India's not only economic dependence on England, but even intellectual development to a large extent. Similarly, because of the comparative economic backwardness of the North East, the social and consequently academic and intellectual developments also felt the effect of this.[4]

Before the onset of the colonial rule, the region had its own vehicles of carrying forth historical consciousness of the people and the famous Buranji literature of the Ahom period fall into the medieval tradition of Annals and Chronicles which were external records of the historical consciousness of the time. The trend of writing comprehensive histories of the region, on modern historiographical lines begins with Edward Gait, followed by S.K. Bhuyan who besides writing on Assam's relation with the British, made available to researchers many Buranjis by compiling, editing and translating them. Gait and Bhuyan were followed by a number of historians. But the main trend of history writing in the pre-1947 period and years that closely followed and were heavily influenced by liberal ideas of empiricism and documentation with very little attempts at critical interpretative analysis. From the 1950s onwards, a methodological progress was seen in the writings of H.K. Barpujari. With him began a trend which shifted somewhat from the solely empiricist tradition of the earlier period. Barpujari has dominated historical writing in Assam in the post 1950s period not only by his own writings but by a guiding numerous research scholars in their quest for historical knowledge. From the end of the 1960s a new trend in the development of the historiography of the region came to be seen in the writings of scholars like Amalendu Guha and Hiren Gohain. These scholars have attempted a more comprehensive understanding of the various phases from historical materialist standpoint. They have thus posed the first real alternative to positivist historiography in the region. They have thus initiated a trend which it develops as Kosambi or R.S. Sharma and others developed it for other parts of India, will lead to historical writings which would not remain at the level of chronicles, documents or narration but would go down to studying the sequence of development in socio-economic formations. Manorama Sharma in her article, written in the 14th Session of the North East India History Association narrates that the main problems in developments of historical writings in the North East India has been a serious shortcomings in the methodological and theoretical orientation. One major area to which all historians of the region has to give special importance is the field of oral history. As Paul Thomson has written, "the term oral history is new. But it does not mean that it has no past. In fact, oral history is as old as history itself. It was the first kind of history."[5] Mahadev Chakravarti in his Presidential Address in the 19th Annual Session of the North East India History association at Khima, 198 stresses the importance of culture as an important domination in writing the comprehensive cultural history of the North East and apprehends threats from internal and external agencies to fossilize the indigenous culture.[6] In the words of K.N. Panikkar, the present attack on indigenous culture is due to the fact that "... within culture is embedded immense possibilities of challenge and resistance against all forms of domination."[7]

The trend of historiography in Tripura can be divided into two parts viz history writing under Princely Tripura and Post Princely days. One of the important sources of history of Tripura is known as Rajmala which was written during the time of Maharaja Dharma Manikya (1431-1462 AD). The literary meaning of Rajmal is "the garland of kings", was in fact the court history of Tripura. The King entrusted the task of writing the oral tradition of Tripura to Durlabhendra Cantai, the High priest, and the Court-poets, Banesvar Deva Sarman and Sukresvar Deva Sarman who composed the first volume. Subsequently, some other kings continued to patronize the task and the book in six volumes were produced which narrates the account of 15th to 19th century Tripura. The name of this famous work is Sri Rajmala, according to Kali Prasanna Sen, though "Sri" does not occur in any colophon. This book is written in Bengali verse. The first four parts (khanda) contain a very useful and extensive commentary of Kaliprasanna Sen, and their poet-authors are Durlabhendra Cantai, Banesvar, Sukresvar (Vol. I) Rana-Catur Narayan (Vol. II), Gangadhar Siddhanta-Vagisa (Vol. III) and Durgamani Uzir (Vol. IV). Though Sri Rajmala is a state chronicle of Tripura, written in Bengali verse, later on translated in English by Dr. N.C. Nath (Vol. I to IV) from Tribal Research Institute, Govt. of Tripura in 1999. There are many facts of this book which are based on myth and belief and in that way it lessens the gravity of historical treatise. While verifying the facts, the good faith of author be checked in drawing historical conclusion. But the Rajmala written by Kailash Chandra Singh in two volumes is a valuable document which unfolds the functioning of party politics in the administration and it seems more authentic and has been referred by many scholars in recent history writing of the State of Tripura.

The books written by colonial historians as officials of East India Company and British Paramountacy do reflect the trend of history writing on Tripura. Rajmala or An Analysis of the Chronicles of the Kings of Tripura by Rev. James Long, was the first booklet in English which unfolded the history of Tripura to the world. It was first published in the *Journal of the Asiatic Society* in 1852 which was reprinted in Dacca in Isan Press in 1911. It has long been out of print. S.C. Chaudhuri, published this book in a revised edition in 1978 from Firma KLM (Pvt), Lts., Calcutta. The approaches of history writing of James Mill is reflected in the book of E.F. Sandys, "History of Tripura" first published in 1915 and later republished in 1997 by the Tripura State Tribal Cultural Research Institute and Museum. Mr. Sandys was a manager of the Chakla Roshnabad, a British officer and sometime was Private Secretary to Maharaja Bir Bikram Kishore Manikya. The books characterize ancient Tripura as the period of Hindu Tripura, Medieval Tripura as Mahomeddan period and Modern Tripura as English period. The utilitarian and pragmatic concept of enlightenment school of historians is reflected in the writings of Sandys. This book depicts the Tripura-British relations, State's Eastern Boundary issues and status of Chakla-Roshnabad vis-a-vis the Muslims rulers and the British Government. There are other books viz. Alexander Mackenzie, the History of North East Frontiers of India, Delhi 1981 (Reprint); C.U. Aitcheson, A Collection of Treatise, Engagements and Sanads Relating to India and Neighbouring countries, Vol. II, Mittal Publication, New Delhi 1997 (Reprint); B.B. Robert Smart, Geographical and Statistical Report of the District of Tipperah, the Bengal Secretariat Office, Calcutta, 986; B.C. Allen; E.A. Gait; C.G.H. Alen; H.F. Howward, Gazetteers of Bengal and North East India, Mittal Publishing

Delhi, 1984; K.D. Menon, Tripura State Gazetteers, 1975; Imperial Gazetteer of India, Oxford, 1908; Grierson, G.A., Languages of North East India, Vol. I, Delhi, 1987 (Reprint); T.H. Lewin, The Hill Tracts of Chittagong and Dwellers Therein, Calcutta, 1869 and Wild Races of the Eastern Frontier of India, Mittal Publishing, Delhi, 1984; W.W. Hunter, A Statistical Account of Bengal, Vol. VI, D.K. Publishing House, New Delhi, 1973 (Reprint). These books represent the facts of colonial time and in so many places, inaccuracy and biasness of imperial rule is reflected. Hunter depiction about the then Tripura is confined within the periphery of Agartala and its adjoining places and the socio-account of all tribes have not been touched accurately. The Reports of Political Agents during Bir Chandra Manikya is an important source of history and that too makes a contradiction with the accounts of Kailash Chandra Singha about the court history of Tripura.

There are some valuable sources of history of Tripura which were written by individual writers, nobles under Princely Rule in India viz. Achut Charan Choudhury, Srihatter Itibritta (in Bengali), published by Upendranath Pal Choudhury, 1317 B.E.; Brajendra Chandra Datta, Udaipur Bibaran, Rajdhani Agartala Press, 1340 T.E.; Col. Mohim Chandra Thakur, Deshya Rajya (in Bengali); Nawadwip Bahadur, Awarnajhuri (manuscript from in Bengali), published in Tribeni Patrika, Calcutta, 1916; Radha Mohan Thakur, Kok-Borak Maa (in Bengali script, Tripura Bhasha); Chaitanya Jantra, Comilla, 1900 A.D.; Tripura Katha Mala, Tripura Bhasha Vidhan; Kali Prasanna Gupta Vidyabhusan, Panch Manikya, Agartala 1351 T.E (1941 A.D.); Suprasanna Bandÿopadhyay, Tripura State Gazette Sankalan, Education Department, Government of Tripura, 1971; Somendra Chandra Debbarma, Census Bibarani, Census Office, Tripura State, 1932; Tripur Chandra Sen, Tripura Deser Katha (1626-1715), Agartala, 1372 B.S. (in Bengali); Maharaja Kumar Sahadev Bikram Kishore Dev Barman, Princely Tripura's Constitutional Act, 1351 T.E. (1941 A.D.), Agartala, 2002; Sambhu Chandra Mookherjee, Travel and Voyages between Calcutta and independent Tipperah, Reis and Rayyet Office, Calcutta, 1987. This literature, though not written in the methodological form of scientific history, but it provides ample information and knowledge from where, the socio-cultural history of Tripura can be framed. The development of Bengali language as the official language owes its origin in the writings of these luminaries of the time. The trend of history writings of nobles and officials of the State of Tripura contributed to some extent in the promotion of composite culture of the State.

With the advent of the British in the Eastern India, attempts were made to annex the Territory of Tripura State to that of the British India, but successive kings of Tripura, beginning from Krishna Manikya, foiled the mechanism of British officials, protégés of the sultans of Bengal. They succeeded to a great extent to maintain its separate entity as a Princely State till its merger with the republic of India in 1947. The administration of the State was transferred to the Dominion Government on 15th October, 1948 and the State of Tripura became a part "C" State of the Indian Union. In 1956 when the Indian States were reorganized, Tripura became a centrally administered Territory. When the Territorial Council Act of 1956 was passed, the Tripura Territorial Council was formed with 32 members headed by the leader of the Congress Party S.L. Singh as the Chairman. The Government of Union Territories Act which came into existence on July 1963, provided an opportunity for a Legislative Assembly to be filled by persons by direct election. Under this Act first popular Ministry of Tripura was installed on July 1963. In 1970, Chief Commissioner was designated as Lt. Governor. On 21, January 1972, Tripura became a full State of the Indian Union.

The trend of history writing in Tripura after the accession of this State into India Union is reflected in many domains of socio-economic life of the State. The book of Debabrata Goswami on *"Military History of Tripura (1490 to 1947),"* published from Tripura State Tribal Cultural Research Institute & Museum, Government of Tripura in 1996 stresses the intermingling of the martial traditions of the plains and the hills. Academic study of war history is a recent phenomenon. Annals of wars, whenever maintained, mainly aimed at eulogizing a particular hero or to narrate about the people. Such materials are so mixed up with imaginary attributes that it is even difficult to shift out any accurate account then reconstruct the historical facts. But Dr. Goswami has tried to project the military skill and acumen of the Tripura rulers which helps us to understand the social history of Tripura in a broader way. He admits that the armed forces of a country no longer function in isolation, but as an integral part of the nation.[8] Goswami justifies the need of military history in Marxian tradition. According to the Marxian interpretation when the State "emerged, as the result of the disintegration of the primitive communal system and the society's split into opposing classes, the need arose for specially organized armed detachments, placed above society and called upon to suppress the exploited masses in the interests of the exploiting upper crust, and to wage wars of aggression."[9] Karl Marx admitted, "the history of the army brings out more clearly than anything else the correctness of our conception of the connection between the productive forces and social relation."[10] While narrating the military history, he admits the importance of resources and geographical location matter much. The elephants of Tripura was an object of attraction for the invaders. Though, the rulers of Tripura did not raise regular army. The soldiers were conscripted during an attack and used their own traditional weapons like bows and arrows, khadgas etc. Dhanya Manikya during 15th century proved himself capable to inundate the camps of his enemy. In the middle of the 16th century, Vijay Manikya too proved his bravery by his surprise attack on enemies. Amar Manikya's battle formation in the style of "Garuda Vyuha "of the ancient days to face and defeat his powerful adversaries—was an example of military exploits.[11]

Recently, there are some books which have been published from Tribal Research Institute, Government of Tripura, Agartala in English and Bengali, indicates the emergence of new information in farming the socio-economic history of the State. This institute publishes "TUI" a quarterly research journal on tribal life and culture. Bidrohi Reang Neta Ratanmani (1993, in Bengali) by Tarit Mohan Dasgupta; Tripura in the Eighteenth

Century with Samser Gazi against Feudalism (1995); Sri Rajmal Vol. III English version (1996) by P.C. Dhar; Tripura Administration Report-1872-1878 (part I) and part II (1878-90); Introducing Malsoom (1996) by Ramendra Narayan Sen; The Darlong of Tripura (1996) by L. Darlong; Shrenimala (Re-print in Bengali, 1996) by Col. Mohim Thakur; Deshiya Rajya (in Bengali, 1996) by Col. Mohim Thakur; Pancha Manikya (Re-print in Bengali, 1996) by Kaliprasanna Sen; The Chakmas of Tripura (1998) by Panna Lal Majumdar; The Rupinis of Tripura (1998) by Upendra Rupini; Tripura Desher Katha (Re-print) Bengali, 1998 by Tripur Chandra Sen; Survey Settlement of the Chakla Roshnabad (1892-1899) (Re-print) by Samrendra Debbarma (1998); Census Bibarani 1931 (Re-print, 1998) by Samrendra Debbarma; Customary Laws and Practices in Reangs of Tripura (1998) by B.K. Kilikdar; Rajmala, Vol. I to IV (1999) by Dr. N.C. Nath; The Murasings (1999) by R.K. Acharyya; Art and Architecture of Tripura (1997) by Ratna Das. These books enrich the trend of regional history writings and the tribes of the State.

Tripura in the light of Socio-Political Movements since 1945 (Progressive publishers, 2004) by Bijan Mohanta deals with the socio-political advancements in Tripura through tribal and non-tribal people. Their movements speeded up the March of Tripura from Monarch to Democracy and shaped the lives and destiny of the people of the State. J.B. Ganguly, *Economic Problems of Jhumias of Tripura*, Calcutta, 1969, the Benign Hills: A Study in Population Growth problem, 1963; and his recent book, *An Economic History of North East India (1826 to 1947)*, Akansha Publishing House, 2006, B.K. Roy Burman, *Demographic and Socio-economic Profiles of the Hill Areas of North-East India*, J.B. Bhattacharjee, *Trade and Colony: the British Colonization of North East India*, NEIHA, Shillong and "*Some Documents of Economic situation in Tripura, 929-1936: a Study of the Impact of Great Depression,*" published in J.B. Bhattacharjee (ed.) *Studies in the Economic History of North East India*, Har-Anand Publications, New Delhi, 1994 Bani Prasanna Misra, *Socio-Economic Adjustments of Tribals, Case Study of Tripura* Jhumias, People's Publishing House, New Delhi; Ranjit Kumar

De (ed.) *The Statistical Account of Tripura*, Uppal Publishing House, New Delhi, 2000 and the book of Prabhas Ranjan Bhatatcharya entitled Economic Transition in Tripura, Vikas Publishing House, New Delhi, 1993, Reflections on the History of Tripura by Dipak Kumar Chaudhuri, published from Bhasa, 2006 and others are the examples of the writings of economic history of Tripura.

The book written by K.B. Jamtia on *Modernity and Tradition : A historical Study of the Jamatias of Tripura* published from Akshar Publications, 2007 and Introducing Malsom of Ramendra Narayan Sen and Omesh Saigal's book on *Tripura: Its History and Culture*, Concept Publishing House, 1978 and the book of J. Ganchoudhuri on *Tripura and the Reangs of Tripura*; Ram Gopal Singh, *The Kukis of Tripura*, manifest the trend of writing the history of the tribes in relations with the history of the Greater India. These writings have tried to fill the gap of the history writing of India in relation to the North- East India which was felt by the historians of the region and that too has promoted partially the sense of exclusion in the mindset of the people of North East India.

Sukhendu Debbarma's book on *Origin and Growth of Christianity in Tripura*, Indus Publication, New Delhi, 1996, Dr. Dwijendra Lal Bhowmik, *Tribal Religion of Tripura*, TRI, Government of Tripura 2003, the book of Dr. Palit on Religions of Tripura do manifest the trend of writings the history of *Buddhism, Hinduism and Christianity in the State of Tripura* and it certainly upholds the rich cultural tradition of the State.

The political history of the State of Tripura has been touched by the writings of H.K. Sur, *British Relations with the State of Tripura 1760-1947*, Sarswati Publication, 1983; Mahadev Chakravarti, Jyotish Dutta and Vishmadev Bhattacharya, Ratna Das, Rajmala, 2002; D.K. Choudhuri, *The Political Agents and the Native Raj-Conflict, Conciliation and Progress, Tripura between 1871 to 1890*, Mittal Publications, Delhi, 2002; Dwijendra Chandra Datta and Suprasanna Bandyopadhyay, Rajgi Tripurar Sarkari Bangla, 1976 and N.R. Choudhuri, *Tripura in Transition*.

Thus, it can be concluded that the recent writings on the history and culture of Tripura as enumerated above is the testimony which made help to bridge the gap of socio-cultural contour of Tripura with the rest of India. It has also manifested the rich cultural tradition of India particularly when we visualize the art and architecture and cultural of the State as depicted in the work of Smt Ratna Das; K., Lahiri; N.K. Bose and others. With the pace of writing the history of post-colonial history of North East India, the history of Tripura too finds proper space in the field of political, economic, tribal and religious history of the land.

Notes

1. Shrutidev Goswami, (1993): "Progress of Historical Research in North East India, A Survey", in the Proceedings of North East India History Association, Fourteenth Session, Jorhat, p. 355.
2. Ratnakandi and Arjundas Katakai edited by Surya Kumar Bhuyan, (1983): Department of Historical and Antiquarian Studies, Gauhati, p. Introduction, III
3. Ibid.
4. Manorama Sharma, (1993): *op. cit.*, p. 369.
5. Ibid., p. 383.
6. Mahadev Chakravarti, (1998): Presidential Address Booklet of NEIHA, 19th Session, Kohima, p. 14
7. D. Goswami, (1996): *Military History of India*, Tripura State Tribal Cultural Research Institute & Museum, Government of Tripura, Agartala, p. 2
8. Ibid., also see, Yeveny, Dolgopolov, (1981): *The Army and the Revolutionary Transformation of Society*, Moscow, p. 9.
9. D. Goswami, *op. cit.*, p. 2.
10. Ibid., p. 171.

6

SINO-INDIAN CONFLICT OF 1962 & NEHRU

Ajai Kumar Misra

"My own picture for the future is a federation which includes China and India, Burma and Ceylon, Afghanistan and possible other countries. If a world federation comes that will be Welcome."[1]

This was version of Jawaharlal Lal Nehru, which he has mentioned in his Autobiography. It appears from the above statement of Pt. Nehru that he was confident about an amicable solution of the Sino-Indian Border dispute which was outcome of McMahon Line. Before discussing in detail about Sino- Indian relations, let us have a look on the historical Simla Conference in which the Boundaries between India & Tibet were settled. This conference was held in Simla from October 1913 to July 1914. The McMahon Line was a product of this conference.[2] In this conference the British representative Sir Arthur Henry McMahon demanded the creation and delimitation of an Outer Tibet as virtually a separate entity, and An Inner Tibet where China was to be retaining administrative rights. Strong pressure to bring about this was applied in Simla talks themselves and also in Bejing where the British Minister declared "The patience of His Majesty's Government was exhausted and...unless. The Simla Convention is signed H.M.G. will hold themselves free to sign with Tibet."[3]

In July the British Government declared that China has rejected the 'Convention' and any separate arrangements Britain might sign with anyone in Tibet would be regarded as null and void. In March 1914 McMahon had induced Xazha a representative of Tibetan local administration, to sign at Delhi, secretly and apart from the open Simla talks, a map which placed several of Tibet's south eastern counties within the British India Empire. Not only this, many months before the Simla Xazha had been coached by the British delegate Sir Charles Bell political officer-in-charge of Sikkim and a major theoretician and practitioner of frontier expansionism. Thus Simla Conference was mere formality[4] Xazha's action was condemned and repudiated by the Lhasa's authorities along with the Chinese Government The map of McMahon Line as border line was published till 1938, when China was pressed by imminent Japanese invasion. The Chiang Kaishek government of that time also refused to accept the Line, after which, it was withdrawn Thus Simla conference ended without signature of the delegation of China. Thus Simla Conference was secretly signed by the British & Tibetan representative. The Simla conference produced no agreement in which the Government of China was a party McMahon himself admitted that it was a great failure that he left India without having secured the formal adherence of the Chinese Government to a Tri-partite Agreement[5] After the refusal of the Chinese Government the map disappeared from the British Indian The Simla agreement provided much grounds for the international lawyers and was to be sieved over again and again in the Sino-Indian relations.

The British Government always treated the Simla Conference as a failure. Because the Government of India had been unduly anxious to secure the best terms for Tibet and the Chinese always denied That Tibet as a sovereign state and not accepted the terms of Simla Conference. Not only had this have the two Governors of Assam in British India also questioned about the validity of McMahon Line. In a letter published in the *Times,* London on 3 September 1959 Sir H.J. Twynam a former Governor of Assam wrote

As it is now well known since began publicizing maps indicating that the Frontiers of India stopped at the foot hills on the northern Bank of Brahmputra the Government of India both British Indian have laid stress on what is called McMahon Line have pursued on active policy of exploration an penetration into the vast hinterland lying between Brahmputra Valley and the Himalayas. But the McMahon Line, which sought to serve the main crest of the Himalayas as frontier does not exist and never existed.[6]

An other former Governor Sir Robert Reid observed—As late as September 1936 an Assam Government letter recorded that the 1914 convention was never published mainly because Chinese Government failed to ratify it and nothing was done to give effects to McMahon's recommendations for extension of administration in the Tawang area. "He further wrote that Captain Lightfoot visited Tawang region in 1938. Reid also revealed the attitude of Tibetan Government towards Tawang, where he found Tibetan Administration fully operative. They regarded the adjustment of Tibet-Indian boundary as a part and parcel of General adjustment of boundaries contemplated in the 1914 Simla Convention. If they could with our help secure a definite Sino- Tibetan boundary, they would have course, be glad to observe the Sino-Tibetan border as defined in 1914. They had been encouraged in thinking that His Majesty's Government sympathized with this way of regarding the matter owing to the fact that at no time along since the Convention and Declaration of 1914 had the Indian Government taken steps to question Tibetan rights and British authority in the Tawang area. On the Simla agreement Viceroy Lord Hardings wrote:

> We recognize that consideration of eastern part or India-Chinese portion of North - Eastern Frontier did not form part of Functions of the conference and we therefore request that the views and proposal do not carry the endorsement of Government of India. As soon as we have time to examine this we shall address you're Lordship Hardings never followed this.[7]

Thus McMahon proposals were also not endorsed by the

Government of India also. The Chinese also rejected McMahon's proposals. On 21 November 1962 the Times London exposed a specific outcome of forward policy perused by the Government of British India in 1914 when it produced a map depicting India's frontier in North Eastern sector. It showed the McMahon Line as a border as well as the border that existed earlier revealing the area bounded by the McMahon Line and earlier border line. According to this cartographic exposition, places like Tawang Bomdila Rupa and Walong lie in this area bounded on the north by the pre-McMahon Line and the south by McMahon Line frontier line. The McMahon Line, which sought to serve crest of northern frontier and led to a border war between India and China, never recognized by either the Government of British India or China, thus naturally becomes a matter of amusement and consternation.

After independence the Indian Ministry of States published two white papers on Indian States in 1948 and 1950 in which authoritative maps carrying the legend boundary undefined for the entire western sector from the trijunction of India, China and Afghanistan borders to Karakoram Pass and further east till it descends Kangra district of Himachal Pradesh. The legend was repeated in the trijunction of India, China and Nepal. In the eastern sector McMahon Line was shown as though a clear boundary line but marked as Undemarcated. In 1946 the Indian Army accepted the Karakoram Range as the northern boundary of India in the western sector. This state of northern boundary was the product of the then deputy secretary of Foreign Department of British India, Sir Olaf K. Caroe, who in 1938 pressurized the Government of China after invasion of Japan, fabricated the official maps and raised a claim that China had formally acquiesced to the British annexations of Tibetan territory in India's north east. Prof. K. Zacharia, first Director of the Historical Division Ministry of External Affairs was also of the same opinion. Pt. Nehru's several statements in the Parliament in August-September 1959 were based on Prof. Zacharia's opinion. In 1961 Sir Caroe revealed the fact that in 1959 the Indian High Commission in London had sought his help in this matter.

The opinion of all Foreign Secretaries, who served in office from G.S. Bajpai up to T.N. Kaul was that in the western sector, India's Northern frontier was delineated approximately along the Karakoram range which formed watershed in the region, but in 1938, on the initiative of Sir Caroe the Survey of India maps were unilaterally altered to register an equivocal Political claim to the effect that east of Karakoram Pass this boundary extended in the North East up to Kuenion range. A study of Survey of India maps published in the ninety thirties reveal that in the eastern sector, the boundary was along the foothills of the Himalayas, however since 1938 the maps were altered showing the McMahon Line with the word "Boundary Undemarcated."[8]

At the Bangdung Conference in 1955 the Chinese Premier Zhau Enlai made it clear that there are a number of discrepancies in the Chinese Maps. He also said that the border lines with some neighboring countries are yet to be finalized. The surreptitious alterations made in Survey of India maps, however, became a primary cause for creating widespread misapprehension among the Indian public about the western sector of the boundary, and also that the Chinese were making unjustified claims over a large number of area south of McMahon Line. Nehru was a very typical devil's workshop and successfully blurred the vision of Indian people.[9]

On 13th November 1935 the Assam Government regarding position of Tawang commented "As regards the connection of Tawang with Tibet is concerned the Governor in Council believes that Tawang is more or less independent territory, but holds some indirect allegiance with Tibet…It may be that owing to this indirect connections with Tibet the Dzongpons of Tawang consider that they have an authority to grant Kingdom Ward permission to enter Tibet. So far as information goes, there has been no change in recent years in the attitude of Tibetan Government in respect of their part of the frontier."

In August 1936, a conference was held at the Government House Shillong in which all important officers of North East frontier participated in which it was agreed that the Government of India should not press their claims to Tawang Twynam's suggestion that an alignment more suitable for boundary line than the McMahon Line could be found further south, in the neighborhood of Dirang dzong, was accepted. On 1st October 1949 after liberation from Chiang Kaishek yoke Peoples Republic of China was established. India was among first countries to recognize

The new Government of China. The emergence of a strong united China was immense significance to India which has over 2000 kilometer long border with China's Tibet region. In a statement in Parliament, Pt. Nehru clarified the reason of recognizing the new government. He said :

> Very great revolutionary changes have taken place in that Country. Some people may approve of them, others may not. It is not a question of approving or disapproving. It is A question of recognizing a major event in history, of Appreciating it and dealing with it. When it was quite Clear, about three months ago, that the new Chinese Govt. Now in possession of practically the entire mainland of China, was a stable government and there was no force Which likely to supplant it, we offered to recognition to the new government and suggested that we exchange Diplomatic relation.[10]

In 1950 India and China faced an important task of a defined clearly marked Boundary line. When China decided to move troops in Tibet, India faced a new reality of giving special interests and extra-territorial rights of the early 20th century inherited from British-India Govt. At the same time the ruling class of India was also against the Chinese supremacy over Tibet. At this time Nehru expressed that the British policy of claiming special interest in Tibet could not be maintained by India.K.M. Panikkar, Indian ambassador to China, was assured by the Chinese authorities that, though, China regarded Tibet as an integral part, it had no intention of using power to settle the issue. It wanted a negotiated settlement with Tibet's representatives. When Chinese troops entered Tibet, India deplored the timing of action because it would give powerful support to those who opposed China's entry into United Nations and its Security Council. Five days after Chinese troop's entry into Tibet India expressed surprise and regret that China should have ordered the advance of its troops into Tibet especially when a Tibetan delegation had decided to proceed to Beijing immediately for negotiations. Inspite of all these developments India recognized Tibet as an integral part of China, but harped on extra territorial rights. China welcomed India's declaration that it had no political or territorial ambition in China's Tibet, but ignored India's claim to certain rights, but hoped the problems relating to Sino-India diplomatic commercial and cultural relations with respect to Tibet may be solved through normal diplomatic channels. The Sino-Indian differences over Tibet flowed from divergent approaches to Tibet's autonomy. In the debate in Parliament over Tibet, Nehru not mentioned the differences and only said that he had insisted on Tibet's autonomy within Chinese suzerainty which he explained was not same as sovereignty. Sino-Indian correspondence on Tibet broke off with this. Two members of the Tibetan delegation on their way to Bejing met the officials of India's External Affairs Ministry in New Delhi. In the year 1950 the rulers of China sent troops to check the both—centrifugal & centripetal forces in Tibet. On 7th November 1950 in Lok Sabha Nehru said "Since Tibet is not same as China it should ultimately the wish of people Tibet should prevail and not any legal or illegal constitutional arrangements...whether the people of Tibet are strong enough to assert their rights or not, is another matter." The Indian leaders feared the comparative outlook of the Indian masses Would certainly assume dangerous dimensions, so they decided it must be destroyed through the hysterical nationalism. To keep up the tempo of such hysteria it must be essential to keep the border issue and Tibet alive. The most Effective remedy would be a war which bred contempt and hatred. Once the Chinese were pronounced as enemy, the masses of India would not like to here any good reports about them.

Coming to the east front Nehru had already ordered Indian administration to be extended through NEFA, as the tribal belt beneath the McMahon Line had been struck a thistle in the throat of India since 1947, when Chinese troops advanced towards NEFA, replaying a question in Lok Sabha, Pt. Nehru said, "Maps of China for the last thirty years have shown a certain area of that area as not part of India...Our maps show that McMahon Line is our boundary and that is our boundary...and we will not allow anybody to come across that boundary."[11] On bilateral level political tussle over boundary line was going on, at international level Indian efforts to brought the Chinese Government on World Level was in process. Pt. Nehru was personally of the opinion that bilateral issues may be resolved through dialogues. During these days the world was polarizing in two blocks, one was under USA, while the other was USSR group. In the circumstances a treaty was signed between China and India at Bangdung in 1954, this treaty was based on five new principles of co-existence. These principles for a year or two were heavily stress both in Delhi and Beijing, included respect for territorial integrity, non-aggression, non-interference in each other's internal affairs, equality and mutual benefit, and peaceful co-existence. In this conference India also recognized China's sovereignty over Tibet.[12] This step was taken by India after suggestion Chinese leader Mao.[13] In this conference China assured India about Autonomous status of Tibet in Chinese territory. (watt p. 725-726) The Chinese Premier Zhau Enlai visited India in 1956 and after detailed discussion between the two Prime Ministers Nehru wrote.

Premier Ahan Enlai referred to the McMahon Line and again said that he had never heard of this before though of course the then Chinese Government had dealt with this matter and not accepted this line. He had gone in this matter in connection with the border dispute with Burma. Although he thought that this line, was established by British Imperialists, was not fair, nevertheless, because it was an Accomplished fact and because of the friendly relations which existed between China and the countries concerned, namely, India and Burma, the Chinese Government was of the opinion that they should give recognition to this McMahon Line.[14]

International law recognizes such oral agreements as being binding and valid even less precise and less categorical oral declarations than the other made by Prime Minister Zhau Enlai in the current case have been held to be binding agreements.

Zhau Enlai's declaration accepting McMahon Line is more Authoritative and hence more persuasive because it is a communication of commitment deliberately made by a Head of State to another. Subsequent events culminating in China's recourse to violence against India, however were to show that while India took Panchsheel as code of international conduct, to China they meant a code of temporal sing tactics-a temporary device to lull India into a sense of security until China' s military capabilities were adequate for implementing its postulated goal of territorial expansion. By the end of 1959 the border situation was worsening. The Prime Ministers of India and China met in New Delhi in April 1960 in an effort to explore avenues which might lead to a peaceful settlement. The sole out come of their talks was a decision that officials of the two countries should meet to examine all relevant documents in support of their respective stands and draw up a report for submission to the two Governments. Meanwhile it was agreed that the steps be taken to avoid frictions and clashes in the border areas. Officials of the two Governments accordingly met and held three sessions of Bejing, New Delhi and Rangoon between Junes to December 1960. In fulfillment of their assigned task, however the Chinese Government took no steps to reduce tension. On the contrary the Chinese forces continued to violate Indian Territory. In June 1960 the Chinese troops intruded to Taksang Gompa in the Eastern Sector, in September they crossed into Sikkim near Jeltpa Pass, and in October they went up to Hot Spring in Laddakh. In May 1961 there was an intrusion into Indian Territory in Western Sector and in July a Chinese patrol crossed the Eastern Sector in Kemong Frontier Division of NEFA.

The year 1962 was marked by a dramatic intensification of Chinese coercion which was characterized by observers as a Yellow invasion of India. It was an Asian nation invasion in other Asian Nation for mere border dispute in an era of Panchsheel and the Bangdung treaty. Chinese forces during 1962.

Made spectacular advances deep into Indian Territory, constructed new roads and military bases and finally staged a full-fledged military invasion in India both in the western and

Eastern Sectors of India-China border. In January 1962, some Chinese civil and military personnel crossed the borders in the Eastern Sector near Longju and proceeded to Roi village half a mile in India. In April and May, patrols were carried out by Chinese forces in the Chip Chap area of Laddakh. On 30th April they issued a threat that they would extend patrolling to the entire boundary. On 8th September, a Chinese force intruded into Indian Territory in the north-western corner of the Eastern Sector across the Thagla Ridge. This was the first major instance of Chinese forces crossing the established boundary in the Eastern Sector and intruding into NEFA. Ironically, this crossing took place at a time when the Indian Government was seeking cooperation of the Chinese Government on holding the preliminary discussion to reduce tensions and to consider the boundary question on the basis of the report of the officials of the two governments. In spite of this invasion India did not abandon efforts of restoring peace in area. In a note of 6th October 1962, the Government of India expressed her willingness to hold further discussions to restore the status quo. Their military activities had already secured Chinese a sizable area of 12000 squire miles in the Western Sector. Beginning on 20th October 1962, Chinese activities took a new tern and suddenly flared into a massive military invasion of India's northern front from Laddakh to NEFA. The attack continued for about a month and Chinese forces captured an additional 6000 squire kilometers of Indian territory in the Western Sector and 20000 squire kilometers in Eastern Sector. The Chinese attack took place at a time when Pt. Nehru wet off London to attend a Conference and after returning India he again left for Colombo on 12th October. A week later, the launched a massive attack and overran Indian posts in the eastern Sector in NEFA. The Indian army commander in NEFA fled without any efforts at Resistance leaving the door wide open for China to walk in. There was a great cry in the country and feeling of panic about Chinese Intention. It was thought that the Chinese would come rushing into the plain and occupy Assam. After this China announced suspension of military operation on 21st October 1962. In support of their action the Chinese Government in their unilateral cease-fire declared.

In the past two years, first in the western and then in the eastern Sector of the Sino-Indian border, Indian troops crossed the Line of Control between China and India, nibbled Chinese territories set up strong points for aggression and provoked a number of Border clashes. Relying on the advantageous military position had occupied and having made full preparations the Indian troops eventually launched massive armed attack all along the Chinese Frontier Guards on 20 October 1962. The Chinese Frontier Guards all along maintained maximum self-restraint and forbearance in order to avert any border conflict. However, all these efforts of China proved of no avail and the Indian acts of aggression steadily increased. Pressed beyond the limits of endurance and left no room for retreat, the Chinese Frontier Guards finally had no choice but to strike back resolutely in self defense.[15]

In two letters written to President Kennedy on 9 November 1962, Nehru described the situation as really desperate asked for wide ranging military help.

He also sought British help. The Chinese troops returned back after unilateral cease fire, but this invasion left many question unanswered. India took many years to recover from this tragedy. Nehru never recovered from this blow and perhaps it was a major factor in his death in May 1964. At the pinnacle of his outstanding career, he had to face attacks from his political opponents. He was forced to demand resignation of his most favorable defense minister Krishna Menon. His policy of Non-Aligned Movement was derailed by a socialist country. Not only had this Congress Party lost three parliamentary seats in by-elections. Not only this, India's relation with other countries was also effected. The western countries began to pressurize India on Kashmir issue. In these circumstances, he had no option but to shift his foreign policy towards Soviet Block, which was a major change its policy of Non-Alignment Movement which was a turning point in world history. In spite of all the reveres factors India used to support China for her entry in UNO and in other world organizations.

A natural question arises why this Sino-Indian conflict took place and who was really responsible for the entire episode. Obviously Nehru's policies.

At this point, are criticized. But were Nehru and his policies only responsible? Some persons see him as a native fool who was blinded by settlements and failed to safeguard native interests while others are of the opinion that Nehru refused to settle the boarders with China on a very reasonable terms offered by China and instead followed from 1959 a forward policy which provoked the Chinese to attack in self defense. Dr. Bipin Chandra does not agree with either view.

Dr. Chandra says "Nehru's understanding to the Chinese history had convinced him that China should not be isolated and pushed into a corner, but should be brought into the community of nations and its revolution humanized." He did not want to participate in any conflict with China as it would be a disastrous for both countries. On 7th December 1961 in Lok Sabha he said that a huge elephant of countries was sitting on the border of country and we should not ignore. He further said that after Chinese revolution, he was of the opinion that the border of the country is safe. Nehru's long statement in Rajya Sabha explained about not wanting "to spend too much on the military, about the emphasis on building one's own strength as that is the only security, no country that is not industrialized is militarily strong today. And the real thing before us was to strengthen India industrially and not superficially, by getting an old gun or an odd aircraft."[16]

Nehru understood that Chinese occupation of Tibet meant a common boundary with attendant conflicts, but he also saw that China did not think of expansionism yet, as it had no big problem to solve. Nehru was shocked at the scale of attack, as he had thought at there may be occasional skirmishes here and there, but not an invasion of this type. He did not anticipate the nature of attack, rather than in the foreign policy he pursued. A further mistake that he committed was the panic in appealing to USA and UK for help it is now agreed that India's defeat at China's hand in 1962 was not the result of Nehru's native faith in Chinese friendship and utopian pacifism and consequent neglect of India's defense preparedness. On the contrarily, between 1949-50 and 1962, the strength of Indian Armed Forces doubled and that of Indian Air Forces from seven combat squadrons in 1947 to nineteen in 1962. Nehru was well aware and had been warning of the possible border clashes with the Chinese since 1959, but neither the political nor the military leadership anticipated the precise nature of the Chinese attack, and were therefore taken by surprise. Apparently, the military leadership thought in terms of either border clashes or a full-scale war in the plains of Assam, but not about the possibility of a limited deep thrust and withdrawal. Despite of Nehru's warning in 1959 much professional had not gone into the planning for a war in the Himalayas. It was a failure of logistics, of intelligence, or rather of analysis of intelligence, of coordination of wings such as the military and air force, etc. However, in spite of all the shortcomings, as head of government, Nehru can not be excused.

Every strong Chinese government had tried to integrate Tibet. But Tibet wanted independence. Nehru accepted the Chinese position on Tibet in 1954 Panchsheel agreement without getting a quid pro quo on the border, which was possibly a mistake. Only in 1959 did Zhou EnLai claim territory in Laddakh and NEFA this is in wake of the Khampa revolt and flight of Dalai Lama to India with many refugees. China accused India of instigating the Dalai Lama and objected to the asylum. When clashes took place between India and China on the border, the Soviets remained neutral. In April- May 1962 a number of incidents occurred. According to V.P. Dutt:

> "China had arrived at a new theoretical understanding of its own national interests. It had despaired of a peaceful solution to the outstanding problems with the United States and the fulfillment of its primary objectives, namely the return of Taiwan ... acceptance of China as a great power, seat in the Security Council... it had now come to believe that the international balance of power was shifting in the favor of he socialist camp in view of Soviet advances in rocketry and ICBMs and that the time had come for the adoption of an uncompromising and militant line to compel United States to make concessions to China." [17]

It is unbelievable that the Chinese attack on India had little to do with issues between India and China, but was a reaction to a feeling of isolation, abandonment and frustration. By attacking India they have wanted to topple Nehru or at least push India into the western camp so that the USSR could have no illusions about Indian non alignment and would have to rethink its policy of peaceful coexistence, which the Chinese figured, was leading to their isolation.

According to V.P. Dutt, "Deng Xiaoping said later to an Indian delegation of which he was also a member that it was Khrushchev who was responsible for the 1962 war."[18] The debacle of India-China war in no raises doubts on the correctness of Nehru's basic thrust in foreign policy. This was an unusual occurrence in the days of Cold War. Nehru had been right in pursuing a policy of friendship with China even if it ended the way did it. It was in India's national interest of not having another hostile neighbor. India's espousal of China's right to have a seat in UN was not given up by Nehru even after the Indo-China war since he rightly believed that the western power's isolation of China pushed her into becoming more irresponsible.[19]

In a convocation address at JNU K.P.S. Menon the first Foreign Secretary said:

> "when Zhou Enlai came India in 1960 after first blood was drawn on the frontier, we missed an opportunity to improve relations then there was a faint hope that a settlement could be reached under which the Chinese Government would recognize the Mc Mahon Line, which no previous Chinese government had recognized in return of some disputed Aksai Chin. I deliberately say 'disputed.' Because the maps, treaties, agreements, and other documents on which both sides rely can not be said to place the boundary, as convinced by either party beyond the reason of doubt or the need for negotiations. The watershed principle on which we have heavily relied on other sectors of the frontier is in the Aksai Chin area, not in our favor. Moreover it cannot be forgotten that Aksai Chin is of no importance, because it is the link between two historically troublesome regions Tibet and Xinjiang. A careful study of Sino-Indian frontier by Alistair Lamb under the auspices of Royal Institute of International Affairs,

> London, has come to the conclusion that it is a matter for regret that before the crisis of late 1962 was reached and it may be a point of no return was passed, India did not attempt to offer for few concessions which she could in all justice have made rather than perished in her declaration of absolute right..."[20]

The ruthlessness of the Chinese action, the continued concentration of Chinese troops along the border and her refusal to accept any community procedure for the settlement of the dispute do not rule out the possibility of future attack by China... However, the recent introduction of new factors in Sino-Indian relations has raised the hope for a possible détente. Observers are of the opinion that India's China policy has been undergoing significant change as reflected by Prime Minister Indira Gandhi's New Years press conference in 1969. The small gestures raise a hope that a reasonable settlement of boundary dispute is possible.[21]

Notes

1. Jawaharlal Lal Nehru, (1953): *Autobiography*, London: The Boodle Head, p. 608.
2. Surry P. Sharma, *India's Boundaries and Territorial Disputes*, Delhi: Vices Publication, p. 5.
3. Charan Shandilya (1999): *India-China Relations*, Kavi Nagar-Ghaziabad: Sunder Lal Institute of Asian Studies, p. 33.
4. Ibid., 34.
5. Ibid., 35.
6. Ibid., 36.
7. Ibid., 36-37.
8. Ibid., 40.
9. Ibid., 40-41.
10. Ibid., 46.
11. Ibid., 55.
12. Chandra Bipin and others, *India After Independence 1947-2000*, Calcutta: Penguin, p. 164.
13. Ibid., 150.
14. S.P. Sharma, *op. cit.*, p. 99.
15. Ibid., p. 59-62.
16. Bipin Chandra, *op. cit.*, p. 166.

17. Quoted by Bipin Chandra, ibid., p. 169.
18. Quoted by Bipin Chandra, ibid., p. 169.
19. Bipin Chandra, ibid., pp. 169-170.
20. Charan Shandilya, *op. cit.*, p. 145.
21. S.P. Sharma, *op. cit.*, p. 196.

7

ARUNACHAL PRADESH
A Matter of Dispute Between India and China

Amit Kumar Pandey

In present times most of the border disputes have been resolved but one area remains where this issue is alive and real; it is between China and India. The area in question is Arunachal Pradesh, which means "land of dawn lit mountains" or "land of rising sun." Arunachal Pradesh is located in the North East corner of India and bordered on north by Tibet region of china and east by Myanmar. Arunachal Pradesh given a status of Union Territory in 20th January 1972 and the state of Arunachal Pradesh bill was passed by the parliament in 1986 and with effect from 20th February 1987; Arunachal Pradesh became 24th state of Indian Union. Even though Arunachal Pradesh is one of the thirty states of India, China still claims of it as a part of Tibet autonomous region.

Before the territorial dispute between China and India emerged in Arunachal Pradesh, the first ancestors of the tribal groups migrated from Tibet during pre historic period. Even though ancestors were there, little is known about the history of Arunachal Pradesh, recorded history is only available in the

Ahom chronicles from the sixteenth century; the British christened 'originally known as North East Frontier Agency (NEFA)' took administrative control Arunachal Pradesh and it remain under this rule until 1948.

The major cause of China and India territorial dispute, which deprived peace from Arunachal Pradesh, is from immediately after Chinese Revolution in 1911. At that time, Qing Dynasty, the lost Chinese Dynasty, fell and the Emperor of Qing Dynasty resigned. As a result, China, Tibet and Mongolia became equal and separate countries. In these three countries, Tibet and Mongol tried to be approved internationally as independent states, and undertook to be international society. However, on the other hand, Han Chinese Republicans started small war to subjugate reigns of Government of Tibet and Mongol. Therefore, they could not be independent states at that time.

In 1912-13, the British Raj made agreements with tribal leaders that defined the area that was known as NEFA. British rules could have very small impact on the isolated, self sufficient in terms of economy and militarily uncontrollable tribal peoples. In order to arrange this conflict in 1913 and 1914, the British administrator Sir Henry McMohan drew up the 550 mile McMohan Line as the border between India and China in Shimla, during a conference which also discussed the Tibetians and Chinese border. This conference is called Shimla Conference, regardless of this reconciliation; the McMohan Line was rejected by Chinese Government in 1947. The map showing McMahon Line and NEFA is as follows:

Following this dispute, the Chinese troops crossed the McMohan Line on 26 August 1959. They abandoned this in 1961 but in October 1962, they crossed the line with force. A as a result, Sino-Indian war broke out. The Chinese extended the frontier as they intruded deeper and deeper.

However, this war did not go for a long time. In 1963, the Chinese agreed to withdraw back to McMohan Line and also returned Indian prisoners of this war at that time.

Even though, both India and China found a peaceful solution to the border dispute in late 1980s, officials from two

McMAHON LINE
Lhasa
Migyitun
Longju
NORTH-EAST
FRONTIER AGENCY
Sadiya
BHUTAN
Brahmaputra R.
INDIA
ASSAM
BURMA
E.
PAK.
Imphal
0
100
200 mi.

countries have met more than fifteen times to argue the Arunachal Pradesh but China still claims that 90,000 sq.kms. of land in Arunachal Pradesh and does not recognize the North Eastern state as a part of Indian territory.

The Strategic Importance of Arunachal Pradesh for India

Coming to the strategic importance of Arunachal Pradesh in Chinese parlance the following need to be recognized:

- Arunachal Pradesh provides strategic depth to India's Brahmaputra Valley and India's other North Eastern states.
- Arunachal Pradesh provides security to Bhutan on it entire Eastern flank by geographical contiguity.
- Bhutan would be then be in a pincer group of China on both it flanks if Arunachal Pradesh is given away. This would be detrimental to India's security.
- China's borders would then rest on the plains of Assam; India might as well write off its other North Eastern states.
- The Chinese obsession with the Arunachal Pradesh Region is totally strategic in its aims.
- In any future conflict with China and if India singly or in coalition with some other power develops offensive capabilities against China, this region offers the shortest cut to China proper and to Tibet.
- India's communications infrastructure in this region developed in World War II for US military aid to China is existent and can be further improved.
- Arunachal Pradesh offers all-wealthier lines of communication to India for military needs to the Tibet border as compared to Aksai-Chin.
- In terms of any air operations by China in this region, Arunachal Pradesh would provide multi-layered air defence deployments on the ground as deterrence.

- The region is rich in terms of mineral and natural resources prospects.

There are many more reasons that one can state but the major ones should be enough. Arunachal Pradesh is of vital strategic importance for the territorial integrity and defence of India's North East states and should be non-negotiable.

Fresh phase of India-China border row on Arunachal Pradesh

As Arunachal Pradesh was voting for a new assembly on 13th October 2009, China revived its old claim to the states territory by objecting to the Prime Minister Manmohan Singh's visit to the state on 3rd October. It is to be recalled that Chinese foreign ministry spokesman Ma Zhaoxu said on October 13

> "The Chinese Government's position on the disputes area has been consistent and clear. China expresses its strong dissatisfaction on the visit by the Indian leader to the disputed area in disregard of China's grave concerns. We urge the Indian side to take China's solemn concerns seriously and not to stir up trouble in disputed area with a view to ensure the sound development of China-India relations."

India promptly responded by asserting that such outbursts would in no way help to resolve boundary dispute between the two countries. Rejecting Chinese claim over Arunachal Pradesh finance minister Pranab Mukherjee said in press conference that Arunachal Pradesh is an integral part India and the just concluded assembly election has proved that it was held under the Indian constitution.

But in recent meet on sideline of regional summit of ASEAN premiers of both countries Dr. Manmohan Singh and Wen Jiabao seeked to dispel the impression that two countries see each other as a threat. A recurring theme in high level China India dialogue is the idea that there is sufficient space in the political and economic domains of the world for both these countries to rise peacefully without threatening each other's security.

It is regrettable indeed that China stirs up border row through media despite India's best attempts to Chinese concerns. But in recent meet of the premiere of both countries China and India shows a positive gesture towards their relationship. The official comment regarding to visit of Dalai Lama to Arunachal Pradesh made in advance by the Chinese foreign ministry spokesperson did not blame India. If relations between two giant Asian countries develop in optimistic manner, it will be beneficial for the overall development of this region and peace in particular.

Notes

1. Jaideep Saikia, (2007): *Frontier in Flames: North East India in Turmoil*, Viking Books.
2. www.wikipedia.org
3. www.southasiaanalysis.org
4. www.kanglaonline.com
5. *Frontline*, Friendship First, 20th November 2009
6. Ibid., *China Factor.*
7. http://www1.american.edu/ted/ice/images4/McMahonLine.jpg accessed on 2nd November

Section II
Insurgency

8

ALIENATION AND INSURGENCIES IN THE NORTH EAST INDIA

B.B. Kumar

Introduction

The North Eastern region of the country had the state of Assam and the Princely states of Manipur and Tripura when India became free on 15 August 1947. Today the region has seven states of Assam, Arunachal Pradesh, Manipur, Meghalaya, Mizoram, Nagaland and Tripura. We have four Autonomous District Councils in Assam under the provisions of the Sixth Schedule of the Constitution of India. Today, the number of ADCs and the Tribal Councils exceed a dozen. The autonomy demand started in the Naga Hills district of Assam and the Naga National Council was then the only insurgent outfit in the region. The Nagas got their State in 1963, but the problem did not end. The Nagaland was replicated many times; the insurgent outfits mushroomed.

The present state of affairs in the region is due to interaction of diverse psychological, historical, social, political and economic factors. Some factors have colonial roots; yet there are others which are due to our mishandling the North Eastern affair. Different sections of the people have developed deep sense of perpetual grudge, antagonism and mistrust for each other, lack of the sense of belonging and the communication gap. The Central leadership, barring Mahatma Gandhi, is charged with having agreed to the Cripps Mission proposal of 'Grouping Assam with East Pakistan.' The vested interest groups try to perpetuate the memory that Nehru abandoned the people of Assam in the face of Chinese aggression.

Colonial Historiography

The British, during their rule of over 100 years, misinterpreted history and culture of the region; created the myths of race. They invented the myth of core-fringe conflict and that of isolation, which the Indian historians and ethnographers parroted and over-emphasized. They also created artificial barrier between the hills and the plains of the region by introducing Inner-Line Regulation in as early as 1973 to prevent plains people from visiting the hills—Naga Hills (now Nagaland), Mizo Hills (now Mizoram) and Arunachal Pradesh. The colonial historiography ignored age-old links not only between the region and the rest of India, but also between the hills and the plains of the region. Our own historians, on the other hand, did nothing to bring the perceptional change about the region. Here, it needs mention that none of the Indian historians, except Tapan Roy Choudhury and Irfan Habib, did study the history of North East India as a part of the history of India. Even they included the history of the medieval period of Assam only in the appendix of *The Cambridge History of India*, Vol. I (1982). Thus the region does not find proper place in the history of India. In this connection, it needs mention that such trend of colonial historiography is not confined only to the North East region, but also to the South.[1] The trend of non-inclusion of the regional history in the history of India, especially of the Medieval and the British periods, is rightly criticized as the 'Ganga Valley Bias.'[2] Here it needs mention that Indian historians have many failures to their credit. As mentioned above, they failed to incorporate regional histories in the broader frame of the Indian history. Their blatant ignorance and irresponsible act becomes shocking when we find that a paper on the North East was categorized as non-Indian in a volume of the Indian History Congress.[3] It is strange that the struggle of the Khasis, Jaintias, Nagas, Mizos, Manipuris, etc. against the British did not find legitimate place in the history of the freedom struggle. It is, no doubt, a serious lapse on the part of the Indian historians and the nation was weakened by the same.[4]

An important reason for the spread of insurgency in the North East region was the alienation and weakening of the sense of belonging generated by the myth of isolation. The artificial barrier created by the British prevented national freedom movement from penetrating to certain areas of the region. It was often claimed that the Inner Line Regulation was devised to ensure the identity of the tribes and to prevent their exploitation. Ironically, the tribal identity is not discussed therein. The hollowness of such claims is proved by the fact that the British frequently interfered in the internal affairs of the tribes and the former monopolized the trade of the latter's produce.[5]

The first colonial historian of modern India was James Mill, whose History of British India, published in 1818, has most negative colonial impact on the Indians, especially on the members of Indian Civil Service. The book, considered to be the most mischievous by Max Muller, was used by the candidates of Indian Civil Service Examination. His opinion about the book is revealing:

> "The book which I consider most mischievous, nay, which I hold most responsible for some of the greatest misfortunes that have happened to India, is Mill's History of British India, even with the anti-dote against its poison, which is supplied by Professor Wilson's notes."[6]

Edward Thompson and G.T. Garratt wrote that "it would be absurd to imagine that the British connection will not leave a permanent mark on Indian life."[7] The statement is correct so far the English educated Indians are concerned. Uncritical acceptance of the colonial views on our history and culture is too glaring. Our scholars, especially the anthropologists and historians by and large, have ceased to question the colonial myths and lies. H.K. Barpujari, an eminent historian from the North East, borrows the expression from the European history and says that Assam had maintained its 'splendid isolation.'[8] Suhas Chatterjee uses the expression in Mizoram's context.[9] There is ample proof that Surma valley was ruled by Bhashkarburman of Kamarupa. K.L. Barua, however, does not agree. For him the hills separating the two valleys of Brahmaputra and Surma are insurmountable,[10] whereas, in reality, even the Himalayas are not. It may not be out of place here to mention that Indian historians of the North East followed the foot-prints of colonial scholars and carried the biases of the latter ones in their writings, be it H.K. Barpujari *(Assam in the days of the Company;* Guwahati, 1963), J.B. Bhattacharjee (*Cachar under British Rule;* New Delhi, 1977), Sruti Deva Goshwami (*Aspects of Revenue Administration in Assam, 1826-1874;* Delhi, 1987). H.K. Barpujari heavily relies on colonial sources for writing the history and follows the pattern of British historians of India who wrote how India was colonized (Ramsay Muir and others) and administered (Dowel and others). Bhattacharjee and Goshwami also followed the same line.[11] S.K. Bhuyan, H.K. Barpujari, S.K. Barpujari, J.B. Bhattacharjee (*The Garos and the English*; New Delhi, 1978), Helen Giri (*Khasis under British Rule;* Shillong, 1992), Hamlet Bareh (*History and the Culture of the Khasi People;* Calcutta, 1967), Milton Sangma (*History and Culture of the Garos;* New Delhi, 1991) in their studies of the British relations with the tribes of the North East mostly followed the traditions of Gait, Mackenzie, Shakespeare, etc. They relied mostly on colonial sources, followed their technique and carried their biases and outlook.[12]

Ethnicity

Racist Interpretation of Society/Myth of Race

The British colonialists gave racist interpretation of Indian society. The myth of race created divisions in Indian society. In the North East, it was Aryan-Mongolian divide. Edward Gait, in his 'A History of Assam', has given strange racist twist to the history of the North East region by mis-interpreting the terms Asur and Danav in Aryan non-Aryan dichotomy frame.[13] Apart from fabricating and strengthening the myth of race, the colonial scholars over-emphasized the migration of races. For them, the Indian land mass, the vastly fertile and abundantly gifted by nature, was empty till the arrival of the Munda/ Austric, Dravidian, Aryan and the Indo-Mongoloid/Kirata people were only the immigrants. This was just absurd and mischievous proposition. Gait, either did not know or he safely ignored the fact that Puranic mythology of Deva, Danav and Asura point to the same ancestor Kashyapa for them and their enemy Devas. It needs mention here that Vritra was an Asura, a Brahmana and a Vedic Rishi (seer). Indra was Vritraghna (killer of Vritra), Asuraghna (killer of Asur), and Brahmaghna (killer of Brahmana). Thus as Rigveda testifies Vrittra was both Asura and Brahmana.

Myth of Isolation

The North East India was linked up with rest of the country geographically, culturally, politically, historically and in many other ways. Contrary to the myth of isolation, the region was never an isolated one in the past. Similarly, intra-regional isolation was also a myth.

Links and the Myth of Isolation

A land route, from Peshawar (now in Pakistan) to Parvatipur (now in Bangladesh), via Vazirabad, Lahore, Jalandhar, Saharanpur, Lucknow, Tirhut and Katihar,[14] keeping Ganges mostly to the right, extended upto Assam.[15] The southern route branched off at Kajangal in Rajmahal to Gangasagar (Kolkata)[16] and the other one crossed Ganges there and extended to Kamarupa. Bhaskarbuarman, the king of Kamarupa and the Chinese pilgrime, Yuan Chuang must have used the same route to come to Kajangal from Kamarupa[17] to meet Harsha. From Kajangal to Kanauj, Harsha followed the Southern and Bhaskar Varman and the Chinese pilgrime the

Northern one.[18] That route extended from Brahmaputra valley/ Kamarupa upto Yunnan province of China.[19] There were several routes linking Bramaputra valley to Tibet.[20] One or Two routes linking Brahmaputra Valley to Myanmar via Manipur were comparatively more difficult.[21]

Manipur, like Assam, was also not an isolated area. Johnstone[22] and A. Phayre[23] testify to the human movement from India to South-East Asia via the land routes through Manipur. Captain Doon writes:

"There can be no reasonable doubt that a great Aryan wave of very pure blood passed through Manipur into Burma in pre-historic times."[24]

Intra-regional communication routes in the North East India were also not lacking. We had land routes linking Upper Assam to Cachar,[25] Brahmaputra Valley to Manipur and Tripura through Cachar[26] and with Jayantiapur[27] and Bengal.[28]

Region as Part of the Country

Politically, the North East region of the country had inter- and intra-regional linkages since the ancient days.

It is true that Assam, except for sporadic invasions and brief occupations, did not come under Muslim rule. But it is not true that the State during pre-Medieval period remained out of India. As R.C. Majumdar writes, "The effective hold of the Guptas on this kingdom (Pragjyotish) is indicated by the currency of the Gupta era in this kingdom for about five hundred years."[29] He further writes: "Thus an independent and powerful kingdom of Kamarupa arose out of the ruins of the Gupta Empire."[30] Similarly, the king of Davaka (present day Doboka in the Kapili valley of Assam) was also the vassal of the Gupta emperor, Samudra Gupta.[31] According to the same source, "Even in later times, we find a king whose name ended in Gupta fighting on the banks of Brahmaputra.[32] The Chiefs from neighborhood of Brahmaputra paid homage to the emperor Yashodharman.[33]

According to R.K. Mukherji, Bhaskarvarman, the king of Kamarupa, was a vassal of Harsha.[34] It is well-known that the king of Kamarupa beyond Brahmaputra was an ally of

Harshavardhana, but the later was a senior alley[35] and the former acknowledged the superiority of the latter.[36]

Indian concept of Sovereignty is enshrined in *Chakravartitva* linked to the performance of Rajasuya Yajna (which was performed only thrice) and *Ashwamedh Yajna* (horse-sacrifice). Usually the Indian monarchs satisfied their urge of becoming universal or all India sovereign (*sarvabhauma, asamudrakshitish*) and to realize the political unity of India by performing *Ashwamedha*. It is significant that the kings of Assam also performed the same. King Bhutivarman performed Ashwamedh once and Mahendravarman and Sthiravarman each did it twice.[37]

Another significant point is that at certain periods, the kings of Brahmaputra valley ruled over other parts of the country. Assamese kings ruled over Pundravardhana during the reign of Bhutiburman and his successors, including Banamala.[38] Bhaskarvurman ruled over the provinces of Gauda, Kalinga, Udra and Koshala. It was perhaps obtained from emperor Harsha during Danasagar ceremony at Prayag, as Harsha gas great regard for Bhaskarvarman. Kings of Bhauma dynasty of Assamese origin ruled over Orissa and neighbouring areas for about 400 years.[39] Devapala attacked Assam in early 9th century and was victorious.[40]

The link of the region with rest of the country in pre-historic period is well-known. It finds numerous mentions in the epics and the Puranas, such as subjugation of Pragjyotishpura king, Bhagadutta by Arjuna during Rajasuya Yajna,[41] defeat of Vajradutta, the king of Pragjyotish,[42] king of Manipur[43] by Arjuna during Yudhisthira's Ashvamedha. Among the tribals of Arunachal Pradesh, Mishmis claim king Bhishmak, and his daughter Rukmini belonging to their community. We have numerous such legends in the North East. *Nag-Kanya* Ulupi belonged to this region. Tejpur of Lower Assam was supposed to be the capital of Vanasur, the father of Usha, who was married to Shri Krishna's son Aniruddha. It needs mention that Tejpur stands for legendary Sonitpur, as *tej* in Assamese and *sonit* in Sanskrit mean blood.

Intra-Regional Isolation

It is not true that hills and plains of the North Eastern region remained mutually isolated and cut of from each other. Some of the points supporting my stand are: *(a)* Brahmaputra valley is a very narrow one surrounded by the hills and high mountains in all the directions. Yet the valley had many longest ruling dynasties which was possible only if the dynasties ruling in the vallies controlled the neighbouring hills as well, as the Ahoms in the Brahmaputra valley and Meithei kings in Manipur ruling for almost 600 and two thousand years respectively, did. Tripuri kings, similarly, ruled over parts of the plains areas of East Bengal. *(b)* Many tribes, and even the individual clans, have legends of common origin with neighbouring tribes and plainsmen. *(c)* The keen observation exhibit unprecedented ethnic mix disproving isolationist theory. *(d)* Legends of migration of different tribes point towards all the direction linking them to wide areas. (e) Indian tradition, as Mahabharata says, does not accept racist myth and considers Kiratas to be Kshatriyas of good birth.

It is true that North East region, like rest of the country, has immense linguistic, cultural, social and religious diversity. But there are also strong threads of unity, which the colonial scholarship and its continuing tradition highly ignore. Ignoring the fact of unity and cohesiveness weakens the sense of belonging and thereby strengthens alienation in a region suffering from bottleneck psychology. The uniting factors, if listed, are numerous. However, some of them need mention. As for example, almost all the languages of India follow 'SOV' (subject, object and verb) pattern, except, of course, Kashmiri and Khasi. Score-system of counting supposed to be the trait of Munda languages. But even many Naga dialects, such as Chang and Sangtam, and a language like Bengali exhibit the trait. Languages of different families have inclusive and exclusive plural of first person.[44] Lexical borrowing is numerous. In reality, there is need to study Indian languages taking India as a 'Language Zone.'

With few exceptions, clan-exogamy was practiced throughout India among tribes and castes.[45] There was a trend to absorb the distinct and diverse ethnic elements.[46] The concept of the Supreme-being, the creator is shared by different communities.[47] There was a tendency among the colonial scholars to deny the Hindu past of many communities in the North East India or at best to declare them to be neo-Hindus. The mischievous "Hindu Conversion Theory" was put forward keeping in view the colonial desire of proselytization. Some examples may make this point clear. Garib Newaj, the king of Manipur (1709-1748), is said to have converted to Hinduism. But his forefathers built Hindu temples and therefore, were already Hindus.[48] King Khyamba (1467-1507), born 12 generations before him built Vishnu temple, which still exists at Bishnupur.[49] King Khongtekcha (765-784) was the devotee of Lord Shiva and Devi. He regarded Hari (Vishnu) as the Supreme Deity.[50] Even Garib Newaj's father was a Vaishnava, and two Kali temples were built during his reign.[51] Contrary to what is propagated, Garib Newaj, favoured Ramanandi form of Vaishnavism in place of Vaishnavism of Chaitanya School.[52] Another example of Krishna Chandra (1780-1813) and Govinda Chandra (1813-1832), the last kings of Cachar may also be cited here. The myth of Hinduization, in their case, is exhibited by the fact that their ancestor Vikramadityapha (1410-1469) established a city called Lakshmindrapur (present day Dimapur; Lakshmindra, Lord of Lakshmi, the Goddess of wealth) after installing a stone image of Lakshmindra (Vishnu) in a temple.[53] Bhubaneshwar Vachaspati, during the reign of Surdarp Narayan (1707-1732), prepared the manuscript of Narad Puran. This was done on the command of Chandra Prabha, the king's mother and the widow of the king Tamradhwaj Narayan.[54] According to a silver coin, discovered at Maibong and issued by the Cachari king Yaso Narayan Dev during 1583, he was a worshipper of Har, Gauri, Shiva and Durga.[55] A conch shell, depicting ten Avataras of Lord Vishnu, was carved during the reign of Bir Darpa in 1671.[56] These examples amply prove the hollowness of the myth of Hinduization.

Some prominent British colonial functionaries wanted separation of the Naga and other Tribal areas of the North East from the rest of the country. Their strategy, commonly known as Coupland Plan, of the formation of a separate Crown Colony or Hill State in NE region could not succeed as the independence came a bit too early for them after Second World War. The Memorandum from the Naga Hills district to the Simon Commission, mostly signed by the employees of the Deputy Commissioner's office of the Naga Hills district, was British inspired which presented confused identity claims. Naga representatives wrote about themselves thus:

> "Our country within the administered area consists of more than eight Tribes, quite different from one another with quite different languages which can not be understood by each other, and there are more Tribes outside the administered area which are not known at present. We have no Unity among us and it is really the British Government that is holding us together now."[57]

About the mixed ethnicity even of a single tribe, Hutton writes:

> "It would be impossible to give any general description of the type of the Angami features, as it varies from village to village and even from house to house in a remarkable degree. The flattened nose and slightly oblique eye of a decidedly Mongolian type may be seen side by side with a straightness of eyes and nose that might be purely Aryan."[58]

The seeds of separation, however, were shown in the Simon Commission Memorandum. It said,

> "If the British Government, however, wants us to throw us away, we pray that we should not be thrust to the mercy of the (Indian) people who could never have conquered us themselves, and to whom we were never subjected but leave us alone to determine for ourselves as in ancient times."[59]

The Naga Nationalist Council, the only secessionist outfit in early decades of Independent India, vide its resolution dated 19 June 1945, wanted Naga Hills district to remain in India as a part of Assam. But, it changed its stand soon. The moderate voice of "Nagas under autonomous Assam in free India" was never heard from that platform again. The NNC, vide its resolution dated 10 February 1947, demanded self-determination. The demand was based on:

(i) Ethnic distinctiveness.
(ii) Distinct Social Life, way of living, laws and customs, etc.
(iii) Different Religion—Animism and Christianity.[60]

The facts mentioned above clearly show the colonial roots of alienation. But there are other factors also, which strengthened and further complicated the situation. Pt. Nehru, as demanded by the moderate Nagas, conceded the formation of Centrally Administered Naga Hills Tuensang Area (NHTA) by uniting Naga Hills district of Assam and Tuensang Division of the then NEFA (now Arunachal Pradesh) and then Nagaland State, which were dully formed in 1957 and 1963 respectively. The formation of Nagaland initiated a series of demands leading to the re-organization of North East India and the formation of new states of Meghalaya, Manipur, Tripura, Mizoram and Arunachal Pradesh.[61] Creation of new states, ADCs and Autonomous Councils continues; Small States Syndrome persists as usual.[62] Ethnicity related problems ceased to ebb.[63]

Nagaland was created waving any criteria of area, population and local resources for the statehood. This also created resource-rich area in the State and resource starved areas in its neighbourhood. These factors naturally whetted the desire of the non-Naga elites for power and privileges leading to new States' demands. The Central and the State governments ceased to effectively counter the signals that (i) violence and (ii) social distancing pays. Meitheis felt neglected when Naga Hills district of Assam attained Statehood, whereas Manipur, a two thousand year old monarchy remained just a Central administered territory. This brought further alienation among them. While moderate Nagas enjoyed the fruits of statehood, the secessionists continued with their myths, mis-information campaigns and propaganda,[64] making the people to believe that the statehood was the result of their armed struggle. The cult of Gun and assertion of separate identity became the dominant trend. A vicious circle of the alienation and use of arm for autonomy was the result. The worst sufferer in this game was the Assamese Hindu society. Its internal cohesion was shattered. Every community claimed to be distinct with separate administrative unit.

North East is the most densely administered region of the country with the replication of Nagaland and multiplication of administrative units. It is also the most liberally centrally funded region of the country. In spite of these favorable factors, the states have failed to deliver. The benefits hardly percolate to the grass-roots. The region is mal-administered; there is huge leakage/pilferage of resources. Terrorist outfits manage to get their share from the development funds. Insurgency in the region initially started as a cottage industry; now it has taken the shape of medium range industry and is bound to take the shape of heavy industry, if the present trend continues. Extortion by the terrorist/secessionist outfits is rampant.

A rampant tendency in the region used to be to blame the Centre for all the ills of the region and to overlook the deficient role of the state governments. Of course, some of the problems needed greater Central attention. The problem of illegal migration from Bangladesh is one such problem.[65] The other one is to ensure proper utilization of the Central funds. Self-seeking groups of the region have developed vested interests in perpetuation of alienation, insurgency and insurgency. We have failed to plug the help from the neighbouring countries, especially, Bangladesh and China. Now Paresh Barua of ULFA is supposed to be in China. ISI openly helps subversion; helps insurgent outfits.

The weakest front for us in fight against insurgency and terrorism—ethnic, Maoist and Islamist, is the intellectual one. These outfits receive direct and indirect help from a section of our intellectuals, especially of the left variety and certain human rights groups. Central Government is following the wrong policy of signing cease-fire agreement even when half a dozen law breakers pick-up gun, kill a few persons and declare the formation of an outfit. These outfits continue to indulge in recruitment and extortion activities even during so called ceasefires. Dominant insurgent outfits, such as NSCN (IM), form nexus with them and spread their influence and strength.

Notes

1. B.B. Kumar, Dialogue, 1.1 July-September 1999, Editorial, p. 9.
2. S.N. Pandey, "Regional History and Studies in History of Manipur," *Dialogue*, 1.1, p. 58.
3. *Proceedings of North East India History Association (NEIHA), Session XVII*, p. 68; Sajal Nag quotes O.P. Kejarival.
4. B.B. Kumar, "North East India: Crisis of Perception and Credible Action," *Dialogue*, 1.2, p. 80.
5. Ibid.
6. Max Muller, *India: What can it teach us?*, p. 28.
7. Edward Thompson and G.T. Garratt, (1962): *Rise and Fulfillment of British Rule in India*, Allahabad, (Reprint), p. 654.
8. *NEIHA Proceedings*, XVII, p. 66.
9. Suhas Chatterjee, (1985): *Mizoram under British Rule*, Delhi, pp. 180-81.
10. *NEIHA Proceedings, Session XVI*, p. 40.
11. Kumar, *op. cit.*, p. 81.
12. Ibid.
13. Sir Edward Gait, *A History of Assam*, Reprint (Guwahati, 1994), pp. 11-14.
14. Dr. Motichandra, *Sarthavah*, Patna, 1953; p. 12.
15. Ibid.
16. Ibid.
17. N.N. Vasu, *Social History of Kamarupa*, p. 151.
18. Ibid.
19. *Motichandra, op. cit.*, p. 127.
20. B.B. Kumar, (2000): *The Border Trade in North East India: The Historical Perspective*, pp. 12-22; in *Border Trade: North East India and Neighbouring Countries*, Gurudas Das & R.K. Purkayastha, New Delhi: Gait, *op. cit.*, p. 171.
21. A. Mackenzie, (1981): *The North East Frontier of India*, Reprint, Delhi, p. 64.
22. J. Johnstone, *My Experience in Manipur and Naga Hills*, p. 280.
23. A. Phayre, *History of Burma*, p. 3.
24. Dun, *Gazetteer of Manipur*, p. 6, foot-note.
25. S.L. Baruah, *Presidential Address, NEIHA, XVI Session, Proceedings*, p. 10; quoted from Cachar Buranji.
26. Ibid.
27. Ibid., quoted from *Jayantia Buranji.*
28. Gait, *op. cit.*, p. 285.
29. R.C. Majumdar, *The History and Culture of the Indian People: The*

Classical Age, Bharatiya Vidya Bhavan, p. 90.
30. Ibid., p. 91.
31. Majumdar, Raychaudhury & Dutta, *An Advanced History of India*, p. 140.
32. Ibid., p. 144.
33. Ibid., p. 147.
34. R.K. Mukherji, *Harsha*, p. 44.
35. Professor H.P. Barpujari acknowledges the same.
36. Majumdar, Raychaudhury & Dutta, *op. cit.*, p. 150-51.
37. H.K. Barpujari, (ed.), *The Social History of Kamarupa*, Vol. I, pp. 306-07
38. Ibid., p. 201.
39. Vasu, *op. cit.*, Vol. III, pp. 11-12.
40. Barpujari, *op. cit.*, p. 157.
41. Mahabharata, Sabha Parva, 26.7-16.
42. Maha., Ashwa, 7.6.
43. Ibid., 79-81.
44. B.B. Kumar, (1994): "North East India: Need for a Fresh Look," in *The Administrator*, p. 10; Mussoorie: Lal Bahadur National Academy of Administration, Vol. XXXIX, No. 4.
45. Ibid.
46. Ibid.
47. Ibid.
48. *Dialogue*, Vol. 1, No. 2 (1999), p. 92.
49. R.K. Jhalajit Singh, *A Short History of Manipur*, p. 84.
50. Ibid., p. 51.
51. Ibid., p. 118.
52. Ibid., pp. 133-36.
53. R.M. Nath, (1978): *Foundations of Assamese Culture*, Guwahati, p. 71
54. Vasu, *op. cit.*, p. 244.
55. Nath, *op. cit.*, p. 240.
56. Vasu, p. 243.
57. Quoted in B.B. Kumar (2005): *Naga Identity*, New Delhi: Concept Publishing Company, p. 21.
58. Hutton, *The Angami Nagas*, p. 21.
59. Kumar, *Naga Identity*, p. 143.
60. Ibid., p. 146.
61. See for detail see B.B. Kumar, (1996): *Re-organization of North East India* (Facts and Documents), New Delhi: Omsons Publications.
62. B.B. Kumar, (1998): *Small States Syndrom in India*, New Delhi: Concept.

63. B.B. Kumar (ed.), (2007): *Problems of Ethnicity in the North East India*, New Delhi: Astha Bharati & Concept
64. Kumar, *Naga Identity*, pp. 161-167.
65. For detailed information see B.B. Kumar (ed.), (2006): *Illegal Migration from Bangladesh*, New Delhi: Astha Bharati & Concept.

9

CONFLICT TRANSFORMATION IN NORTH EAST INDIA
Core Issues and Challenges

Rajib Handique

I

Introduction

The term 'North East India' is a geographical expression that includes the seven states of Assam, Arunachal Pradesh, Manipur, Meghalaya, Mizoram, Nagaland and Tripura. Of late, Sikkim has also been included in this conglomerate for certain purposes. The term 'North East India' is generic and it must be acknowledged that this area is a repository of unparalleled diversity both in terms of biodiversity as well as culture. It is an area that forms a meeting ground of different bio-geographic as well as cultural realms. The moist tropical climate coupled with the altitudinal variations makes this area one of the richest habitat mosaics in the world. In fact, three different bio-geographical zones meet here in the North East India—The Indian (Afro-Tropic), Himalayan (Palearctic) and Indo-Malayan making these forests among the richest terrestrial regions in the world in terms of bio-diversity (Kakati: 2009). This multiplicity of habitats also meant existence of multiple zones for man-nature interaction. Over a period of time, such interaction might definitely have led to development of different cultural traits, customs and traditions that prolonged living in a particular locale normally entailed. This was a development that was slow and evolved through ages. This might have also led to creation of exclusive societies with cultural characteristics that differentiated them from the 'others.' It is for such reasons that approximately 240 ethno-linguistic groups live in this area, creating matchless diversity. There are a lot of people who are averse to the use of the word North East India. A leading magazine *'Outlook'* (16 November 2009) recently carried an article on Arunachal where a film maker Moji Riba rightly says, "A Naga tribal is as alien to me as he is to you. Then why should we be clubbed together as the North East?" It is for such reasons that adequate care needs to be taken to understand the diversity of the North East India and for all practical reasons not consider it to be a homogenous entity.

At the same time, North East India is considered as one of the most complex Conflict Zones in the world. Since India's independence in 1947, we have not seen a single decade of calm political atmosphere in the region. Transforming these conflicts into positive constructive relationships and outcomes form one of the biggest challenge before the academia and policy makers.

II

On Conflict Transformation

Conflict transformation is relatively a new terminology that has emerged as a constructive academic response to violent conflict. The perspective adopted by advocates of conflict transformation is different from Conflict Resolution or Conflict Management. This term has been extensively used by John Paul Lederach in 1980s after his intensive experience in Central America. (Lederach: 1980)

The change that the practitioners desire is to move from violent and destructive patterns towards capacities which are creative, responsive, constructive and nonviolent. Conflict transformation understands peace as embedded in Justice. It emphasizes the importance of building right relationships and social structures through a radical respect for human rights and life. It advocates non-violence as a way of life and work.

Conflict transformation may sound accurate to those engaged in constructive change efforts that include and go beyond, the resolution of specific problems. According to Lederach, Conflict Transformation is more scientifically sound as it is based on two verifiable realities: (i) Conflict is normal in human relationships, and (ii) Conflict is a motor of change. Thus 'transformation' provides a clear and important vision because it brings into focus the horizon towards which we journey—the building of healthy relationships and communities locally and globally (Lederach: 1980, 1989).

Conflict resolution is a well-known and widely accepted term in both practitioner and research communities and it has a defined field for more than half a century. At its most basic, the language of resolution implies finding a solution to a problem. It guides our thinking toward bringing some set of events or issues, usually experienced as very painful, to an end. There is a definitiveness and finality created in the language when we add "re" to "solution" We seek a conclusion. *Resolution's* guiding question is this: How do we end something that is not desired?

Transformation directs us toward change, to how things move from one shape to a different one. The change process is fundamental to this guiding language. By its nature, when we add "trans" to "form" we must contemplate both the presenting situation and a new one. *Transformation's* guiding question is: How do we end something not desired and build something we desire?

Resolution often focuses our attention on the presenting problems. Given its emphasis on immediate solutions, it tends to concentrate on the substance and content of the problem. This may explain why there has been such a predominance of literature on negotiation technique within the field of conflict resolution—from popular airport bookstands to the halls of major research institutes. In short, resolution is content-centered.

Transformation, on the other hand, includes the concern for content, but centres its attention on the context of relationship patterns. It sees conflict as embedded in the web and system of relational patterns. We can take this a step further. Both resolution and transformation claim to be process-oriented. Resolution, however, sees the development of process as centered on the immediacy of the relationship where the symptoms of crisis and disruption take place. Transformation envisions the presenting problem as an opportunity to engage a broader context, to explore and understand the system of relationships and patterns that gave birth to the crisis. It seeks to address both the immediate issues and the system of relational patterns (Lederach: 1980).

This requires longer-term vision that goes beyond the anxieties of immediate needs. Transformation actively pursues a crisis responsive approach rather than one that is crisis-*driven*. The impulse to resolve leads towards providing short-term relief to pain and anxiety by negotiating answers to presenting problems. Those answers may or may not deal with the deeper context and patterns of relationships which caused the problems.

Finally, each perspective has an accompanying view of conflict. Resolution has tended to focus primarily on methods for de-escalating. Transformation involves both de-escalating and engaging conflict, even escalating in pursuit of constructive change. Constructive change requires a variety of roles, functions, and processes, some of which may push conflict out into the open (Lederach: 1980).

In summary, transformation includes, but is not bound by, the contributions and approaches proposed by resolution-based language. It goes beyond a process focused on the resolution of a particular problem or episode of conflict to seek the epicenter of conflict.

III

Conflicts in North East India

Every conflict in the world is unique, characterized as they are by the peculiar contextual factors. Though there might be certain common factors in some conflicts which might in turn be of help in putting them in categories, yet, the very difference in the nature of actors and the nature and the methods of articulating the conflicts adds to the uniqueness of every conflict.

Most of the conflicts in the world today are intra-state conflicts. The dissolution of the USSR marked the end of an era in which a single international conflict in the form of the Cold War had dominated the international system. Subsequently, the 1990s saw profusion of internal or intra-state conflicts, ethnic conflicts, conflict over secession, etc. Such conflicts are normally unlike the struggles for competing centres of power of the genre that had characterized international conflicts for most of the 360 years since the Peace of Westphalia (1648). Rather such conflicts reflect the fragmentation and breakdown of state structures, economies and whole societies. Globalization and neo-liberalism have created situations where such conflicts thrive and expand. The first decade of the 21st Century is likely to see proliferation of intra-state conflicts especially in the developing Third World ((Ramsbotham, Woodhouse, *et. al.*, 2005: 4)

Conflict in North East India may also be clubbed under 'new wars' as well as under—'wars of the third kind' where communities seek to create their own states in wars of 'national liberation', or which 'involve resistance by various peoples against domination, exclusion, persecution, or dispossession of lands and resources, by the post colonial state.'

Kaldor characterizes the 'new wars' in terms of political

goals (no longer the foreign policy interests of states, but the consolidation of new forms of power based on ethnic homogeneity); ideologies (no longer universal principles such as democracy, fascism or socialism, but tribalist and communalist identity politics); forms of mobilization (no longer conscription or appeals to patriotism, but fear, corruption, religion, magic and the media); external support (no longer superpowers or ex-colonial powers, but diaspora, foreign mercenaries, criminal mafia, regional powers); mode of warfare (no longer formal and organized campaigns with demarcated front-lines, bases and heavy weapons, but fragmented and dispersed, involving paramilitary and criminal groups, child soldiers, light weapons, and the use of atrocity, famine, rape and siege); and the war economy (no longer funded by taxation and generated by state mobilization, but sustained by outside emergency assistance and the parallel economy, including unofficial export of timber and precious metals, drug-trafficking, criminal rackets, plunder) (Kaldor : 1997).

North East India has long been suffering with the conflicts within and outside. Of its seven constituent states (Sikkim not included for this purpose), only Arunachal, Meghalaya and Mizoram are comparatively less conflict ridden today. Mizoram had a history of insurgency and Meghalaya and Arunachal has also been affected by the conflicts in their neighbourhood. The conflicts galore in Assam, Manipur, Nagaland and Tripura are well-known.

IV

Structural Dimensions: Identity, Colonialism and the Indian State

There are some underlying factors that have helped develop and sustain Conflicts in North East India. This is an area that lies at the confluence of migration from both the east and west. It is an area where conflicts relating to identity have developed and flourished. In fact, the history of North East India is different and so is the colonial experience. The same can also be said of the post-colonial experience. Structural deficiencies and unequal power relations inherent in the Indian state forms the basis of most struggles in North East India. The history of the region is different and it is a fact that this region was politically never an integral part of any of the Indian empires that developed in the ancient or the medieval periods of history, perhaps barring the short period of Mughal occupation in 1662-63.

However, the cultural connections with mainland India are conspicuous all throughout the history of the region. This region is well represented in the various legends including the epic *Mahabharata*. There was constant inflow of ideas from the west and both the Brahmaputra and the Barak river valleys were culturally and otherwise influenced by the happenings in the rest of mainland India. The great saint and social reformer of Assam Srimanta Sankardeva visited other parts of India, while the great Sikh Guru Tegh Bahadur was one of the numerous visitors to Assam. History has records of settlers who were part of invading forces to Assam. Thus Assam represented a country that had interaction with rest of the world and was not insular per se.

At the time of British occupation, the region was very sparsely populated and had large forested areas. These forests were regarded as a bar to the prosperity of the Empire. British policies initially led to establishment of state's proprietorship of land (which was considered as communal property) followed by alienation of the same to imperial capital interests. This led to large scale transfer of land to non-indigenous people. There was unprecedented transfer of 'wastelands' to tea planters which were funded by foreign private capital. At the same time, forced immigration of people from outside was encouraged to serve the plantation interests.

Extension of agriculture was actively pursued by the colonial government more as a means of augmenting the land revenue. The forests were considered as an obstruction to agriculture rather than otherwise and consequently a bar to the prosperity of the Empire. (Ribbentrop: 1900: 134). British authorities were conscious from the very beginning of the fact that unless the vast tracts of wastelands were brought under tillage, neither the resources of the Government, nor the condition of the people could be improved. As early as 1832, circulars were issued inviting settlers to Assam through respective collectors to populous districts of Bengal, viz., Dacca, Tipperah and Mymensing offering wastelands rent-free for a term of years after which, settlement would be made for the portion brought under cultivation (Barpujari : 1992 : 48). Assam's forests have always been put under new pressures when the influx of refugees from East Pakistan moved northwards into Assam. They used to have on their side the general British assumption that settled agriculture was a far more productive and stable means of land (forest) use. In the twenty years ending 1950, the immigrants from East Bengal had turned some 1.5 million acres of forest into settled agriculture.

On the other hand, some scholars like Nel Vandekerchkove and Bert Suykens of the Ghent University opine that migration itself is insufficient to understand problems like that of violence and conflict in Bodoland. They contend that colonial forestry and tea estates created certain restrictive structures that changed the livelihood pattern of the involved communities (Vandekerchkove: 2008). They put the entire development under a paradigm of 'tribal entrapment', where the forest policies and the plantation economy pushed the indigenous population into the periphery of an enclave economy.

The Brahmaputra valley and the Surma Valley especially were subjected to new population pressures during the colonial period. All these led to marginalization of the people. Parts of the hill areas of North East India were saved from this trouble by the Inner Line Regulation, which primarily did not allow persons from outside these areas to own land there. However, this part of the country was always affected by the events and changes in the Assam valley as they were all linked up to the metropolis through the valley.

Thus, the 'influx' of people from the other parts of India to the North East was a colonial phenomenon. This phenomenon was very unique to Assam and is very distinctly recorded in the colonial sources. The census reports are replete with statistics revealing the significant inflow of population from other parts of the sub-continent. The map of the following nature and depiction is not to be found in Census reports of other state of colonial India.

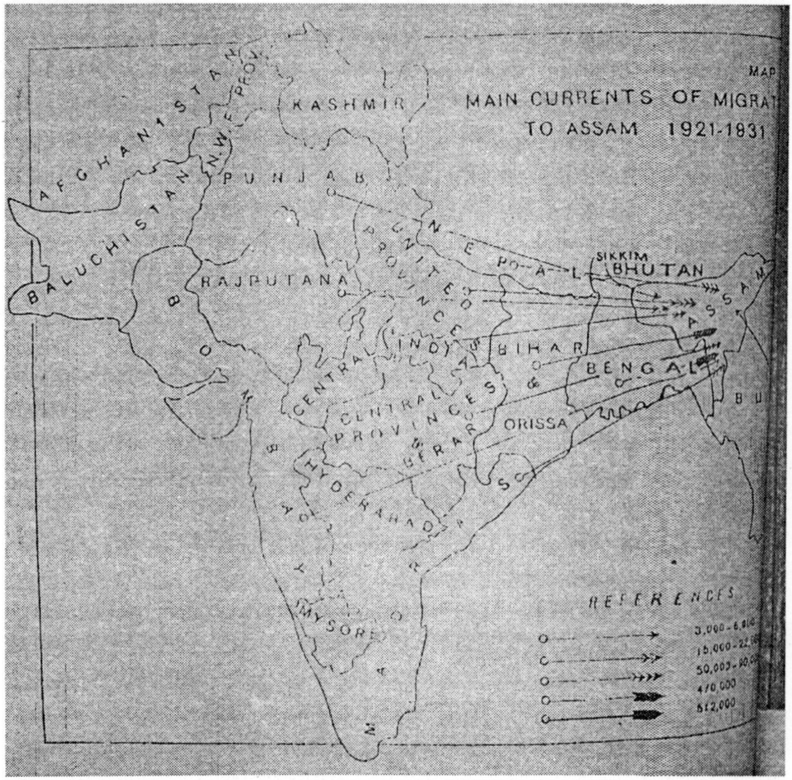

(*Census of India*, 1931: 41)

The influx of people from other parts of the sub-continent to Assam was forced by the circumstances which the colonial economy demanded. In a way all these immigrant 'new-comers' were part of the colonisers and might therefore be viewed as part of the 'other.' The trade and industry were carried on by people all drawn from outside. The national movement helped in bridging the divides and there was already much assimilation through a process that normal living together entailed. Many of such erstwhile 'outsiders' were already making contribution to the cultural life of Assam. In this context, we may mention the name of Jyoti Prasad Agarwalla, whose contributions to the world of music, art and literature in Assam remains unparalleled. Moreover, the indigenous and the immigrants were all ranged against the colonial masters till independence. However, there was brewing conflicts that were discernible to the British administrators themselves. The Census Report of 1931 refers to the growing communal animosity between the Hindus and the Muslims, especially in the Eastern Bengal and Sylhet. C.S. Mullan, the Census Superintendent of Assam further mentions:

> "It will be of intense interest to observe whether the Assamese language itself against the inroads of which the tribal languages of the plains have, for hundreds of years, put up such a stout fight—will, in its turn, be able in the future to defend itself against a new and a very powerful invader in the shape of Bengali which, with the coming of the Eastern Bengal settlers, has established itself firmly in all the districts of lower and central Assam." (Census of India, 1931:181)

Such a powerful portrayal of the emerging conflicts and its admittance by the British colonial masters did not auger well for the future in any way. The irony remains that the same conditions persisted and the conflicts and ruptures discernible to the British escaped the attention of the leaders of the newly independent country. It was only normal to expect a resolution or transformation of the conflicts that originated in the colonial era in the new found atmosphere of freedom and goodwill.

Colonial ethnography and the colonial construct of the 'other' in the context of Assam affected the understanding amongst the people of the region. Several of these ethno-national divides were created during the colonial period but remained dormant during the freedom struggle. Many colonial writings are in fact valuable ethnographic document which help us to understand many facets of the British colonial state. A series of monographs were published on the Assam Hill tribes by the

British administrators. Those monographs were published by Mcmillan and Company, London, by direction of the Government of Assam (Census 1931: 205). The stereotypes created through such accounts create powerful perceptions which have affected the understanding of the natives of North East India.

An important feature of any colonial discourse is its dependence on the concept of fixity in the ideological construction of otherness (Said: 1993: 8-9). The British colonisers have in fact entrenched the 'feudal' and maybe the 'archaic' on the society they have helped civilize and modernize. This fixity as the sign of cultural/historical/racial difference that is embedded in the discourse of colonialism creates powerful perceptions that is very difficult to be effaced easily. The ethnographic writings found acceptance in spite of their shortcomings, in many colonial discourses and many native writers are said to have followed them. Independent modern India needs to review and if need be deconstruct this colonial understanding of the natives of North- East India. This paradigm shift is absolutely necessary to do away with many of the colonial prejudice that continues to divide people and stand on the way of growth of modern India.

Finally it remains that the population that entered North East India and especially Assam was not required to return to their homeland as the North East India became part of independent India. They remained in the region as remnants of the colonial state but also as potential threats to the culture of the indigenous. Such a situation was unique to North East India. After independence, the same paradigm of colonial underdevelopment continued and unabated influx of population from other parts of India and Bangladesh. The indigenous became a minority or was on the verge of becoming one in their own land. The new post-independent Indian state therefore was not viewed as essentially different from the British colonial state. The 'brown sahib' readily had stepped into the shoes of the British colonial masters. This came to be emphasized profusely by critiques of the new Indian state who wanted a change in the existing structure and also by those who wanted secession. The ethno-national divide and feelings of marginalization remained as important factors in the post colonial state.

At the same time, North East India is governed with many exclusive laws like The Armed Forces Special Powers Act, 1956, the IMDT Act (now repealed). This aggravates the ethno-national divide which is cited as the causal factor on the basis of which the negligence in not securing the frontiers or not showing any concern for the preservation of the unique cultures of the North East India is built up. Under the circumstances, the processes of assimilation and integration prove counter-productive.

V

The Development Paradigm

The adverse impact of colonial under-development and the very nature of the enclave economy have created alienation amongst the indigenous people of North East India and have bred insurgencies.

It needs to be emphasized that the economy of North East India and especially of Assam continued to be a source of animosity as it remained extractive with the indigenous population enjoying only fringe benefits. At the time of independence and the early 1950s, Assam's per capita income as well as productivity of its main crop, i.e., rice was higher than the all India average. During the sixties of the last century when foreign exchange crisis hit India, Assam's tea and jute provided the much-needed foreign exchange; oil from Assam saved part of the foreign outflow. Assam was in fact industrialized at the start of the century (Madhav: 2007).

Despite all these developments, as well as nationalization of oil and coal industries after independence, benefits to Assam economy was marginal. Oil, Coal, Railway, Tea were particularly 'enclave' industries. Neither the Government of Assam nor the people, except getting some limited employment opportunities benefited much. Profits from these industries were transferred outside the state (Madhav: 2007).

However, Assam could achieve a growth rate of 4% during the period 1960-61 to 1969-70, as compared to the all India rat of 3 per cent. During 1970-71 to 1979-80, the growth rate of Assam was just 3 per cent compared to an all India average of 3.6 per cent. The growth rate of the economy reveals a condition of stagnation for Assam. Compared to the all India average growth rate of 5.6 per cent and 6.8 per cent, Assam could manage just 3.6 per cent and 2.7 per cent during the period 1980-81 to 1989-90 and 1993-94 to 1998-99 respectively. On the Human Development Index, Assam ranked 26 in 1981 and 1991 amongst 32 states (Madhav: 2007). The unemployment figures hovers above 20 lakhs. This state of economy has been used by the ultras in their propaganda, while un-employment youth provides the necessary recruits for these organizations. Lack of good governance and corruption has deteriorated the situation even more.

The process of development in India is mostly tops-down and creates a non-participatory development paradox. Anything which is tops-down is paternalistic and has the potential to create conflicts. Development is viewed by the marginalized as development of the 'other' and the Client-Patron relationship gets aggravated if it falls into the ethno-national divide. Under the circumstances, the underdevelopment of a group is often blamed on the development of 'the other.' Consequently, reactive polarizations develop on ethnic lines and are egged on by newer groups from the middle-class.

VI

The Periphery-Mainstream Discourse

Perceptions have always played an important role in conflicts and North East India is no exception to this. Central to such perceptions is the peripheral existence of North East India in the core academic discourses. It is now an established fact that the history of Assam was never a part of the greater Indian History text books and that it took almost half a century after independence to put the story of the valour of Lachit Borphukan in the Indian national perspective.

The physical remoteness of the region connected as it is with a corridor comprising of 2 per cent of its entire boundary, coupled with the remoteness in the psychological domain of mainland India has adversely fed alienation in the indigenous population and has affected the integration process.

That North East India is yet to be properly understood is an accepted fact. The very titles of some of the remarkable books written on the area indicates the predicament and the uncertainty that prevails—*Strangers in the Mist* (Sanjoy Hazarika), *India Against Itself* (Sanjib Baruah), *Periphery Strikes Back* (Udayon Misra), *Durable Disorder* (Sanjib Baruah), *Troubled Periphery: The Crisis of India's North East* (Subir Bhowmik).

A popular viewpoint is that India ends with Bengal in the east. Facts like non-inclusion of river Brahmaputra or of any element of North East India in the national song of the country add to the strength of the discourse. The situation created during the Chinese incursion in 1962, when the Prime Minister of India Pt. Jawaharlal Nehru bade farewell to Assam still reverberates in the psyche of the people especially of the older generations. Perceptions created around facts are very powerful in creating differences and intensifying divides.

VII

Security Dilemma and the Conflict Situation in North East India

Security is considered by all modern states to be of preponderant importance. Security of the state from external aggression or threat and from internal disturbances has always been accorded the utmost importance by policy-makers.

The response of the state to the complex conflict situation in North East India has largely been largely reactive, security-centric and statist. Security centric approach of the state blurs the focus on the actual and underlying causes of the conflict and helps keep the conflict going. It even adds new conflicting dimensions to it. Under the circumstances, the militants are regarded as cause of conflict per se and there is a belief generated especially in the security establishment that the conflict would be over if militants are 'wiped out.'

Such an approach goes against the basic contention of conflict transformation, which views peace as a continuously evolving and developing quality of relationship. Military mite can only help in temporary de-escalation of a conflict but cannot resolve a conflict, not to say of transforming it. In fact, such acts create the proverbial security dilemma that in turn helps in prolonging the conflict and creating mistrust. Hot pursuit mostly leads to human rights violation and disruption of normal ways of life. This alienates the people more and the insurgents usually garner the sympathy.

Insurgencies like that in North East India have changed the security perspective of the state. Armed forces normally kept ready to battle intruders or fight against foreign countries for defence or aggression are compelled by the state's security concerns to take centre-stage to fight their own countrymen to maintain internal security and prevent disintegration of the state. Such interventions of the armies have caused certain security dilemmas, which form part of a wider phenomenon of self-perpetuating protracted social conflicts. Considering the fact that many of such conflicts are identity conflicts, using armed forces consisting of personnel drawn mostly from other ethnicities itself create alienation and dilemma of immense proportion.

'Security Dilemma' is understood by most conflict analysts as the mechanism though which fear can lead to or sustain violent conflict. Any solution of a conflict can be generated only if the adversaries trust each other to keep the promises. The more mutually vulnerable the actors are, the more acute the security dilemma becomes and consequently more diminished the level of trust. In extreme cases, the security dilemma may incite conflict actors to strike the first blow out of fear of being subjected to a surprise attack otherwise. 'Kill them before they kill you' becomes the guiding dictum. Under such harsh conditions the fact that the 'them' constitutes actors who stand up in defence of some dimensions in a conflict is often forgotten. This kind of defensively motivated first strike is referred to as pre-emption and often leads to escalation of violence and even to war that no one wants, not even the side that initiates the fighting. Such situations are normal in North East India.

Thus, adoption of an exclusive statist and security-centric approach often leads to oversight of the structural or fundamental dimensions of a conflict and often transform insurgencies or armed social movements into terrorism. It creates a situation where the security agencies appear helpless and sometimes clueless as terror acts continue to be perpetrated by faceless 'terrorists.' This increases the sense of public insecurity and may lead to anarchic psyco-social turmoil of entire societies. The security agencies under the circumstances contrive to harp on the cowardice of the terrorists (insurgents) and demonize their adversary even more. Sometimes such demonization is carried to an extent where reconciliation becomes impossible.

Mitigation of Security Dilemma is therefore considered an important form of conflict management which might ultimately lead to conflict transformation. Ways of reducing vulnerability could include supporting human rights training for military forces and the police, demobilizations, disarmament, starting and documenting re-conciliation processes, etc. Most importantly, the academia and general public must come out of the clutches of a thinking that conforms to the security centric approach of the establishment and start articulating newer alternatives.

VIII

Epilogue: Ideas as Suggestions

It is very difficult to suggest solutions to the multi-layered conflict situation in North East India. The intricacies involved are multifarious and multidimensional. There is every reason to believe that there is need for change, that too of a structural nature by the entire India. Thus one may think of change that is not entirely North East India centric.

One of the ways of effecting fundamental change in understanding the conflict situation may be through changing the perspective in which subjects in humanities and social sciences are taught. While teaching such subjects in schools and colleges, it is often overlooked that religion, caste, creed, etc., are social constructs. Scientific methods of studying history need to be emphasized. Needless to say that history of North East India should be included in the text books of history so that new generations of Indian citizens develop a basic understanding of the region. History has more often been a narrative of dividers and not of connectors. At the same time, contesting historiographies lay at the root of many a conflict. We need to re-look at some of the ideological constructs related to immigration and the son-of the soil theory. This reinterpretation may go a long way in changing the psychological contexts in which alienation in North East India is bred.

This also calls for revisiting and reinterpreting colonial constructs and ethnographies that still dominate the knowledge landscape of the land. This is necessary to understand certain divisive prejudices and constructs that evolved during colonial times and continued to help in breeding conflicts in post-independent India. The Census Reports are a case in point, where categorizations in terms of religion, language and ethnicity sometime work against convergence of national energies. Therefore reinterpretation of the colonial knowledge—colonial records and ethnography is of utmost necessity.

Moreover, the security-centric and statist view of conflicts should be replaced with a more positive and humane approach where structural dimensions of the conflicts get properly addressed. Treating conflict situations as law and order problems and adopting repressive measures often lead to human rights violation, which in turn helps in creating and sustaining conflicts.

Real decentralization of power may be an important step towards conflict transformation. Constitutional safeguards for securing the cultural identity of the indigenous people would definitely contribute towards conflict transformation. We may consider thinking and acting upon a concept of 'United States of India' in place of 'Union of India.' Development would then have a bottoms-up approach so that the client-patron divide gets bridged. Good governance is an imperative for mitigating conflict in any country. To this may be added the urgent need to fight the real enemy of the country i.e., corruption.

Conflict transformation attaches great attention to understanding people's perceptions of how identity is linked to power and to the systems and structures which organize and govern their relationships. This is particularly important for people in regions like the North East India, who feel their identity has historically been eroded, marginalized, or is under deep threat. Under such circumstances processes must address the ways in which structural relationships symbolize and represent the perceptions. Understanding the roots of perceptions remains the key to successful conflict transformation. Unfortunately the perceptions of the indigenous people of North East India have never been studied with due importance.

Moreover, considering the divides created by the existing conflicts and the demonization of the 'other' coupled with a large degree of dehumanization, it has become imperative to seriously consider setting up of Truth and Reconciliation Commissions. Such commissions might help in mending fences and building bridges. Forgiveness is a political necessity to building peace and reconciliation is necessary to sustain it.

Finding indigenous solutions to the problems of India including North East India is imperative to transform the existing conflicts. Importing and imposing alien notions and solutions on indigenous problems/conflicts may not help in Conflict Transformation. We may develop our own Indian concept of sovereignty which may have a more inclusive connotation in place of the euro-centric notions of sovereignty as absolute and indivisible.

In a region like the North East India characterized by ethno-political movements, the traditional paradigms of assimilation and tops-down integration appear paternalistic and have the potential to breed and sustain conflict. Therefore, multi-culturalism should be promoted by the government and the media. Cross-cultural dialogue and civil society interactions should always be encouraged. It may be better to cause a paradigm shift from the existing 'unity in diversity' to 'diversity in unity' model. Sometimes processes of assimilation and integration prove counter-productive and are looked upon with suspicion.

There should be more emphasis on the new paradigm of 'celebrating differences' in terms of ethnicities and cultures. Celebrating difference happens towards the end of a conflict, when conflicting parties enter the realm of atonement and forgiveness. Former enemies are reconciled to the point where differences are not only tolerated, but even appreciated. Many never reach this stage, which often includes formal acts of acknowledgment and apology on behalf of previous generations, and general acceptance that a shared future is now more important than a divided past. This involves deeper levels of peacemaking and cultural peace-building that stretch from revisions of formerly polarized official accounts and media representations, through pluralization of education and stories told in school textbooks, and eventually on to learning everyday experiences that affect localized transmissions of memory within communities and families. (Ramsbotham, Woodhouse, et. al.: 2005: 244-245). Under the circumstances, identities themselves become softened and transformed, as a broadening of self-understanding combines with a re-perception of other as fellow human beings. Transformation of this kind may be difficult but may not be impossible. The academia linkages and people's love for Peace may be worked upon towards this glorious end.

References

Barpujari, H.K. (ed.), (1992): *The Comprehensive History of Assam,* Vol. V, Guwahati.

Holsti, K., (1996): *The State, War, and the State of War,* Cambridge University Press.

Kakati, Kashmira, (2009): "How Green really is my valley?," in *The Hindu Magazine,* Sunday, October 4.

Kaldor , M. and B. Vashee, (eds.), (1997): *New Wars : Restructuring the Global Military Sector,* London.

Lederach, John Paul, (1980): *The Little Book of Conflict Transformation,* New York.

Madhav, Jayanta, (2007): "The Movement of Economic Development," in Sonowal Paramananda (ed.), *Insurgency and Economic Development in North East India,* Guwahati.

Mullan, C.S., (1932): *Census Report of Assam, 1931, Secretariat Printing Office,* Shillong.

Ramsbotham, O., Tom Woodhouse and Hugh Maill, (2005): *Contemporary Conflict Resolution,* Cambridge.

Ribbentrop, B., (1900): *Forestry in India,* Shimla.

Said, Edward W., (1993): *Culture and Imperialism,* London.

Vandekerchkove, Nel and Bert Suykens, (2998): "The Liberation of Bodoland : Tea, Forestry and Tribal Entrapment in Assam," in *Journal of South Asian Studies,* Vol. XXXI, No. 3, December, pp. 451- 471.

10

INTEGRATION, ILLUSION AND ANOMIE

Bhawani Singh Shekhawat

August 15, 1947, by the midnight stroke, India awakened to an added agenda of responsibilities, to defend the newly acquired freedom, to take the country to progress and development and to prevent further Balkanisation of an already truncated nation. The responsibility was indeed heavy and awesome but it did not deter the assortment of individuals who had assembled to give India her first indigenous constitution, which came into force on January 26, 1950. The constitution was not a simple parchment of paper, it was indeed the Deed of Destiny, dexterously designed and immaculately contrived to remove all impediments and roadblocks to progress and contain fissiparous tendencies let loose in the wake of partition. The challenge ahead was to convince the people that the partition was a one-time exception to gain freedom and not a licence to indefinite vivisection of the divided nation. This called for a renewed attempt to keep the flock together through the time honoured device of national integration that unites people but sans assimilation because these two words have different connotations and produce varying effects. Integration implies unity of diverse segments of population divided on the basis of ethnicity, religion, language and regional differences whereas assimilation stands for defacing and destroying all identities and hence a dreaded word for multiple ethnic identities who fear an enforced acculturation of their separate entities. It is for us to now examine to what extent we have succeeded in maintaining this ethno-religious balance. In the pages that follow an attempt will be made to find out to what extent the Indian leaders have maintained this thin balance to protect the fragile unity of our nation, particularly in the volatile North Eastern Diaspora.

Geo-Political Roots of Alienation

The North East, comprising of seven sisters is a land-locked region, a veritable ethnographic museum of nationalities, inhabited by a plethora of tribes speaking a variety of over 400 languages and dialects, professing several faiths and covering an areal tract stretching 2,55,083 square kilometers which shelters 3,84,95895 inhabitants as per the census, of year 2001. The diaspora of North Eastern India is a historian's puzzle, an anthropologist's dream and dialectician's delight. But the region is also a statesman's dread because the area is heavily forested in lower altitudes of south and is snow-clad in the upper altitudes of north. It is interspersed by a complex riverine system and is surrounded on practically all sides by alien nations. It shares ninety eight percent of borders with foreign countries such as Bangladesh, Myanmar and China and only two percent border is tagged to the Indian soil. The region is rich in swamps where terrorist crocodiles breed and proliferate. It is also a fertile ground for guerrilla warfare. Among the states of this region, Nagaland alone epitomises the ebullient ethos, rising hopes and motivational urges necessary to create a foco-nucleaus of insidious insurgents and guerrilla Warriors. In the words of V.K. Anand "The jungles of Malaya, mountains of Greece and 'the slushy paddy fields Vietnam can all be found together in Nagaland."[1]

To this, the partition of sub-continent in 1947 added its own hazards. In the undivided India, there was a direct rail and road communication to this region through Bangladesh but partition snapped those links and access to the region is now through a 20 kilometer narrow strip of land called the Siliguri corridor which is flanked on either side by Nepal and Bangladesh and touches Bhutan in the north, thereby converting it into a very tenuous link which if snapped, shall cut off all communication links with the entire North East and its seven states and endanger India's territorial integrity and national sovereignty. Apart from this geo-political constraint, there are other variables too such as ethnic distinctiveness resting on Mongolian authenticity, geographical propinquity with Nepal, Bhutan, Bangladesh, Burma and China, a religious divide between Trident, Crescent, Cross and animism, a bewildering linguistic mosaic, nefarious anti-India activities of foreign Christian missionaries, subversive acts of Inter Services Intelligence Organization of Pakistan and espionage agents of diverse nationalities such as those of Bangladesh, Saudi Arabia, China, USA, and erstwhile Soviet Union that make this area secessionism-prone. To this one may add the unrelenting wave of foreigners entering into this area from Bangladesh and native job seekers and entrepreneurs from different parts of India such as Bihari labourers in tea plantations, Punjabi transport barons and ubiquitous Marwari traders and business tycoons from neighbouring states who add to the economic distress of the locals and fuel the embers of alienation and exacerbate the xenophobia against outsiders and the result is a demand for secessionism. One can identify these alienating factors in some details below, in order to understand how they inhibit patriotic sentiment and impede national integration.

Complex Territoriality

As stated earlier, the North Eastern India is a geographically complex territorial tract which is separated from the mainland by vast distance and access to this region is only through the 20 kilometers stretch of a narrow strip called the Siliguri neck which runs between Nepal and Bangladesh from Kishanganj in Bihar to Cooch Bihar in West Bengal. In northern tip touches Bhutan and this complex territoriality of the area makes it too sensitive and vulnerable both in peace times as well as in war. Any frontal attack to cut off this life line will not only separate and severe the seven sisters from the mainland, there would be a lot of collateral damage to commerce and trade as the oil pipe-line from Assamese oil fields also runs through this tiny strip of land.

The Siliguri neck like the Chicken's neck in Punjab is vital to the security of India, being the sole source of rail and road connectivity with this region. But there is a seamy side also to this facility. The corridor also provides easy access to smugglers, militants and fifth columns who have a free run in this little space and who if pursued, can escape to Nepal, Bhutan or Bangladesh to have safe sanctuary.

Ethnic Divide

In addition to this vast distance separating this region from the rest of India, which creates a sentiment of alientation, the region is surrounded by nations of similar Mangolian ethnicity, owing to which people develop some sort of affinity with them. There is a common perception in this region that as the crow flies, Hanoi is nearer than New Delhi. Tibet is just 50 kilometers away by crow flight. The Mainland China borders Arunachal Pradesh and is just 150 miles away from Nagaland. This helps our hostile neighbours to stoke the flames of insurgency in the region without throwing their own troops in the inferno of a prolonged battlefield. This provides the added advantage of keeping the pot of insurgency boiling while the promoter remains anonymous and incognito. In a country, which is littered with history's cinders to fuel communal strife which led to the country's partition in 1947, unabated insurgency, aided and abetted from abroad, when confounded with confessional religious rigidity, creates an artificial Hindu-Christian, Hindu-Muslim as also inter-ethnic unbridgeable divide which is the major causal factor of alienation and secessionism.

The geographical divide not only promotes ethnic affinity among the locals with the neighbouring countries having similar ethnicity, it also prevents mentle bonding between mainland

Indians and people inhabiting the seven sisters. The abysmal ignorance of mainland Indians about this region and its inhabitants is yet another inhabiting factor which prevents a closer mentle bonding and encourages separation. Obviously distance cannot be reduced but greater and quicker connectivity can be provided to change the mindset of locals who hate the hegemonistic political designs of mainland Indians and looks upon them as economic oppressors or a colonial adjunct.

Museum of Nationalities

Assam has been a crucible of diverse cultures brought about by migrating ethnic communities. "Down the ages groups of people have been coming to the banks of Brahmputra in search of peace and shelter. Nobody can say whose footprints were those on the fertile valleys of the Lohit, whether Tibetan, Burmese, Thai, Mangol, Kirat or Aryan" observes Palhi Saikia quoting an unnamed author.[2] Over the years, the region has been a mute witness to an uninterrupted wave of migrants of varied ethnic groups crossing into it in driblets from Tibet, Thailand, Mynamar and South China which has made it multi-ethnic. Ethnic multipolarity has given rise to the phenomenon of multiple-identity formation of migrant groups, each zealous to preserve its ethnic distinctiveness. Small wonder the Nagas, Mizos, Khasis, Garos, Jaintias and Ahoms got statehood and remaining neglected segments of Bodos, Kacharies, Missings, Lalungs, Kukis and other like-minded groups are agitating to carve out their own ethnic enclaves within India if conceded constitutionally and outside India, if prevented through successful insurgency. To this one may add the dimension of clandestine cross border nocturnal migration from Bangladesh, which is in the nature of irregular, illegal, unauthorized and undocumented migration.

The point is that a multi-ethnic society can absorb the shocks of such migration and even assimilate diverse ethnic groups if that does not change its basic demography and migrant groups remain a trickle and do not become a torrent. In the latter case, migration induces insurgency. The unremitting wave of Bangladeshis into Tripura has changed its demographic structure so drastically that the erstwhile tribe is reduced to an abysmal minority in its homeland accounting for just 25 per cent of Tripura's total population; the rest 75 per cent being the Bengalis. In Assam too the undocumented Bangladeshi exodus from across the border poses a serious threat to the local Assamese community who apprehend being reduced to a minority in its own habitat on the pattern of Tripura. The continued influx of Chakrnas in Arunachal Pradesh and Kukis of Burma in Manipur touches an emotive umbilical chord among the natives who fear being swamped by unwanted aliens into their homeland. Mufti-ethnicity has thus created inter-ethnic feuds in the region and the entire region is in the coils of a python. The central movement is at its wits ends and is doling out one ad hoe solution alter another in the fond hope of controlling inter-ethnic dissent and dissonance, which is the chief cause of unabated insurgency in the region. Its failure to seal porous border effectively and provide strict vigilance on border will continue to encourage illegal undocumented emigration, which will further inflame passions and exacerbate native-migrant dichotomy.

Confessional Divide

Religious diversity provides an inflammable dimension to the seemingly peaceful political situation. The polyglot state of Assam is the biggest and the largest state in the North East both in terms of territory and population and is inhabited in most part by Hindus who constitute an absolute majority. But how long they would be able to sustain this status is open to question. The unabated, large scale infiltration of Muslims from Bangladesh has not only made the Muslims the second largest numerical group in Assam accounting for more than 25 per cent of population of Assam, there is a fear that in the next ten years, Assam is likely to be declared the second Muslim majority state after Jammu and Kashmir if the unchecked immigration of Bangladeshi Muslims is not stopped. The Christians too constitute a sizeable chunk of population. Many of the tribal groups are fast being converted to Christianity. A very large percentage of Padam tribe of Assam has already been converted to Christianity.

In addition to Assam, three states of North Eastern India have a clear Christian's majority. They are Meghalaya, Mizoram and Nagaland. Nagaland lacks even national symbols and its state language is English. States like Manipur, Tripura and Arunachal Pradesh though Hindu dominated at present are unlikely to retain this status for long if the rate of conversation to Christianity is any indication. While one cannot object to people accepting any religion, the problem of North East is singularly different. The Christian converts in the states of Nagaland, Mizoram and even in Meghalaya are being inoculated in the tradition of separatism. Zapu Angami Phizo was the first Naga tribal in North East India to unfurl the banner of rebellion and his characteristic refrain was Hindu India versus Christian Nagaland. Unlike the Christians in the rest of India who are second to none in upholding their innate Indianness and loyalty to the nation, the converts in North East are bitten by the bug of separatism and this is entirely due to the influence of foreign missionaries who had injected the virus of separatism in the new converts, purposively to keep them away from Indian mainstream.

Here it would not be out of place to mention that not only foreign Christian missions, even the British never thought of keeping these tribals in India and they had coined the word ab-origins to indicate the non-Indianness of these tribal groups. Governor Robert Reid had plan in place to carve out a separate independent state in North Eastern India by amalgamating some areas of Burma into it. He justified it on the grounds of history, language, religion and ethnicity. The seeds of separatism were sown by the British and the emerging plant was manured and watered by foreign Christian missionary groups each one of whom had ulterior motives in keeping these tribals out of the mainstream of India by emphasing their differences with and separateness from the rest of Indians. Small wonder, the diaspora today is a hot bed of secessionism. Confessional rigidity has only cemented this separateness.

Linguistic Mosaic

Linguistic diversity is an Indian reality. The linguistic survey of India published-in 1927 listed 1625 mother tongues that included 199 languages and 544 dialects. The census of India 1961 recorded speakers of 101 languages. About 73.3 per cent Indian speak Indo-Aryan languages whereas 24.5 per cent speak, Dravindian languages, such as Tamil, Telegu Kannada and Malyalam.[3] Sir John Straitchy once observed, "What is India. There is no such country............. India is the name, which we give to a great region including a great multitude of different countries. The differences between the countries of Europe are undoubtedly smaller than those between the countries of India. Scotland is more like Spain than Bengal is like Punjab........... It is probable that not less than fifty languages which may rightly be called separate are spoken in India."[4]

This linguistic plurality is also reflected in the North Eastern states. Here every tribal group speaks its own language or dialect and there is a staggering variety of mother tongues spoken in this region. One may enumerate some of them. In Arunachal Pradesh alone 168 languages and dialects are spoken, followed by 192 in Assam, Mizoram and Meghalaya, 87 in Manipur, 112 in Tripura and 95 in Nagaland.[5] In Naga areas one tribal does not understand the language/dialect of his neighbour because 42 Naga tribes have an equal number of languages/dialects. The All India Radio tried to beam news bulletins for Nagaland in Nagamese which was formed by taking linguistic bits from different Naga languages/dialects, but it was hardly understood by all sections of Nagas and the experiment failed. Thus apart from, ethnic, religious and other differentiations linguistic heterogeneity is yet another dividing factor in the North East.

Why Secessionism?

Diversities such as these can be found in other parts of India too but there is no demand for seceding out of India except in Tamil Nadu, Punjab and Jammu and Kashmir. Separatist voices were heard in Rajya Sabha in 1962 on behalf of Tamils by the late C. Annadurai who later on gave it up fearing that a truncated Dravidian state would not be able to defend itself against any powerful neighbour. The Punjab and Kashmiri separatism is being fuelled by our hostile neighbour Pakistan. Being border states both get clandestine support in terms of men and material, money and armament from Pakistan. Even more importantly Pakistan provides a safe sanctuary to Punjabi and Kashmiri insurgents in addition to valuable logistic support in times of operations. But secessionist slogans are a normal occurrence in each one the seven states of North Eastern India. The big question, therefore, is why the North Eastern region is the hub of secessionism? Why are antinational separatist groups proliferating there? Why is there no end to secessionist sentiments? The answer cannot be simply a religious divide, ethnic differentiation or linguistic diversity. These factors are found elsewhere too in India but they have not led to any secessionist movement. Why then in North East alone such movements are gaining momentum?

To find the answer some soul searching and deep delving is necessary, howsoever unpleasant and painful it may be. The answer lies in the history of this region, which shows that this area is a late entrant to Indian mainstream. Prior to the British, no Indian ruler governed this area. "It was never a part of India during the ancient and medieval period. The Mauryan Empire, the Gupta Empire, the Delhi sultanate and the Mughal Empire were not able to include Assam. However, there was a close cultural interaction between the two since the times of ancient Indian civilisation. That is evident from the iron pillar inscription of Allahabad, the ancient Chinese traveller Hieun Tsang's account on cultural interaction and exchanging visits between ancient Kamrup kingdom under Bhaskar Varman and Harshavardhana in Kanauj. The Mughals had tried to invade Assam as many as 17 times, but the Ahom rulers successfully resisted and retained sovereignty of their kingdom. This glorious past of Assam is the source of inspiration and pride for the people living in Assam. It is, however, true that although Assam was not politically a part of medieval India, it practised the Hinduite traditions and customs."[6] Muslim entry into the

Brahmaputra Valley commenced with the Turki invasion in 1206 under Mohammad Baktiar, followed by Mughals. At one stage in the seventeenth century, the Mughals succeeded in capturing Assam up to Kamarupa. It was the Ahom ruler, Rudra Singha, who formed a confederation with the Chutiya King and finally threw the Mughals out of Assam in the Battle of Saraighat. Assamese are proud of this feat and can never stop speaking about their great military achievement.

Being largely a dense forest region, with scarce communication facilities and hardly any source of income, this region did not attract the attention of rapacious conquerors from north and remained largely outside their influence and control. It was a tribal infested area which later on came under the spell of wandering tribes of Burma, Thailand and Tibet and though its rulers became Hindus after being baptised into the Hindu fold through "the Aryanisation of Indo-Mangoloid stocks"[7] by Hindu priests. Till then they were outside the pale of authority of any Indian monarch. Even the East India Company got entry into this area through a commercial treaty with the Ahom King in 1793. The native rulers were engaged in fratricidal warfare among themselves and very often came in conflict with their powerful neighbour Burma. For long they remained under the control of Burmese rulers and it was only in 1926, that the army of East India Company inflicted heavy damage on the Burmese and got this area under their control by signing the Treaty of Yandabo in the same year. Later on the British captured Naga, Mizo, Khasi Jaintia hills and brought the entire area under their unified control. Complete control over Assam was established in 1842. In 1874, a separate province of Assam was created.

This more than anything else makes many people in this region think that it were the British who defeated them and brought them under their control and sovereignty like the other parts of India and hence with the final departure of the British in 1947, this region too became independent and ceased to be a part of independent India. To this one may add Indian governments indifference and its notional consent to let Assam merge with East Pakistan in 1947 which left an indelible scar on the psyche of an average Assamese that they were like an unwanted child of India who but for the Herculean efforts of Lokpriya Gopichand Bardoloi, would have gone to Pakistan. Sanjoy Hazarika in his book 'Strangers in the Mist,' recalls how Jawaharlal Nehru had agreed to let go Assam into East Pakistan and on being asked if it was not a betrayal of the Assamese people, Nehru replied "Assam could not hold up the progress of rest of India."[8] Nehru even tried to persuade Gopichand Bardoloi to accept this by saying "Assam must make some sacrifice for India's independence."[9] The Chinese invasion of India in 1962 and their deep penetration into Assam further embittered Assamese feelings. The Assamese felt let down by Jawaharlal Nehru's rueful statement during this war that "My heart bleeds for Assam." The Assamese took it to be a sign of Indian inability and weakness to defend Assam. All this created a feeling of alienation among the people of these seven states.

Strangers in the Indian Mist

To this one may add the role of Manipur and Tripura rulers. Manipur had proclaimed its independence on 1947 and had set up a constituent assembly to draft its constitution. It joined Indian Union in November 1949, some say under duress. Tripura joined India on October 15, 1949.[10] The state of Arunachal Pradesh was originally North East Frontier Agency (NEFA) during the reign of the British and the Chinese still do not recognise it as a part of India and maintain that this was done by a British officer Sir Henry McMahon who drew an arbitrary McMahon Line to democrat Indo-Chinese borders in 1913-1914 and amalgamated this area into India. This area was named NEFA in 1914. China never recognised the validity of McMahon Line. The same thing the British did in western India where they forcibly annexed Afghan territory and named it, North West Frontier Province (NWFP). In the latter case the Durand line was also arbitrarily drawn and Afghanistan never recognised this Durand frontier. Nor does she accept this area belonging to Pakistan. It is a moot question why when all other Indian states had distinct names, only these two states were not given appropriate names and continued to be addressed as North East Frontier Agency (NEFA) and North West Frontier

Province. The perception in China and Afghanistan is that they are the illegitimate offspring's of India, perhaps even aliens.

Thus, British conquest and annexations both in western and eastern India created two territorial entities called NWFP and NEFA and unlike in the case of rest of India where every province was given a distinct historical or linguistic name, these two territorial identities viz., NWFP and NEFA were not given such names. NEFA became Arunachal Pradesh in 1971 when the Indian Parliament passed the North Eastern Areas (Reorganization) Act in 1971. China disputes India's claims to the area of Khinzamane, Bumla and Longchu in Arunachal Pradesh.[11]

The Sino-Indian boundary line is 3,350 kilometers long. Between 2005 and 2007, there have been 300 Chinese incursions and 10000 Chinese soldiers are concentrated across the Tawang sector of China.[12] China is claiming 90000 sq. km of India's land whereas India is seeking 36,846 sq. km from China besides 5080 square km of land ceded by Pakistan to China.[13] China has made deep incursions into Demchok area in Ladakh area and here the Chinese build-up "can cut off supply lines for Leh on Manali-Leh route without encountering Indian defences."[14] In the Ladakh region, the Chinese can bring infantry and armed columns through Charding La, Jara La and Toshigong. In Uttarkhand, areas near Barahoti have been violated.

In Tawang sector, in Narnkha Chu and Sumdrong Chu, China wants to straighten the border from Kharsangla to Indo-Bhutan border. Through its creeping acquisitions, China has already got several hundred kilometers of Indian territory, says Kiren Rijiju, the M.P. from Arunachal Pradesh.[15] The Chinese have built all-weather motorable roads on their side of border, whereas only three posts in Arunachal Pradesh can be accessed by road. The reminder can be reached only by foot patrol. The government of India has cleared the construction of 608 kilometers of road in this sector at a cost of Rs. 9092 crores but the work is proceeding at a snail's pace.

As of now China is provocatingly upping the ante in a bellicose and revanchist manner. Having wrung concessions from India, China is now demanding territorial concessions from Bhutan on the Tawang sector, which is a critical corridor between Lhasa and Assam. Since it overlooks the chicken neck that connects India with the entire North East, its military and strategic significance cannot be overemphasized or ignored. Having gobbled up Tibet, China is seeking territorial connections not only in the name of ethnicity or Han connection between Tibet and Tawang. But also on grounds of Buddhist ecclesiastical ties between the two regions, which creates tutelary ties of long standing. In pursuance of its diplomacy, China has forcibly separated two regions from Tibet-Amdo, the birthplace of present Dalai Lama and Kham where Buddhist influence was undisputed but China separated them from dominant Tibet with impunity and the principle of tutelary ecclesiastic relationship was rejected in this case but ironically is being applied to Tawang region in utter violation of the same principles. Those being espoused now in the case of Tawang were rejected in respect of Amdo and Kham. Obviously China wants settlement of border disputes on vacuous principles, hence "India needs a more nuanced, realistic and leverage-playing approach"[16] to put relations with China on an even keel.

In view of these historical antecedents it is not difficult to understand why the people in this part of India consider their links with India a disputed legacy. Assam joined India in 1826, Garo's area was subjugated in 1866 when a British officer was appointed in Tura in that year and Mizo areas came under British domination in 1895. The Nagas were brought under British control in 1914. Tripura joined India on October 15, 1949 and Manipur in November 1949.

This shows that North Eastern region is a latecomer to the Indian scene. It is inhabited largely by people of Mongolian stock who speak their own languages and dialects and is separated from India by vast distance which makes the entire diaspora a little different from the rest of India and successive ill-conceived polities of Government of India have only deepened and widened the chasm between this region and mainstream India, owing to which a feeling of alienation has grown here and this has resulted in fanning the flames of secessionism. It has created pockets of discontent and discontented people are turning to secessionism as a solution of their problems.

Notes

1. V.K. Anand, (1980): *Conflict in Nagaland,* Chanakya Publications, Delhi, p. 21.
2. Pahl Saikia, in Dipankar Sengupta and Sudhir Kumar Singh (ed.), (2004): *Insurgency in North East India,* Delhi: Author Press, p. 58.
3. Bhawani Singh, (1990): *Indian Politics: Ideology and Ecology,* Jaipur: Printwell Publishers, p. 31.
4. Quoted in Nariman D. Palmer, *Indian Political System,* 2nd edition, Boston, USA: Houghton on Miffm, p. VIII.
5. Bhawani Singh, *op. cit.,* p. 3.
6. Dilip Gogoi in Dipankar, Sen Gupta and Sudhir Kumar Singh, *op. cit.,* p. 40
7. N.S. Narahari, (2002): *Security Threats to North East India,* Delhi: Manas Publication, p. 5.
8. Ibid., p. 39.
9. S.K. Sinha, (1998): "Insurgency in Assam," *Journal of United Service Institution of India,* Vol. VIII, No. 553 (July-September), p. 429.
10. Chandra Bhusan, (2004): *Terrorism and Separation in North East India,* Delhi: Kalpaz Publications, p. 26.
11. N.S. Narahari, *op. cit.,* p. 19.
12. *India Today,* October 15, 2007.
13. Ibid., p. 39.
14. Ibid., p. 40.
15. Ibid., p. 42.
16. Brahma Chellaney, (2004): "Don't Get Cowed Down," a write-up in *Times of India,* New Delhi, 2 October, p. 10.

11

PARADOX OF ASSIMILATION AND ALIENATION IN NORTH EAST INDIA

Rakhee Bhattacharya

Introduction

Mountainous North Eastern Region of India has been the sufferer of history. While looking at the colonial period, Sanjib Baruah[1] narrates that this region came under British East India Company in 1826, at the end of the Anglo-Burmese war. During that time, under the Yandabo Treaty, the king of Burma renounced all claims and agreed to be away from future interferences with the principality of Assam and with its contiguous states. Eventually, with the end of Anglo-Burmese war, this entire region became the territory of British India. Manipur retained its status as a kingdom under British protection though its autonomy eroded over time. Advent of British was purely to understand the economic and strategic worth of this region which together with the vast tracts of uncultivable and uninhabited lands caught the fancy of the British who used them in the most productive and profitable way for generating surplus; not for recycling it back into the region, but for serving their own interest. But as Baruah[2] argues, when the British found the lands in the valleys and foothills suitable for large-scale commercial plantations like tea, they came in direct confrontation with people of this region like Nagas, whose hunting and food gathering activities were disrupted due to such land grab. In words of Baruah, 'Naga-British encounter was one of the most violent chapters in the history of British conquest in sub-continent. There were ten violent 'punitive expedition' against Nagas between 1835 to 1851.' The last major military encounter between them took place in 1879, when Angami Nagas seized British military base in Kohima. The usual trade transactions between the hills and plains people across this frontier were severely disrupted due to the introduction of Inner Line Regulation of 1873 by the British in the name of preserving indigenous cultures in tribal areas and also to protect the plains villages from tribal raids. But according to Scott[3] people had continually moved from hills to plains and from plains to hills to supply manpower, and to do commercial activities. The policy of isolation by the British has made the people more conscious about their ethnic identity. For their economic and strategic interests, the colonials have ruthlessly isolated North East India by drawing boundaries with its close Southeast Asian allies, and introduced the policies of distinction for the people of North East from rest of India. Colonials have emphasized the concept of preserving 'tribal'[4] identity of North East. Since the region never had any cultural link and geographical accessibility with other parts of India, therefore its truncation from its close neighbours on the other side truly made it 'isolated.' Trade, economic and cultural transactions with neighbours and between the hills and plains across this frontier came to a standstill. Such policies of seclusion of the region combined with its geographical isolation from rest of India, reflects an isolationist mindset. The creation of tea and oil economy by the British by using labourers outside the region had served as an 'enclave economy' amidst the ethno-traditional economic set-up, which could never be successful in bringing opulence and welfare to the people of entire region. In words of Kumar,[5] 'their (colonials) policy of gradual segregation of the tribals and non-tribals, hills and the plains; segregation of the tribal population by introduction of the 'Inner Line Regulation', creation of 'non-regulated', 'backward' and 'excluded' areas/tracts was able to break centuries of historical, cultural, social and religious continuum and connectedness. The colonial theories/myths—the myth of race, core-fringe conflict, isolation, colonial misinterpretation of history and culture further deepened the impact' of such isolation and has finally alienated the region from rest of India.

Post Independent Policy: Assimilation or Alienation

After independence of India, the question of North East India's modernization and linkages with the rest of India has always been contradicted with the preservation of its rich ethno-cultural identity. Nehru[6] persistently felt the necessity of respecting 'tribal' sentiment, which is clear from his writings that 'the problem of tribal areas is to make the people feel that they have perfect freedom to live their own lives and to develop according to their wishes and genius. India to them should signify not only a protecting force but a liberating one. Any conception that is ruling them and that they are the ruled, or that customs and habits with which they are unfamiliar are going to be imposed upon them, will alienate them.'

The ruthless 'restructuring of North East India' by colonial rulers has forced the region to remain at the periphery, and even in post colonial era, this peripheral status was never been broken, rather North East became further away from mainstream due to its persistent political-economic swings along with Nehru's policy of protection. This had to set a gradual resentment in the region and manifested in way of separatism, secessionism, insurgency, and above all a terrible hatred and denial for 'mainland.' So over the years, any attempt of cultural convergence with mainstream has been termed as 'cultural imperialism' by the new generations of North East. On the other hand, such gap in connection and understanding has also created misnomers in 'Other India' about 'North East India.' As rightly argued by Miri[7] there can be broadly two views of North East India. They are view from inside and view from outside. The outsiders' view imagines North East as a unitary entity, inhabited by vaguely differentiated 'tribal' people, who seem 'racially distinct' from Indians elsewhere. And the insiders' diverse view caters to tribes, communities, languages, ethnicity, culture, tradition etc. Miri has termed insider's view as 'egocentric predicament.' Such egocentricity amongst insiders and misnomers amongst the outsiders have pathetically widened the problem of integration both within 'North East India' as well as with 'Other India.'

But the government always was aware of the absolute lack of development and infrastructure in the region. The regional economies remained simple, heavily deficient and dependent on the rest of the country. Multiple development agenda therefore were taken with injection of huge funds to develop the region, thus North Eastern Council, Ministry of Development of North Eastern Region have been created. Attempts were focused and funds were directed towards development of infrastructure and economy. But due to large scale endemic corruption and leakages in the political system in North East, such funds systematically were misutilised and the region failed to take advantage of India's modernization. Also, the development initiatives of Indian government miserably failed to reach the grassroot, but it succeeded in creating an elite urban tribal class, who has started enjoying the fruits of life, by acquiring a modern identity and by receiving tribal benefits vertically for many generations from the government. The rest are utterly deprived off, poor and voiceless, giving rise to horizontal inequality within the region.

Issue of Identity & Rise of Insurgency

Such attempts of assimilation and development initiatives from 'New Delhi' without the voices of local people were never accepted in the region. Different ethnic groups in North East India were rather utterly confused after India's independence and were not sure about their place and their identity in the independent India. In 1945, when a Naga Tribal Association was formed, their primary concerns were:

- What would be their role in the future in India?
- Whether they were a part of the Indian nationality?
- How would they exist in future and what would be their safeguards for the present?

In fact Naga nationalists have never accepted the Indian identity and any kind of assimilation with Indian union and started their actual movement for political sovereignty since 1950s and Indo-Naga conflict continued since then. Indian govt. has tried with several measures and tactics but was not successful to solve their issues. As Nagas[8] think that the measures were half-baked, incomprehensive, exclusive, out of political in context and content, traditional in methods and adhoc in nature, which were applied to divide the Naga people and their struggle for political identity. For example according to them creation of Nagaland state has greatly weakened the spirit of nationalism among Naga people.

The fear for survival and issue of identity eventually then became common among the people of North East and made them politically aware and active. It was realized that, participation in political process required solidarity and unification of the tribes to equip themselves to combat the hegemony and dominance of the prospective post-colonial state of India and more importantly, to resist being taken for granted and be able to assert their rights to decide the future course of action. Thus anger and frustration at the near total lack of development and marginalization have created strong feelings against the Indian union in the region among many of the deprived tribes and also amongst the people of the plains. The wide-spread anti-India sentiments and secessionist tendencies were successfully exploited by the insurgent groups. Apart from this, economic backwardness, lack of opportunities, a persistent inflow of illegal immigrants from neighbouring countries like Bangladesh in states like Assam and Tripura, and then percolating to rest of the region has imposed an additional threat to the people of North East, which has fast changed the landscape of the region. Such major issues have gradually given birth to several non-integrative warfares, movements for sovereignty and right to self-determination and finally manifested as militant organizations. For example Assam being one of the richest states in India in terms of her natural resources like oil and gas was deprived off from having economic benefits, as people of Assam think so. This sense of deprivation has given birth to a sense of grievance and finally culminated to militancy and given birth to deadly outfits like ULFA, which had surfaced more than a quarter century back in 1979, with a vow to free Assam from 'Indian Colonials.' The following statement made by Arabinda Rajkhowa, Chairman ULFA, in 2007[9] can make ULFA's sovereignty movement in Assam clear.

> 'ULFA (United Liberation Front of Asom) was formed with the determined aim of re-establishing a Sovereign Independent Assam, presently under Indian colonial occupation. The objective of our national liberation struggle is to free the indigenous people from Indian colonial oppression and exploitation, the ultimate goal being to establish a society on the principles of scientific socialism. Assam belongs to all the indigenous peoples of Assam. But the divisive and oppressive Indian subjugation has deprived us of our common heritage of the Sovereign rights over our land. It is with these solemn national and social objectives that ULFA was formed on this day 28 years ago.'

Assam being one of the richest reservoirs of natural resources in India has the potential to become a self-sufficient, economically stable and modernized core state of India like Gujarat. But the history has given it an altogether different identity, as an unstable periphery of a landlocked region without many economic opportunities, beset with nature's fury as well as men's folly like poverty, ethnic and linguistic clashes, near total absence of any infrastructure, exploitation, infiltration from across the border, subsistence living for most of the populace and extreme deprivation. Lack of development has resulted in dissipation of energy in unnecessary conflicts and separatist movements in the region for a long time. ULFA is one such reflection, which had surfaced more than a quarter century back in 1979, with a vow to free Assam from 'Indian Colonials.'

This dominant outfit was formed in April 1979 at the deserted Rong Ghor premises in Sibasagar when a handful of youth had assembled and pledged to liberate Assam from the rule of New Delhi. No one cared to take that event seriously at that moment, but in course of time ULFA became so prominent that for a brief period in early 1990s it was running a parallel administration in some pockets. The outfit emerged from All Assam Students Union, with an initial issue of anti-immigrant agitation and then its rise was linked with the coming of AGP Government in power.[10] The outfit's movement aims at sovereign Assam, though illegal influx from Bangladesh was one of their initial priorities. A group of bright, vibrant and young people was committed to fulfill their dream of 'independent Assam', which would bring prosperity to its 'indigenous people.' But this euphoria has vanished long back, its ideology and commitment disintegrated and dissipated over the years and the objectives of ULFA lie in tatters now, with its mass base having been eroded. It has now become just another terrorist outfit and a non-state actor, its plea for sovereignty only a camouflage to destabilize Assam and prevent it from attaining any stability. Its systematic extortion has further impoverished the people and driven industries outside the region and prevented new ones from coming up. This has also given rise to a 'parallel insurgent economy' in the State, and its illegal transactions have made the state economy extremely porous. Assam, the nodal state of North East thus eventually came to dominate the news due to such militant outfits and insurgency activities and became a threat to security, in the process of getting further alienated from the rest of India.

Insurgency: Present Form & Future Threat

The region today is extremely vulnerable due to various insurgency related activities, especially in the states like Nagaland, Manipur, Assam and Tripura. To counter such violence, Government of India had introduced Armed Force Special Power Act in 1958, under which Indian army had enormous power relating to counter insurgency operation. Such draconian government measure had further aggravated the anger of the people of the region. The mindset of North East today refuses any kind of assimilation with the rest of India without resolving their existing problems. Naga movement is one of the world's oldest movement and they refuse to accept themselves as part of India till today. Unless their right to self-determination and a separate Naga national identity is recognized, this movement is unlikely to die and they would continue to blame Indian government to resolve this issue by saying that the government lacks sincerity and honesty for a peaceful solution.

Situation is more complicated today due to cross border support and connectivity and poses a challenge to the security of the entire India. Around 14 countries are involved today in the insurgency operation in the region. Over the years, assistance and support of various kinds from various external agencies have found their way into the various militant outfits here, making it even more volatile. Apart from Bangladesh, Pakistan, China, Myanmar, Bhutan, Nepal, there are also other countries like US, Australia, Singapore and Thailand, Malaysia, Sri Lanka which act as conduits for such assistance flowing to the militant groups operating in the region in one way or the other.[11]

While looking for the foreign hand in region's insurgency issue, Bhaumik[12] has mentioned that 'Bangladesh backs almost all North Eastern Indian militant groups—the guerillas from Assam, Meghalaya, Manipur and Tripura have around 125 camps, smaller hideouts and safe houses in its territory. The NSCN has several bases in CHT but ever since it started negotiating with India in 1997, these camps have not been functional.' The recent arrest of Arvind Rajkhowa from Bangladesh justifies Bhaumik's argument and the friendly pro-Indian gesture of Awami League government of Bangladesh. Bhaumik[13] further says that 'the most powerful rebel army on Burma's western borders, the Kachin Independence Army (KIA), developed close link with North Eastern separatist groups like Naga National Council (NNC), the National Socialist Council of Nagalnad (NSCN) and the United Liberation Front of Assam (ULFA). They first helped the Naga rebels to reach China in 1966 and then they trained and armed NSCN and ULFA and at least two Manipuri rebel groups. Pakistan and China and then Islamist regime in Bangladesh, have aided and abetted rebel groups from North East as part of a deliberate design to destabilize India's frontier regions. Chinese support for these rebels started in the mid 1960s and is said to have ended in the early 1980s, but there are some fresh indications that Chinese intelligence are in touch with at least two North East Indian rebel groups after India signed a nuclear deal with the United States and decided to enter into a 'strategic partnership' with them. Pakistan and Bangladesh continued to support rebel groups from the North East, providing them sanctuaries and safe houses, weapons and training facilities.'

Another threat that we see in North East insurgency is the growth of a strong parallel insurgent economy that has taken deep roots in the region, whose funding primarily comes from corporate sector, development fund of government, illegal extortion in the form of taxation, levies and kidnapping. This has twisted the economy of the region to a large extent. Local political and bureaucratic link to the insurgent outfits has made an unholy nexus to hinder solution and development. The Annual Report of the Ministry of Home affairs, Govt. of India, 2000-2001[14] admitted that insurgency in this region has grown like a 'Cottage Industry', whose sole objective was to 'make easy money.' Evidence says that both financial and training support along with arms supply is pouring from cross border countries. This has twisted the economy of the region to a large extent. Local political and bureaucratic link to the insurgent outfits has made an unholy nexus to hinder solution and development.

Concluding Remarks

The question remains can North East India and the secessionist mindset of its various insurgent groups be brought to reconciliation and integration with the rest of India or will it be allowed to drift away, creating possibly a situation like Myanmar in this region, deprived and oppressed, poor and marginalised? The answer is simply NO. Rather the solution needs to be found out through a way of integration.

It is important therefore that the tremendous psychological

gap that exists between North East region and the rest of India needs to be bridged through collaboration, cohabitation, meeting of minds and understanding. In this regard we need to understand and thoughtful that the people of North East when go out of the region should be accepted without any racial discrimination and also inside the region, they need to accept the outsiders with dignity but not by treating them as foreigner. People of North East need to understand that India has infinite resilience to accept cultural diversities therefore North East's cultural mosaic can never be under threat from India. Above all government must do everything to create confidence that it is committed to promote a system of governance and security that is based on the rule of law, which can provide a lasting solution to all existing problems by creating hope. The mosaic of issues must find an inclusive approach for a solution, which involves the people of the state and their economic betterment. Institutes for knowledge, excellence and strategy need to be established. Co-operative security and peace-building measures, both within the region and with the international neighbours can successfully lead to growth and development for all. Unless this is done, the geopolitics of the region soon manifests itself in some other form.

People of the region need to feel like being an integral part of India, but not only as a group of people who wield the bargaining power on the benefits like special category, tax exemption and reservation. To my mind, this is a hindrance to promote the true spirit of Indian citizenship among them and their sense of participation and assimilation with India's socio-economy and culture. Secessionism also can never solve their economic and other woes, because none of the states in the region has enough resources to make for a viable state but remaining as a unit in the Indian federation may solve their problems, with efforts from both sides, which are increasingly becoming spontaneous and visible. Only time can say whether right measure that are being spoken off so far can rewrite the troubled history of North East.

The region therefore desperately needs resurgence through multiple economic opportunities that are opening up with 'India's modernity.' It is these opportunities that can usher in an era economic sovereignty in North East India. All this while, Central assistance was pumped in generously for various developmental programmes, for rehabilitation of surrendered militants, for meeting the rising security related defense expenses, but enormous leakages and misutilisation and untimely evaluation had hindered and prevented achievement of the scheme deliverables. Time is of essence here, and urgency is the need of the hour to contain and stop insurgency operation from spreading and to restore the lost ethno-cultural and economic links across the border to regain people's confidence. Only regional cooperation, not conflict, can improve people's capability index to revive its economy. The whole of North East India for that matter can rightly be claimed as 'embedded' between the two fastest growing economies of the world—India and China. Also, North East India, South-West China and South-East Asia can be a 'triangular economic zone' and can bring prosperity to this region through appropriate vision and initiatives where The region can remain a pivotal partner, it is in this light that the national perspective for development of North East India and its assimilation process shall have to be charted out. Only with an approach towards integration rather than fragmentation and division can make the region a 'geographical heart land' of an emerging North East India, having a vibrant socio-economic and cultural fabric.

Notes

1. Sanjib Baruah, (2005): *Durable Disorder: understanding the Politics of Northeast India*, New Delhi: Oxford University Press, pp. 104.
2. Ibid., pp. 104.
3. James C. Scott, (2005): "Hill and Valley in Southeast Asia ... or why the State is the Enemy of the People who Move Around . . . or . . . why Civilizations Don't Climb Hills." Paper submitted at symposium on Development and the Nation State. Washington University, St. Louis, 2000, available at http://www.artsci.wustl.edu/~symp2000/jscott. Cited by Sanjib Baruah *Durable Disorder: understanding the Politics of Northeast*

India, New Delhi: Oxford University Press, pp. 103.

4. The word tribal is commonly coined and used by the British ethnogaphers and rulers, as cited by S K Choudhury & S M Patnaik in the introduction of "Indian Tribes and the Mainstream," in S.K. Chaudhury and S.M. Patnaik, Rawat Publications, New Delhi, 2008, pp. 2.
5. B.B. Kumar, (2007): "Ethnicity and Insurgency in India's North East," pp. 17, in of B.B. Kumar (ed.), *Problems of Ethnicity in the North East India,* New Delhi: Concept Publishing Company, New Delhi.
6. Nehru wrote the forward of Varrier Elwin's, "Philosophy of NEFA" NEFA Administration, Shillong 1957. Cited by H.N. Das, in "Ethnic Aspirations and Insurgency in the North Eastern Region of India," in B.B. Kumar (ed.), *Problems of Ethnicity in the North East India,* New Delhi: Concept Publishing Company, pp. 84.
7. Mrinal Miri, (2007): "Two Views of the North East," p. 3, in B.B. Kumar, *Problems of Ethnicity in the North East India,* New Delhi: Concept Publishing Company.
8. *Morung Express,* (2008): "A Step by Step Transformation of the Indo-Naga-Burma-Naga Conflict," Yaronsho Ngalung, 2nd June.
9. Arabinda Rajkhowa, (2007): "India Committing Genocide in Assam," *The Telegraph,* 30 October, available at (http://telegraphnepal.com/news_det.php?news_id=1362).
10. Dinesh Kotwal, (2001): "The Contours of Assam Insurgency," *Strategic Ananlysis: A Monthly Journal of IDSA,* March, Vol. XXIV, No.12 available at http://assamchronicle.com/index.php?option=com_content&task=view&id=5&Itemid=43.
11. G.M. Srivastava, (2009): Director General of Police, Government of Assam has made this statement in the seminar organised by Maulna Abul Kalam Azad Institute of Asian Studies at Guwahati on 'Addressing Security and Development Issues in Assam' on 28th March 2009. This report has also come out in *The Assam Tribune,* 29th March 2009.
12. Subir Bhaumik, *Troubled Periphery: Crisis of India's Northeast,* Sage, New Delhi, pp. 156.
13. Ibid., pp. 154.
14. Cited by Sajal Nag in "Politics of Secessionism and Economy of Insurgency", Srikant Dutt memorial lecture delivered in New Delhi 2006.

12

EXTERNAL INFLUENCES ON THE NORTH EAST INSURGENCY

Anand Kumar

Introduction

North East India has been in turbulence since independence of the country, making it as a major trouble spot from the internal security point of view. A large number of groups are active in this region, with their demands varying from independence to self-rule. A plethora of ethnic groups are also clamouring for special rights and the protection of their distinct identity. To get some of these demands met insurgent groups have indulged in armed violence against the state and security forces. They have also resorted to killing of other ethnic groups or even to fratricidal killings. This situation has often prompted Indian state to take counter-insurgency operations. Under pressure from the Indian security forces the North East insurgents have found it expedient to seek support from the neighbouring countries. Forces inimical to India's interest have tried to take advantage of this situation. The insurgent groups have also managed to get support from some countries as same ethnic groups reside on both sides of the border. In some other cases, a purely client-patron relationship has existed. This kind of relationship existed between the insurgents and the arms smugglers of Southeast Asia or the Mafiosi of Bangladesh.

This paper tries to examine the role played by various external powers in sustaining the insurgency in North East. It argues that situation in North East would be vastly different, once these external forces stop influencing the insurgency in this region. The external powers have been supporting insurgency to weaken the India state.

North East: Providing Favorable Conditions for Insurgency

North East India has been facing insurgency since 1956 due to feelings of ethnic separatism among its inhabitants. Besides this region has all other enabling conditions which a terrorist or insurgent outfit might need for continuing their activities. Ninety eight percent of North East is contiguous to international border which allows terror outfits to get sanctuaries in Bhutan, Myanmar, Bangladesh and even China. In these countries they also get facilities for training and procure arms and ammunition from there. Ineffective administration in northern Myanmar, state-sponsorship from the intelligence agencies of Pakistan and Bangladesh and a regular flow of funds from the smugglers of narcotics from the Golden Triangle make their operation further easier.

Beginning of International Linkages

The North East insurgent groups started developing their international linkages immediately after the independence of India. Nagas were the first to raise the banner of insurgency. The process started when the father of the Naga insurgency, Angami Zapu Phizo, chief of the rebel Naga National Council (NNC), left the Naga Hills in 1956 to fight for an independent Naga homeland from London after traveling through East Pakistan and Switzerland. He continued his activity from there till his death in 1990. His agenda is now being pursued by his daughter Adinno Phizo, who has succeeded him as the NNC president, and is also based in London.

The government of India outlawed NNC in 1972 and started a major counter-insurgency operation finally resulting into the controversial Shillong Accord on November 11, 1975. Under this agreement Nagas agreed to accept Indian constitution, surrender arms and ammunition and join the Indian national mainstream.

However, a splinter group of around 140 NNC cadres did not accept Shillong Accord and formed a new insurgent group called the National Socialist Council of Nagaland (NSCN) under the leadership of Thuingaleng Muivah, Isak Chisi Swu and S. S. Khaplang. This new group was launched from bases inside Myanmar in 1980. In due course, the NSCN emerged as the most radical and powerful insurgent group fighting for the Naga cause. The outfit split in 1988 because of the clannish divisions among the Nagas.

The Naga insurgency in northeast is taken as mother of all insurgencies in North East. They were the first group to raise the banner of rebellion and also started providing arms training and other logistic support to outfits such as the United Liberation Front of Asom (ULFA), formed in April 1979 to fight for a 'sovereign, Socialist Assam.' The ULFA started sending its cadres for advanced 'military training' at the hands of the Kachin Independence Army (KIA), an anti-Yangon rebel group in Myanmar, from 1988 onwards.

ULFA set up its first camp in Bangladesh in 1985 in the Moulvi Bazaar district. By 1990 the outfit had also established its Pakistani contact. Its top leaders including Paresh Barua traveled to Afghanistan through Pakistan's North West Frontier Province where Pakistani Inter-Services Intelligence (ISI), assisted them to meet Gulbuddin Hekmatyar, a top Afghan Mujahideen leader of the time. ULFA also set-up well-entrenched bases inside southern Bhutan mainly in the district of Samdrup Jhongkar, bordering western Assam's Nalbari district by the end of 1990 and early 1991.

ULFA moved to Bhutan after the Indian army launched 'Operation Bajrang' in November 1990 and subsequently 'Operation Rhino' on September 14-15, 1991. Though the information regarding Operation Bajrang had leaked thereby allowing top ULFA leaders to escape to Bangladesh, the Operation Rhino was extremely successful as tactical surprise was achieved this time.[1] In Operation Rhino 431 hard core elements including 46 top leaders were arrested along with 299 supporters and trainees within few weeks. Sixteen ULFA camps were destroyed and material seized established ULFA's link with KIA, NSCN and the Liberation Tigers of Tamil Eelam (LTTE) and the existence of sanctuaries in Bangladesh.

ULFA chose southern Bhutan as a base as this area was not very well policed and thick jungles provided them suitable hiding place. Subsequently, Bhutan was also chosen by other insurgent groups like the National Democratic Front of Bodoland and the Kamtapur Liberation Organisation (KLO). The terror groups also preferred Bhutan as it was easy for them to carry out attacks across the border in India and return back to their safe hideouts in southern Bhutan. Bhutan with a small army was hardly in a position to take any effective counter-insurgency operation. It took 12 years for Bhutan to launch operation against the insurgents.

Bhutan's War on Terror

The presence of Indian insurgents and terrorists in Bhutanese territory was causing damage to the Indo-Bhutan ties, which is excellent otherwise. India has been persuading Bhutan to take action against these groups since 1998. The virtual illegal occupation of southern Bhutan by the terrorists posed a serious challenge to its sovereignty. The state had actually started withdrawing from these areas by closing down various institutions and commercial places. The terrorists were also hampering economic activities in Bhutan besides affecting its trade and commerce. Work at large industries such as the Dungsum Cement Project was suspended. Educational institutions in terrorist-infested areas were closed down. Trade, agriculture production and other commercial activities in several districts of the country were disrupted. Ordinary citizens were not feeling free to even travel across the country. Many became victims of threats, coercion and extortion. Unprovoked attacks by the militants against Bhutanese nationals inside the country, as well as those traveling through Indian state of Assam resulted in loss of innocent lives.

This situation forced Bhutan to take military action against Indian insurgent groups under the codename "Operation All Clear" on December 15, 2003 to oust them from its territory. At the time of the operation there were over 3,000 heavily armed Indian separatists belonging to three different groups, the ULFA, NDFB and the KLO based in Bhutan. They were operating from 30 camps inside the kingdom.[2] Out of these 30 camps, 13 camps belonged to ULFA, NDFB had 12 and rest five camps were of KLO.

Before opting for this operation Bhutan had tried to persuade insurgents to leave the kingdom peacefully. But after several round of talks spanning over six years, it had become almost certain that the militants had no intention of leaving the soil of Bhutan. In all the meetings that were held between Bhutan and the insurgent groups, Bhutan sent its top officials. On the other hand insurgents were represented only at the middle level. Some ULFA leaders even said that the leaving of Bhutan was as good as bidding goodbye to their cause for which they were not ready.[3] Bhutan however wanted to remove a major irritant in its relationship with India though it faced serious threats from the militants.

The Bhutanese king was dithering before taking military action as he was not sure of the military power of Bhutan. Its forces were not used for more than a century. Bhutan also knew that an action against the insurgents would make them hostile against the Bhutanese citizens and even Royal Bhutan Army. Most importantly Bhutanese had to travel through Indian territory to reach southern Bhutan.

It has been suggested by some that the decision to take military action against the militants was also expedited by the formation of the Bhutan Communist Party (Marxist-Leninist-Maoist) on April 22, 2003.[4] This party wanted to smash monarchy and establish a 'true and new democracy' in Bhutan. It was also feared that one of the insurgent groups KLO based in southern Bhutan was in league with the Bhutanese and

Nepalese Maoists. Thus the emerging Maoist threat could have forced the hand of the king who was already under the pressure of India to act against these groups.

Whatever may be the reason behind the Bhutanese military action, one thing is sure that Bhutanese action did set an example of cooperation in counter-terrorism in south Asia. The amount of risk taken by Bhutan to uproot the terrorists from its territory has only increased the importance of its action. Even countries like Bangladesh were prompted to say that they have sealed their borders with India to prevent Indian insurgents fleeing Bhutan or Myanmar from entering its territory. It also took sporadic actions against insurgents operating from its territory. But such actions were kept secret to buttress Dhaka's official stand that no Indian insurgents were operating from that country. There were indications that Myanmar was also tightening noose on Indian insurgent groups like the NSCN-K and the ULFA, which have bases in the country.

Insurgents Seeking Help of China

During the course of Bhutanese military operation it became clear to insurgent leaders that they would have to vacate Bhutanese territory. This prompted, ULFA 'chairman', Arabinda Rajkhowa, to appeal to the Chinese leadership on December 25, 2003, to provide safe passage to the insurgents from Bhutan for temporary shelter in China. Rajkhowa in his fax communication to the Chinese leadership said, "We have come under massive attack of Indo-Bhutan joint forces and our combatants have been forced to retreat up to the Sino-Bhutan border due to all out air and artillery campaigns."[5] Beijing however turned down the ULFA request and asked its frontier forces to remain vigilant against any effort by the insurgents to move into their territory.

This however does not mean that China has not been involved with North East Indian insurgents. Indian insurgents had not only visited China in the past for help, but had received assistance from sources within the country. NSCN-IM 'general secretary', Thuingaleng Muivah, admitted that Naga insurgents had, in the early days, obtained arms from China and Pakistan.

Even the NSCN (K) chief, S.S. Khaplang has admitted that Nagas have taken help from China and Pakistan in the past.[6]

The core leadership of the People's Liberation Army (PLA), an insurgent outfit active in Manipur was trained in China. Though the ethnic rebel armies of the Naga and the Mizo hills had received military training in China before them, the Chinese only tried to politicize a few Naga leaders such as Thuingaleng Muivah, the present general secretary of the NSCN. Muivah had some exposure to Marxist-Leninist ideology before he led the first batch of Naga rebels to China in 1966 at the beginning of the Cultural Revolution. But there was no attempt to politicize the Mizos or most of the Nagas, who were devout Christians. China merely wanted to use them against India to counterbalance the continued Indian support to the Tibetans. But the PLA's core leadership-the first batch of eighteen "Ojhas" (pioneers) went through heavy political training. The Chinese had hopes they would coordinate their struggles with the Indian Maoist groups and strengthen the cause of the Indian revolution.[7]

China trained and armed several batches of Naga, Mizo and Meitei since 1966. But this help stopped by the early 1980s. By then, however, Bangladesh's military rulers, who had come to power by the bloody coup that killed the country's founder Sheikh Mujibur Rehman, had revived the Pakistani policy of sheltering, arming and training rebel groups from North East India. Almost all the separatist groups in the North East-Nagas, Mizos, Meiteis, Tripuris, and now even those from Meghalaya-have subsequently received shelter and support in Bangladesh.

Recent reports however indicate that North East insurgents are once again trying to take the help of China as the political environment in Bangladesh has become unfavorable to them with return of Shaikh Hasina to power.[8] Since October 2009 ULFA's Commander-in-Chief Paresh Barua is believed to be somewhere close to the Myanmar-China border scouting for help to relocate its bases.[9] China in recent times has also emerged as a major source of weapons for North East insurgents and Maoists. Barua also visited China several time to procure weapons.[10] He also sells them to terror outfits such as National Democratic Front of Bodoland, National Liberation Front of Tripura, All Tripura Tiger Force and Maoists.[11]

Bangladesh: A Safe Haven for North East Insurgents

Bangladesh has been a safe haven for North East insurgents since East Pakistan days. Though officially Bangladesh government asserts that it has "never allowed or assisted insurgent groups of any country for acts against that country and this policy was being pursued by the Government consistently and rigorously", the actual policy of Bangladesh government is completely different.

Pro-Insurgent Record of the Successive Bangladeshi Governments

Indian insurgents have received support under all regimes in Bangladesh. Under the BNP led governments this support has been direct. However, when Awami Legue is in power insurgents get support of only a section of Bangladeshi security establishment. As a result, almost all North Eastern groups engaged in insurgency in North East have established their camps in Bangladesh. Begum Khaleda Zia in her last stint as leader of the Opposition had hailed these insurgents as "brave freedom fighters" carrying out a "heroic battle against an oppressive regime."

When Sheikh Hasina came to power for the first time, she disbanded most of the "overground" training camps of these insurgents but could do nothing to those going "underground" with the assistance of various government intelligence agencies. It was during the Awami League's regime that the ULFA leader Anup Chetia was arrested, convicted and jailed, while there were up to four attempts on the life of the leader of the group's armed wing, Paresh Barua.

This forced Paresh Barua to leave Dhaka for Karachi. He returned to Bangladesh again after the victory of BNP in the elections. Though Karachi was safe, it was too far off and it was difficult to run a rebellion in Assam from there. Besides, Barua also owns a number of businesses in Bangladesh that funded his once-powerful group.

These insurgents and their leaders were jubilant when the Khaleda Zia's Bangladesh Nationalist Party came to power after the parliamentary elections in October 2001. The BNP led ruling coalition did not disappoint these groups either.

The insurgency in Manipur has also received support from Bangladesh. The United National Liberation Front (UNLF) was formed on November 24, 1964, under the leadership of Areambam Samarendra Singh to establish an independent socialist Manipur. This outfit shared a close 'political relationship' with the then East Pakistani regime, and in 1969 underwent military training in that country. The group is also said to have backed the Pakistani Army during the Bangladesh liberation war in 1971. In December 1968, a break away group of the United National Liberation Front (UNLF), led by Oinam Sudhir Kumar, established a government-in-exile called Revolutionary Government of Manipur (RGM) with headquarters in Shylhet, in the then East Pakistan. The RGM was backed by Pakistan. However, the Meitei secessionist movement received a serious jolt when most of its leaders were arrested during the Bangladesh liberation war in 1971. Subsequently, the UNLF also became close to China with a team headed by N. Bisheswar Singh proceeding to Lhasa in 1975 to ask for Beijing's assistance. The UNLF is also close to the NSCN-K and has training camps in Myanmar and Bangladesh. In recent years insurgency has got intensified in Manipur and situation has become further complicated with rise of Islamist groups like PULF.

Similarly, in Tripura, both the major outlawed rebel groups—National Liberation Front of Tripura (NLFT) and All Tripura Tiger Force (ATTF) fighting for independent tribal homelands have operated from bases in adjoining Bangladesh. Tripura shares 856-kilometer-long border with Bangladesh with at least 70 percent of the boundary unfenced and with concrete pillars separating the two countries. But Dhaka denies the presence of Indian rebel bases in their territory. The role played by Bangladesh has been an important factor behind the continuation of insurgency in Tripura.

Arms Smuggling

Bangladesh has also been supporting insurgency in North East by freely allowing smuggling of arms to take place from its territory. The Bangladesh police and coastguard stumbled across a huge consignment of sophisticated illegal arms and ammunition, when they raided the Government-controlled Chittagong Urea Fertilizer Limited (CUFL) jetty on April 2, 2004. Reports indicated that, in this seizure, the smugglers were unloading the weapons with help from local police.

The Awami League after coming to power has restarted investigation into the Chittagong arms seizure. It has unmasked the government officials and agencies involved in arms trafficking. The investigation has now also conclusively proved that the arms were meant for northeast insurgents.[12] The arrested smugglers have revealed that senior political leaders along with civil and military intelligence chiefs of then Khaleda Zia government were involved in the botched arms shipment.[13] The Shaikh Hasina government prosecuted two former Bangladesh Army generals, Major General Rezakul Haider Chowdhury and Brigadier General Abdur Rahim, who headed the National Security Intelligence (NSI).[14] They were prosecuted for facilitating the landing of Chinese arms meant for insurgents in India's North East and for trying to smuggle these arms into India. It is also reported that Paresh Barua himself supervised the unloading of arms.

There were several seizures of this kind in the year 2003. Substantial caches of arms have been recovered from Chittagong and its three hill districts; Bogra in northwestern Bangladesh (this was the largest earlier seizure); and even from the capital, Dhaka. Cox Bazar in Bangladesh has emerged as a major port for supply of illegal arms and ammunition to North East insurgents.[15]

Fratricidal Killings among Insurgent Outfits in Dhaka

The insurgent groups using Bangladesh territory for terror operations against India have often indulged in fratricidal killings. This has further confirmed the presence of these groups in that country. Besides, there has also been action against these groups from the Bangladesh security agencies often to keep the internal security situation under control. Dhaka has however denied all such incidents just to prove that insurgents are not using its territory.

In November 2009, the Shaikh Hasina government in Bangladesh took a significant step towards improving bilateral relations with India when it detained two top leaders of the United Liberation Front of Asom (ULFA)—'foreign secretary' Sashadhar Choudhury and 'finance secretary' Chitraban Hazarika and handed them over to India.[16] Subsequently, they have also handed over ULFA chairman Arabinda Rajkhowa, his bodyguard Raja Bora and the Deupty Commander-in-Chief of ULFA Raju Barua. This has provided a much needed impetus to counter-terror cooperation in south Asia. But there are other top insurgent leaders who are still residing in Bangladesh. They are Ranjan Daimary of the pro-sovereignty faction of the National Democratic Front of Bodoland (NDFB), Biswamohan Debbarma of the National Liberation Front of Tripura (NLFT) and Ranjit Debbarma of the All Tripura Tiger Force (ATTF). Paresh Barua has already managed to escape on 'Bangladeshi passport.' However, the current cooperation of Bangladesh would pacify New Delhi to some extent.

Weakening Support Base of North East Insurgents

Except for Manipur, insurgency in whole of North East is on a decline. Insurgent groups like ULFA, NLFT, ATTF, NDFB etc. have been considerably weakened. After 9/11 international opinion has decisively turned against terrorism. This has also resulted in ULFA being branded a terrorist organization by the US. ULFA was considerably weakened when Bhutan launched its operation against it in December 2003.

Along with the international situation domestic situation also turned against the outfit. There have been desertions in its rank. In several insurgent outfits of North East rank and file was disgusted with their leadership. While they were facing hardships, the leaders were enjoying opulent lifestyles in Bangladesh. Organizations have also faced stress on the grounds of ideology. The discontent in the organization even led to split in ULFA. The organization has now been divided into pro-talk and anti-talk factions. This decision has also prompted the most deadly 28 battalion to declare ceasefire and opt for talks. The constant operation of Indian security forces has also not made life of the cadres of insurgent outfits any easier.

ULFA has tried to replenish its cadre base by reaching out to new sections. It attempted to recruit cadres from Adivasis or tea tribes. It also tried to indulge in terror acts in concert with other insurgent outfits. But these tactics were not very helpful.

ULFA's International Linkages helping it to continue insurgency in Assam

ULFA suffered major reverses in the Bhutanese operation. Even the counter-insurgency operations of Indian security forces in North East have been quite successful. Despite all this ULFA has not opted for ceasefire or peace talks because it is still able to run rebellion from its camps in Bangladesh and Myanmar. Though its Commander-in-chief Paresh Barua has been forced to leave Dhaka he still has good contacts in Bangladesh. Till very recently most of ULFA's top leadership was based in Bangladesh. The business interests developed by ULFA in Bangladesh are another major reason why this outfit is reluctant to come to the negotiation table.

Role of Pakistan and ISI

Pressure in Myanmar led groups like ULFA to establish contacts with the ISI and Afghan Mujahideen in Pakistan.[17] In March 1994 the Assam Assembly was informed that some 200 ULFA militants have reportedly received training with the help of Pakistan's ISI, many of them in Afghanistan, over the previous two years.[18] This relationship only deepened in subsequent years. Pakistan and its external intelligence agency ISI have tried to spread their tentacle in North East through the Indian insurgents groups (IIGs). ISI wants to achieve its own objectives through these groups. For ISI, Bangladesh has become an operational zone for bleeding India and ensuring a large deployment of the army in the east away from Kashmir and the border with Pakistan. Besides, it is also interested in creating an independent Islamic nation carved out of India to avenge separation of Bangladesh. ISI has been involved in funding, training and arming these rebel groups in order to keep India's hand tied. The game-plan of ISI has been known since at least August 7, 1999 when Assam police achieved a major breakthrough, busting an ISI network in the state, arresting 31 people, including two ISI officers and 27 militants belonging to different Islamic militant outfits.

To facilitate its work, ISI has tried to take the help of fundamentalist elements within Bangladesh government, army, bureaucracy and intelligence. The ISI has been instrumental, either directly or through the Pakistan High Commission in Dhaka, to develop a nexus between Indian insurgent groups (IIGs), Islamic fundamentalists and criminal elements in Bangladesh. Besides assisting terrorists in the procurement of arms, ammunition and explosives, the ISI has been arranging meetings of terrorists of different hues to coordinate their activities. The ISI has also been helping IIGs in obtaining weapons and explosives from different places, including Thailand.[19]

A report placed in the Assam State Assembly on 6 April 2000 stated that the Assam police had in its possession plenty of evidence to show that the top ULFA leadership was in close touch with certain officials of the Pakistani High Commission in Dhaka. The ULFA leaders had also been traveling to Pakistan regularly and the Pakistani officials in their High Commission in Dhaka arranged for their passports in various Muslim names.[20]

In April 2002 ISI took a major initiative to unite several Islamic rebel organizations in Assam and across the North East, with major insurgent groups of the region receiving instructions to impart training to these rebels. As many as 14-odd Islamic extremist groups operating in Assam were approached to unite under the banner of the All Muslim United Liberation Forum of Assam (AMULFA).[21]

They also attempted to rope in several Manipur-based Islamic outfits like the Peoples United Liberation Front and the

Islamic Liberation Army. Through this effort the ISI wanted to step up disruptive activities. The Pakistan High Commission in Dhaka organized a meeting in this regard. This meeting was attended by three top leaders of the ULFA and the ISI in charge for North Eastern affairs. The meeting held in January 2002 was to finalise the arms training for the Islamic rebels where the ULFA gave in to the ISI demand.

On May 9 and 10, 2002 sixty three representatives of nine Islamic groups including Rohingya forces, the Islamic Oikya Jote and the ULFA met in Ukhia to form the Bangladesh Islamic Manch, a united council under HUJI's leadership. The Manch has big plans and it dreams of creating a larger Islamic land than the territorial limits of Bangladesh to include Muslim areas of Assam, north Bengal and Burma's Arakan province.[22]

In recent times, ISI has further intensified its focus on North East. Its plan to turn North East into a volatile region was once again proved when Assam police arrested a Bangladeshi national S.M. Alam in January 2008. He was a top-ranking member of the Bangladesh Islamic Chhatra Shibir, the student wing of Jamaat-e-Islami, and was engaged by the ISI as its "North East in-charge." He allegedly worked as a conduit between the ISI and the region's outfits with Ulfa's help. Alam reportedly selected 40 youths from 24 outfits across the region for training in Pakistan-occupied Kashmir.[23] This indicates that now a large number of insurgent groups in North East have been pushed into the clutches of Islamic militants.[24] The ISI had directed ULFA to buy arms for the small outfits of the region from the profit accrued from its businesses in Bangladesh. The small outfits have always been nourished by bigger militant groups in the region, but an external agency's efforts to feed them gave a new dimension to militancy in North East.[25] This also indicated a seamless link between ISI, Jamaat, Bangladesh Islamists and IIGs.

Myanmar

Myanmar has been another favorite base for Indian insurgents for three important reasons. The insurgents used this country as a safe base after East Pakistan (Bangladesh) became unavailable to them immediately after liberation of Bangladesh. Myanmar is also used as crucial link zone through which rebels could go to China for training and weapons. It also provides as safe training and regrouping zone where new recruits can be taught guerrilla warfare and active guerrilla units can be shifted out to when under pressure in India.

The policy of Myanmar towards Indian insurgent groups has been mixed. The insurgent outfits were actively supported by Myanmar as a counter to India's support for pro-democracy activists in Myanmar. IIGs cross Myanmar's heavily forested but porous border to be trained not only in Kachin but also in China and Thailand. The drug trade further strengthened their activities, with Myanmar's insurgent groups (like the Kachins) cooperating with Indian insurgent groups like ULFA and NSCN.

These groups have also allowed the setting up of training camps for terrorist outfits like ULFA. This support can be attributed to the fact that such groups on both sides have been fighting against the state and more importantly ethnic affinity has deepened such collaboration in case of Nagas. The Naga tribes are present on both the sides of the border and therefore they found it easier to operate from Burma with the help of their brethren. The Naga rebels had set up a powerful base in Somra Hills facing Manipur. Sinkaling Hkamti and Noklak have served as the headquarters of Naga Federal Army in the 1960s and 1970s.[26]

Although during the 1990s the Tatmadaw (military) signed about 17 major ceasefires with rebel groups, two dozen armed opposition groups are still active in pockets around Myanmar's remote border regions, including the Karen National Union, the Shan State Army (South) and the Karen National Liberation Army. Such armed groups have found common ground with insurgents in India and they collectively set up the Indo-Burma Revolutionary Front in May 1990. The aim was to create a vast network for financial and ammunition exchanges. Although it soon disintegrated due to internal disputes, it had brought together major insurgent groups like Kachin Independent Army (KIA), National Socialist Council of Nagaland-Isak Muivah

(ISCN-IM), United Liberation Front of Asom (UNLFA), United National Liberation Front-Manipur (UNLF-M), and the People's Liberation Army (PLA) from both sides of the border.[27]

Following improvement in relations, India and Myanmar conducted joint military operations—'Operation Goldenbird' (May 1995) and 'Operation Leech' (1996). In the 'Operation Goldenbird' the Indian and Myanmarese Armies launched a pincer attack on a group of some 200 Indian insurgents along the border with Mizoram. Up to 60 ULFA and other Northeast Indian insurgents were killed and several others arrested during the 44-day offensive. The insurgents were returning to their bases in India after procuring a huge consignment of arms from Bangladesh. This military co-operation has been generally continuing between the two nations despite some ups and downs in recent years.

In the year 2000, ULFA signed a deal for joint operations with United National Liberation Front (UNLF). ULFA described the agreement as a 'fraternal bond sealed to fulfill certain tactical goals. But actually this agreement was reached as ULFA by this time under pressure of Bhutan was scouting for new safe havens. ULFA was eying the UNLF's bases and training facilities in Myanmar and Bangladesh. As UNLF enjoyed excellent equations with the Junta in Myanmar ULFA apparently tried to take advantage of this.

Myanmar has not decisively turned against IIGs. In December 2001, as many as 192 UNLF cadres, including some top leaders, were 'arrested' by the Myanmarese Army. All of them were set free by February 14, 2002, in four phases. At the same time the regime in Yangon kept promising Indian leaders of support in checking cross-border insurgency. Similarly, Meitei rebels of Manipur captured inside Myanmar were set free instead of being handed over to Indian authorities.

Myanmar's stand towards the North Eastern insurgents is ambiguous. Their army has been selective in targeting Indian rebels. As a result, despite occasional crack-downs on the NSCN Khaplang, the ULFA and PLA, rebels have been functioning from there without any difficulties. According to Indian militants, no Burmese government would be able to dismantle all NSCN camps or ULFA bases in Myanmar, as some of the Tatmadaw officers have very close ties with the leaders of these groups, who have been using the Sagaing Division as a launch pad for their trafficking and terrorist activities. It has been reported that after fleeing from Bangladesh in 2008, ULFA's[28] battalion and a group of Kamtapur Liberation Organization took shelter in Myanmar (Sagning, Lunglang, and Huweit) under the protection of NSCN (K).

Thailand

Thailand, too, has been a favourite location of some of the top North East Indian insurgent leaders. This country has been used by the North East insurgents as a sanctuary for striking arms deals and holding strategy sessions. Indian government has been persuading Thai government not to let their territory used by these groups. In the mid-nineties, the Royal Thai Navy seized an illegal arms shipment of the People's Liberation Army (PLA) of Manipur. They also arrested ten PLA cadres who were holding Bangladeshi passports. Thai Navy also managed to seize two tons of weapons from them. This has been the only instance where Thai authorities have acted against northeast militants who have been using this particular sea route to ferry military hardware to their bases.

Generally, Thai authorities have not been cooperating with India. Naga leader Muivah was arrested from the Bangkok International Airport on January 19, 2000. But this arrest was more due to the internal security reasons of Thailand as Thai authorities suspected that he would indulge in some terror activity inside Thailand. The action was not at New Delhi's persuasion. It is also believed that Muivah and the NSCN-IM chairman, Isak Chisi Swu, have been living in Bangkok for more than 20 years now, own apartments and have business interests in the Thai capital. When the stock market in South East Asia crashed, NSCN (IM) lost over Rs. 10 crore.[28]

Sri Lanka

In case of Sri Lanka state has not been directly involved. But an important non-state actor the Liberation Tigers of Tamil

Eelam (LTTE) has maintained links with northeast insurgents. Though this link was known for a long time, only recently a material proof of link between ULFA and the LTTE has been found. This evidence emerged on October 19, 2009 when the Indian Army's 19 Kumaon Regiment seized some documents along with a large cache of weapons and explosives buried in a pit in a forest in the district of Tinsukia. These documents were related to ULFA's financial transactions and one of them stated that the group paid Rs. 2.3 million to the LTTE to buy weapons from them.[29]

Some of the ULFA arms consignments have even been traced to the Khmer Rouge in Cambodia. A deal brokered in 1993 by General Bo Mya's Karen National Union (KNU), an anti-Yangon guerrilla group was apparently clinched by ULFA's self-styled foreign secretary, Shasha Choudhury, who visited the KNU base at Manerplaw, on the Thailand-Myanmar border.

Conclusion

Despite the overwhelming international consensus evolving against international terrorism, the forces inimical to India are yet to curb their covert and overt support to insurgent and terrorist groups operating against India in North East. Though the government of Bangladesh under Awami League has acted against the Indian insurgent groups and fundamentalist Islamist groups, they have often been supported by the Directorate of General Forces Intelligence (DGFI), a section of Bangladeshi army, and the ISI. No doubt, the successful Bhutanese operation against some North East insurgents created a positive impact and prompted other neighbouring nations like Myanmar and Bangladesh to tighten noose on these groups, it has not made insurgent outfits completely defunct. The insurgent outfits have successfully managed to shift their bases from one place to another. When the Chinese support to northeast insurgents stopped in 1980s, Bangladesh emerged as a major support base. Now when Bangladesh has tightened noose on them, the insurgents have once again turned to China and Myanmar. To ensure peace in northeast, India will not only have to encourage northeast insurgent outfits to come for negotiation, but also increase diplomatic pressure on countries who are providing safe havens to these insurgents. Unless the supply lines of these terror outfits are broken they can not be brought to their knees or even encouraged to negotiate with the Indian government. Steps should also be taken to disrupt the business interests of some of these organizations in neighbouring countries so that once more incentive behind keeping insurgency alive is lost.

Notes

1. B.G. Verghese, (2002): *India's Northeast Resurgent*, New Delhi: Konark Publishers, pp. 58-59.
2. Anand Kumar, (2003): *Bhutan's Offensive against the Terrorists*, Institute of Peace and Conflict Studies, Article # 1258, 28 December, at http://ipcs.org/article/bhutan/bhutans-offensive-against-the-terrorists-1258.html
3. Ibid.
4. Wasbir Hussain, "Insurgency in India's Northeast Cross-border Links and Strategic Alliances," *Front line*, Volume 17, New Delhi, at http://www.satp.org/satporgtp/publication/faultlines/volume17/wasbir.htm
5. Ulfa knocks on China's door, *The Times of India*, 29 December 2003, at http://timesofindia.indiatimes.com/india/Ulfa-knocks-on-Chinas-door/articleshow/388334.cms
6. Samir K. Purkayastha, (2003): "Olive branch to Tangkhuls—on khaplang's trail," *The Telegraph*, February 05, at http://www.telegraphindia.com/1030205/asp/frontpage/story_1640366.asp
7. Subir Bhaumik, "Ethnicity, Ideology and Religion: Separatist Movements in India's Northeast," in *Religious Radicalism and Security in South Asia* edited by Satu Limaye, Robert Wirsing and Mohan Malik, Asia-Pacific Center for Security Studies, Honolulu, Spring 2004, pp.232-233 at http://www.apcss.org/Publications/Edited%20Volumes/ReligiousRadicalism/PagesfromReligiousRadicalismandSecurityinSouthAsiach10.pdf
8. Arijit Sen, "ULFA trying to shift base to China, says Assam CM," at http://ibnlive.in.com/printpage.php?id=105756&section_id=3
9. ULFA Eyeing China for Shelter, Commander in China-Myanmar

Border, IANS, October 29, 2008 at http://www.thaindian.com/newsportal/south-asia/ulfa-eyeing-china-for-shelter-commander-in-china-myanmar-border_100112644.html

10. "China, new hideout of top ULFA commander Paresh Baruah," ANI, 1 June 2009 at http://www.thaindian.com/newsportal/india-news/china-new-hideout-of-top-ulfa-commander-paresh-baruah-2_100199528.html
11. Paresh Baruah, (2009): "Buying Chinese arms for Maoists: Ulfa duo," *The Times of India*, 19 November, at http://timesofindia.indiatimes.com/city/guwahati/Paresh-Baruah-buying-Chinese-arms-for-Maoists-Ulfa-duo/articleshow/5248310.cms
12. "Arms found in Bangladesh meant for Indian insurgent group," *IANS*, June 9th, 2009 at http://www.thaindian.com/newsportal/world-news/arms-found-in-bangladesh-meant-for-indian-insurgent-group_100202554.html
13. "Zia government behind botched ULFA arms shipment, court told," *IANS*, 5 March 2009 at http://www.thaindian.com/newsportal/world-news/zia-government-behind-botched-ulfa-arms-shipment-court-told_100162786.html
14. Dhaka to prosecute 2 former spy chiefs smuggling arms for Indian rebels, IANS, 18 May, 2009 at http://www.thaindian.com/newsportal/world-news/dhaka-to-prosecute-2-former-spy-chiefs-smuggling-arms-for-indian-rebels_100194036.html
15. Saswati Chanda and Alok Kumar Gupta, (2004): "Pakistan-Bangladesh Nexus in Abetting Insurgency in India's Northeast," in Dipankar Sengupta and Sudhir Kumar Singh (eds.), *Insurgency in North East India: The Role of Bangladesh*, New Delhi: Authors Press, p. 279.
16. Border Security Force arrest two ULFA leaders along India-Bangladesh border, *The Times of India*, 7 November 2009 at http://timesofindia.indiatimes.com/india/Border-Security-Force-arrest-two-ULFA-leaders-along-India-Bangladesh-border/articleshow/5204738.cms, also see "Assam unveils Ulfa leaders caught in Bangladesh," *The Telegraph* (Kolkata), November 8, 2009, at http://www.telegraphindia.com/1091108/jsp/nation/story_11714009.jsp#
17. B.G. Verghese, p. 58.
18. Ibid., pp. 59-60.
19. Sultan Shahin, (2004): "India frets over Pakistan-Bangladesh nexus," *Asia Times online*, March 6, at http://www.atimes.com/

atimes/South_Asia/FC06Df02.html

20. Jaideep Saikia, (2002): "The ISI Reaches East: Anatomy of a Conspiracy," *Studies in Conflict & Terrorism*, Routledge, Volume 25, Issue 3 May, pp. 191-192.
21. Shankhadeep Choudhury, (2002): "ISI move to unite ultras in the North East," *The Times of India*, 21 April.
22. Alex Perry, (2002): Deadly Cargo, *Time*, 14 October, at http://www.time.com/time/magazine/article/0,9171,364423-2,00.html
23. Nishit Dholabhai, (2008): "ISI funds N-E rebels, says agent," *The Telegraph*, January 18. http://www.telegraphindia.com/1080118/jsp/northeast/story_8796908.jsp#
24. Nava Thakuria, "ISI Spreads a Net in Northeast India," *The Seoul Times*, http://theseoultimes.com/ST/?url=/ST/db/read.php?idx=6239
25. Nishit Dholabhai, (2008): "ISI funds N-E rebels, says agent," *The Telegraph*, January 18. http://www.telegraphindia.com/1080118/jsp/northeast/story_8796908.jsp#
26. Pradip Saikia, (2009): "North East India as a Factor in India's Diplomatic Engagement with Myanmar: Issues and Challenges," *Strategic Analysis*, New Delhi, Vol. 33, No 6, November, pp. 880-881.
27. Pradip Saikia, *op. cit.*, p. 881.
28. Sajal Nag, (2008): "Funding the Struggle: Political Economy of Insurgency," in Pushpita Das and Namrata Goswami (eds.), *India North East: New Vistas for Peace*, New Delhi: Manas Publications, p. 42.
29. Syed Zakhir Hussain, "ULFA-LTTE links come to light," 21 October 2009 at http://www.thaindian.com/newsportal/uncategorized/ulfa-ltte-links-come-to-light_100263580.html
    M.R. Narayan Swamy, (2009): "LTTE not only armed, trained ULFA too," Former Rebel, *IANS*, November 15, 2009 at http://www.thaindian.com/newsportal/uncategorized/ltte-not-ony-armed-trained-ulfa-too-former-rebel_100275139.html

13

INTER-TRIBAL CONFLICTS IN THE NORTHEAST INDIA AND THE PROBLEM OF SOCIAL EXCLUSION
The Reangs' Imbroglio of Mizoram

K.N. Jena & Bindu Ranjan Chakama

Introduction

India is a home of hundreds of tribal communities. They constitute almost seven percent of the India's total population. They are mostly concentrated in central India and Northeastern region. In the North East, all the seven states have huge number of tribal population.

Inter-tribal conflict is the dominating feature in the politics of today's North East. The conflicts between Nagas and Kukis, between Kukis and Paitees in Manipur, between Karbis and Dimasas in Karbianglong district of Assam, between Chakmas and Mizos (Lushai)[1] and between Mizos and Reangs (Brus)[2] of Mizoram etc. are some of the common examples of such intra-tribal conflicts that India faces today in the North Eastern region.

Such conflicts have been characterized by creation of under ground groups, attacking against each other accompanied by arson, torching down of houses, looting and disappearances and extra-judicial killings of many innocent lives leading to gross infringement of human rights and creating a serious law and order problem for the government of India.

This paper has made a brief attempt to the study the causes of such inter-tribal conflicts and the dimension of social exclusion emanation from such inter-tribal conflicts with reference to the Brus' imbroglio of Mizoram.

I

Anthropological and Political History of Tribal Communities in the North East

As stated above, the North East is a home of several tribal communities. In physical anthropological look, they share greater proximity with the people of South-East Asia. In other words, in ethnographical perspective, they are different from the people of mainland of India. Therefore, often people of mainland India also mistake to identify them and consider as either subject of Nepali origin or foreigner belonging to a country of East or South-East Asia. There is a common perception even among those who has little knowledge about these tribal groups that they speak in the same language and either do not have or have marginal socio-cultural differences among these tribal groups. Let not include the people of mainland India, even majority Bengalis and Bengali intellectuals of Tripura still maintain similar perception despite living for years with nineteen such constitutionally recognized tribal communities within the state.

Of course, it is undeniable fact that there are some common characteristics among these tribal communities. They are mostly highlanders, as they live in the hilly areas. Their society is still a traditional with primordial outlook and affiliations. Jhum (slash and burn) cultivation is the principal source of livelihood for many of them. A part from hunting of animals in jungles as a technique of food gatherings, they also collect different food items including green vegetables and folk medicines from forests to meet their traditional food habits and medicinal requirement. Their traditional houses are mostly made of woods and bamboos. Therefore, forest occupies a central position in their life. Domestication of animals such as buffaloes, dogs, goats, pigs and birds like mynah and parrots etc. and weaving of traditional cloths with traditional instruments made of wood and bamboo are some popular professions among most of these tribal groups.

But, despite that, the perception about socio-cultural commonality among the tribal groups of North East is not correct. These tribal communities, albeit, their near identical physical proximity in term of physical traits with the people of South-East Asia, yet they differ in term of religion, language, traditional dresses, and other customs and practices. The Naga population itself is an amalgamation of several Naga tribal groups, who themselves do not share common cultural values and traditions. So to say, the there is wide diversity among the tribal population in the North East itself.

If we look at the political history of these tribal groups of North East, during pre-British and even British's periods, most of these tribal groups were being ruled by a chief (head of the community), who exercised his powers and influence on his subjects independently. During British's period, although the British colonial administration interfered on their affairs and sufficiently eroded the independent political status as enjoyed by them, yet the British primarily followed the policy of 'indirect rule' vis-à-vis these tribal groups. It allowed them to retain political autonomy and declared those areas, sometimes, as *'Excluded Area'* and sometimes as *'Backward Area'* to suit their administrative purpose.[3] Therefore, instead of animosity, the feeling among many of these tribal groups was cordial and supportive to the British policy in India. Moreover, many of the tribal groups such as Naga, Mizo, Garo, Khasia, Jayantia, Kuki, and Paitee etc have been converted to Christianity and British Missionaries extended their assistance and undertook many welfare and development activities, which brought in them profound changes in their socio-economic lives. When the British administration was making preparation to end its prolonged colonial rule in the Indian sub continent, these tribal groups, instead of happiness, voiced their disenchantment and remained apprehensive about their political future of being subjugated to the people of mainland India and loosing the institutional protections that they enjoyed from the British colonial administration.[4] Therefore, unlike the mainland India's people, who openly expressed their anti British voices and took part in various anti-British agitations, these tribal communities were not very much inimical to continuation of British colonial administration, if not in mainland India, at least in their areas.

The problem of inter-tribal conflicts during British period was rarely found, although there were a few such instances like the Chakma-Lushai conflict. Politically, these tribal groups were not as conscious as they are today during the British period. Therefore, in ethnic term, they were not as assertive as they are today. Moreover, the British colonial administration did not give any room for conflicts as such conflicts would have threatened their political interests in many respects.

II
Origin of Intra-Tribal Conflicts in the North East

The origin of intra-tribal conflicts in the North East can be traced to the British colonial disengagement policy from the Indian sub continent. As noted above, the British colonial administration acted as a deterrent against the outbreak of such conflicts. It is also stated above that these tribal groups considered themselves as different from the people of mainland India and expressed their apprehension about being overtaken by the people of mainland India after the withdrawal of British rule. The withdrawal of the British rule and feeling of xenophobia led to the generation of ethnicism. This lead to inter tribal conflicts as it had led to delineation of boundary ethnic division creating disharmony and suspicion among many tribal groups who once lived as peaceful neighbours.

The Nagas were the first to raise their anti integration voice as they favoured to remain independent and retain independence over the Naga inhabited areas. Very soon, Naga National Council (NNC) led by Phizo was formed to begin a strong organized anti India movement. After marginalization of the NNC, Nationalist Socialist Council of Nagaland (NSCN) was formed to spearhead the Naga independent movement. Following the foot steps of the Nagas, Mizos under Mizo National Front (MNF) and many other tribal groups such as Tripuris, Kukis began armed insurrection against the government of India. But ethnic nationalism and ethnic insurgency in the North East has been accompanied by exclusion of some ethnic groups. For example, thousands of Kuki, Hmars and Paitees communities also live in the Naga designated territory of Manipur. But, while fighting for Naga independent homeland with the integration of all Naga inhabited areas, the Naga political movement did not consider the political interests of these tribal groups thereby creating exclusion against them. The same was true to the MNF of Mizoram. As an organization, it was predominantly represented by the Mizos and did not include other tribal groups like Brus and Chakmas who live in large number as their neighbours in the Mizo hills. Tribal insurgency in Tripura also excluded the non Kokborok speaking tribal communities such as Darlong, Chakmas, Mogs, and Lushais etc. Remaining apprehensive about the future of their identity and political future, many of these excluded tribal groups such as Kuki, Brus etc. formed similar armed group to fight against two mighty forces-the government of India and the dominant ethnic groups who created exclusion against them. This has heightened ethnic tension and communal violence throwing them at political loggerhead.

The concepts of indigenous and non indigenous and sons of the soil and outsiders have been other factors for inter tribal conflicts in many parts of Northeast India. The indigenous Arunachalese tribal groups such as Adis, Mismis, Monpas, and Simpo etc. consider the Chakmas and Hajongs as non indigenous in Arunachal Pradesh and therefore, to them, these two tribal groups are outsiders. The Mizos also maintain similar perception towards the Chakmas and Brus of Mizoram. Such perception leads to exclusion of some tribal groups by other tribal groups. In other words, ethnocentrism that refers to suspicion of outsiders and evaluation of others' culture in term of one's own culture has played an important role in generation of inter tribal conflicts in many parts of the North East.

Psychological factor which explains ethnic conflicts in term of group comparison has also been a source of inter tribal conflicts in the North East. Due to continued animosity and distrust among many tribal groups, group comparison on the basis distribution of available resources, and social benefits and opportunities among distinct tribal groups has been an important determining factor in inter tribal relations in the North East. Many backward ethnic groups remain apprehensive of going extinct if they fall behind. The Reangs of Mizoram, the Kukis of Manipur are some of the examples of such ethnic groups. The feeling of frustration or relative deprivation among these disadvantaged groups made them feel that they are also rightfully entitled to the goods and conditions which according to them, they are capable of attaining or maintaining, if the social means are made available to them.

Power plays the key role in furthering and determination of interests. When the competing claims of legitimacy among different ethnic groups clash, it yields to dynamics of ethnic politics. It is characterized by arguments and counter arguments about who will be represented most and how. This ultimately creates the ground of ethnic confrontation. The Naga-Kuki conflict in Manipur, the conflict between the Reangs and Mizos and between the Chakmas and Mizos of Mizoram can also be explained with the help of this power conception theory.

Above all these, the dominant tribal groups have followed the policy of assimilation and expulsion against the non dominant tribal groups. The dominant Mizo community of Mizoram favours either Mizonization of non-Mizo tribal groups or expulsion from Mizoram.

It appears that anarchic situation continues to determine inter-tribal relations among different belligerent tribal groups.

During such conflicts, the competing tribal groups have employed different strategies to ensure survival, protect and promote their interests. There have been military confrontations, economic blockade, (Nagas against Meeteis of Manipur, the Mizos against Chakmas of Mizoram, the indigenous Arunachalese tribal groups against Chakmas and Hajongs of Arunachal), severance of community based relations as it is seen between Karbis and Dimas of Assam, between Nagas and Kukis of Manipur, between Mizos and Reangs of Mizoram. During these conflicts, the non dominant and disadvantaged tribal groups have been the worst affected. Apart from being excluded from social benefits and opportunities and fundamental rights as laid down in the Indian constitution, they also become victims of internal displacement. The Reangs' imbroglio of Mizoram can be explained from this perspective.

III

Genesis of Reangs' Imbroglio and Dimension of Social Exclusion

Who are the Reangs? What are their demands? What is the popular perception of the Mizos about the Reangs? These fundamental questions need to be addressed to study the genesis of the Reangs' imbroglio of Mizoram.

Reangs are still one of the primitive tribes recognized by the government of India. Apart from Mizoram, where they are mostly concentrated in Western part of Aizwal district, Reangs are also found in large number (2nd largest tribal group) in Tripura and in small number in the Chittagong Hill Tracts (CHT) of Bangladesh. In Tripura, Kanchanpur sub-division of North Tripura district that shares physical boundary with the western part of Aizwal district has the largest Reangs' concentration.

The exact population figure of the Reangs of Mizoram is contestable, as there has been no such popular survey on population of Mizoram on ethnic wise. Nevertheless, it is believed that there are near about fifty to sixty thousands of

Reangs in Mizoram. A large number of Reang families living in Mizoram started arriving in Kanchanpur Sub-Division under North Tripura District since 29/10/1997. The influx continued mainly for about a year covering period from 29th October, 1997 to end of September, 1998. As per initial reporting, total population of such internally displaced Reangs were 35,178 persons including children. After setting up of Relief Camps, an exercise of verification of population and relevant records was organised on the basis of Head Counting.

Reasons for Exodus

The following are the major reasons of exodus:

1. The demand for creation of a sperate Bru Autonomous District Council under the Sixth Schedule of the Indian constitution was resisted and opposed by the dominant Mizo community of the state. This has created ethnic tension between the Mizos and the Reangs accompanied by threatening and intimidation.
2. Ethnocentrism in the Mizo society that has developed non tolerance of cultural pluralism has formed the basis of traditional rivalry of the Mizo community against their non dominant ethnic neighbors.
3. Killing of a Mizo Forest Officer, allegedly by some Reang miscreants on 29 October 1997 that had resulted retaliation from the Mizo community.

The Reangs being nomadic in nature have been the most uneducated among all the tribes of Mizoram. The policy of ethnic assimilation against the disadvantaged tribal groups like Reangs has Mizonized many of the Reangs over the last couples of decades. Apart from being converted into Christianity, many Reangs,[5] over the decades, have also adopted Mizo names. But, despite such cultural assimilation, the dominant Mizos never took the Reangs as their own people. Therefore, they have excluded them from all types of social benefits and opportunities. Till the end of 1990s, the Reangs of Mizoram did not launch any political movement against such social and political injustices. However, in the first half of 1990s, some educated Reang youths raised their voice against such injustices. They organized the geographically scattered Reangs of Mizoram to fight against in such inhumane discrimination. Very soon, as apart of political movement, they demanded creation of a Bru Autonomous District Council (BADC) with the major Bru inhabited areas of Aizwal district of Mizoram that infuriated the dominant Mizo ethnic group. In other words, such a demand is not acceptable to the greater Mizo society, leading to ethnic tension between the Mizos and the Brus. The ethnic tension finally erupting into ethnic conflict led to displacement of most of the Brus and 35,000 of such displaced Brus took shelter in relief camps located in the Kanchanpur Sub-division of North Tripura district in 1997. Since then, they have been living in the makeshift camps for the last one decade. The government of India has been providing ration to the displaced Brus through the government of Tripura since their arrival.

As per as the third question is concerned, the popular Mizo perception is that the Reangs are not the original inhabitants of Mizoram. They have come either from Tripura or the CHT of Bangladesh. Therefore, their demand for a separate BADC is not acceptable to the Mizos. This perception of the Mizos about the Reangs of Mizoram, *albeit*, can not totally ruled out, yet generalization of all Reangs as not original residents of Mizoram does not have any empirical validity. Some Reangs due to practice of jhum cultivation and in search of suitable plot for such cultivation might have crossed the CHT and Tripura, but Reangs have been living in Mizoram along with other tribes for long. It is, because of that, Reang is a recognized as a Scheduled Tribe community in Mizoram. The demand for a separate BADC may not be accordable, but as like other fellow citizens of India, they are entitled to enjoy all social benefits and opportunities and fundamental rights laid down in the constitution of India.

Original Habitation of the Reangs Displaced persons in Mizoram

Most of the Reang Refugees who took shelter under the above exodus were originally resident of about 100 habitations in Mammit Sub-Division of Aizawl District. Important habitations from where they came in large numbers are Hrengdil, Darlak, Bunghnum, Taidor, Mathuampara, Dintharpara, Malthuampra and Tumpanglui. A few families from Lunglei district of Mizoram and adjoining areas of Assam also migrated and took refuge.

Location of Relief Camps in North Tripura

The Reang Refugees were provided shelter in six Relief Camps in two areas -one on the western side of Jampui Hills in the nearby areas of Dasda -Anandabazar road and on the eastern side of Jampui Hill in the nearby areas of Damcherra-Khedacherra road. Most populus camp is at Kashirampur (Naishingpara). Other camps are Longtharaikami (Ashapara), Hezacherra (all in Dasda Anandabazar road), Kaskau, Hamsapara, Khakchang (all are in Damcherra-Khedacherra road).

Social Exclusion of the Reangs in the Relief Camps

The displaced Reangs of Mizoram also face social exclusion in the relief camps. As citizens of India, they are entitled to enjoy the basic civic amenities such as health care and educational facilities. Enteric diseases have taken a heavy toll of the displaced Reangs-men, women and children. Officials of the Tripura Government confirmed 210 deaths in 1998 alone.[6] They do not have proper health care facilities. There are two Primary Health Care Centers (PHC) under the Directorate of Health Services, Government of Tripura-one at Anandabazer and another at Dasda, nearby by the relief camps. But due to shortage of doctors in these PHCs, they hardly can take the medical consultation of the doctors. "There were only two doctors and a few bags of medicines to cater to eight camps," said A. Tuisarai Bru, vice-president of the Bru National Union (BNU), in the Gachiram Para camp, which is the biggest camp and which houses 18,000 refugees.[7] The situation has not improved as yet in the relief camps.

There are also no educational facilities for the children. The Reangs of Mizoram are not acquainted with Bengali. But, accepting one English medium School in Kanchapur sub divisional town run by the Tribal Welfare Department, Government of Tripura, English medium schools are rarely found in and around the relief camps. Therefore, the Bru children are the worst sufferers.

Statement Continued

The government of India and the government of Mizoram and the leaders of the displaced Brus held tripartite talks several times to solve the imbroglio of the displaced Brus. But, efforts have failed so far due to some intransigent attitude maintained by the government of Mizoram regarding the actual population figure of the displaced Brus in Tripura and the modalities of rehabilitation and consideration of their political demands. Therefore, the imbroglio of the displaced Brus still continues to remain unaddressed. In other words, the Brus, despite being citizens of India whose constitution calls for equality of justice without any discrimination on the basis of race, culture and place of birth, continue to be excluded from the framework of the state of India.

Conclusion

India is a liberal democratic country. As a multinational country with presence of cultural pluralism, the framers of the Indian constitution realized that India could stand united and integrated in the future only if it recognized its diverse cultural values. Therefore, cultural pluralism was recognized as an integrating force for United India. However, the values of cultural pluralism faces a stiff challenge in Mizoram where the dominant Mizo community has followed so far the assimilitionist approach of ethnic integration against the non dominant tribal groups such as Reangs, Chakmas etc. But, unlike the Chakmas, who have an autonomous district council of their own, the Reangs are the worst victims of such policy of cultural assimilation. Rajiv Gandhi, the former Prime Minister of India, in his address to foundation ceremony of Mizoram state in 1987 reminded Mizos the values of cultural pluralism of India and asked them to give equal treatment to other minority tribal communities within the state. But, ethnocentrism has continued to guide the greater Mizo society creating either no or little room for socio-cultural enrichment of disadvantaged groups like the Reangs of Mizoram.

While the demand for a separate BADC may not be accordable, but Mizoram as a part of India and as a federated unit of India, it is its responsibility to follow the sanctity of the Indian constitution in ethnic integration and accord the fundamental rights as laid down in the constitution as step of inclusionary measure to provide justice to the Brus as fellow Indian citizens. At the same time, the government of India must take some pro active involvement to find out an early solution of the Reangs' imbroglio without remaining confined only with providing rationing facilities. It must be emphasized that justice for these displaced people can not be established unless they are able to return back to their homesteads and some of their concerns are not addressed.

Notes

1. There is no any such community in the name of Mizo. The term 'Mizo' is a Lushai language. It means high. The Mizos are actually Lushais, although they now see it in derogatory perspective. In Tripura Board of Secondary Education, Lushai, not Mizo, is taught as an optional language. Similarly, in the Chittagong Hill Tracts of Bangladesh, they are still recognized as Lushai. The Chakmas popularly call them as Kuki.
2. The Reangs prefer to be recognized as Brus. Therefore, both the terms 'Bru' and 'Reang' carry similar connotation and have used interchangeable throughout the paper as and when suited.
3. A. Mackenzie, (1989): *The Northeast Frontier of India*, New Delhi: Mittal Publications.
4. Sagal Nag, (1998): *India and Northeast India: Mind, Politics and the Process of Integration-1946-1950*, New Delhi: Regency Publications.
5. *The Observer*, 8 February 1999.
6. *Frontline*, Vol. 15, No. 15, July 18-31, 1998.
7. Ibid.

14

ETHNICITY, IDENTITY CRISIS AND THE ETHNIC RESURGENCE IN THE NORTH EASTERN REGION OF INDIA

C.D. Amar

Whether it is the case of Haiti, Somalia and Kosovo of 1990s or Ukraine and Georgia of the first decade of 21st Century, no region in the world is untouched by the serious situation created by the ethnic resurgence. As far as South Asia is concerned, it is grappling with the issue since the very inception of the cold war. However, as this paper wishes to discuss the phenomenon taking place in the North Eastern Region (NER) of India as the by product of the sense of alienation, it doesn't go in detail about the problem being faced by other states. However, the devastating nature of ethnic conflict of Sri Lanka and the serious divides that are there in between 'Bhutias' and non-Bhutias in Bhutan and between 'Tharus' and 'Madhesis' in Nepal etc. should essentially be kept in mind.

I

Before going to have an in-depth study of the ethnic resurgence as the by product of the alienation and also of the factors responsible for creating the sense of alienation it is essential to know that the word 'Ethnicity' is derived from the Greek word 'ethniko' and in the words of Anthony D. Smith, the term ethnicity means to have the awareness about solidarity among the group of people on the basis of shared belief, common culture, religion, language and ancestry, presence of common historical memories and association with specific territory and homeland."[1]

Ethnicity remained a driving force of solidarity till the cold war but the way the resurgent ethnicity has produced conflicts and violence of devastating nature-both within state and across the border since last two decades has made it one of the serious challenges of the present day international society. The gravity of the situation can be realized from the fact that more than 75 per cent of the ongoing conflicts of the post-cold era are the ethnic conflicts.

II

Though different from the ethnic conflicts of other regions in more than one way, the situation in South Asia is also extremely grim. The devastating outcome of the conflicts between the Sinhalese and Tamils might be cited to exhibit the magnitude of the situation.

The North East Region of India has been a highly sensitive area. NER, it is to be noted, is a generic term which includes seven Indian States; Arunachal Pradesh, Assam, Manipur, Meghalaya, Mizoram, Nagaland and Tripura. These are commonly known as the 'Seven Sisters.' Except the princely States of Tripura and Manipur all other states were the parts of British colony of Assam. The post-colonial era witnessed the role played by language, one of the main components of ethnicity, in the creation of the new states i.e. Arunachal

Pradesh, Manipur, Meghalaya, Mizoram and Nagaland.

Except Assam, Manipur and Tripura all other states are predominantly inhabited by tribal people. The ratio of the non-tribal and tribal people in Tripura, Assam and Manipur is 60:40. Thus the sizeable section of the people of even the said three states is tribal. Evidently the overwhelming majority of the people of NER is tribal and of Mongolian origin.[2]

Both Mongolian and non-Mongolian tribes have their own ancestry, heritage and place of origin. Each of them has its own unique ethnic, religious, cultural and lingual identity. It is the uniqueness of their respective ethno-religious and cultural identity that generates the feeling solidarity among them.

III

The people of each tribe consider their ethno-religious and cultural identity as highly sacrosanct. Any kind of sacrilege against their identity is intolerable to them. They can go to any extent for the preservation of the purity of their identity-even the killings on mass scale, violent struggle for separate statehood and even for having an independent and sovereign state. The deep rooted sense of alienation that breaded the resurgence of ethnicity and ethnic conflicts is nothing but the outcome of the attempts to temper with the identity of the tribes of the region. The first of them was the annexation of states by the British Empire. Assam was the first state to be annexed. The other states were annexed subsequently.

The demographic structure of Assam changed after the annexation. The British Government appointed the educated Bengalis on the administrative posts. The Biharis in general and tribes in particular migrated as the labours. Marwaris then filled the vacuum that existed in the trading field. The British Government also introduced English education and allowed the people of the mainstream to migrate freely in the state. No doubt, all this initially led to the interaction of the Assamese with people of mainstream, and thus the assimilation with Hindu religion and culture. However, subsequently the

Assamese started considering it as a blow to their ethno-religious and cultural identity and that generated the sense of alienation among them. The resurgence of ethnicity was the by product of this feeling. The demand for the statehood within the territorial integrity of India and the demand for independent and sovereign state for Assamese might be considered as the natural consequences of the aforementioned development.

For their calculated politico-strategic and economic interests the British government not only pursued the policy to keep the states, other than Assam, isolated from rest of India but also left no effort to aggravate the feeling of alienation and thereby the resurgence of ethnicity in the people.

Secondly, whatever might have been the intention behind keeping the people of NER constitutionally under the category of the Scheduled Tribes of the mainstream of India, the people of the said region considered the this deed against their independent identity and self-respect. They felt that they had intentionally been kept under the category of the Scheduled Tribes and thus were treated as outcast Hindus or untouchables like the Hindu Scheduled Tribes. The constitutional status given to them also became a contributory factor in deepening their hurt.

Thirdly, the migration from India's mainstream also breeded a sense of insecurity and thereby the rise of ethnicity and ethno-religious conflicts. Instead of intermingling with the people of Hindu religion, the people of NER considered the "Hinduization," termed as "Sanskritization" and highly injurious for their ethno-religious sanctity. This made them extremely conscious to protect the purity of their ethnic identity.

Fourth, what essentially was needed on the part of the national leaders was to make genuine efforts to understand the sentiments of the people of NER and thus to become their trustful friends. Regrettably they failed to develop any mechanism for the emotional integration. A critique has aptly written that "instead of breaking the legacy of imperialist rule, undoing the arbitrary and irrational British method of administration and formulating a coherent policy to buildup organic relations between tribal mass and rest of the people, they took them as granted ignoring the alienated mindset of the people, provided forces of vested interests to fish the troubled water."[3]

Finally, the way hostile and unfriendly neighbours such as China, Bangladesh, Myanmar and Pakistan have exploited the Indian government's failure it has inflicted an unreparable damage to the national integration. They have left no efforts to aggravate the anti-India mindset and also provided patronage and assistances of both military and non-military nature to the insurgents.[4]

IV

Born by the feeling of alienation, the resurgent ethnicity has given rise to ethnic conflicts of very serious nature. These conflicts are of three kinds. First are the conflicts between the ethnic groups and the people of the rest of India in general and the government of India in particular for having a separate statehood within the territorial boundaries of India. These conflicts may be termed as the Inter-ethnic conflicts. The struggle initiated by NCHR in Nagaland was the first conflict of this kind. Manipur and Mizoram also witnessed such movements subsequently. In Assam, the ULFA's struggle is for an independent and sovereign state whereas the Bodos are fighting for separate homeland within territorial integrity of India.

The conflicts fought between the dominant ethnic groups (both ruling and non-ruling) and the marginalised are the conflicts of second category. These conflicts might be termed as the Intra-ethnic conflicts. The conflicts between the Meities and non-Meities of Manipur and between the Nagas and Kukies of Nagaland etc. are the examples of intra-ethnic conflicts.

The conflicts between the people of the same religion and also of the same origin are the conflicts of third category. Termed as the Intra-religious conflicts, these can be seen in Tripura and Asssam. In Tripura the Bengalese are fighting against the migrant Bangladeshi Bengalese as they consider migrant

Bengalese the outsiders. In Assam both Hindus and tribal are fighting against the migrant Bengalese as both of them consider migrant Bengali a threat to the purity of their respective identity.[5]

V

Whatever be the nature of conflicts, they have left serious implications. Whereas the demand for sovereign and independent state threatened the sovereignty and territorial integrity of India, the demand for separate homeland within the territorial integrity would make the country topographically and demographically altered giving further rise to ethno-religious conflicts. The outcome of the division made on the basis of language is there before the country.[6]

Secondly, undoubtedly the superpowers have not intervened in the disguise of humanitarian intervention as was done by them in the other parts of the globe, the hostile neighbours, however, as stated earlier, have left no stone unturned to make India destabilized and unsecured. Except Bhutan, India doesn't have congenial relations with any of the neighbouring states. The way China, Myanmar, Bangladesh and since recent past Pakistan also have been providing shelter, patronage and assistances of both military and non-military nature might be cited as the examples of nefarious design of the hostile and unfriendly neighbours.[7]

Third, the resurgence of ethnicity and subsequently the eruption of the ethnic conflicts have also damaged the economy badly. The ethnic groups mainly target the basic infrastructure essential for the development. Frequent blockade of roads and call for 'band' for long duration, sometimes for more than 74 hours, the restrictions imposed for the use of natural resources of their respective domain and the boycott of the goods of the rest of the India have serious repercussion on the economy of NER in particular and the economy of the nation in general. The violence against the people of the mainstream also has dangerous implication as these people are the backbone of the economy of NER.[8]

Fourth, the ethnic conflicts have produced highly serious humanitarian issues. The rehabilitation and resettlement of victims i.e. the handicapped, widows, widowers, orphans and jobless etc. indeed are the implications of serious nature to be borne both by Central government and State Government.[9]

Fifth, as the ethnic resurgence also is the hostile attitudes and feeling of hatred of a particular ethnic group against another ethnic group, it has adversely affected the harmony and mutual adjustment of the society.

Finally, the resurgence ethnic nationalism has proved detrimental to the process of nation building, as people of various tribes adhere to different ethnic loyalties undermining the predominance of states.[10]

VI

Instead of tending to the discontent of people, the governments sought to tackle the problem militarily considering the problem as the problem of the maintenance of law and order. No doubt, that brought calm for time being but ultimately the military measures made the situation more perilous as the people also retaliated militarily. The government then also adopted wrong mode of settling the problem. Without having the clear-vision of the geo-ethnic dimensions of the conflicts it resorted to the method of territorial solution. That, however, altered the demographic structure giving further rise to the ethnic conflicts.

As the cause of the resurgence of ethnicity lies in the deep rooted sense of alienation and that, as stated earlier, is the result of injuries caused to the identities of the various ethnic groups of the region, any effort for the comprehensive and the lasting solution must address the factors that led people to construct a shell of ethnic identity around them rather than opening up. Through the confidence building measures (CBM) the government must also convince the people that neither government nor the people of the rest of India are inimical to them; they rather respect their unique ethno-religious and cultural identities. The CBM should have the active involvement of NGOs, media, intellectuals and the people of all sections as their participation is essential to make the efforts successful. Both the ruling and non-ruling elites and the political parties, then, must have the courage to disassociate themselves from those who are creating and aggravating the strife for their narrow gains. Finally, use of military measures should only be made for the protection and preservation of peace and tranquility.

Notes

1. Anthony Smith D., (1981): *The Ethnic Revival* (Cambridge), See also K.M. de Silva, (2001): "Ethnicity and Conflicts in South Asia," International Studies, New Delhi, 38(1), pp. 53-56.
2. R. Upadhya, *North East Violence*: An overview, downloaded from Internet http://www.cionet.org/wps/sap01.
3. Monirul Hussain, (2004): "Nationalities, Ethnic Processes, and Violence", in *India's North East, in Peace Studies: An Introduction to the Concept, Scope, and Themes,* by Ranbir Samdar (ed.) New Delhi, pp. 291-314.
4. Sanatomba Kangujam, *Ethnic Discourses in The North East: In Search of Alternative Paradigm,* downloaded from Internet, No. 2.
5. P. Sahdevan, (1998): "Internationalization of Ethnic conflicts in South Asia : A Conceptual Enquiry," *International Studies,* New Delhi, Vol. 35, 3, pp. 338-40.
6. Lt. N.S.I. Narhari, *Socio Ethnic Conflicts in the North East: Four Case Studies,* downloaded from internet no. 2.
7. Sibasis Chatterjee, (2005): "Ethnic Conflicts in South Asia : A Constructive Reading," *South Asian Survey,* Vol. (12) (1), New Delhi, pp. 75-87.
8. M.S. Prabhakar, (2009): "Identity Politics : Where it is leading," *The Hindus,* New Delhi, June, 4.
9. U. Bhaskar Rao, (1967): *The Story of Rehabilitation,* New Delhi, see also Ross Mallik, (1998): *Development Ethnicity, and Human Rights in South Asia,* New Delhi, pp. 7-8
10. Urmila Phandis and Rajat Ganguli, (2001): *Ethnicity and Nation-Building in South Asia,* New Delhi, pp. 6-7.

15

INSURGENCY IN ASSAM
A Case study of ULFA

Swati Thakur

The purpose of this paper is to focus upon the genesis of insurgency in the state of Assam and the rise of insurgent group like United Liberation Front of Assam (ULFA). When India attained independence the then Naga Hills district was the only area which witnessed an armed uprising. Today, after more than sixty years of independence the entire area is engulfed in unrest, spawning a large number of militant outfits, each demanding independence and secession from India. The state of Assam deserves a special mention, as Assam is one state which has been well integrated with the civilization of the country, sharing its culture, belief system and linguistic characteristics. Still it witnessed the growth of insurgency. Insurgency began in Assam in 1979[1] almost after three decades of independence. This paper discusses the reasons that alienated Assam, ultimately leading to the growth of insurgency. Before that it is important to understand what insurgency is and that it should not be confused with terrorism.

What is Insurgency?

Insurgency is often regarded as a form of terrorism. Terrorism and insurgency are two different concepts. Insurgency is a movement—a political effort with a specific aim. This sets it apart from terrorism, as it is the method available to pursue the goals of the political movement.[2] "Insurgency is an organised armed struggle to capture state power. It is a challenge to the existing state of governance. It is a revolt against inadequate governance, which failed to meet the economic, socio-political, ethno-cultural and physical security needs of various communities, especially those on the periphery.[3] The insurgents aim to control the population by subverting its loyalty to established authority. This is achieved through intelligent propaganda to mobilise popular support for their cause alongside terror-inspiring violence designed to demonstrate the inability of the government to provide security to citizens."[4] Insurgency has emerged as one of the biggest challenges before the Indian government particularly in its North Eastern part.

Genesis of Insurgency in Assam

Insurgency does not develop instantaneously and without notice. Every movement has an incubation period specific to it. Long term alienation of the region resulted in insurgency. The rise of insurgency in Assam can be traced by having a look in the history.

The discovery that tea could be easily cultivated in Assam caused an expansion of British imperial activity. Britishers annexed Assam in 1826,[5] incorporating it into British India. As a result large numbers of labourers from the rest of India moved to Assam. Further expansion of commercial activity and linkages with the entry of a large commercial Marwari merchant class into Assam, brought the province closer into a British Indian orbit.[6] Britishers also brought English knowing educated Bengalese for assisting in administration and thereby opened a floodgate for the Bengali-speaking people particularly Muslim peasantry to migrate from the densely populated Bengal to the fertile lands of Bramhaputra valley. Bengali officials, who held important positions in administration managed to introduce Bengali as the language of the courts and Government schools of Assam in 1837.[7] The British also ignored the demand for replacement of Assamese as language of courts and of educational institutions. However, as a result of protracted protests by Assamese intellectuals, Assamese became the language of schools and courts. The linguistic clash of the migrant Bengalese and the native population therefore, generated a socio-cultural conflict between the two groups. "Assamese people consider the Bengalese as a hostile ethnic group guilty of committing cultural genocide in Assam."[8]

Despite their hatred of Bengalis, Assam remained closely linked to the cultural current of India and ethnic Assamese fought shoulder to shoulder with the freedom fighters against the British power. After Independence the flow of large-scale Hindu refugees from East Pakistan to Assam aggressively increased and disturbed its demographic balance. The Assamese middle class took it as a threat. They feared that they would be marginalised in their own land. Seeds of alienation, which were sown in the British era, started germinating. In 1950 with a view to countering linguistic chauvinism of Bengalese, Assam Sahitya Sabha, a literary organisation adopted a resolution and demanded that Assamese should be accorded the status of Assam's official language. Asom Jatiya Mahasabha. This linguistic conflict gradually turned into a major political controversy in the state.

Alienation of Assamese was further aggravated by the common perception among the Assamese that the natural resources of their state were being exploited by the Center, and that little benefit was being accrued to Assam. "A myth of Assam's vital importance to India grew in the 1970's, a period in which, before the development of Bombay High, some 70 per cent of India's then marginal crude production came from Assam, saving India much foreign exchange. Additionally, large quantities of tea for export, was produced in Assam and earned India valuable foreign exchange. The Assamese grievance was that little from that profit of crude production and tea, went to

Assam. Which could have been amicably made Assam richer.

The alienation of Assam continued, after years of independence. After the independence of Bangladesh, immigration from this newly formed nation caused a further demographic and social shift in the region. This ultimately proved harmful to the indigenous people of the North East who were swamped in certain areas by these new immigrants. Already scarce jobs and resources were further stretched as the competition for them increases. Educated, unemployed youths sometimes had no option but to take up the gun after becoming frustrated with the sad state of affairs. The central government had been historically unsympathetic to the troubles of the region. The Central Government had turned a blind eye to the pressing problem of immigration; it did not draw any approach to put down even legitimate demands in the region.

Economic underdevelopment of Assam further fueled insurgency. The Central Government failed to developed large-scale industries in the region, thereby making the region poor and under developed as compared to rest of India. The tea industry and the oil refineries, established during the British era in Assam were the only industries worth mentioning. There was a feeling in Assam that these industries catered more to the needs of the people outside the northeast than within it. There was a consequent lack of economic and industrial development and thus prosperity and jobs were hard to come by. Thus poor and unemployed youths were drawn towards armed political movement.

Poorly developed communications and transport links were additional factors that gave rise to insurgency. Political isolation resulted because of this. The region as a whole was "walled off" from the rest of India. People outside the region seem to have little idea as to what was going on in the North East. Residents of the North East believe themselves to be a distinct group who are shunned by the central government and the rest of the people of India. Political isolation gives rise to feelings of frustration and neglect. Some people in the North East started feeling that the region was never a part and should not be a part of India. These in turn give rise to feelings of intense ethnic nationalism, where some people desire to take the matters into their own hands. They perceived that they would be able to do a better job at administering themselves than the central government. The desire to be masters of their own destiny and not live on the pittance of others leads some to take up insurgency.

The Central Government failed to bring Assam and the North Eastern region in the manifold of India. Neglect of education sector by government of India and failure to generate means of employment made the youths of the region easy targets of insurgents groups. Youth of Assam by the decade of seventies started feeling that their future lies in establishing a separate country called Assam. This would give them the freedom to shape their future according to their will.

It was because of these reasons that Assam witnessed rise of several insurgent groups, significant among them was the United Liberation Front of Assam (ULFA). ULFA is still active in the region.

Rise of ULFA

After the formation of Bangladesh, a huge influx of immigrants filled Assam. The demography of the region changed further. Assamese fear of alienation and feeling of exceptionalism was brewing. In this climate of insecurity and chaos, the largest of the insurgent movements in Assam, the United Liberation Front of Assam, or the ULFA, was born. In 1979, at the city of Rang Ghar, the seat of power of the former rulers of Assam, the Ahoms, ULFA declared the desire for independence and secession of Assam, from the Indian Union.

The Assamese people, who had gradually developed an emotional distance from the centre under Congress Government for overlooking the illegal migration for its short term political game found ULFA as their saviour. On August 26, 1979 some of the political, cultural and literary organizations including Assam Sahitya Sabha also joined the movement and formed a common platform known as Asom Gana Sangram Parishad (AGSP - Committee for the Assam People's Struggle) with a view to coordinate a statewide campaign on this issue.

ULFA considers itself a "revolutionary political organization" engaged in a "liberation struggle" against state terrorism by India for the establishment of a sovereign, independent Assam. ULFA's stated objective is the attainment of "Swadhin Asom (independent Assam)."[9] It does not consider itself a secessionist organization, as it claims that Assam was never a part of India. It claims that among the various problems that the people of Assam are confronting, the problem of national identity is the most basic, and therefore it seeks to represent "independent minded struggling peoples" irrespective of race, tribe, caste, religion and nationality. Assam as perceived by ULFA was federal in character.

The ULFA sought to establish a federal, independent state that could also be home to non-Assamese. Because of this objective, ULFA, weakened its support among its key potential support base, the Assamese. The idea of a federal, independent Assam was a non-starter, given the military preponderance of the Indian Army, the ambivalence of the Assamese towards the idea of independence, and because non-Assamese indigenes were just as distrustful of the Assamese as the Assamese were of non-indigenes. As a result ULFA stuck to its "Swadhin Asom" objective.

ULFA maintained that India's national mainstream had no meaning when the country's leadership failed to meet the aspiration of their people. They argued that independent political power was the only option for the organised ethnic group of this State that remained in seclusion for centuries. For them ethical solution to socio-economic and socio-political malady could be possible only through revolutionary changes it could be evolved only by independent political power. The Assamese people, who had gradually developed an emotional distance from the centre for overlooking the illegal migration for its short term political game found ULFA as their saviour.

From 1979 till early in 1990, ULFA developed its strength in upper Assam and engaged in selective acts of extortion and terrorism. By the late 80's, ULFA boasted of running its own parallel government in upper Assam. At its height, the organization boasted of some 1,250 active members, with numbers of sympathizers and political and tacit support in varying degrees from members of the ruling AGP, and a number of armed camps in upper Assam, on Indian soil. The evolution of ULFA into an organization capable of running a parallel government met with little opposition from the Indian Army, curiously. At least this was so, initially. Perhaps the Center was too busy fighting fires in the Punjab and in Kashmir and was waiting for an opportune time.

ULFA gradually grew up as a violent terrorist group and emerged as a parallel Government in Assam. They maintained huge resources to sustain and strengthen themselves.

Resources of ULFA

ULFA adopted militant and unlawful means to generate resources. "The chief sources of income of these outfits are narcotics trade originating from Myanmar and extortion. Also, the needle of suspicion points to certain international terror groups, certain hostile neighbouring countries like China, Bangladesh, Myanmar and religious expansionists."[10]

The ULFA is also credited with some bank robberies during its initial stages. Now it is widely reported to extort businessmen, bureaucrats and politicians for collecting funds. "In 1997, the Chief Minister of Assam accused Tata Tea of paying the medical bills of the ULFA cultural secretary Pranati Deka at a Mumbai hospital."[11]

The ULFA has been accused of using money proved the central government for various developmental projects. There are reports of collusion of government servants, including senior IAS officers with insurgent groups. "Initially, the politicians started siphoning or large scale diversions of development funds in collusion with spineless bureaucrats. After that the insurgent outfits intervened and started taking a major share of the deals. The non-governmental organizations (NGOs) mostly run by the politicians in the name of housing of rural poor, watershed projects. Only five percent of the amount is used the real work rest of the money received as grants from central government is siphoned out.[12] Venkaih Naidu, former Union Rural Development Minister, during the meeting of Rural

Development Ministers of the region at Shillong on June 14, 2001, warned that "the Centre would stop disbursing rural development funds to those states where bulk of the funds go to the coffers of extremist outfits."[13]

In many case collusion between insurgent outfits and police has been reported. Police has in many cases provided support to these outfits. "In Assam there were cases of desertion from the service, collusion and illegal arms sale to the ULFA by policemen. Two policemen disappeared with their arms and the ULFA insurgents, they were guarding and joined ULFA camps. Chief Minister Saikia issued a statement after this incident that 500 police constables recruited in Assam during AGP regime between 1985 and 1987 had ULFA links and four of them were actually being trained in ULFA camps in Kachin state in Myanmar.[14] There was media report of the sale of arms to the ULFA from an armory in Sibsagar district by two constables in September 1992.[15] It was also reported that ULFA received prior information about army raid during operation Bajrang from top IB officer, having cordial relation with the outfit.[16]

The militant activities pursued by ULFA like frequent bombing and killing of innocent people could be seen as deviation them from their path. Today ULFA itself has become the biggest cause of underdevelopment of the region. No sovereign government can allow any such movement to operate in its boundary which could lead to its disintegration. Thus Government of India started movement to counter insurgency.

Counter Insurgency Operations

In its counter-insurgency operations India uses military force but its use is circumscribed by the clear understanding that the ultimate solution will have to be a political rather than a military one. The most important element of the army's counter-insurgency doctrine is the limitation on the use of force. Though this restraint was originally imposed by Nehru, the army has assimilated this as an attitude when it engages in counter-insurgency operations. "The army's role is seen as limited to creating the conditions for the political process to resume ('restoring normalcy' in army parlance) rather than militarily defeating the insurgency."[17]

The Government of India has classified ULFA as a terrorist organization and had banned it under the Unlawful Activities (Prevention) Act in 1990. Concurrently, Government of India started a military offensive against it, named 'Operation Bajrang' 'Operation Bajrang' conducted by Army could control the menace of ULFA to some extent. "The operation was suspended in April 1991 and Assembly elections were held the same year in June. The Congress defeated the AGP and formed its Government led by Hiteshwar Saikia. The ULFA took the defeat of the AGP as a challenge and resumed its violent activities. The Army had to launch another operation, known as 'Operation Rhino' in September 1991. Initiative of the then Assam Chief Minister Hiteshwar Saikia and pressure from army made about 4000 ULFA cadres to surrender to the Government. 'Operation Rhino' was withdrawn and the Government used surrendered members of the ULFA (known as SULFA) for assisting in counter insurgency measures."[18]

The Asom Gana Parishad (AGP) returned to power in 1996 Assembly election. The AGP had been covertly supporting the insurgency movement in Assam. Victory of AGP came as a boon for ULFA to accelerate its militancy. However, strong counter insurgency measure taken up under unified command of army and para-military forces not only weakened the ULFA considerably but also forced its leaders to take shelter in neighbouring foreign countries like Bangladesh, Bhutan and Myanmar. The AGP Governments peace initiative for a political resolution failed because of the precondition of ULFA leaders on their core demand of sovereignty.

In 2001 election Congress came to power and Tarun Gogoi became the Chief Minister. In the year 2004 UPA government came to power at center. Efforts were made to bring ULFA on dialogue table.

In 2004 ULFA put forward a set of three preconditions for talks and negotiations with the Indian government:

- The talks should be held in a third country.

- The talks should be held under United Nations supervision.
- The agenda of the talks should include the sovereignty of Assam.

Spelling out the UPA government's new policy to counter militancy in the strife-torn Northeast, Union Home Minister P. Chidambaram ruled out the possibility of signing ceasefire agreements with any militant group unless it first laid down arms and abjured violence. The minister, who was replying to a calling attention motion in the Rajya Sabha on the killings in Assam's troubled North Cachar Hills district, said: "since I took over, I have not entertained this kind of ceasefire. A militant group must first abjure the path of violence, surrender and lay down arms, and then we can talk about any other problem they may have."[19]

The ULFA dropped the first two preconditions and offered to talk with the government. The Government of India was not ready to negotiate on the issue of sovereignty. Therefore no conclusion could be reached.

Future of ULFA

By June 2008 ULFA appeared divided. "The A and C companies of ULFA declared unilateral ceasefire on 24 June 2008."[20] "A joint communiqué from A and C companies of ULFA's 28 Battalion in which they have declared unilateral ceasefire for facilitating peace dialogue to resolve the conflict and urged both the State and Central government to reciprocate."[21] This approach was different from ULFA approach. According to some analyst the ceasefire was made to pressurise the top brass of ULFA to sit on negotiation table with the Government of India. But the top brass of ULFA expelled the leaders of 28 Battalion. This group later renamed itself as ULFA (Pro-talk).

The Pro-talk ULFA met the Chief Minister of Assam and submitted the Charter of Demands to the Prime Minister through him. The most significant among these demands was the demand for, "Full autonomy within the framework of Indian constitution." The agenda of sovereignty of Assam was dropped. This shows the willingness among a large section of insurgent group to come to the main stream.

In October 2009, Government of India initiated the first round of formal talks with the pro-talk faction of the ULFA. This has brightened the hope for a peaceful Assam, where there would be no place for any insurgency and insurgent groups like ULFA, which have become militant in character.

Conclusion

Insurgency is defined as a "political effort with a specific aim." But, today insurgency in the region is just a euphemism for criminal terrorism sans any ideology and with the sole intent to kill unarmed men, women and children. Insurgency today has adversely affected the healthy social environment of Assam, because of the fear that it puts on the minds of the people. The law and order situation has deteriorated. Because of the fear of armed insurgents as well as security forces, who are merely doing their job as ordered by the Government, the common man has to consciously restrict his movements, curfews and 'bandhs' only add to their problems.

It may not be wrong to say that insurgency and underdevelopment are two sides of the same coin. They go hand in hand. This is true at least in the context of the problems faced by the North Eastern States today. Initially it was the lack of development which created conditions for the rise of insurgency, but now, ironically, insurgency itself is becoming the main reason for the lack of development.

The Government of India should pay greater attention to the North East. Instead of looking at problems from the vote bank politics, there is need to understand the genuine grievances of the Assamese and redress the past wrongs. Assam may be geographically too far away but they are a great people with a sense of history and belonging to proud cultural milieu.

The need of the hour is to take measures to free this area from the meanace of insurgency.the first step towards tackling insurgency could be; to make the administration provide good governance. An efficient, effective and accountable administration, which sincerely and adequately meets the needs of the people, would be the most viable counter-insurgency mechanism.

The focus should be on evolving the peace-promoting role of education, and an attempt should be made to explore how education can bring about an understanding of the sources of conflict, promote conflict management, and contribute to post-conflict resolution and reconciliation. Given the comparatively high rates of literacy obtained in the North Eastern states, this approach deserves serious attention.

The irritant of ULFA may be removed. If Assam can be made as safe as the Punjab, and a conducive atmosphere for investment created in Assam, there is hardly any question that the citizens will have a renewed respect for the Government of India, which will only deepen with an improved economic climate. The recent talks with ULFA Pro-talk have raised the hopes for a peaceful solution to the problem of insurgency.

Notes

1. ULFA was formed in this year.
2. http://www.terrorism-research.com/insurgency.
3. Paolienlal Haokip, "Counter Iinsurgency in North East: A Counter Perspective", *Manipur Online,* August 25, 2005.
4. Chaman Lal, "Terrorism and Insurgency," *Seminar,* Nov. 1999.
5. H.K. Barpujari, (1980): *Assam in the Days of the Company, 1826-1858—A Critical and Camprehensive Study,* Delhi: Spectrum Publication, p. 21.
6. Prasenjit Medhi, (2001): "Insurgency in Assam: Genesis, Evolution and Solutions," *Bharat Rakshak Monitor,* Volume 3(4), January-February.
7. Sanjib Baruh, (1999): *India Against Itself: Assam and Politics of Nationality,* University of Pennsylvania Press, p. 58.
8. H.M. Bareh, (2001): *Encyclopaedia of North East India,* Volume II, Delhi: Mittal Publication, p. 194.
9. M.S. Prabhakara, (2009): "Looming shadow of insurgency," *The Hindu,* March 31.

10. Pallavi Barua, (2008): "North East where insurgency is a Cottage Industry," *Assam Times*, 16 June.
11. http://en.wikipedia.org/wiki/United_Liberation_Front_of_Asom#Major_activities.
12. E.N. Rammohn, "Blue Print for Counter-insurgency in Manipur," *Faultline*, Vol. 12, pp. 8-9.
13. *Sentinel*, June 15, 2001.
14. *The Hindu*, August 23, 1991.
15. *Sentinel*, Guwahati, September 2, 1992.
16. B.P. Routray, "The Revolution Comes Full Circle," *Faultline*, Vol. 13, pp. 126-127.
17. Rajagopalan, Rajesh, "Insurgency and Counter-insurgency," *Seminar*, July 2009.
18. R. Upadhyay, *United Liberation Front of Assam (ULFA): A Deviated Movement?* http://www.southasiaanalysis.org/%5Cpapers14%5Cpaper1307.html.
19. http://www.satp.org/satporgtp/countries/india/states/assam/timelines/index.html.
20. Sushanta Talukdar, (2008): "Two Companies of ULFA Battalion Declare Ceasefire," *The Hindu*, June 25.
21. Ibid.

16

CHILDREN OF NORTH EAST
Trauma Revisited

Kumkum Singh

Alas, regardless of their doom,
the little victims play!
No sense have they of ills to come,
Nor care beyond today.

— *Thomas Gray (1747)*

These lines, appropriately describe the state of children of North East India. The children of this region have to experience an environment which is not conducive for proper growth as this region has a long history of terrorism, internal disturbances and imbalanced economic development. Despite the natural beauty which can inspire a best from the child, what we witness today is exactly opposite. They have grown up in an atmosphere of mistrust both with the centre and local police.

Although today the problem has to an extent been brought under control with peace prevailing in most of the region except in some parts of Assam, Manipur, Tripura and Nagaland, the scars left by violence in this region are a reality as a child of yesterday is today's youth and he has spent his childhood by waiting for his father to return and his mother struggling to keep the household fire burning and being part of the protest movements against authorities to locate her missing husband. Sometimes as in the case of Tripura where when big businessmen went missing the property could not be passed immediately to the wife as a period of ten years is required to elapse to declare the person dead. This period was not only a period of mourning for the family it was also a struggle to make their ends meet and many rich families had to live in penury. The children had to go through psychologically traumatized experiences. They are being deprived of their basic rights as recommended by Convention of Right of Children held in USA (UNICEF).

The NE region, has become a deprived state. 'Deprivation', in this context, is defined as "...a state of observable and demonstrable disadvantage relative to the local community, or to wider society or nation to which individual, family, or groups belong to."

—*Townsend*

The region is legging behind in development in comparison to other states of India. The average deprivation index of this region is 35.74% with highest in Assam (49.93%) and lowest in Mizoram (17.98%) (Sarvalingam and Sivakumar). They calculated the deprivation index by taking into account poverty line (1999-2000), Illiteracy rate (2001) and Infant Mortality rate (2001).

Despite government's efforts the deprivation is prevalent in North East region. It has affected the people of the region and children in particular. The development of a child is determined by heredity as well as environment he is living in. Biological development is most vulnerable to the effect of prolonged deprivation, drug, malnutrition, lack of medical facility at the time of child birth, stressful situation at the time of pregnancy etc. This has negatively affected the biological endowment of the people of this region. It has been transmitted from one generation to another; the process is called "Cycle of

Deprivation". The genetic endowment provides a person's potentiality for growth and behavior and if this is disturbed it affects the personality of the child. Likewise unhealthy environment also plays a major role in proper personality development of the child. Environment of the region is not development friendly. Kidnapping, burning of the schools, hospitals, institution is a routine there. The child is constantly witnessing the burning of schools, industries, hospitals etc. and also the murder of his friends, parents and relatives. The result is the feeling of insecurity, fear, hostility frustration, low self-confidence and low self-esteem.

The term 'deprivation' is being used in a variety of ways. The 'Psychological Abstract Index' list over two dozen types of deprivation. Such as cultural, social, economical, linguistic, education, environment, emotional etc.

An attempt will be made in the present paper to find out the possible psychological effects of various types of deprivations caused by the terrorists' activities on the children of the region and also how the recommendations of Convention Rights of the Child are bring violated.

Deprivation of Basic Needs

It refers to the nonfulfillment of the basic needs of individuals, such as food, clothing, shelter etc. (Violation of article 27-right to have food, clothing and shelter). Though region is primarily an agriculture based region the poverty level of this region is quite high in comparison to other states of India. 31.22 per cent individuals are below poverty line in this region. Terrorists have destroyed their agriculture lands, burnt their schools, industries etc. Most of them have no employment, thus, they are unable to fulfill even the basic needs of their children. The children are either developing feeling of insecurity, lack of self confidence, juvenile delinquency or joining terrorist group to fulfill their basic needs. They are lured by the terrorists to join their groups and become terrorists.

Educational Deprivation

It stems from lack of educational facility to the children

(Violation of article 28-right to primary education). Average illiteracy rate in this region is 31.39 per cent. Most of the children of this region do not enjoy the facility of education in far flung areas and those schools which do exist have problem of resources and being closed down due to lack of good teachers and some of them were closed during the time when terrorism was at its peak. Those children whose ill luck was to see their parents, siblings or relatives being captured at gunpoint, the research on them do show a permanent effect on them. An effort should be made in this region to see that primary, secondary and higher education is within the reach of all the children. Developmental programmes which compliment the growth of small scale industry in this region like agricultural products, weaving and growth of traditional arts should be a priority. Special care centers for children affected due to violence should be established and the government should take full responsibility of these children. Proper mechanism to promote good practices for early childhood care and development for children should be given first priority. Emphasis should be to enhance primary net enrolment to near 100 per cent and educational programs should be made in such a way that all children should be able to participate in and benefit from the education process. The overall aim should be to increase access and improve quality of education. The support of private sector in this field is vital in establishing day care centers, increasing schools in interior and remote hamlets and to consolidate schools in rural and urban areas. Boarding facilities can also be extended. Extended class room programme should be introduced in far-flung areas and equitable distribution of teachers should be done.

Health Deprivation

Healthy citizens are an asset to any nation and an effort should be made to provide all citizens free health care through a network of health centers, basic Health Units and hospitals. In this region infectious disease and childhood illness, non-communicable diseases such as alcoholic diseases, heart disease and malnutrition are common. HIV/Aids is also a reality along with psychological problems which needs specialists to deal with victims of violence who though no mistake of theirs have found themselves in a state where depression, feeling of inferiority, irritability, aggressiveness, hostility, depression and insecurity take roots.

Emotional Deprivation

A child has a right to be loved, cared for and looked after by his/ her parents but the children of this region have been witness to incidents where their parents were either underground or were busy leading movements against state. Many of them found themselves growing up without the direction which is so necessary for the overall development of children who can be good citizens later on.

Bonds of Togetherness Missing

Any society which does not take care of its social environment has to pay a big price in terms of stability at social front for family is the first school of a child. The state should protect the child from all quarters of maltreatment but the programs which are specially to prevent abuses such as drug abuse, child labour and adoption of those children who have lost both their parents, if it not carried out in the right spirit, will result in anti social activities and a feeling of loneliness which can give rise to depression. Diversity is a big challenge to our country and administrators of this region in particular. The feeling of preservation amongst the communities and the feeling of superiority amongst one tribe against another has been causes of conflict earlier and it is a matter of concern even today. Care should be taken that this multi ethnic, cultural region should be given due respect and social programs are so devised that this region develops more understanding and co-operation with each other. The various festivals of this region should call for celebration and a reason to celebrate the rich diversity by the people here.

Conclusion

As a nation we should aspire that our society and our

children are spared the agony of deprivation of hunger, destitution which so often affects their innocent lives. The way a child grows and the experiences he has, will decide the way he will contribute to the society and the nation. The innocence and goodness of our children should be protected to beautify their lives and our societies. This all can be a reality if the efforts are in the right direction and along with the intentions and desire to work for a peaceful North East India which is the first vital ingredient for the child's growth and for the development of the society.

References

Winnicott, Donald W. (1984): *Deprivation and Delinquency*, London, The Winnicott Trust.

http://129.3.20.41/eps/hew/papers/0412/0412004.pdf.sarvlingam

http://www.unicef.org/crc/files/rights_overview.pdf

17

MANIPUR IN SEARCH OF A NEW DAWN

Anju Rawat

The inception of terrorism took place with the armament civilisation in 20th century. It is not an ideology but a method, a process and also an equipment, which is utilise by any state, political party or separatist orgnisation to achieve its vested interest.

Generally, insurgency and terrorism are considered as one, but there is basic difference between them. Terrorism is not always linked with insurgency but insurgency can not exit without terror.[1]

North East region has natural beauty, serenity, and exotic flora and fauna of the area is an invaluable resource for the development. It is rich in economic resources but sadly is one of the least developed and most problematic areas.[2]

Manipur or the "land of Jewels" was the last kingdom to be incorporated into British India in 1891. It was also the battlefield between the Japanese and the allied forces during Second World War. A Union Territory since 1956, Manipur attained full statehood in 1972. This land of flat, central plains surrounded by rugged mountains is home to more than 30 tribes speaking 29 dialects contributing to a rich cultural heritage.[3]

In the world various tribes and sub-tribes are fighting for formation of smaller states along the ethnic lines. In Manipur, as many as nine underground outfits are separately trying to tear this small state which has total area of 22,327 sq. km. and a 2000 year old written history as a part of the North Eastern region.[4] There are two sections of people; One, which wants a portion of it to integrate with neighbouring states which was born only in 1963, others, demanding creation of different 'homeland' by reorganising its territories.[5] They believe that Manipur was 'forcibly merged' with India in October 1949.

Manipur is a cesspool of natural and man-made problems. Political violence, murders, bombing, kidnapping, extortion by militants etc., are common in Manipur. The people of Manipur have their own distinct identity, culture, ethos, own way of life and self governing system. They feel that Manipur is being subjected to political, economic and social discrimination and is being systematically marginalized and pushed to non-dominant entity in India. The sense of alienation has manifested itself in several forms, the most common is the rebellion against the central authority either in demand for greater autonomy or secession. The causes of terror and insurgency in Manipur are as follows:

Historical and Geographical Conditions are the base of unrest. The British colonial policy has sown the seeds of separatism in the region. Between 1874 and 1934, the tribal populations were administered under a succession of extraordinary provisions that segregated those categories called "non regulated" or "excluded area."[6] 'The Line Regulation of 1874' prohibited access to these areas to all "outsiders" except those who obtained special permission from the government. By this regulation tribal people were separated from the people of the Plains.

The other thing responsible for isolation of North Eastern states is its geographical conditions. Naturally these states were nearly cut from rest of India. This psychological pain troubled the people of this area. Manipur has limited road, railway lines and air services so it's difficult to move about freely. The ironic fact is that ninety percent of the border of North East is international while only two percent is connected with India.[7] This makes it very easy for the infiltrators to enter this region.

The **problem of infiltration** in Manipur has aquired dangerous magnitude. Its long border with Myanmar both in the east and in the south is porous that makes the infiltrator's work of coming in a child's play. The tribal community faced a mass silent invasion in the political, economic, social, cultural and physical structure of the indigenous people. These infiltrators find easy access to government jobs and bank loans to set up the business in the states. Using the numerical advantages they have begun suppressing the tribals. Government of India is not able to check it. Infiltration has become a medium of economic backwardness.

Economic inequality is also generating unrest in Manipur. India's North East is where south and south-east Asia meet. It formed a bridge with the rest of India, in the British colonial time. The North East region was a single economic zone and the GDP in the region was more than that of national average. But after independence the GDP of the region fell much below the national average. The economic development faced a setback due to the lack of infrastructure, particularly communication, transportation and power.

The planning policies of both central and state government are faulty. The implantation of projects and programs is even worse. Corruption is rampant and all these factors have contributed in poverty rate of the states going higher than national average as shown in the table:

The above figures of poverty of the North East as compared to national average reflect the paradoxe of development.

Political independence is an instrument of getting economic freedom but unfortunately, this phenomenon is not for Manipur.

Political Motives

The violence in the North East India is linked with the grievance of people, which can be traced back to the colonial

Table 1

POVERTY RATE OF THE NORTH EAST

State	*Percentage of Poverty*
Arunachal Pradesh	33.47
Assam	36-09
Manipur	28.54
Meghalaya	33.87
Nagaland	32.67
Tripura	34.44
Mizoram	19.47
All India	28.10

Source: Economic Survey of India 2002/2003/2004.

policies by post-colonial process of nation formation. Their role in the making of the nation has been constantly decreasing. In the present time the North East has 8 per cent of total population but less than 4 per cent representation in parliament for decision making: for example, the representation in Lok Sabha and Rajya Sabha is as shown in Table 2:

Table 2

REPRESENTATION OF NORTH EAST IN PARLIAMENT

State	*Rajya Shaba*	*Lok Shaba*
Arunachal Pradesh	1	2
Assam	7	14
Manipur	**1**	**2**
Meghalaya	1	2
Mizoram	1	1
Nagaland	1	1
Tripura	1	2
Sikkim	1	1
Total	14	25
All India	250	545

Source: North East Council.

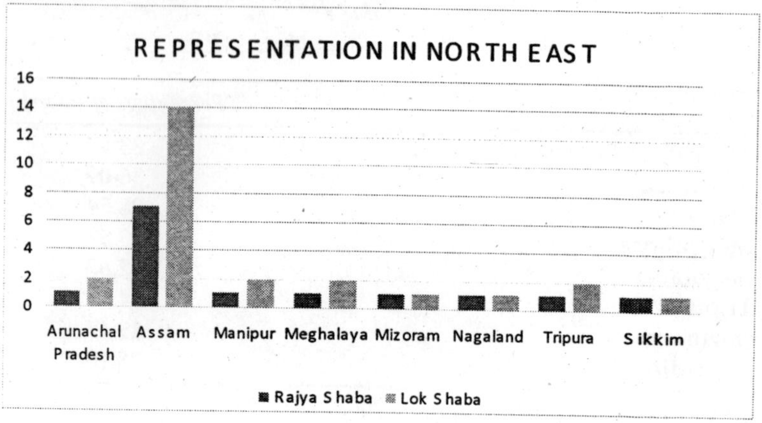

Education and Unemployment

Education is a life-long process of learning and thereby achieving optimum potential of one's innate capabilities as a man, in diverse facets of one's personality. When the emergence of new states in the North East generated hope and there were tremendous job opportunities and the explosion of expectations. It is heartening that the literacy rate in Manipur is 42 per cent against the national percentage of 36 per cent but education system failed to provide them technical and vocational training. Due to it the problem of unemployment kept on accumulating higher volumes and insurgent groups were easily able to lure people into anti-national activities. For example in 2001/2002 the unemployment rate of the states depicts the following dismal state (see Table on 253):

In the backdrop of increasing population, poverty and slow pace of economic development, the unemployment problem has assumed a chronic and complex character in the Manipur.

Social and Cultural Reason

Social structure of North East India is many fold. More than 75 major population groups and subgroups inhabit the region, speaking more than 500 languages and dialects of which there are about 168 in Arunachal Pradesh, 95 in Nagaland, 87

Table 3
UNEMPLOYMENT RATES IN NORTH EAST INDIA

States	*Rural Male*	*Rural Female*	*Urban Male*	*Urban Female*	*Total*
Arunachal Pradesh	1.7	-	0.3	1.7	3.7
Assam	6.2	14.3	6.2	28.9	55.6
Manipur	**1.9**	**1.1**	**5.3**	**4.4**	**12.6**
Meghalaya	0.4	-	1.3	3.2	4.9
Mizoram	1.6	0.6	0.5	0.5	3.2
Nagaland	2.1	-	6.9	7	16.0
Tripura	1.5	8.4	6.2	20.1	36.2
All India	**2**	**1.4**	**4.5**	**8.2**	**16.1**

in Manipur, 100 in Tripura and 200 in Assam, Meghalaya and Mizoram.[8] Manipur represents a unique fusion of different racial and linguistic elements and Manipur agitation has roots in linguistic sentiments. The ethnic group is demanding autonomy for protecting their land, culture, conserving their language, customs and traditions.

Ethnic identity has always been a complex issue in Manipur. The valley at the heart of the state is inhabited mainly by the Meiteis along with Pangals (Manipuri Muslims) and the hills are home to as many as thirty three recognized tribes which are Aimol, Anal, Angami, Chiru, Chothe, Gangte, Hmar, Lushai, Kabui, Kachanaga, Tangkhul and Thadou etc.[9] The complexity of demographic configuration, emerging community conflicts, and violence erupting out of such conflicts, shapes into particular patterns.[10]

External factors

There are internal as well as external reasons of unrest and violence in Manipur. The unstable situation helped in easing the inflow of out side help to the violence of separatist elements. They receive help from China, Pakistan, Bangladesh and Myanmar. These countries aid insurgent groups in spreading violence by providing financial support or establishing training camps.

But the real reason for strength of these organizations is our internal weakness. Demoralization and inefficient administration, lack of political foresight as well as colonial way of thinking by the government are also responsible for this problem.

Insurgent Groups

The insurgency finds its roots in the history. Manipur rebels raise the question about the constitutionality of the merger agreement of 1949 with India. In Manipur the internal dynamics is different. With backwardness, deprivation, exploitation and lack of economic development, the region has become a breeding ground for protests, which has led to insurgencies. Practically every state in the entire North East fosters one or more insurgent groups fighting for the establishment of varied goals ranging from creation of homeland within the Indian Union to outright secession.

Terrorist, Extremist and Insurgent groups of the North East are as follows:

Table 4

TERRORIST, EXTREMIST AND INSURGENT GROUPS OF THE NORTH EAST

State	*Number*
Assam	34
Manipur	36
Meghalaya	3
Nagaland	3
Tripura	30
Mizoram	1
Total	107

Source: India Terrorist Groups: State-wise List February 2003.

All the above groups have been declared as 'Unlawful Associations' under the Unlawful Activities (Prevention) Act, 1967 (Articles 37 of 1967 Act).

Conclusion

'As the medicine is administered, the disease increased' such is the case of Manipur. Its problems go on increasing though the remedies are found and implemented. A number of economic packages have been given to this area during the last few years but the situation constantly worsens rather than improving.

Suggest below are some observations and recommendations which if understood and implemented can make a substantial step towards attributing to Manipur the well deserved glory of being India's Jewel :

- The local parties and governments always blame the central government for ignoring the North East region but it is not fact. Infact the centre has sectioned a number of economic packages for this area but the state government agencies appointed to utilise the funds have centralized them at few places, depriving the region of equitable distribution of resources.
- Manipur is rich in natural resources and local people possess an extraordinary dexterity at handicraft and handloom but their art is not being utilised properly to bring financial returns to them.
- There is a great scope in tourism sector but there are no proper arrangements for package tours, etc.
- Insurgency in the region is not merely a law and order problem but a complex issue of ethnic struggle. The traders are not in a position to do the business freely. The terrorists and local group extort enormous money from them by threatening them.
- Some communal groups, student leaders, and leaders of local parties are involved in encouraging unrest in the region.
- Separatism and violence in the states is the result of unemployment among the youth. But the fact is the youth from this area do not want to go out either for employment or for starting a profession.
- The help received by voluntary organisations should

be properly used for the purpose for which it is given. It is necessary to supervise and stop its mis-utilisation.

- Cultural troups from rest of India should be made to perform in North East. Various sports festivals on National level as well, should be oranised in the region. This may help connecting them with rest of India.

Some rethinking is necessary on the part of both the government and the people of the region to replenish the elixir of peace and harmony in this beautiful land and to sustain the normal flow of life.

Notes

1. S.N. Saksena, (1985): *Terrorism-History and facets, in the world and in India,* New Delhi: Abhinav Publication.
2. Dhurba Rizal & Yozo Yokota, (2006): *Understanding Development, Conflict and Violence: The Case of Bhutan, Nepal, North East India and the Chittagong Hill Tracts of Bangladesh,* Delhi: Eastern Book Corporation.
3. *Yojana—A Development Monthly,* December 2009, Special issue on 'FOCUS-MANIPUR.'
4. Phanjoubam Tarapot, (2003): *Bleeding Manipur,* New Delhi: Har Anand Publication.
5. Ibid., 2003, p. 11.
6. Archana Upadhyav, (2006): "Terrorism in the North East, linkages and implications," *Economic and Political Weekly,* 2 December 2006, pp. 4993-4999.
7. Ibid., 2006, p. 4993.
8. Source: Northeast Council.
9. S. Mangi Singh, (2009): "Ethnic conflict and Demand for Contiguous Homelands," *Yojana—A Development Monthly,* December 2009, Special issue on "FOCUS-MANIPUR."
10. Oinam Bhagat, (2003), "Patterns of Ethnic Conflicts in the North East: A Study on Manipur", *Economic and Political Weekly,* 24 May, pp. 2031-2037.

18

RETROSPECTING KUKI MILITARY ORGANISATION (WARRIORS) IN THE LIGHT OF *SAWM-INN*

Th. Hethang (George) Haokip

The Kukis, since time immemorial have always felt that, the territories they inhabited belonged to them, and in that, they claimed to have been a nation of warriors, ruled as a nation and protected by their principle hereditary Chief independently in a country supposedly in their ancestral land called, *Zalengam* or Kukiland. This can be necessitated from the traditional way of Kuki Military Organization, *SAWM* (better known by the Mizos as *Zawlbuk*[1]) in the erstwhile *Zalengam* or Kukiland which according to them were in existence in pre-colonial period.

SAWM-INN infact is a Bachelor's Dormitory. It was usually constructed at the adjacent of the Chief's house and this purposely served as a military garrison for Kuki warriors. Therefore, *SAWM* is an institution where all the lads of a Kuki village live together and are trained in various kinds of activities. To some eminent scholars, 'the members of this *SAWM* consist of all the able bodied young boys of the puberty age group, and this peer group constitutes the Kuki Warriors. They congregate to sleep together at night after their sundry chores, *Lawm-tha Kon* (cultivation works) to learn the indispensable art of conventional warfare ranging from fundamental practices of a healthy living to taking up social responsibility.'

The formation of Kuki Warrior (*SAWM*) or their amalgamation in a uniform military organization can be attributed to the nature of inter-tribal hostilities and feuds that were prevalent amongst tribes in recent years. And the very intention behind the formation of Kuki Warriors was initially to draw the readily available necessary manpower/fighters for deployment in times of emergency,[2] which subsequently surfaced into regular standing army/warriors.

They rendered free and compulsory services to the village with the Chief himself as the supreme Commander of the armed forces. He paid personal and undue attention towards the military forces and led the supreme authority over them either in time of war or during peace.[3]

The Kuki Military Organisation consists of infantry and artillery. Cavalry and Naval force were however never known to them. The arms divisions of infantry, used weapons like Sword, Spears, and Bow & Arrows. Muzzle Guns and bullets (*Thihnang*) too became popular and were widely used by them in later years, while the artilleries used indigenous made cannon (*pum'pi*), with various kinds of iron and metallic substance as its bullets which were manufactured by the village *Thih-Kheng Pa* or the village blacksmith. He has in him the highest dexterity in black-smithy and his duty was to rendered free services in manufacturing and repairing of various war weapons for the warriors. They were skillful and could manufacture a good numbers of guns *(Thal/Thihnang)* and cannon *(Pumpi)* in a single day.[4] The efficiency of the warriors in the combat thus, depends mainly upon the ability of the *'Thih-Kheng'* to produce weapons.

History has also proven that, the Kuki Warriors were daring to fight gallantly and ferociously against their enemies that too, till the last breathe of their lives. One inherent typical national character of the Kukis is their sense of stubbornness and refusal. They indeed were hostile to outsiders and were not the one to submit before any alien authority unless forcibly subjugated.[5] They recognized no other authority but only the Chief. With this temperament the Kuki warrior firmly stood even against the mighty Britishers whose legend goes *"the sun never sets in the British Empire."*

The Kukis are well known for their outstanding techniques in guerilla warfare. They often carry out sudden attacks and ambush their enemies by rolling down huge stones in steep area. To, P.S. Haokip, 'Their skill with regards to stone-traps called *Song-khai/Song-thaang* is genius. The traps involved the collection of large load of huge stones, which were then placed on wooden planks. These planks were fixed to a rope against a tree, just above the roads, where the enemies were likely to pass through.'[6]

And apart from their vital defensive role, the Kuki warriors in the *SAWM* also had the privilege to impart technical and practical knowledge especially in the art of handicrafts like making of *Beng-kong* (basket for carrying fire woods), *Long-Kai* (basket for carrying paddy), *Nam* (String used for carrying the basket), *Guo-dal* (winnowing materials), *Pheh* (mat) etc. These products were instrumental and served various purposes. Moreover, at times of leisure, they would engage themselves in sports activities like *Kibot* (wrestling), *Lhai chop* (Long Jump), *Kung-Kal* (High Jump) etc. Stories of their fore fathers, legends, folk songs etc. are also taught and told. These oral histories were handed down from generation to generation.

A paradigm shift however took place in the institution of SAWM after the treacherous attack of the ferocious Pawis in later years. The SAWM which was once the backbone in the arena of the village socio-political scenario took the character of a scattered form due to the ill fated defensive strategy, but it continues to exist on a smaller scale at different houses of the village.

> T.S. Gangte writes, "The Pawis had been surreptitiously planning to attack the Lhungtin village by surprise. It so happened that one night, when all the able-bodied young-men of Lhungtin village slept in their dormitory, the Pawis stealthily came and butchered them, killing instantaneously as many as 80 able-

> bodied young men. As a result, the Hangshings were scattered and fled in different directions. Most of them were found to have settled down among the Paites. The one that gave a serious impact besides all other repercussions was that the institution of SAWM which was centralized took the character of a scattered form due to defensive strategy. Such a different form of SAWM, though it still continues, exists on a small scale at different houses where there are girls."[7]

This was further intensified and escalated with the intervention of the British in their internal affairs which ultimately led to their dispersion and subjugation. The enmity with the British had began since the time of Warren Hasting in 1777 A.D. to the close of the great Anglo-Kuki war, 1917-19 and then finally, during the course of the World War II.

Thus, in examining the above given analysis, it would be prudent to state that, the conventional atrocities/war owing to tribal feuds and hostilities were limited. It confined to the village level and in that, the respective concerned warriors under the able leadership of their particular village Chief were only responsible for the war. War in good faith was the order of battle in those days. In short, inter-tribal feuds or chaos in the form of *Gal-Lu lah* (Head Hunting) were of frequent incidence and happenings.

However, in highlighting the episode of the Anglo-Kuki war of 1917-19, the Kukis organized themselves basically on the line of their Clan's seniority. For instance, Pu Chengjapao Doungel, Pipa of the Kukis and Pu Lhukhomang Haokip (Pache), Head of the Haokip clan took the overall responsibility in defending their ancestral land, *Zalengam* or Kukiland.[8]

They organized and convened political meeting at regular intervals. And it was when the notice for raising the second labour corps in the hill areas of Manipur reached the knowledge of Kuki warriors, a meeting of all the Kuki Chiefs was held at Jampi immediately and the meeting unanimously passed a resolution pledging to maintain the unity of the Kukis in resisting the government efforts to fulfill their demands by fanning out "*Thing-kho le Malcha-pom*" (Chilies tight in the fire-wood) to every Kuki village as a mark of an open declaration to fight against their common enemy i.e. the mighty Britishers. The events became a great historic memory to the Kukis which subsequently came to be known as the great Anglo-Kuki War of 1917-1919 better known as the Kuki Rebellion in the history of India's struggle for freedom. The Kukis hope for recovering their ancestral land and lost prestige was once again revived during the course of the World War II under the leadership and banner of Netaji Subhash Chandra Bose and his Indian National Army (INA). This however proved to be a failure once again and thereby only subjected them to disperse in the entire Indian sub-continent with the status, "Minority in Ghetto" with no Political Unit among them.[9]

However, the present Kuki Revolutionary organization like the KNF (Kuki National Front) and the KNA (Kuki National Army) under the banner of UPF and the KNO, formed on 18th May, 1988 and 5th August, 1988 respectively, has taken up the initiative to revive and restore the past glories that they once had in the past.[10]

To conclude, the continuation of SAWM by the Kukis with much modification in the form of a revolutionary organization till date has depicted the zeal of their quest for a free nation state. And in relation to this, a number of memorandum and reminders were sent off many a times to the concerned authority for the creation of a Kukiland (*Zalengam*) within the frame work of the Indian Constitution.[11] They were the first tribe to vigorously rebel and counteract against the British in lieu of their freedom. They indeed are a freedom loving people. Therefore, it needs a vivid retrospection.

Notes

1. Chitta Ranjan Nag, *The Mizo Society in Transition*, pp. 12-13.
2. T.S. Gangte, (1993): *The Kukis of Manipur*, Gyan Publishing House, New Delhi, p.133.
3. Bertrams Carey and H.N. Tuck, (1976): *The Chin Hills: A History of the People, British Dealings with them, their Customs and Manners and Gazetteer of their Country*, Delhi: Cultural Publishing House, p. 3.

4 P.S. Haokip, (1998): *Zalengam, the Kuki Nation*, KNO Publication, April, p. 78.

5. See, S.M.A.W. Chisti, (2004): *The Kuki Uprising in Manipur, 1917-1920*, Guwahati, Delhi: Spectrum Publications, 58.

6. Ibid., p. 78.

7. T.S. Gangte, *op. cit.*, p. 135.

8. P.S. Haokip, *op. cit.*, p. 142. (Revised Edition with Additional Text).

9. The Kukis are found in India, Burma and Bangladesh till today.

10. The Kukis believed that the formation of a Revolutionary Organisation in the late eighties crystalised from their Traditional Military Organisation called *SAWM*.

11. Nehkholun Kipgen, "Founder President of the KNF" Why not Kukiland for Kukis," *The Shillong Times*, 1st October 1998, and see also, *Ahsijolneng*, Annual Magazine, KSO, Shillong, 2007, pp. 16-21.

19

HUMAN RIGHTS
Response and Challenges with Special Reference to North-East

Amita Sonker & Shalini Gupta

Sixty-two years is a very small span in a nation's history. Nevertheless, this span for India, as sovereign, socialist, secular democratic republic, was a very significant one. After two centuries of colonial rule India emerged as an independent nation for the first time in modern history and began its "tryst with destiny." But today we need to remind ourselves as to what promises we had made to ourselves at the outset? What path have we traversed over the period? Where do we stand today?

One is reminded of Jawaharlal Nehru's words: ".... The ambition of the greatest man of our generation has been to wipe every tear from every eye, that may be beyond us but as long as there are tears and sufferings, so long our task will not be over ...."[1]

There has been significant progress in the field of economics, science and technology but the question arises have we been able to provide the minimum condition essential for the development of the unique characteristics, which nature has bestowed every Indian with, as a human being irrespective of one's race, religion, caste, creed and color, gender or any other social origin, birth or any other status. In short what has been the state of human rights enshrined in our constitution?

To understand human rights in the North East, it is imperative to look into historical background and the special constitutional arrangement of the region. The region comprises of states of Arunachal Pradesh, Assam, Manipur, Meghalya, Mizoram, Nagaland and Tripura and recently Sikkim has also been included. It is known for its ethnic, linguistic, cultural, religious and physiographical diversity.

Human rights are a big issue in North East India, especially in Assam, Manipur, Nagaland and Tripura. Human rights of individuals are "those conditions of social life without which no man can seek in general to be himself at his very best. Human rights have to do with allround development of the human being in harmony with that of his fellow beings in the totality of the relations in a society.[2]

Since independence most part of the North East has remained afflicted with insurgent movements having goals ranging from outright secession to autonomy of varying measures. Magnitude, intensity and duration of the armed struggle have made North East synonymous with insurgency. Is insurgency at such a vast level the result of wrong strategies followed so far?

The post-colonial era witnessed to have the role played by language in the creation of new states i.e. Arunachal Pradesh, Manipur, Meghalya Mizoram and Nagaland. By product of deep rooted feeling of alienation, the ethnic conflict are of three kinds, the first of them are the conflicts between the ethnic groups and the people of the rest of India in general and government of India in particular for having a separate statehood within the territorial integrity of India and also the conflicts to have sovereign and independent states. The ethnic conflicts have produced highly serious humanitarian implications such as the rehabilitations and resettlements of victims i.e. the handicapped, the widows, orphans and unemployed. Mis-governance resulting largely from an unplanned and hurried imposition of modern institutions of governance and administration on indigenous societies enjoying since ages a good measure of self rule also made for the feeling of "Otherness" encountered in the North East.[3]

The response of the central government to unrest has been to deal with violence militarily instead of addressing its underlying causes and conditions. What has heavy militarization resulted into, what is the position of state government and police of the states? The answer is 'a total collapse of Law and Order.' It would not be out of place to say that the governments of North East States, particularly Manipur, Nagaland and Tripura have abdicated their constitutional obligation and are being run by the center with the help of army and Para military forces.

Army Act (Special Powers) 1958, revised 1972, under section 4 of this act, any personnel of the Indian army above the rank of Jawan, can shoot to kill, destroy property, search without warrant or arrest anyone who has committed, is suspected of having committed, a cognizable offense and to invoke this provision the officer need only be "of the opinion that this is necessary to do so" under section 6, no legal proceedings can be brought against the army personnel without the permission of the central government, in other words with this act, the Government of India has imposed an undeclared emergency in the state. Preventive Detention Laws, 1985 (TADA), National security Act (NSA) 1980, were also used to curb insurgency.[4]

Human rights have been taken beyond the realm of the philosophical statements or moral principles and accorded a practical shape by their incorporation in the constitution and domestic laws of the lands. North East presents an area where harassment of general public at the hands of army of independent India began in the mid 50's, in fight against the Naga insurgency.

Strafing of civilian areas and the "grouping of villages" turned army operations into full fledged war making more distinctions between combatants and non combatants, though now the overall situation has improved. Military still has an upper hand, while harassments at checkpoints and aggressiveness during search and cordon operations are stoically accepted as part of normal life in the North East, people express their resentment and agitate for their rights when a major incident involving large scale destruction of life and property of the civilian population results from indiscriminate unprofessional attitude of administration.

The state Human Rights Commission in Assam and Manipur has no jurisdiction in regard to violation of human rights by the members of the armed forces and therefore cannot entertain any complaints against them. The groups involved in the human rights activities too have come under repeated attacks, as the killing of Cheniram Nath and Dashrat Singh testifies.[5]

What has been army mode of operations? It is through "Specific Information." Acts of disappearances, secret killings this is commonplace in the state. Manipur is very high on the list of human rights violation, involving many deaths, torture and destruction of property. Pranam Singh case of July 2000, the Gang rape of M. Mercy Kabui, October 2000, 13 Bazaar Massacre, Manorama Rape case 2004, and enforced disappearances in the region present the grim picture of the state of North East.

Universal declaration of human rights has not received much attention from the international community especially in the developing countries of the world. The rights include civil and political rights and economic, social and cultural rights; a misplaced hierarchy has put the civil and political rights concern mainly with worth and dignity of the individual higher and above the economic and social rights that are crucial to individual rights and well being of the community. The economic and social rights incorporate as the directive principal of the state policy are now being acknowledged significantly, in context of nation building, and socio- economic transformation based on the principal of democracy equality and justice.[6]

A review of human rights in North East is, essential to include the state of economic and social rights of the people regardless of the fact that most of the rights in North East present a gloomy picture. Sikkim Chief Minister Pawan Chamling spoke of criticality of the governance in North East state and need to deliver basic services to people. He talked about sustainable development and the need to protect the environment and ensure public interest. But who is opposing the states in conserving natural resources and using them competently in an environmental friendly manner? Can anyone object to the delivery of basic services to the venerable and poor?

Neighboring country Bhutan's concept of 'Gross National Happiness' based on good governance, preservation of cultural heritage, economic development and environmental protection can be an answer to solve this regions problems. It definitely is an idea worth exploring.

During the reorganization of the states in North East, A pertinent question was ignored that the territory in question must have revenue sources to meet its administrative and non developmental expenditure. The role of the state should be to build human capabilities and enlarge human choices. Governance if it is to promote development has not to be just pro people; it has to be owned by the people. The people can shape their own governance which can protect them and save them from all types of humiliations in their daily life. Government has to be accountable in every branch, executive, legislative, judiciary and forces of law and order. State civil society should help in building capacity, which will meet the basic need of all people particularly women, children and poor. It should also ensure that the human development is sustainable.[7]

Complaints of human rights violation pertaining to North East

The states of North East are found to be occupying, bottom positions, both in terms of the number of complaints per 100,000 population.

(a) While the complaints handled by NHRC have

increased 26 times since 1994-95, the North East has registered an increase of 30 per cent. The rise is due to awareness among people but in North East the case is not so.

(b) Major share of complaints are against army and Para military forces. 17.5 per cent in 2003-04 and 22.5 per cent in 2004-05.

(c) The complaints against army and Para military forces constitute a small fraction less than 0.5 per cent of total complaints in country as a whole. But it is sizable in North Eastern state. 17.5 per cent in 2003-04 and 22.5 per cent in 2004-05.[8]

Since NHRC can only investigate and make recommendation people has sought refuge in Guwahati High Court, which has intervened a number of times in favor of citizen rights. The other human rights which are violated in the region are lack of educational infrastructure, lack of proper employment, public distribution system, non existent public health care and extreme poverty. We should keep in mind that India has always been a nation of unity in diversity, even insurgents are people of India and their anti national activities are not normal crimes, they are a sign of a bigger problem at the root. A gross discontent lies at the heart of it. Acts such as AFSA 1958, Assam Disturbed ACT 1955, have also added to the mistrust for the government.

Now I will like to focus on rights of women and children in the North East. What efforts are being made by all concerned on protecting this section of the society? Case of Manipuri women stands out. The 1981 report of National Human Development shows that inspite of bad socio-political situation in the state, they stand next to Kerala in health, economic and socio-political participation, and their literacy level is also well above the national average. The women movement on 12 December 1939, against artificial scarcity of rice is a well recorded movement; they did not sit at home when their children were crying of hunger. It is observed in Manipur as Women's War Day. "Meira Paibi" (torch bearer) movement is where elderly women take lead in solving day to day social problems which are part of Manipuri women and their sisters in the other states.

But few facts regarding the pitiable state of women in North East blatantly stare in the face:

- Widows of the insurgents are forced to earn for their livelihood and survival of their children.
- Increasing responsibility within and outside household has resulted into declining health of women.
- Fear psychosis and sleepless nights are the common features among Manipuri women.
- Torture and rape of women by armed forces is an ugly truth.[9]

Tales of torture during twenty year long insurgency in Mizoram contain gross violation of human rights. Most of the families were broken as women were raped and men were forcefully put behind the bars. Most of the children had single parents and even schools and church were not spared. Gangrape became common during this time. At Zawlsei, a blind and mentally retarded woman was gang raped. One woman at Kelsih village was hit by a stray bullet fired from Aizwal; her arm got fractured. B. Vanlalzari, a mizo lady was sentenced to life imprisonment but fortunately the then Mijo Student Union filed a case in Supreme Court. She later became a free citizen and got reinstated in her job. The people of Mizoram in general do not carry good memories of the insurgency period. For these people life will never be the same again.

Since the 80s Tripura is bleeding from the wounds of insurgency. Innocent people are killed by militants or get killed during ambush or cross fire. The result is always huge loss of property and lives. Unlike other regions of North East in Tripura the problem has ethnic dimension. In 2002 it was reported that the total number of displaced persons due to insurgency was 58,758 and only a few were able to return home. And two thirds of the displaced people are living in makeshift camps or away from their homes. Kidnapping in this area has also revealed an unseen unheard dimension of life as when a person is abducted or killed the bereaved family is not able to get proof of death which in turn leads to the issue that how should be the settlement of inheritance be resolved for wife and children. One such example in 1996 a tea magnet in Tripura Shri Jogabrata Chakraborti was abducted and despite the ransom asked being paid he was killed. This turned the wealthy family into overnight becoming poor for no legal rights could be established for according to law of the land, Indian Evidence Act 1982 is completely silent to take care of such situation. Section 108 of this act says that a person who has disappeared can be considered dead only after seven years. An effort in the direction is being made by the Tripura amendment bill 1999.[10]

In North East region two forces are operating simultaneously; one is of democracy, ecology and culture and the other of insurgency, terrorism and corruption. Social intervention at community level has helped in fighting the impact of insurgency in this region. Organizations such as Bodo Women Justice Forum formed on 20th February 1993 is mainly concerned with issues of peace and human rights. In Guwahati first regional women's convention was held from 17-20 December 1997 where 1500 participants from over a hundred tribal groups participated. The official slogan was "women for peace and progress." According to a Khasi tribe participant convention is a new awakening for women to realize their power to heal the wound of war and hatred and to work for unity and progress. To strengthen these groups their must be political will and encouragement from the society so that they can have a far lasting influence in the region.

Children of Manipur

In a seminar in Imphal "Effects of trauma and violence on children and adolescent", it was reported that 50-60000 persons in the state are suffering from mental ailments, citing insurgency-related problems as main factor, the feelings of insecurity and growth of violence has led to the rise in mental disturbance in children.

The reason why most of the students study outside the state is not because they do not want to study in Manipur, but because of frequent *bandhs* and strikes. The children are devoid ot a healthy environment to grow due to constant presence of terror. The need of the hour is concentrated and holistic efforts towards creating a conductive environment promoting blooming of Psycho-Socio recovery as social reintegration of children affected in the armed conflict situation in the region.

The need today is to launch a people's movement for realization of basic human rights and fundamental freedoms of people of North East. Academic institutions, citizen groups and media persons from state outside North East can play a vital role in this endeavor.[11]

Ancient Indian culture followed the concept of "Vasudhaiva Kutumbkam" meaning the entire world is one family. Atharva Veda said as cow protects her born even at the risk of her own life so one should enlarge one's heart. Same sentiments were echoed by Jesus Christ and Holy Quran. In the west Rousseau Locke, Thomas Jefferson in 17th and 18th centuries kept up the flame. In 20th century emphasis on human rights charter of United Nations which is preamble reaffirmed. "Fundamental Human Rights, in the dignity of the human person, in the equal rights of men and women of the nations large and small." This dream can be changed into reality if we work honestly. In the language of the Buddhist monk "The snow has fallen, but don't be sad, after the snowfall comes the warmth of sun."

Notes

1. V.I.K. Sarin, (1980): *India's North East in Flames*, New Delhi: Vikas Publishing House, pp. 11-15.
2. Rajinder Sanchar, (2004): *Human Rights Perspective and Challenges*, New Delhi: Gyan Publishing House.
3. Anuradha Dutta and Bhyan, *Genesis of Conflict and Peace: Understanding North East India*, New Delhi: Akansha Publishing House.
4. P.K. Saksena (1999): *Human Rights: Fifty years of India's Independence*, New Delhi: Gyan Publishing House.
5. Dhurba Rizal & Yozo Yokota, *Understanding Development Conflict and Violence: The Case of Bhutan, Nepal, North East India and*

Chittagong hill tracts of Bangladesh, Eastern Book Corporation.

6. H.M. Barch, (2001): *Encyclopedia of North East India,* Vol. II, Delhi: Mittal Publication.
7. *Dialogue,* Volume 5, No 4, Jan. 2004.
8. P.K. Saksena, (1999): *Human Rights: Fifty years of India's Independence,* New Delhi: Gyan Publishing House.
9. National Seminar on *Impact of Insurgency on Women and Children in North East Region,* Aizwal Mizoram, 17-18 September 2002, A Report, pp. 33-34.
10. Ibid., pp. 41-42.
11. Ibid., pp. 45-46.

Section III

Society, Culture and Economy of North East India

20

PREPARING THE NORTH EASTERN ECONOMY FOR THE ASEAN LINKAGE

Gulshan Sachdeva

Introduction

The North Eastern region of India is known for its ethnic, linguistic, and cultural richness and diversity. There has been plenty of literature on all these aspects of the region. In recent years, security related issues have also been discussed in detail. The economic literature on the region broadly discusses its unique economic institutions, "economic backwardness" and failure of economic policies in the region.[1] The "mainstream" economic literature on the North East generally argues its economy in the context of "neglect" theory. It is also frequently suggested that to end this neglect, massive developmental assistance from the Central Government is required, which in due course would also end discontent, insurgency and terrorism in the region. This paper argues, instead that failure of economic strategy for the region is not because of any so-called economic neglect but because of wrong assumptions and inappropriate economic policy framework, which have created an unbalanced economy and destroyed the basic institutions of market economy. There is an urgent need to question usual myths surrounding the region, create market institutions and start working towards linking the region with the ASEAN neighbors. It is further argued that to take full advantage from its proximity to the ASEAN market, the region needs some fundamental changes in its land and labour policies in addition to improvements in infrastructure and security situation in some of the states.

The Region

The North Eastern Region, traditionally known as the land of seven sisters, comprises the States of Arunachal Pradesh, Assam, Manipur, Meghalaya, Mizoram, Nagaland and Tripura, with about eight percent of the country's geographical area and about four percent of its population. Their combined contribution to the national economy is around two percent. In 2002, Sikkim is also included in the group. Historically, successive legal and administrative decisions taken between 1874 and 1935 gave the areas of the North East distinct identity. The British administration initially treated the hill areas as "Non-Regulated Areas", then declared them as "Backward Tract" and, lastly, "Excluded Areas" and "Partially Excluded Areas."

Statistics are available in plenty about the number of races, tribes and their sub-groups, ethnic groups, cultures, religions, languages and dialects spoken in this region but broadly speaking there are three distinct groups of people—the hill tribes, the plains tribes and the non-tribal population of the plains. The majority of those living in the plains are Hindus and Muslims while a substantial proportion of hill tribes in Meghalaya, Mizoram and Nagaland are Christians. Geographically, apart from Brahmaputra, Barak (Assam) and Imphal (Manipur) valleys and some flat lands in between the hills of Meghalaya and Tripura, the remaining two-third area of the region consists of hilly terrain. Most of this hilly portion is either owned, or controlled or managed, by tribes, clans or village communities. The most populous part is the

Brahmaputra valley which constitutes about 22 per cent of the region.

The pace of development in the hill areas and plains differs considerably. The valleys are economically active areas, the Brahmaputra valley being the most active. Tribal population constitutes only about one-fourth[2] of the population of North East even though in four States—Mizoram, Meghalaya, Nagaland and Arunachal Pradesh—tribals are in majority. In Mizoram, which has one of the highest literacy levels (88 per cent) in the country, second only to Kerala (91 per cent), they constitute as high as 95 per cent of the population.

On the one hand, the region is diverse and heterogeneous. On the other hand, it is quite homogeneous; the social stratification found in other parts of the country is not present in the North East. The tribal societies in the hill areas are egalitarian. This results in better social indicators for most of the hilly States of the region.

On 26 January 1950, North East India consisted of the State of Assam and the Union Territories of Manipur and Tripura. However, to fulfil the political aspirations of the local people several new States, beginning with Nagaland in 1963 and ending with Mizoram in 1987, have been created. Further, there has been an increase in the number of districts in the tribals States of the North East. Mizoram with a population of only about nine lakhs (2001) has eight districts. Administratively today the North East has eight States, 76 districts, more than 400 Community Development Blocks and about 245 towns. However, despite the creation of several new States, the basic problem of integration and balanced economic development remains.

North East in Indian Planning

During the colonial period, the institutions and infrastructure in India were mainly developed to serve colonial interests.[3] In the initial years of planning after independence, regional economic development was still not really on agenda. The emphasis was on concentration of limited resources on those areas and regions which could give maximum returns to tackle the problems of food security and heavy dependence on imports for capital goods. Very little attempt was made at regional desegregation of national planning. Emphasis on industrialization during the second plan led to some industrial regions. Although some problem regions like Damodar valley, refugee rehabilitation etc. were identified, they were not part of any regional development strategy. Till that time, States of North East were not discussed as a "problem" region as per capita income of Assam was among the top few States.

In the third Five Year Plan, the concept of balanced regional development was discussed in detail. The policies through which the balanced regional development was supposed to be achieved were selection of industrial location (both for public and private sector), use of large projects as nuclei of regional growth, technological development, education and training and labour mobility. It was asserted that "from the decisions regarding location of projects in the public sector which has been reached so far, it is apparent that there will be a fair measure of dispersal and various regions will have significant share in industrial development."[4] Despite these policy pronouncements, the third plan document also noted that "the level of development depends to a considerable extent on the availability of competent administrative and technical personnel and on the growth of a class of small and medium sized entrepreneurs...*Attention should be given to these aspects of development, for they point to handicaps which cannot be removed merely by providing resources to an under-developed region*" (emphasis added).[5] This was an important observation, which was ignored in later plan documents. Overall, the thinking was that that "development of regions and the national economy as a whole have to be viewed as parts of single process.... Excessive emphasis on the problems of particular regions and attempts to plan for their development without relating their needs to the requirements of the national economy has to be guarded against, for in the final analysis, it is as integral parts of the country that different regions can best hope to realize their full potential for growth."[6]

Fourth Plan outlined that "differences in development

between State and State arise out of variations in activity in the three sectors-cooperative, private and public" It was argued that in the cooperative and private sector, actions of the Central government could influence very little. In the state sector it was outlined that directions in which the Centre can help are: (1) allocation of Central assistance; (2) location of Central projects; and (3) adjustments in procedures and policies of national financial and other institutions. Apart from weightage given to backward states in the allocation of central assistance, programme for Small farmers, Marginal farmers, Drought Prone Areas, Dry Areas, Tribal Areas and industrially backward areas were taken up. The Planning Commission also issued guidelines for the formulation of district plans. Despite these steps there was a sense of frustration in the Fifth Plan when it said that in the reduction of regional imbalances "the measure taken so far have not had any appreciable impact."[7] It argued that *"there has been an unfortunate tendency to define the needed efforts merely in terms of financial magnitudes. Organisational and institutional aspects of the resource development problem of the backward regions have not been attended to."* (emphasis added).[8]

North East as a region started figuring prominently in planning literature from the early 1970s, particularly after the reorganization of States in the region. The establishment of North Eastern Council (NEC) in 1972 was acceptance of the fact that this region needed special institutions and incentives for development. In the Sixth Five Year Plan, under the sub plan approach, greater emphasis was placed on Special Tribal Plan, Hill Area schemes and the programmes handled by the North Eastern Council.[9] Contrary to the Third Plan, where it was argued that the Central government cannot influence much the private sector initiatives in backward areas, under the Sixth Plan, Central policies were also designed "to provide incentives to private entrepreneurs through schemes of concessional finance, seed/margin money scheme, Central investment subsidies scheme, tax reliefs, specific interest subsidies for engineer entrepreneurs and so on."[10] These policies were in addition to resource transfers and public sector programmes.

One of the main objectives of the Seventh Plan was also

the "adoption of effective promotional measures to raise the productivity and incomes of the poorer sections of the population, poorer regions and poorer States."[11] The Plan also emphasized the need for decentralisation of planning and development administration below the State level, particularly in the context of agricultural and rural development programmes. It urged the States to take steps towards four important aspects of a decentralised district level planning setup. These were (a) effecting functional decentralization (b) effecting financial decentralization; (c) the establishment of appropriate planning mechanism at the District level; and (d) establishment of appropriate budgeting and reap-propriation procedures.[12] In the eighth and ninth Five Year Plans, there were very little direct references of problems regions. In both these plans, North Eastern States were discussed broadly within the category of Special Area Development Plans like Hill Area Development Plan (HADP), NEC etc.[13] One of the major concerns of the Mid Term Appraisal of the Ninth Plan as well as the Tenth Five Years Plan is that of widening regional disparities.

While emphasizing the importance of balanced development for all States, the Tenth Plan document included a State-wise break-up of the broad developmental targets, including targets for growth rates and social development. For the first time a separate volume State Plans was included. The document declares that, "the adoption of planning and a strategy of State-led industrialization was intended to lead to a more balanced growth in the country. It was expected that, over time, inter-State disparities would be minimized. Plans and policies were designed to provide more investments to the relatively backward areas. Nevertheless, socioeconomic variations across States continue to exist today."[14] It further said that some of regional imbalances have narrowed down, but most have grown over time.

To tackle the problem, it was argued that the emphasis would be on effectiveness, quality, and reforms and not so much on volumes of investment alone. According to the document, the "core element in the Planning Commission's strategy towards reducing regional disparities would be the targeting of less developed areas with provisions of funds for capital investments and innovative delivery mechanisms linked to institutional reforms."[15] For the first time a special portion of the document deals with North Eastern States. According the 10 Five Year Plan "the trauma of partition, political evolution and insurgency combined with the geographical location, transport bottlenecks, natural calamities, etc., have hindered the progress of the North East, and the region has experienced relatively slower economic growth compared to the rest of the country. Most of the North Eastern States joined the planned development process later than many other States."[16] The Plan documents outlines the special measures initiated by the central government like the Special PM packages, NEC, non lapsable central pool of resources, Department of Development of the North East etc.

The Eleventh Five Year Plan argues that it is the collective endeavour of the Central and State governments to form appropriate polices for the region. The plan document has emphasized connectivity (road, rail, air, inland waterways, and telecommunications) as the key area for the development of NER. In addition, it has been recognized that economic activities will be generated through interaction with neighbouring countries.[17]

Understanding Economic Policy Framework for the North East

Above analysis shows that the policies of regional development provide some scattered information about the North East. Although, many of the recent government documents do provide some special mentions of the Northeast, they are not shown as part of any coherent strategy. They also do not clearly mention any linkages or diversions from the earlier policies.

It seems that due to special constitutional arrangements, historical background as well as geographical location,[18] the Central government has been trying to integrate the North East Region with the national economy through certain policy framework. It has accepted the right of tribals to retain their

FIGURE I

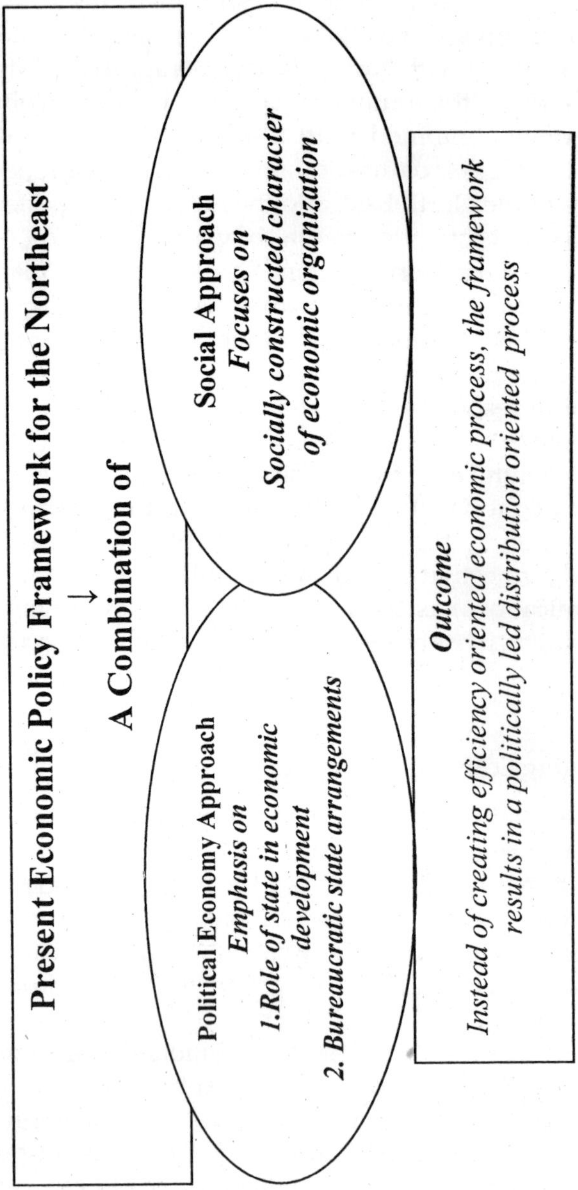
Present Economic Policy Framework for the Northeast
A Combination of
Political Economy Approach
Emphasis on
1.Role of state in economic
development
2. Bureaucratic state arrangements
Social Approach
Focuses on
Socially constructed character
of economic organization
Outcome
Instead of creating efficiency oriented economic process, the framework
results in a politically led distribution oriented process

way of life and identity and has sought to integrate them through democratic means into the federal frame of the Constitution of India. The policy framework for the region so far is guided by a combination of political economy and culture. The main focus of the *political economy approach* is on the relations between the State and the economy. Therefore, in this approach, the role of the bureaucratic state arrangements is strongly emphasized. The *cultural approach,* however, focuses on the socially constructed character of economic organisation where the economic system is a product of the social order.

As a result of this combined approach, the importance of the bureaucratic arrangements in the process of economic development has been unduly exaggerated. Besides, wherever possible, an attempt has been made by policy makers to work through the unique social and cultural institutions existing in the region instead of imposing new institutions.[19] This special approach has been adjusted with the central governments' policies of a regional planning development model. The major assumption of regional planning is that it would permit the transfer of surplus generated in one region to another. This mechanism was expected to increase aggregate national efficiency through optimum resource allocation.

Under the influence of this policy, various schemes for the development of infrastructure and economy of the North East region have been formulated. The schemes include the formation of the North Eastern Council, Hill Area Development Projects and sub-plans, Tribal Area sub-plan, and Tribal Development Agency Projects to name only a few. In addition, these seven States have been declared as Special Category States; they get Central Assistance on the basis of 90 per cent grant and 10 per cent loan. Some public sector units have also been set up in the region. The policies of industrial licensing, concessional finance and investment subsidy, growth centres, as well as freight equalisation of some major industrial inputs have also been used towards economic development. Under the announcement made by the then Indian Prime Minister Deve Gowda in October 1996, all developmental ministries and departments of the Central Government have been directed to earmark at least 10 per cent of their annual budget for the progammes in the Northeast. In case any Central Government Ministry is failed to achieve this target, the unutilized 10 per cent portion is pooled in the Non-lapsable central pool of resources which will be re utilized to finance developmental projects in the Northeast. Creation of a separate Department of Development of North Eastern Region (DONER) is another new initiative by the government.

Further, to protect tribal interests, policies of less interference with the cultural traditions and customs of the tribal people are being followed and additional political and administrative framework has been provided for the region. Under the sixth schedule of the Constitution, the concept of Autonomous District Councils has been applied.[20] The councils are responsible for looking after the social, economic and minor criminal and civil matters of the tribal people. More specifically these councils are empowered to make laws with respect to: (a) Land; (b) Forest; (c) Water course; (d) Shifting cultivation; (e) Establishment of village and town and its administration; (f) Appointment of, or succession to chiefs or headmen; (g) Inheritance of property; (e) Marriage and divorce and matters relating to any other social customs.

Restrictions have been imposed on the rights of citizens of other states as well as non tribals from the same state from to acquire landed property in some parts of the Northeast. The regulation of Inner Line Permit prohibits entry of outsiders into Arunachal Pradesh, Mizoram and Nagaland without a permit, and debars a non-native to acquire any interest in land or the produce of land. Tribal belts and blocks have been constituted in the plains areas to prevent land alienation from tribals there.

Economic Outcome and Development Trends

The development strategy followed by the Centre and State governments has created a totally unbalanced economy in the North East. There are differences among all States of the region with respect to their resource endowments, levels of industrialisation as well as infrastructral facilities. On the whole, all these economies are underdeveloped agrarian societies with very weak industrial sectors and inflated service sectors. The share of agriculture although declined, still much higher than the national average. The industrial sector has mainly developed around tea, oil, timber (TOT) in Assam and mining, saw mills and plywood factories in other parts of the region. The tea plantation industry employs a large labour force, in Assam alone it employs more than 500,000 workers. State sponsored industrialisation—whether sugar mills, jute mills, paper mills or food processing has not been successful. Small scale industries have also not been viable and there is large scale industrial sickness in this sector. Despite changes, the economy of the region remains primarily agricultural. The full potential of this sector has not been exploited. Primitive farm practices of slash and burn (jhum) shifting cultivation in the many of the hills and mainly single crop traditional farming in the plains continue. As a result, the region is not even able to produce adequate food grain to feed its population. The States of the region import food items worth about Rs. 2,000 to Rs. 2,500 crores annually from other parts of the country. Since neither agriculture nor industry has taken off, the pressure for employment is on the service sector (means government service). As a result, this sector has expanded disproportionately (figure 2). Because of low economic activity, the States of the region have resource deficit. Of these limited resources a large portion is spent mainly to maintain the service sector.

The regional average growth rates in the 1980's was slightly lower than the national economy. During this period except Assam, all other economies in the region grew at higher growth rates than the national economy. Growth was close to national economy even in the case of Assam. In the post-liberalisation phase during the nineties, while the national economy is growing fast after initial contraction, overall Northeastern economy has slowed down. As a result, the gap between national growth rates and regional growth rates has further widened. Assam, the largest economy of the region is in a very critical state, both in agriculture and industry. In the decade of eighties, the average rate of growth Assam was more than 4 per cent. In the nineties, growth in Assam was much

FIGURE 2: SECTORAL CONTRIBUTION TO NSDP IN THE NORTH EASTERN STATES (BASE 1993-94)

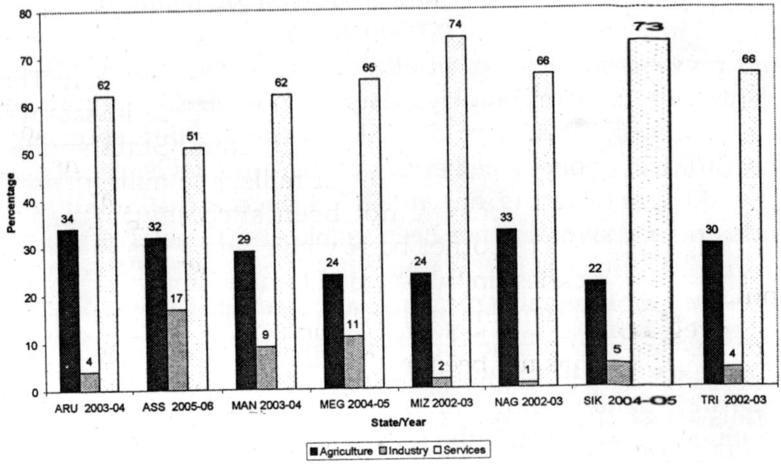

Source: NEDFi Databank

lower. Except Arunachal, the hill economies have not shown much difference in growth rates in the last twenty years or so. Tripura economy in fact has grown fast in the 1990's. As a result of these trends it could be concluded that gap between the northeast and the national economy widened in the nineties. The improved agricultural production and productivity in some pockets of North East, however, indicated that there was a large untapped potential in agriculture.

Similarly, long term trends in the per capita income growth also showed that gap between the national and state growth rates also widened. In these circumstances, there has some rethinking on the development pattern followed in the Northeast. It has been realized for quite some time that this kind of development pattern will not be able to face the forces of liberalization and globalization, unless some serious radical policies are implemented. For that civil society in the region has been engaged in serious debate about different alternatives and their implications. The Central Government took many initiatives, particularly from the mind-nineties. After seeing difficult economic conditions, State governments from the

FIGURE 3: AVERAGE GROWTH RATES IN THE NORTHEAST IN 1980'S AND 1990'S (AT CONSTANT 1993-94 PRICES)

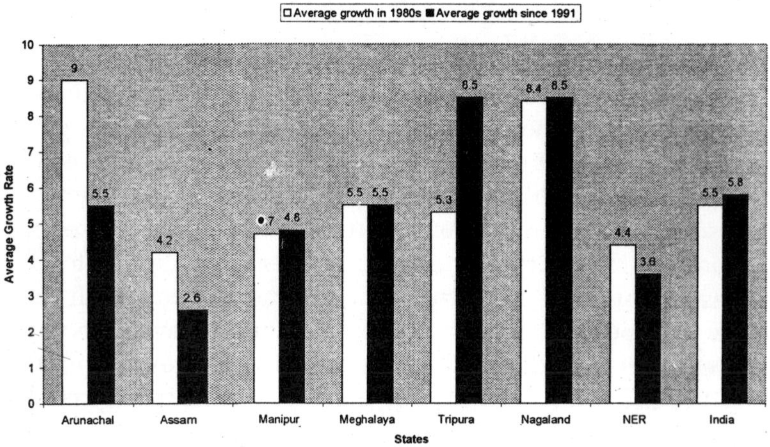

region also initiated many measures to attract private investment. As a result of combination of factors, economic performance in the last few years have improved significantly, particularly in Assam, Manipur and Nagaland (see Table 1)

Table 1

ECONOMIC GROWTH IN THE NORTH EAST 1992- 2011

	8 FYP (1992-97)	*9 FYP (1997-2001)*	*10 FYP (2002-06)*	*11 FYP (2007-11) Target*
Arunachal Pradesh	5.1	4.4	5.8	6.4
Assam	2.8	2.1	6.2	6.5
Manipur	4.6	6.4	11.6	5.9
Meghalaya	3.8	6.2	5.6	7.3
Mizoram	-	-	5.9	7.1
Nagaland	8.9	2.6	8.3	9.3
Sikkim	5.3	8.3	7.7	6.3
Tripura	6.6	7.4	8.7	6.9
India	6.5	5.5	7.7	9.0

Source: Eleventh Five Year Plan, Volume 1 (New Delhi, Planning Commission, 2008).

Although economic growth in the region has improved, it still has to tackle many of the fundamental issues which are continuing to affect its performance.

Demystifying North East

"Complex, mysterious, unique" the region is continue to be referred to in these terms in academic, media and policy circles. Indeed, the region's history, geography, ethnic composition and culture have given it a distinctive character. And selective academic research on disparate subjects like tribal customs, community ownership, gender equations etc., has generated interest. The Central Government deals with these states as "Special category States." Although, over the years, the region has undergone tremendous changes but certain stereotypes have remained. For most people in policy circles, media and academia, it still remains a tribal, neglected, backward, insurgency prone remote frontier. The time has come to question some myths surrounding the region. This will help create a meaningful ground for future policy making.

Any discussion regarding the region starts with its tribal nature. It is almost unanimously accepted as a tribal region. Surprisingly, facts on the ground are totally different. According to 2001 census, only about one-forth of the population of the region is tribal. It is always emphasized that in the four States—Mizoram, Meghalaya, Nagaland and Arunachal Pradesh—tribals are in majority. But tribal majority in these states does not make the whole region tribal. Moreover in today's northeast, tribals are not "head hunters"; on the contrary, a large number of them are educated and have adopted western dress and modes of living. It would be misleading to equate them with marginalized tribals in other parts of the country. Since independence, Indian policy makers have been very sensitive to the tribal nature of the region. Some of these policies we have discussed in the earlier sections. Earlier many scholars critically looked at this protective policy as they found that it had failed to stop alienation of tribal land.[21] Prof. B.K. Roy Burman asserted that as a result of this policy, a process of "state or bureaucracy sponsored neo-feudalisation" was taking place in the region.[22]

In recent years, this policy framework has been under attack from different reasons. The policy of protective discrimination for Scheduled Tribes in the region raises serious questions of justice, and equality for the non-tribal population.[23] As Sanjib Baruah argues, this kind of policy "effectively compromises the constitutional right to free movement of Indian citizens."[24] Moreover, rigid barriers -which aim at restricting outside penetration—are contrary to the processes of contemporary globalization.[25] In these circumstances, it would be more productive and useful if we start treating Northeastern economic problems in a normal way rather than in a "special tribal way." First, the region is not a "tribal region" and secondly, "special solutions" have created more problems than solving it.

Secondly the myth about "neglect" the region needs to be seriously researched. There is obviously some neglect of the Northeast in Delhi politics and national media. There could also be some knowledge deficit. But most vocal writings and speeches regarding "neglect theory" often cite economic figures to show the neglect. Respected national institutions like the Planning Commission are of little help. In fact, some of its main publications have created more confusion. For example, the *National Human Development Report*[26] uses poverty ratios of Assam for Sikkim, Arunachal Pradesh, Meghalaya, Mizoram, Manipur, Nagaland and Tripura. As a result, poverty ratio of States like Nagaland, Mizoram etc. is shown very high, although other indicators like infant mortality ratios and consumption expenditure surveys of the National sample Survey Organistions tell a different story altogether. While using these kinds of figures, many scholars have created theories of neglect and underdevelopment.

There could be any other kind of neglect but the facts about devolution and transfers of resources from the Centre reveal entirely different story. Between 1990-91 and 2002-03, the region received about Rs. 108,504 crores. Assam received about Rs. 43,000 crores from the Centre. Arunachal and Manipur received about Rs. 9,900 crores and Rs. 11,500 crores respectively. Meghalaya received about Rs. 9,000 crores and Tripura's share is about Rs. 14,000 crores. Similarly, figures for the same period for Nagaland and Mizoram are about Rs. 12,000 crores and 9,000 crores respectively. These are gross figures. A portion of that money is also given back to the Central government as repayment on loans and interest payments. Still, the cumulative net devolution from the Centre to the North East for the period between 1990-91 and 2002-03 is about Rs. 92,000 crores. Only grant portion to the region during these 13 years is about Rs. 65,000 crores.[27] So the lack of development could not be because of shortage of funds. Economist and Congress leader Jairam Ramesh has also argued that this kind of public expenditure has become very much part of the problem of the North East.[28] In fact, a significant portion of development funding actually ends up in the hands of underground groups.

Thirdly the importance of high literacy levels in the North East should not be over-emphasised. Although the region has done well due in education because of many socio-historical factors but the region serious problems remain. Despite some pockets of high literacy, the combined literacy rate in the region is 64.5 per cent which is below the national average. Low literacy rates in Arunachal, Assam and Meghalaya are responsible for this. Even in the neighbouring West Bengal, the literary rate is 69.22 per cent. According to 2001 census, 35 out of 72 districts of the region record literacy levels below national average. Even high literacy rates in other districts are accompanied by low educational levels due to high dropout and low standards. Active student politics the culture of *bandhs* in the region have played havoc with the education system. There are enough teachers in the region but many of them are not trained. According to sixth NCERT survey only 45 per cent of total school teachers in the region are trained. The corresponding figure for the national level was about 87 per cent. The situation was particularly bad in Assam and Nagaland where only about 30 percent teachers at the secondary and higher secondary levels were trained. Latest figures from the Ministry of Human Resource Development also indicate that except Manipur, all the states in the region has high gross drop out rates at all stages. Even in a state like Mizoram, which has almost 90 per cent literacy, about

76 per cent students could not complete high school.[29]

Another factor which has to be understood is that major parts of the region face labour scarcity. This is perhaps one of the main reasons for the failure of various labour intensive government schemes like animal husbandry, Jawahar Rozgar Yojana etc. Despite all the talk of outside invasion, labour (both skilled and unskilled) is a big problem with the possible exception of Brahmaputra valley and Tripura. Already outside labour (mainly from Bangladesh, Myanmar, Nepal and other parts of India) is a crucial factor in both agricultural as well as non-agricultural activities. With any increase in economic activities, the problem of labour shortage is expected to be aggravated. Unless the Inner Line restricted areas are opened for outside labour, economic development is going to suffer. Or worse it would be an open invitation to illegal Bangladeshi immigrants.

ASEAN Linkage

Another standard argument in the past has been the disadvantageous geographical situation of the Northeast. This has been argued in writings as one of the main stumbling block for its economic development. This isolated, landlocked region shares less than 1 per cent of its borders with the rest of the country, and the rest with Bhutan, Bangladesh, Myanmar and China. For the most part this international border was artificially created. The result has been the elimination of the region's trade, commerce and other linkages which existed in the pre-partition days. Using the region's two per cent perimeter as a major linkage point with the rest of India and at the same time checking the inflow of goods and people from across the remaining rest of 98-99 per cent has been a gigantic task.

In the last one decade, there have serious discussions on converting this locational disadvantage into a boon because of an increasingly integrated world economy.[30] This is particularly so when all the States of the region are on international borders. In addition, these States are very close to the dynamic South-East and East Asian economies. Most policy makers in the region are excited and optimistic about the idea of linking their economies with dynamic Asia. There were even suggestions that if for security reasons the Government of India is reluctant to open up the natural trade routes, the North East States should ask the Central Government to compensate them for the loss of trade.[31]

These arguments gained momentum at a time when India's "Look East" policy was being implemented.[32] Right from the sixties to the eighties, India and East Asia retained their mutual suspicions. However, the nineties were to mark a significant change in their relations. India had met with limited success in improving its relations with East Asian nations bilaterally during the eighties. The early nineties brought far reaching changes at the global scene. With the collapse of the Soviet Union and the end of the Cold War ideological division of the world ended. After the Soviet collapse, India was also looking for diversification in its foreign trade links. The rapid economic growth of these countries had also made solid impact on the prevailing inward economic thinking in Indian academia and policy elite. Many think tanks in the West had started predicting next century as the Asian century.[33] Against this background, India started working for its "Look East" policy. The crux of this initiative was not just pushing Indian exports to East Asia or attracting investment from the region. The idea was to start an entirely new relationship with the East Asian region in all areas encompassing political, economic, strategic and cultural areas.

These developments were going to have a significant impact on the Northeast. The reason being that there was not only a failure of the economic policy framework in the region but also a weakness of country's foreign policy which had ignored Southeast Asia for a long time. As a result, the North East region was not only cut off from its natural economic partners but also encircled by unfriendly countries. Now with this broad policy changes in India's foreign policy, many scholars and policy makers have started talking about advantages of linking North East with the ASEAN markets.

So far the major border trade activity of the region with Bangladesh and Myanmar is 'unauthorised trade.' The State authorities are fully aware of these activities which function smoothly through unofficial channels. China is an important player in the border trade even though its trading activities are mainly through Myanmar. The major policy issue, therefore, would be to synchronise these realities into Indian trade policies.

There is however, a danger that the hype of linking North East with South-East Asia becoming another myth if we do not prepare the region step by step. While keeping the long term goal in mind, at this point the emphasis should be on creating conditions, both at the policy level and at the ground level, on converting the unauthorized trade into authorized trade. This is not a simple task. The genuine trader will have many practical problems. The unauthorized trade works on the basis of a strong network which involves traders, police, forest departments and, of course, many underground groups and each has its own share in the pie. Apart from infrastructural problems at Moreh, the large number of checkposts on National High Ways 39 and 53 would a create problem in switching over from illegal to legal trade. In most cases, the State governments turn a blind eye to the border trade in illegal items because it creates a lot of economic activity in the region. Since these commodities are not declared legal officially, there is corruption at every turn. With the recent signing of India-ASEAN free trade agreement in goods,[34] many new opportunities for the products of North Eastern region have opened up. But first of all the region should start producing globally competitive products. For that many of the issues discussed earlier like land tenure policies, inner line regulations, Restricted Area Permits, infrastructure, security issues have to be tackled. Otherwise, the region would be a transit point of goods which may create further discontent.

Final Remarks

The relative failure of economic strategy for the region is not because of any so-called economic neglect but because of wrong assumptions and inappropriate socio-economic policy framework, which have created an unbalanced economy and destroyed the basic institutions of market economy. There is no land market for two thirds land area which is under community or clan ownership. There are restrictions on labour movement due to inner line regulations in Arunachal, Nagaland and Mizoram. And investment climate has suffered due to law and order situation and attitude towards outsiders. We need to demystify the region, create basis institutions of the market economy and start working towards linking it with dynamic Asian economies.

In a liberalised economy, any new policy has to be based on some kind of market oriented approach. This framework should concentrate more on economic factors and less on political and cultural factors. The economic factors include labour cost, comparative advantages, technology, efficiency and returns on investment. In a market economy environment, the inefficient economic processes (jhum) and barriers to market entry (inner line regulations, restricted area permits, trading licensees, existing land tenure policies in hilly areas etc.) will clearly make an economic difference.

Although market forces will play a greater role, the State institutions will have to be geared up for the new task. In the last one decade the Central Government has taken number of initiatives which are showing some results. The actual action regarding land policies, inner line regulations, law and order and above all changes in attitude towards investors (read outsiders), however, will begin only at the state level. Once the capacities to deal with these issues are created at the State/ regional level, it is quite natural that Northeast will be able to take advantage from its close proximity to the Asian markets. In the last few years, some of the economies in the region have shown strong signs of recovery, particularly Assam. The process will get further boost with the signing of India-ASEAN free trade agreement in goods.

Notes

1. Nirankar Srivastava, (2002): *Survey of Research in Economics on North East India 1970-1990*, New Delhi: Regency Publications/ ICSSR-NERC, 2000; *North East India: A Bibliography*, New Delhi:

Teen Murti Museum & Library.

2. According to 2001 Census, Tribal Population of the Northeastern region (including Sikkim) constitute 26.93 per cent of the total population. For details see http://www.censusindia.net/t_00_005.html
3. Krishna Bhardwaj, 1982): "Regional Differentiation in India: A note," *Economic and Political Weekly*, April.
4. *Third Five Year Plan*, New Delhi: Planning Commission, p. 148.
5. Ibid., p. 151.
6. Ibid., p. 153.
7. *Fourth Five Year Plan*, New Delhi: Planning Commission, p. 55.
8. Ibid.
9. *Sixth Five Year Plan*, New Delhi: Planning Commission, p. 273.
10. Ibid., p. 276.
11. See *Seventh Five Year Plan*, Volume I, http://www.planningcommission.nic.in/plans/planrel/fiveyr/default.html
12. See *Seventh Five Year Plan*, Volume II, http://www.planningcommission.nic.in/plans/planrel/fiveyr/default.html
13. See "Special Area Development Plans," in *Eighth Five Year Plan*, Volume II, http://www.planningcommission.nic.in/plans/planrel/fiveyr/default.html
14. *Tenth Five Year Plan*, Volume III, New Delhi: Planning Commission, Government of India, p. 1.
15. Ibid., p. 124.
16. Ibid, p. 91.
17. See *Eleventh Five Year Plan 2007-2011*, Volume I, New Delhi: Planning Commission, 2008, pp. 151-164.
18. Some of these special historical and geographical aspects of the region as well as background of special constitutional arrangements are nicely summarized by L.P. Singh, "Problem (The North East: A Symposium on the Problem of a Neglected People & Region)," *Seminar*, No. 336, 1990.
19. While writing the foreword to the second edition of *A Philosophy for NEFA* by V. Elwin, V. (1959), Pt. Jawaharlal Nehru wrote that "avenues of development (for tribal areas) should be pursued within the broad framework of the following five fundamental principles:
    (1) People should develop along the lines of their own genius and we should avoid imposing anything on them. We should try to encourage in every way their own traditional art and culture.
    (2) Tribal rights in land and forests should be respected.

(3) We should try to train and build up a team of their own people to do the work of administration and development. Some technical personnel from outside will, no doubt, be needed, especially in the beginning. But we should avoid introducing too many outsiders into tribal territory.

(4) We should not over-administer these areas or overwhelm them with a multiplicity of schemes. We should rather work through, and not in rivalry to, their own social and cultural institutions.

(5) We should judge results, not by statistics or the amount of money spent, but the quality of human character that is evolved.

20. See Arvind K. Sharma, (1998): "District Councils in the North East," in T.N. Chaturvedi, (ed.), *Fifty Years of Indian Administration: Retrospect and Prospect*, New Delhi: Indian Institute of Public Administration.
21. B.N. Bordoloi, (199): "Land Alienation Among Tribes of North East India: Problems and Policies," *IASSI Quarterly*, Vol. 12, Nos. 3 & 4, 1994, pp. 17-48; M.N. Karna, (1999): "The Agrarian Scene," *Seminar*, No. 366, February 1990, pp. 30-38.
22. B.K. Roy Burman, "Land and Forest Rights," *Seminar*, No. 336, pp. 25-29.
23. Sanjib Baruah, (2003): "Protective Discrimination and Crisis of Citizenship in North East India," *Economic and Political Weekly*, April 26.
24. Sanjib Baruah, (2005): *Durable Disorder: Understanding the Politics of Northeast India*, New Delhi: Oxford University Press, p. 51.
25. For details see Gulshan Sachdeva, (2000): *Economy of the North East, Policy, Present Conditions and Future Possibilities*, New Delhi: Konark Publishers.
26. See table notes at pp. 164-166 and Technical Appendix page 133 in the *National Human Development Report 2001*, New Delhi: Planning Commission, 2002.
27. Authors calculations based on Reserve Bank of India as well as CMIE publications.
28. Jairam Ramesh, (2005): "Northeast India in New Asia," *Seminar*, No. 550, June.
29. *Annual Report 2004-05*, Ministry of Human Resource Development, Government of India, p. 262.
30. See *Gateway to the East : A Symposium on Northeast India and the Look East Policy* in a special issue of *Seminar*, No. 550, June 2005.
31. *Report of (Jayanta Madhab) Committee on Industry*, Volume 1,

Dispur; Government of Assam, 1996, p. 6.

32. For details see Charan Wadhva and Gulshan Sachdeva, (2005): "Indian Perspectives on East Asia," in Charan Wadhva and Yuen Pau Woo, (eds.), *Asian Regionalism: Canadian & Indian Perspectives*, New Delhi: APH Publishing Corp.
33. Sanjaya Baru, (2000): "The Problem," *Seminar* (Special Issue on Looking East), March.
34. C.S. Kuppuswamy, (2009): "India—ASEAN Free Trade Agreement," Paper No. 3364, South Asia Analysis Group, 19 August. http://www.southasiaanalysis.org/%5Cpapers34%5Cpaper3364.html

21

INTERROGATING 'COMMUNITY MANAGEMENT' STATE, MARKET AND COMMUNITY IN ARUNACHAL'S AGRARIAN TRANSITION

Deepak K. Mishra

I. Introduction

In the growing literature on management of Common Property Resources (CPRs), the state, market and community are generally portrayed as alternative institutional mechanisms with varying implications for the sustainability of the resources.

* The paper draws on my on-going work on capitalist transformation in Arunachal Pradesh. Some of the evidences presented here have also been discussed in my earlier works: Mishra (2004) and Mishra (2007). The paper is based on several rounds of fieldworks in Arunachal Pradesh, which were part of different projects. Financial assistance from the UGC, ICSSR and the V V Giri National Labour Institute, Noida is gratefully acknowledged. The author is grateful to the participants of the seminar at the Department of Western History, Lucknow University for their comments and suggestions. The usual disclaimers apply.

State-managed institutional arrangements have been widely criticised for their ineffectiveness in protecting the resources in a sustainable manner. Leakages, corruption and inability to prevent capture by powerful groups and individuals have been discussed as various kinds of 'government failure' in the literature. Market-based alternatives, which generally advocate creation of private property rights or private incentive structures of diverse kinds as a solution to the ubiquitous problems of free riding and coordination failures, have been criticised for the mismatch between private profits, which such policies tend to favour, and socially optimal choices. Such problems typically become important when there is a trade-off between short-term profit maximisation and sustainability in the long-run. The non-commoditised and non-economic benefits and services derived from the resources are typically not taken into account in market-driven policy frameworks. The community-based solutions have been posed as an institutional alternative that performs much better on grounds of equity as well as sustainability in comparison with state and market-based institutional arrangements. The inclusiveness of community managed natural resource management systems, it is argued, results in greater control of resource-dependent populations on the management of natural resources, which in turn leads to a substantial reduction in monitoring and supervision costs. Instead of posing the state, market and community as alternatives, an attempt has been made in this paper to highlight the interconnections among them. By examining the development experience of Arunachal Pradesh, a State located in the extreme northeast corner of India, the paper seeks to examine the interdependent nature of these three institutional forms in the specific context of natural resource management. Rather than posing state, market forces and 'community' institutions as competing and alternative forms of institutional structures, the emphasis here is on the mutually reinforcing nature of the changes in all the above-mentioned dimensions as part of the same, larger dynamics of economic transition in Arunachal Pradesh.

The paper is organised as follows. In the following section, the specificities of the development experience of Arunachal Pradesh has been discussed. In section III, the property rights structures and institutional arrangements for natural resource management in the State have been described. In Section IV, the role of state interventions, expansion of markets and the politics of ethnicity in changing the role, functioning and implications of local institutional arrangements have been discussed. Concluding observations have been placed in the final section.

II. Economic Transformation in Arunachal Pradesh

Because of its ecological and historical specificities, the trajectories of development in Arunachal Pradesh, is markedly different from the rest of the country. Home to more than hundred tribes and sub-tribes, this thinly populated State, remained largely unadministered during the colonial rule. The specificities of the State that remains crucial to the understanding of the process of economic transformation include the following aspects.

The relative isolation of the region during the much of the colonial period and the subsequent establishment and consolidation of governing structures during the post-independence period by the nascent Indian state has left its legacy not only in the structure of governance, but also on the nature of development of the region, earlier known as North Eastern Frontier Agency (NEFA). This meant that the state assumed the role of the prime mover of capitalist transformation. It not only brought labour, administrators and traders from outside, it also played a leading role in the gradual monetisation and commercialisation of the tribal social formations. Being a border region has added new dimensions to the process of development in the region as well. The heavy military presence across the State, particularly after of the 1962 war with China, has had many consequences for the local economy and society. Given the low levels of commercialisation of the economy, the army mostly depends on supply from outside the State even for basic food items; however, the army has influenced the local economy in a significant manner—by monetising transactions, by constructing physical infrastructure of diverse kinds, by creating wage labour markets, by giving supply orders and contracts to locals, by generating demand for local products and also, at times, by creating marketing infrastructures. But all this development has taken place in a context where the structures of governance have remained heterogeneous and fluid. As part of the Nehru-Elwin policy of tribal development, the state has not only recognised the customary rights to forest and agricultural land, but also has legitimised the customary laws of the tribes. Although the introduction of panchayati raj has led to institutional crowding out at the grassroots, for the last few decades the formal and informal structures of governance have coexisted and have influenced each other in diverse and complex ways. This institutional plurality has important implications for the capitalist transformation of the State.

Further, specific legislations like the 'inner line permit', the restrictions on transfer of ownership of any kind of permanent assets including land and houses to persons not belonging to the Arunachal Pradesh Scheduled Tribe (APST) and the affirmative discrimination in favour of local tribal groups in allocation of business contracts, licenses and jobs etc. has also shaped the development process in the State. The ecological specificities of the mountain region have influenced the development of the economy in important ways. Mountain specificities, such as inaccessibility, fragility, marginality and diversity, have been found to have significant implications for the local economies (Jodha 2001). To sum up, the three most significant dimensions of the agrarian economy of Arunachal Pradesh are: the ecological specificities of mountain agriculture; the institutional complexity underlying the use of and access to the various forces of production such as land and labour; and the historical role of the state as the prime mover of agrarian transformation.

III. 'Community Management': Rhetoric and Reality

Social institutions refer to the rules, norms and governance structures to regulate relationships among individual. Social institutions have been described as 'collective action in control of individual action' or a set of rules that order repetitive and interdependent activities among individuals and highlight what actions are required, prohibited or permitted. Institutions reduce transaction costs and facilitate in internalizing the externalities (North, 1990). Collective action, an action undertaken by more than one individual to achieve a common goal, becomes easier in the presence of institutions. The New Institutional Economics School (NIE) has attempted to bring in the role of such rules and ordered patterns of human interaction into the analysis of economic behaviour. However, in conceptualizing these institutional arrangements as outcomes of free negotiations/ interactions among independent individuals such an analysis de-emphasizes the structures of power in designing and sustaining institutional mechanisms. It is important to note that such an argument has also been advanced against the NIE perspective in general (Toye, 1995).

The political economy perspective on institutions, unlike the mainstream neo-classical school, has always conceptualized the economic processes as socially embedded. 'Institutions' were never treated as exogenous. Marxian political economy, in particular, treated such institutional arrangements being determined by the relations of production and productive forces in the society. After the 'rediscovery' of institutions in the New Institutional Economics (NIE) perspective, it will be worthwhile to 'bring in production relations' into the dynamics of institutions for natural resource management. The problem of resource allocation and management gets transformed into a political economy problem once there are multiple claimants to it, with differential access to productive resources (Nadkarni, 1989:20). Markets are not apolitical, asocial phenomena. They are 'not only just socially embedded phenomena, they are sites of the exercise of power in ways which are not reducible either to the tool kit of the new institutional economics or to norms of social embeddedness' (Harriss-White, 2003: 486).

A well-functioning common-property regime is characterized by *efficiency* (low occurrence or absence of disputes and limited efforts required to ensure compliance), *stability* (capacity to cope with progressive changes), *resilience* (capacity to absorb surprises or shocks) and *equity* (shared perception of fairness among members with respect to inputs and outcomes) (Gibbs and Bromley, 1991:26). One of the key problems in community-based natural resource management is to ensure collective action. Ostrom has identified the following features in institutional arrangements as facilitating efficient natural resource management: clearly defined boundaries, congruence between appropriation and provision rules and local conditions; collective choice instruments; monitoring; graduated sanctions; conflict resolution mechanisms; minimal recognition of rights to organize and nested enterprises in case of multilayered CPRs that are part of large systems (Ostrom, 1990: 90). In a recent survey of literature on endogenous collective action, the following contextual variables have been identified as important determinants of collective action: the type of production and allocation functions; the relative scarcity of the good; the size of the group involved; the heterogeneity of the group; the dependence of the group upon the good; common understanding of the group; the size of total collective benefit; the marginal contribution by one person to the collective good, the size of temptation to free ride; the loss to cooperators when others do not cooperate; having a choice of participating or not; the presence of leadership, level of social capital, and a wide diversity of rules that are used to change the structure of the situation (Ostrom, 2000).

The property rights formations in Arunachal Pradesh have undergone substantial changes over the last few decades. The traditional form of land-ownership was collective, although animals, tools and implements were privately owned. Most of the villages had some institutional mechanism like village councils to manage and safeguard property-rights in land and forests. While in some areas the institution of chieftainship was well developed and the individuals derived their rights of ownership from village-chief, in many areas the village-council, consisting of all adult male members was the basic institution of decision-making, conflict resolution and collective action (Das, 1995; Dutta, 2003; Pandey et. al., 1999). The traditional shifting cultivation system was based upon elaborate networks of informal contracts, cooperation, and resource pooling, risk-sharing and mutual insurance mechanisms.

In spite of their low-productivity the shifting cultivation systems did provide a degree of insurance against non-covariant risks, access to various tangible and non-tangible assets through membership of the community as well as a scope for institutional reproduction. However, because of internal dynamics of the system such as non-coverage of covariant risks, absence of fairness in the distribution of agricultural land in terms of quality, lack of sufficient surplus generation and demographic changes as well as the mutually reinforcing interventions by the state and market forces, private property rights over land has emerged in many parts of the state (Mishra, 2001; Roy and Kuri, 2001: 53-59).

Although individualisation of ownership rights over land is the most widely noticed dimension of the transitional phase in Arunachal Pradesh, it is important to note that the collective or communal property rights continues to have diverse context-specific operational meanings. The land under shifting cultivation, generally described as communally owned could also be owned by some specific clans or individual households. Similarly, our field-survey revealed that in the case of privately owned land, the rights of use, occupancy and inheritance are generally enjoyed by the owners, but the right to transfer is often conditional. In some cases 'limited transfer rights' (viz. temporary transfer rights under mortgage, use rights without inheritance rights etc.) and 'preferential transfer rights' (viz. transfer within family, clan or tribe) were found, along with unconditional rights to alienate. The transition to private property rights regime seems to be informal in the sense that even without explicit recognition from the state-institutions, land-market operates in a limited scale. The specificity of the emerging private property regime lies not only in its weak institutional basis but also in the changing dimensions of collective ownership (Mishra, 2002a; 2006).

The emergence of private property over land is often preceded by the adoption of permanent cultivation, which in turn might have followed a gradual shortening of the shifting cultivation cycle or complete abandonment of shifting cultivation. Some of the important features of the agrarian structure in the study area can be summarized as follows: Firstly, the overall character of the agrarian relations in the study region is determined by the predominance of small holders. Secondly, the inequality in the distribution of land ownership, which was nearly absent in the traditional economies of the region, has been gradually increasing in the past decades. Thirdly, landlessness is an emerging phenomenon in the study region, but there may be different processes at work in the emergence of this landlessness while in some villages it is largely because of customary inheritance laws, in others, along with that, indebtedness and rural-to-rural migration have played a role, while in some cases, it is largely caused by immigration from other states and countries. However, by and large landlessness is the feature of migrant non-Arunachalee households rather than that of the indigenous villagers. Fourthly, another significant observation is that normally, notwithstanding the description of the 'traditional' tribal institutions as more egalitarian, women are not the owners of the land although they are often found to be de facto managers of farm operations. Fifthly, transactions in land market were found to be very few in number but they signify the direction of change in coming years. Transfer of land through mortgage, sale and informal contracts were found in all of the sample villages but in few numbers only. Community control over farm land does not simply disappear as a result of emergence of land market. Thus, by and large the agrarian structure represents the characteristics of subsistence, small peasant agriculture.

It is important to note that in relation to commercialisation, similar trends were found by Mishra (2004) both in the interior village having settled cultivation and also in the village nearer to an urban center in West Kameng district. The findings broadly supports the formulation of Demsetz (1967) that as the value of common property resources increases, people are more likely to establish rights over it. However, while rise in the value of agricultural land might be linked with its better quality and productivity in some of the villages, the proximity to the urban centers and roads has caused the increased demand for land in many others. The sale of land to outsiders (only to people belonging to APST communities, but either not belonging to the village or to the same tribe) is rare.

Important changes in the labour relations have also been observed in rural Arunachal Pradesh. The traditional institutional arrangements like cooperative labour-sharing, collective-work and reciprocity have been in the decline. Emergence of rural labour market and increasing occupational diversification has also altered the labour relations in diverse ways. One aspect of these changes is the emergence of waged labour contracts in farm and non-farm activities, but an important dimension of the livelihood diversification strategies of rural households is the increasing reliance on forest based resources to smoothen consumption shortfalls. Mishra (2003) in a field survey in the hilly district of West Kameng in Arunachal Pradesh[1] reported as many as 30 different combinations of livelihoods at the household level. So far as inter-village differences are concerned the developed villages show a greater variability in livelihood combinations than the traditional ones. Broadly speaking two different kinds of livelihoods diversification strategies could be found in this mountainous region. The first one, which is mostly determined by the survival needs of households living in a high-risk, high diversity ecological setting, concentrates on diversification of livelihoods within and around agriculture. Households attempt to combine jhum, terrace and wet-rice cultivation with horticulture, animal husbandry, selling of forest products, casual employment in the emerging rural labour market and, in some cases petty trading. The second kind of diversification is through increasing dependence upon government service, trade and business and large-scale trading in forest products. The later kind of strategy is generally driven by an accumulative motive of relatively better-placed households. However, forest plays a central role in either kinds of diversification, in the first one as a source to mitigate risks and smoothening consumption during seasonal short falls, and in the second as a source of consumables as well as marketable products like timber, and a range of non-timber forest products including medicinal plants. While, historically, forest resources have played a vital role in the survival of rural people, the marketisation of forest product and use of wage labour for collection of forest products are relatively recent developments.

It is well-know that the extent of forest dependency is particularly high among households living in the mountain areas. A recent study conducted in 12 villages of Arunachal Pradesh concludes that on an average 34.48 per cent of the consumption expenditure of the households of the study area were derived from the community forests. Further, around 37.93 per cent of total consumption expenditure of relatively poor households was derived from community forests. On the other hand, 32.02 per cent and 31.06 per cent of total consumption expenditure were derived from community forests for relatively middle income and rich category of households (Mitra and Mishra 2006). Thus, in absolute terms, the richer sections derive more benefits from the community forest. Another study, on the basis of data collected from three villages in West Kameng district notes that while around 24 per cent of total income of the households is derived from forests (A. Mishra 2005). While The extent of forest dependency does not necessarily change as a consequence of increased levels of earnings, but the nature of forest use and the composition of forest products collected changes significantly. While poorer households tend to depend for forest for their survival, better off households operate more in the products that are marketed. Mitra and Mishra (2006) find that the consumption of relatively poor households consisted more of fuel wood and bamboo, leafy vegetables etc., on the other hand consumption of timber was much higher among the rich households. In fact, the study shows that as the income of the households increased the percentage consumption of timber increased but the consumption of minor forest products like bamboo, leafy vegetables reduced.

Thus the nature of forest consumption changes from one dependent on households necessities like food, fuel and fodder, to one based on accumulation motive as one moves across the income ladder. Women are more centrally involved in the former case than in the later. The collection of forest products has been found to be based on product specific gender division of labour. For example a study in West Kameng, Arunachal Pradesh notes that while the contribution of females in the collection of marketed forest products like timber, bamboo and medicinal plants was negligible, women contribute more labour than men in the collection of firewood, grass, leafy vegetables, fruits and roots. In the collection of house building materials men contribute more than that of women (A. Mishra 2005). Commercial extraction of forest products has meant that traditional subsistence activities have been turned into income-generating occupations. Commercialisation has also meant greater interaction with traders and dealers and travel to market places. This has led to a situation where either the entire activity has been turned into a predominantly male activity or a division of labour has emerged where women and children join in collecting the forest products and male members take over the responsibility of selling the products. In either case the cash flows get concentrated in male hands. This is exactly what has happened in Dirang circle of Arunachal Pradesh, where a market for medicinal plants has developed in past few years. In neighbouring Nafra circle, with the opening of pine oil processing units, it is males who have taken over the collection of the oil, while women continue to shoulder the responsibility of collecting household consumption items from forests (Mishra 2007).

This multiplicity and diversification of livelihood sources have altered the foundation of the traditional labour institutions in the area. In the past most of the agricultural works were being carried out by using family and clan labour. Cooperation and labour-sharing were almost indispensable given the low population density and labour-intensive method of cultivation. The institutional arrangements for collective labour mobilization showed considerable tribe-to-tribe variations and it ranged from organized youth labour-groups called patang among the Apatanis to the spontaneous formation of groups under the Haria system in Papumare district (Furer-

Haimendrof, 1980: 43-44; Roy and Kuri, 2001:24). In our field surveys we observed two kinds of labour-sharing processes: generalized and specific (Mishra 2002a; 2006; Harriss-White, Mishra and Upadhyay, 2009). Under generalized cooperative labour-sharing, the entire village worked as a single unit. In such cases reciprocity was generalized and monitoring was a collective responsibility, institutionalized through the traditional village-level decision-making and enforcing structures. Two or more households, independent of other households in the village community, on the other hand, agreed upon specific labour-sharing arrangements. It was found during the field survey that in recent years generalized labour-sharing has been limited to work relating to religious festivals and village commons. In other spheres of economic activities, specific reciprocity was found to be the dominant mode of labour sharing. Under this system two types of sharing arrangements were noticed. In the first case two or more families combine their resources—primarily labour, but sometime other resources like implements, draft-animals as well—to carry out farm and forest related activities. The second form of specific labour sharing is in terms of mutually agreed number of labour days to be exchanged between the participating households. Here the range of cooperation and mutual commitment was found to be narrower than in the first case. Both these forms of specific labour sharing were noticed in all the villages, but the second case is increasingly becoming the standard practice. Under conditions of increasing environmental degradation, low-productivity and prevalence of a variety of risks, these labour sharing arrangements can be viewed as a general bilateral contract that involves resource pooling, risk dispersion and mutual insurance.

In Table 1, we have presented the emerging crisis in the institutional arrangements in the villages in Arunachal Pradesh and the challenges faced by these micro-level institutions. Although it is difficult to establish the causal mechanisms in such an institutional transition, most of these changes can be linked to the processes of increasing individualisation of land holdings, commoditisation of the productive resources and

Table 1

INSTITUTIONAL ARRANGEMENTS AND EMERGING CONFLICTS IN RESOURCE MANAGEMENT: A STYLIZED REPRESENTATION

Institutional Parameters	*Nature of Crisis/ Conflicts*	*Institutional Failure & Responses*
I. BOUNDARIES		
(i) Membership	• Immigration • Rural to urban migration • Shifting of villages to well communicated areas • Multiethnic rural centers	• Denial of participation to new members • Differentiated structure of rights • Accommodation
(ii) Ecological and Geographical boundaries	• Intra-village conflicts over demarcation • State and military establish-ments/ development activities • Unauthorized resource extraction by non-members and members	• Formation of intra village and multi-clan institutions • Mobilisation and demand for compensation • New monitoring arrangements • Reciprocal exchange • Reorganization of boundaries • Softening of allocation rules

II. GOVERNANCE		
(i) Governing body	• Multiple and competing institutional arrangements: traditional village councils/ headmen-vs.-new *panchayat raj* office bearers	• Accommodation of traditional chiefs in new institutional structures • Division of activities; rituals/ religious-vrs. Developmental initiatives
(ii) Governing Principle	• Economic inequality resulting in erosion of consensus	• Reinvention of traditional festivals • Conflict-management through symbolic redistribution
III. ALLOCATION RULES	• Peasant differentiation • Emergence of Tenancy & landlessness • Differential demand for Natural Resources (Timber and NTFP) • Conflict between resource extraction for self-use and commercial extraction activities	• Rising economic inequality • Lower levels of cooperation • Difficulty in collective Action
IV. MONITORING	• Shift of manpower, particularly the young to urban occupations	• Rotation rules fail • Substitution of physical work by monetary contribution • Decline in effectiveness of self monitoring/ switch over from

Institutional Parameters	*Nature of Crisis/ Conflicts*	*Institutional Failure & Responses*
		services rendered by members to paid services
V. CONFLICT RESOLUTION MECHANISMS	• Rise in the number and complexity of conflicts • Availability of Alternative channels for conflict resolution • Increasing gap between the clout of the neorich and the rural poor • Rise in the number of stakeholders in conflict	• Diminished efficiency and popularity of traditional institutions • Formation of multilevel institutions for conflict resolution • Increasing formalisation of procedures • Cooperation and conflict between the formal and informal conflict resolution mechanisms
VI. SANCTIONS	• Monetisation of the sanctions • Weakening of non-material sanctions	• Differential impact upon the rich and the poor
VII. AUTONOMY	• Increasing intervention by government bodies • Increasing power of business and corporate interests	• Formation of multilevel institutional networks • Decline in the effective authority of traditional institutions

Source: Adopted from Mishra (2004).

increasing state interventions. The opening up of state and market activities has led to large-scale immigration and as noted above the rural labour market has been substantially changed by this development. This has not only meant an increasing demographic pressure upon forest resources, but has also changed the nature of resource-consumption by households.

The response of the village communities to these new challenges emerging from demographic and economic changes ranges from passive acceptance to innovative, nuanced and sophisticated institutional responses. In some of the villages, for example, a differentiated structure of rights over forest resources has been developed, which clearly distinguishes between the claims of the original inhabitants and those of the new settlers. When village communities, particularly those in close proximity to urban centers, find it difficult to effectively monitor resource extraction by non-members, they have tried to develop a graduated system of entry fee, which can be both lump sum or ad valorem. With rising economic inequality, however, the allocation rules have been diluted to accommodate the interest of the rich.

The traditional rule that does not specify any quota on forest resources for self-consumption (mainly firewood, timber and bamboo for house construction), fails to monitor the resource-extraction because of relocation of households, in-migration of tenants, government officials and businessmen to the rural areas. But the substantial damage to the institutional structures at the local level has been done by the timber-trade, which has been restricted following an order by the Supreme Court of India. Timber extraction activities paved the way for emergence of a neo-rich contractor class who monopolised the supply contracts and hence the pattern of resource-use was transformed from a need-based one to a profit-oriented one. Apart from the environmental impact of deforestation, the institutional impact was that the traditional rules of resource-use, which had been designed in a resource-abundant context and hence involved almost zero costs of monitoring became redundant so rapidly that communities did not have the social capital to address the problem. The emergence of labour market itself transformed the labour sharing practices and since most of the traditional institutional mechanisms were based upon the implicit assumption of labour-shortage their distributive egalitarianism lost the capacity for conflict-minimisation.

The migration of the relatively richer and younger sections of the population to urban areas has led to the breakdown of collective monitoring and management practices. The attempt to impose a cash fine for absence has hardly altered the scenario. Along with the emergence of private property over agricultural land, the use of common property like forests for individual benefits has led to the creation of alternative institutional mechanisms mediated by the markets. The new institutional space provided by the panchayat raj institutions and the electoral democracy has effectively undermined the legitimacy of the traditional resource management practices. The simultaneous existence of alternative and competing sources of power and authority at the grass root level in some cases has resulted in 'institutional crowding out.'

IV. The Political Economy of Ethnicity and Development

The politics of identity and difference in northeast India has a long and complex history. The colonial project of building the empire and post-colonial politics of nation-building have created the broader context in which the ethnic landscape of North East India has taken shape. The extraordinary ethnic diversity in the region makes its politics more complex and fragmented, but the roots of the fragmented nature of the polity do not emanate from the coexistence of diverse ethnic groups alone, it also has resulted from the multiple ways external forces such as the state and capital have interacted with this diversity. One of the ways state and markets have interacted with and have changed the ethnic landscape of the region, at least since the encounters with colonialism, is the way property rights over crucial livelihood resources have been altered or created. The micro-ethnic communities had their respective institutions of governance at the community level and these institutional arrangements not only regulated the religious and social life of the members, but also governed access to a range of tangible and non-tangible resources that were crucial for the survival of the people.

Depending upon the resource endowment position of the community, its settings and type of economy these rules were different, well-defined or ambiguous, strictly or loosely applied. But the state-induced move towards modernisation and integration of the local economies with the boarder regional and national economies led to significant alterations in the way property rights were created, destroyed or rearranged to suit the demands of the changing economic and political contexts. Often, there is a tendency to view these changes through the binary prisms of 'destruction of the old and creation of the new' institutional forms. A detailed study of the changes in various dimensions of property rights and institutional mechanisms, however, shows that the transition was often complex (Harriss-White, Mishra and Upadhyay, 2009). It involved destruction, survival, adaptation and modifications of the pre-capitalist institutional structures, along with the creation of newer institutional forms. The institutional diversity and complexity that underlies such transitions are to be seen not simply as left-over of the past, but as the defining characteristics of the nature of capitalist transition in the region. What adds to the specificities of the situation is, of course, the continuing significance of the traditional institutions governing access to natural resources. The state and market forces are constantly interacting with and by implication are changing various dimensions of the resource management practices in Arunachal, but as of now, the institutional milieu is defined more by heterogeneity and hybridity rather than by institutional convergence. In a recent field survey in 11 villages in five districts of Arunachal Pradesh, Harriss-White, Mishra and Upadhyay (2009) have found that 'institutional adaptation, continuity and hybridity are as integral to the emergence of the market economy as are the processes of creation of new institutions and demise of others. There is no necessary correspondence between the emerging commercialization of the different productive dimensions of the agrarian economy. These uneven processes are deeply influenced by existing and emerging power relations and by the state.'

As the discussions in the earlier sections show, in Arunachal Pradesh, where nearly 63 percent of forests categorised as 'unclassified state forest' are in fact in the hands of village communities and clans, but the effective control of these forests varies a lot among the communities. Unconstrained individual property rights over land coexist with collective rights in forests. However, irrespective of the precise nature of property rights regime operating at the grounds there is an unmistakable tendency towards de facto privatisation of the ownership or at least use rights over forests. The individual ownership rights, particularly in regards to alienation rights are necessarily subject to community control in many areas (D Souza 2001: 46; Mishra 2006; Harriss-White, Mishra and Upadhyay 2009), but exploitation of forest resources, particularly timber, before the imposition of restrictions by the Supreme Court of India, has no doubt weakened the ethos of collective management. Apart from the environmental impact of deforestation, induced by the wanton exploitation of the 'common' forest for private gains, the institutional impact was that the traditional rules of resource-use, which had been designed in a resource-abundant context and hence involved almost zero costs of monitoring became redundant so rapidly that communities did not had the social capital to address the problem. The emergence of labour market itself transformed the labour sharing practices and since most of the traditional institutional mechanisms were based upon the implicit assumption of labour-shortage their distributive egalitarianism lost the capacity for conflict-minimisation (Mishra, 2002a; Mishra 2004).

Needless to add, the transformation of property relations has fastened the processes of peasant differentiation and landlessness has been increasing (Fernandes and Pereira 2005; Mishra, 2002a). It is important to note that this process of shift from what the communal economy to increasing economic and gender differentiation was not primarily because of factors like internal population growth (although migration from outside has played a significant catalytic role), but because of state interventions in terms of discouragement of shifting cultivation, provisions of incentive to 'progressive' farmers for growing commercial crops etc. The institutional strategies of agricultural extension services in these areas are based on the usual assumptions of an individual male, autonomous farmer as the decision maker in agriculture, which in turn has facilitated the processes of recognition of private property rights over land (Mishra, 2006). In Arunachal Pradesh studies show that although the state has not formally recognised private property rights in land, but has been a passive observer of the systematic informal transition to private property rights. In this informal transition, women, and other marginalised sections, tend to lose out (Mishra, 2003; 2007). Thus, in such contexts, the state, on the one hand, has facilitated the emergence of private property rights through a series of direct and indirect measures,* while on the other hand, by not taking cognisance of the move towards privatisation, it has virtually left the process in the hands of 'traditional' community institutions. These institutions, not withstanding their other strengths as institutions of decentralised, local-level governance, are hardly 'participatory' when it comes to women (Krishna, 2004; Goswami, 2002; Mishra and Upadhyay, 2007).

An important dimension of the development process in Arunachal Pradesh is the reworking of the 'traditional' community identities under the influence of the state-led modernisation drive. It is widely recognised that 'ethnicity is not a primordially given essence, but the outcome of complex socio-cultural and political processes of labeling and identifying people' (Peters, 1998: 400; Collier, 1998). The politics of identity and difference in Arunachal Pradesh, like elsewhere, involves

* The results of this survey indicate that the livelihood combination having the highest frequency is agriculture, combined with forest-based activities, animal husbandry and wage labour. The simpler combination of agriculture, forest and animal husbandry has also a significant presence. So, has the livelihood combination with agriculture, forest, animal husbandry and government service. Together, these three combinations explain the diversification strategy of around 60 per cent of all the households (Mishra, 2003).

considerable rediscovery and invention of the past in the light of the present and it has not only been influenced by the introduction of electoral democracy but also by the unequal distribution of the fruits and burdens of economic prosperity. The ethnic politics in northeast India has been an important aspect of the transition in the region, particularly in the context of the heavy military presence of the state and its relative inability to protect the life, livelihoods and dignity of its citizen (Baruah, 2004). The relative weakness of the state in safeguarding property rights and enforcing contracts typically creates a scope for the emergence of ethnic groups to provide private means of securing property rights (Bates, 1998). Unlike in many of the northeastern states, where this has resulted in the proliferation of numerous insurgent groups defending the interest of specific ethnic communities, in the case of Arunachal Pradesh, it has led to competitions and bargaining among different tribal groups to acquire a larger share of government's resources—a form of 'quiet pressure' exercised from within the system (Mishra and Upadhyay, 2007). Nevertheless, the overall framework of ethnic politics has weakened the 'universal' principles of civic rule to a considerable extent and has provided substantial scope for community leaders and elites to exercise considerable control over the everyday politics of survival and accumulation. This nature of politics has been possible within a specific kind of transition in the economic sphere, which has been shaped by as well as shapes the nature of the ethnic politics in the State.

The other significant dimension of this transition, noted in Harriss-White, Mishra and Upadhyay (2009) is that it is basically the non-agricultural surplus that has been the moving force behind this transition. Secondly, access to political power and resources of the state acted as key factors in the creation and sustenance of this surplus flow. Another source of surplus for the local elites, until recently, was the huge 'profits' from timber trade. Although timber trade was by and large controlled by the large-scale business from outside the State, the local business class, as junior partners and facilitators, managed to corner a substantial share for themselves. Some of them invested the surplus in establishing sawmills, plywood factories and transportation businesses. "Although in the first instance the timber trade appears to be independent of the state, the manner in which the state allowed the plundering of the commonly owned forests for private profit makes it clear that state support and protection was essential for the timber trade. While the forest department of the state government retained control over the supply of permits to cut trees, these permits were issued with such frequency and under such a framework of political patronage that community control over forests remained at best a minor irritant both for the traders," belonging to indigenous tribal groups as well as people from outside the State (Harriss-White, Mishra and Upadhyay, 2009).

Since state support was crucial for the surplus extraction activities of the elites and access to the resources of the state was being governed within the framework ethnic politics, it was quite natural for the elites to protect the institutional diversities that provided a scope for them to exercise control and power at the local level. To put it rather crudely, the ability of the local elites to draw a share from the state's resources or to extract a rent from the state or the outsiders, depended upon their ability to perpetuate the politics of ethnicity and difference on the one hand and also on their capacity to represent their 'community' in the competition over tangible and non-tangible resources. Thus, while state has been influential in initiating the capitalist transition and also in changing the community institution in diverse ways, the overall framework of ethnic politics, in turn, has created the context in which the politics of democracy and state intervention is being played out today.

V. Concluding Remarks

The sustainable ecological practices and institutional mechanisms for natural resource management among many tribal communities have often been projected as an alternative to market-mediated or state-controlled natural resource management. This paper attempts to look at the changes in local-level institutional arrangements for natural resource management along with the changes in agrarian relations in rural Arunachal Pradesh. Along with individualization of property-rights and peasant differentiation, and the consequent changes in labour-use patterns, the 'traditional' institutional mechanisms for natural resource managements face new crises. These institutional arrangements do not necessarily have the social capital to devise new monitoring and allocation mechanisms in the face of rising inequality, heterogeneity of interests and loss of autonomous space for decision-making. Thus, the dynamics of community-level institutional arrangements can probably be better understood by endogenising the emerging power relations in the context of differential access to productive resources rather than an essentialised and homogenised notion of 'community.'

The simultaneous existence of several institutional modes in the rural economy of Arunachal Pradesh, notwithstanding its peculiarities, raises specific doubts about the notion of 'dissolution of the old and emergence of the new' institutional forms that has informed the studies on agrarian changes for decades. Institutional diversity appears not to be an impediment to the development of capitalist relations, but, under the specific conditions mentioned here, it is this diversity and complexity of institutional mechanisms that has helped the tribal elites to accumulate and invest the surplus generated within and outside agriculture. The state, while undermining the authority of the traditional community institutions through its developmental initiatives, nevertheless, has created new spaces for assertion of identities. By invoking the notion of community rights selectively, the tribal elites have not only been able to acquire large chunks of land, but also have been able to 'capture' the local state for their own benefits. In such a context, there is need to move beyond the analytical prism of the state-vs-community or the state-vs.-market framework and to take note of the existing and emerging differentiations within and across the communities.

Notes

1. Jean-Marie Baland and Jean-Philippe Platteau, (1996): *Halting Degradation of Natural Resources: Is there a Role for Rural Communities?*, Rome: FAO.
2. Sanjib Baruah, (2004): "Historicizing Ethnic Politics in North East India," Keynote Address, Seminar on *Inter-ethnic Conflict and Ethnic Crisis in North East India*, Department of Political Science, Dibrugarh University, 16-17 Feb. 2004.
3. Robert H. Bates, (1998): "Comment on Structure and Strategy in Ethnic Conflict," in Donald L. Horowitz in Boris Bleskovic and Joseph E. Stiglitz (eds.), *Annual World Bank Conference on Development Economics*, Washington: World Bank, pp. 371-376.
4. B.N. Bordoloi, (1998): "Tribal land Tenure System and Land Alienation in Northeast India," in *Antiquity to Modernity in Tribal India*, Vol. III, S.N. Mishra (ed.), New Delhi: Inter-India.
5. T. J. Byres, (1996): *Capitalism from Above and Capitalism from Below: An Essay in Comparative Political Economy*, London: Macmillan Press.
6. Paul Collier, (1998): "The Political Economy of Ethnicity," in Boris Bleskovic and Joseph E. Stiglitz (eds.), *Annual World Bank Conference on Development Economics*, World Bank: Washington, pp. 387-399.
7. Alphonsus D. Souza, (2001): *Traditional systems of forest conservation in North East India: The Angami Tribe of Nagaland*, Guwahati: North Eastern Social Research Centre.
8. G. Das, (1995): *Tribes of Arunachal Pradesh in Transition*, New Delhi: Vikas.
9. H. Demsetz, (1967): "Toward a Theory of Property Rights," *American Economic Review*, 57 (May): 347-359.
10. R.K. Deori, (1982): *The Sulungs*, Shillong: Department of Research, Government of Arunachal Pradesh.
11. P.C. Dutta, (2003); *Tribal Chieftanship*, Itanagar and New Delhi: Himalayan Publishers.
12. Walter Fernandes, (nondated) Tribal Customary and Formal Law Interface in North Eastern India: Implications for Land Relations, available at siteresources.worldbank.org/INTINDIA/Resources/walter_fernandes_paper.doc retrieved on 5th Sept 2007.
13. Walter Fernandes and M. Pereira, (2005): *Changing Land Relations and Ethnic Conflicts: The Case of North Eastern India*, Guwahati: North Eastern Social Research Centre.

14. C.J.N. Gibbs and D.W. Bromely, (1991): "Institutional arrangements for Management of Rural Resources: Common-Property Regimes," in F. Berkes, (ed.), *Common Property Resources: Ecology and Community-based Sustainable Development*, Dehradun: International Book Distributor.
15. A. Goswami, (2002): "Introduction," in: A. Goswami (ed.), *Traditional Self-governing Institutions among the Hill Tribes of North East India*, New Delhi: Akansha.
16. Government of Arunachal Pradesh (2006): *Arunachal Pradesh: Human Development Report 2005*, Itanagar: Government of Arunachal Pradesh.
17. Susan Hanna, Carl Folke and Karl-Goran Maler, (1995): "Property Rights and Environmental Resources," in Susan Hanna and Mohan Munasinghe (eds.), *Property Rights and the Environment: Social and Ecological Issues*, Washington: The Beijer International Institute of Ecological Economics and the World Bank.
18. Barbara Harriss-White, (2003): "On Understanding Markets as Social and Political Institutions in Developing Economies," in Ha-Joon Chang (ed.): *Rethinking Development Economics*, London: Anthem Press, pp. 481-497.
19. Barbara Harriss-White, Deepak K. Mishra and Vandana Upadhyay, (2009): "Institutional Diversity and Capitalist Transition: The Political Economy of Agrarian Change in Rural Arunachal Pradesh," *Journal of Agrarian Change*, 9 (4), pp. 512-547.
20. A. Turton Hart, Gillian and B. White, (eds.), (1989): *Agrarian Transformations: Local Processes and the State in Southeast Asia*, Berkeley: University of California Press.
21. Gillian Hart, (1989): "Agrarian Change in the Context of State Patronage," in: *Agrarian Transformations: Local Processes and the State in Southeast Asia*, (eds.), Gillian Hart, A. Turton and B. White, 31-49. Berkeley: University of California Press.
22. N.S. Jodha, (2001): *Life on the Edge: Sustaining Agriculture and Community Resources in Fragile Environments*, New Delhi: Oxford University Press.
23. P.C. Kar, (1982): *The Garos in Transition*, New Delhi: Cosmo Publication.
24. S. Krishna, (2004): "Gender, Tribe and Political Participation: Control of Natural Resources in North Eastern India," in: Sumi Krishna (ed.), *Livelihood and Gender: Equity in Community Resource Management*, New Delhi: Sage.

25. Melissa Leach, Robin Mearns and Ian Scoones, (1999): "Environmental Entitlements: Dynamics and Institutions in Community-based Natural Resource Management," *World Development*, Vol. 27, No. 2: 225-247.
26. Caroline Marak, (2002); "Matriliny and Education among the Garo," in: Walter Fernandes and Sanjay Barbora (eds.), *Changing Women's Status in India: Focus on the North East*, Guwahati: North Eastern Social Research Centre., pp. 159-165.
27. A. Mishra, (2005); *A Study of Economic Transformation, Environmental Degradation and Female Work Participation in Arunachal Pradesh*, Ph.D. Thesis submitted to Rajiv Gandhi University, Itanagar.
28. A. Mishra, (2006): "Occupational Structure and Gender-based segregation in North East India: The Case of Arunachal Pradesh," *Social Change and Development*, 4(1), pp. 125-145.
29. Deepak K. Mishra and V. Upadhyay, (2007): "In the Name of the Community: Gender, Development and Governance in Arunachal Pradesh," in: Sumi Krishna (ed.), *Women's Livelihoods Rights: Recasting Citizenship for Development*, New Delhi: Sage Publications India, pp. 167-208.
30. Deepak K. Mishra and V. Upadhyay, (2008): *Background paper on Agriculture and Allied Sectors*, Arunachal Pradesh State Development Report, draft.
31. Deepak K. Mishra, (2001): "Political Economy of Agrarian Change in Arunachal," *Man and Development*, 23 (3): 40-50.
32. Deepak K. Mishra, (2002a): "Agrarian Structure and Labour-Use Patterns in Rural Arunachal Pradesh: A Case Study," *Arunachal University Research Journal*, 5 (2): 31-56.
33. Deepak K. Mishra, (2002b): "Institutional Arrangements and Agrarian Structure during periods of Transition: Evidence from Rural Arunachal Pradesh," in: *Sustainable Agriculture, Poverty and Food Security: Agenda for Asian Economies*, S.S. Acharya (eds.), Surjit Singh and V. Sagar, Vol. 2, 891-902. Jaipur: Rawat Publications.
34. Deepak K. Mishra, (2003): *Environmental Degradation and Changing Livelihood Strategies in Rural Arunachal Pradesh*, paper presented at the 45th Annual Conference of the Indian Society of Labour Economics, Kolkata, 15-17 Dec.
35. Deepak K. Mishra, (2004): "Institutional Sustainability in Natural Resource Management: A Study on Arunachal Pradesh (India)," *Asian Profile*, 32 (6).
36. Deepak K. Mishra, (2006): "Institutional Specificities and

Agrarian Transformation in Arunachal Pradesh: Changing Realities and Emerging Challenges," *Indian Journal of Agricultural Economics*, 61 (3): 314-27.

37. Deepak K. Mishra, (2007): "Gender, Forests and Livelihoods: A Note on the Political Economy of Transition in North East India," *Social Change*, 37 (4): 65-90.
38. S.N. Mishra, (1983): "Arunachal's Tribal Economic Formation and Their Dissolution," *Economic and Political Weekly*, 18 (43): 1837-46.
39. B.P. Misra, (1979): "Kirata Karyokinesis: Mode of production in Tribal Communities of North East India," in *Agrarian Relations in India*, A. N. Das and V. Nilkanth (eds.), Delhi: Manohar.
40. Amitava Mitra and Deepak K. Mishra (2006): *The Complexities of the Commons: Environmental Resource Consumption Pattern in Rural Arunachal Pradesh*, paper presented at the 9th Biennial International Conference of The International Society of Ecological Economics, New Delhi, December 16-18.
41. D.C. North, (1990): *Institutions, Institutional Change and Economic Performance*, Cambridge: Cambridge University Press.
42. E. Ostrom, (1990): *Governing the Commons: The Evolution of Institutions for Collective Action*, Cambridge: Cambridge University Press.
43. E. Ostrom, (2000): "Collective Action and the Evolution of Social Norms," *Journal of Economic Perspectives*, 14(3): 137-158.
44. V. Ostrom, D. Freny and H. Picht (eds.), (1993): *Rethinking Institutional Analysis and Development*, San Fransisco: ICS Press.
45. B.B. Pandey, D.K. Duarah and N. Sarkar (eds.), (1999): *Tribal Village Councils of Arunachal Pradesh*, Itanagar: Directorate of Research, Government of Arunachal Pradesh.
46. Pauline E. Peters, (1998): "Comment on The Political Economy of Ethnicity" by Paul Collier, in: Boris Bleskovic and Joseph E. Stiglitz (ed.), *Annual World Bank Conference on Development Economics*, World Bank: Washington
47. Assem Prakash and Anil K. Gupta (1997): "Ecologically Sustainable Institutions," in: Smith, Frasser (ed.), *Environmental Sustainability: Practical Global Implications*, Florida: St. Lucie Press, Boca: Raton.
48. N.C. Roy and P.K. Kuri, (1995): "Traditional Institution of Land Ownership and Risk-Coping Mechanism in Rural Arunachal Pradesh," *Resarun*, 21(1-2).
49. N.C. Roy and P.K. Kuri, (2001): *Land Reforms in Arunachal Pradesh*, New Delhi: Classical Publishing House.

50. J. Toye, (1995): "The New Institutional Economics and Its Implication for Development Theory," in J. Harriss, J. Hunter and Colin M Lewis (eds.), *The New Institutional Economics and Third World Development*, London and New York: Routledge.

22

NORTH EAST PROBLEMS
From Economics to Political Economy

Amar Yumnam

Introduction

This paper traces the evolution of national policy in so far as the North Eastern Region is concerned. It elaborates on how regional development policies and programmes in India have been derailed by political considerations right from the end of the Third Five Year Plan. It also explains how the so-called national security perspective has played havoc with the economy and society of the region. The main thrust of the paper is on the issues to be focused in the nation-building process, particularly so given the exogeneity of Indian political institutions to the region. Finally, it emphasises on adopting a development (economic) perspective rather than a security perspective so that the nation building process is carried forward.

GoI Approach

The approach of the Government of India (GoI) to the

development needs of the North Eastern Region (NER) has been well-summarized by the High Level Commission, popularly known as the Shukla Commission thus: The North East tends to be seen as a distant post, some kind of land's end. Yet it was until recently a crossroads and a bridge to Southeast and East Asia, with its great rivers ending in ocean terminals................ the North East must be enabled to grow at its own pace and in accordance with its own genius It cannot he treated merely as a resource region, market dump and transit yard. There is a strong resentment over what is seen as an earlier phase of "colonial exploitation" in which wealth was extracted for others' enrichment such a path of development is not advocated.[1] The lack of or level of development the NER, particularly Manipur, has reached would be evident from the other papers in this issue. My concern in this paper would be to appreciate the basic impacts the policies purportedly meant for development have had on other aspects instead of fostering development.[2] My fundamental argument in this paper is to show how the various policies have rather led to nurturing and fostering political competition rather than economic competition.

The Macrofoundations

Before we come to the microfoundations and the approaches adopted specifically for the region, it would be in place how the regional development policy has evolved in India during the period before 1991.[3] For those who have interest in the general academic aspect of regional balance, there are three must reads written by Myrdal, Hirschman and Williamson.[4] My concern here, however, is with the policy approaches as reflected in the plan and policy documents of the GoI.

The *First Five Year Plan of* India was on a rush order basis. Its main aim was to stabilize and rehabilitate the economy from the devastating effects of the Second World War and the partition of the country.[5] The basic thrust behind the Plan was that without a substantial increase in the production of food and raw materials needed for industry it would be impossible to sustain a higher tempo of industrial development.[6] The Plan recognized that the excessive concentration of industries brings in its wake certain economic and social disadvantages and a wider diffusion of industry is desirable from this larger point of view. Further, if industrial development in the country is to proceed rapidly and in a balanced manner, increasingly greater attention will have to be paid to the development of those states and regions which have so far remained backward.[7] This understanding, however, could not be translated into action as the plan remained essentially a rehabilitation plan and the share of industry in the total outlay was low. The development of industries in India was, till 1991, mainly regulated by the Industries (Development and Regulation) Act, 1951. The First Schedule of this Act gives a detailed list of the industries which are to be under the control of the central Government.[8] In 1954, the Indian Parliament passed a resolution that the basic aim of economic policy should be a socialistic pattern of society. Two years later, the GoI came out with the Industrial Policy Resolution (1956) which had continued to be the guiding principle of India's industrialization policy. This policy resolution notes: In order that industrialization may benefit the economy of the country as a whole, it is important that disparities in levels of development between different regions should be progressively reduced. Only by securing a balanced and coordinated development of the industrial and the agricultural economy in each region, can the entire country attain higher standards of living.

It was in this background that the Second Five Year Plan was formulated. Though it talked of progressive reduction of regional disparities, it essentially remained a plan for the promotion of basic industries and labour intensive consumer industries. It emphasized rapid industrialization and diversification of the economy as the core of development. But if industrialization is to be rapid enough the country must aim at developing basic industries and industries which make the machines needed for further development.[9] It continues: Investment in basic industries creates demands for consumer goods, but it does not enlarge the supply of consumer goods in the short run; nor does it directly absorb any large quantities of labour. A balanced pattern of industrialization, therefore, requires a well organized effort to utilize labour for increasing the much needed consumer goods in a manner which economises the use of capital.[10] But we all are aware of what happened to the Second Plan which was abandoned mid way.

From the angle of regional development policy as well as from the basic thrust of this paper, what is of utmost relevance are the developments during the Third and Fourth Five Year Plans. For the first time, the Third Five Year Plan approached the problem of industrialization from the wider perspective of balanced regional development, and devoted an entire chapter on it. It pointed out: There are many examples both of countries and of regions within a country in which, with limited development in industry, an appreciable rise in living standards has been achieved through the fuller utilization of local natural and human resources. There are also instances of areas around massive projects where no great impact on the levels of living of the people is to be observed. Apart from the basic and capital goods industries and other large industries, there are other industries whose possibilities need to be fully explored such as labour intensive industries of the traditional type, small scale industries of modem type, agricultural processing industries, forest industries, assembly operations, and recreational industries Each region should endeavour to identify, plan for and promote industries which are specially suited to its conditions and for which it can provide relatively greater facilities.[11] This Plan proposed the setting up of industrial development areas in backward regions where basic facilities like power, water and communications are to be provided, and factory sites developed and offered for sale or on long lease to prospective entrepreneurs.[12] It also put forward the concept of large projects as regional growth nuclei. It recognized that balanced regional development involved the preferential treatment of backward regions in the location of training facilities for engineers, craftsmen, etc., training programs to facilitate labour mobility and engender the growth of small and medium entrepreneurs. It also gave importance to dispersal of small scale industries. But most of the various comprehensive statements made by the Third Plan on balanced regional development remained a mere charter of intentions.[13]

By the end of the Third Five Year Plan, it was admitted that in terms of regional development, there has been a natural tendency for new enterprises and investments to gravitate towards the already overcrowded metropolitan areas because they are better endowed with economic and social infrastructure. Not enough has been done to restrain this process: While a certain measure of dispersal has been achieved, a much larger effort is necessary to bring about greater dispersal of industrial activity.[14] The necessity of specific policy instruments designed exclusively to promote industrial development in backward areas was recognized during this period. The Committee of the National Development Council decided in its meeting on 13 September, 1968 to set up two working groups, one dealing with the identification of backward areas and another with the incentives for starting new industries in backward areas.[15] The first one dealing with the identification of backward areas is commonly known as the Pande Working Group and the second dealing with the incentives as the Wanchoo Working Group. These two working groups were set up by the Planning Commission in pursuance of the National Development Council resolution. The Pande Working Group submitted its report on Identification of Backward Areas in February 1969 and the Wanchoo Working Group on Fiscal and Financial Incentives for Starting Industries in Backward Areas in April 1969. Whereas the criteria suggested by these two working groups for identification of backwardness and provision of financial and fiscal incentives might be of little relevance here, I must hasten to add that both the groups put emphasis on identification of backwardness at the State or Union Territory levels. This orientation of the two groups proved to be absolutely consequential for the issue whether it was political competition or economic competition at the countrywide level to be fostered. The basic thrust of the two groups to identify backwardness at the State or Union Territory level and to devise incentives accordingly did not meet the political desires of the larger and economically already more powerful States. Well the rest should be understandable. These later States started their own political mobilizations before the recommendations of the two reports were converted into policy. The politically as well as economically weaker States like Manipur were in no position to match the weight of their larger and stronger counterparts in other parts of the country. The two reports were finally put for consideration in the meeting of the National Development Council in September 1969. The two main decisions taken in this meeting are quite significant.

1. Concessions to be offered by credit and financial institutions for financing industries in backward areas should be available to all the backward areas in all the States and Union Territories. When time comes for decisions, the larger, economically and politically, States could easily prevail their options over those of the economically and politically smaller States; and
2. The criteria to be adopted for identification of industrially backward districts may be settled by the Planning Commission in consultation with the State Governments and the financial institutions in the background of the recommendations of the two working groups. When it comes to investments, the economically and politically larger States would definitely satisfy the requirements of the financial institutions better than the economically and politically smaller States. This static perspective, however, completely ignores the dynamic requirements of building a pluralistic nation almost the size of a subcontinent.

The turnaround was now complete. And it has yet remained there only. The messages emerging from the entire process were as follows:

(a) The backwardness of States like Manipur was to be treated on par with the backwardness of some districts in Maharashtra, Gujarat, etc. This, as mentioned above, would satisfy the immediate static principles of economic optimization, but not the long term dynamic

needs of fostering a nation-wide economic strength and competition; and

(*b*) Whatever the longer-term economic compulsions, the ultimate decision would be based on political weights and political aims driven by short run static arguments. The needs of economically and politically smaller States like Manipur could naturally not fulfil the static principles of optimization better than the larger States.

Such a message for political competition[16] rather than equipping for economic competition on equal footing has had its deleterious impact on the psyches of the larger population of backward States like Manipur, States weak both economically and politically in terms of the national decision making structure. This has completely disoriented the perspective of the political class in the region as well. For the last quarter century or so, the one basis on which the political leaders in the NER have been requesting funds is the need to fight insurgency. This serves the twin purpose of catering to the political orientation of national decision making and stunting the economic articulation of the population in the region. This overall macro perspective of the GoI was accompanied by other national approaches towards the region and region's own weaknesses which together have played havoc with the development process of the region.

The Micro

The NER in the 1950s just could not articulate its own development future.[17] It was during this period that the GoI evolved and adopted an approach towards the region which has fundamentally remained the same till today.[18] The GoI adopted an approach founded on two edifices. The first edifice was one of non-interference into the traditional socio-economic structure of the region. The second was national security perspective. Since the NER could not articulate itself its own development future and given the low level of understanding and appreciation of the region among the policy makers In Delhi, the surest shortcut to policy was one based on security.

So security emerged as the guiding principle for all policy interventions, development or otherwise, in the region. The security principle or rather the insecurity of the GoI drove the GoI to adopt the Armed Forces Special Powers Act (Assam and Manipur) way back in 1958 when there was hardly any insurgency In the region. The GoI could never get rid of its insecurity and abandon the security principle even when it belatedly realized that the NER needed a development agency for transformation. As a result, when the North Eastern Council (which should have been there in 1958 Instead of the Armed Forces Special Powers Act) was established in the early 1970s, it was placed under the Home Ministry. But the Home Ministry could never evolve a development strategy for the region as It is neither competent nor oriented for such a task. This politicization of economic issues has reached its height recently with the requirement of certificates from the Home Ministry for the provincial government to get funds sanctioned from the Ministry of Finance.

The Result

The concatenation of the above three crucial factors—basing national policy for regional development on political weights, region's inability to articulate its own development agenda, and the GoI's approach of basing policies towards the region on security principle—has stunted the evolution of a spontaneous economic awareness in the region, has kept the people of the region occupied in tackling the transitory political issues, and has thus kept them away from articulating any kind of economic agenda for mutual cooperation and competition. This has further had the following unfortunate impacts:

Since no common economic agenda has emerged, it was not costly for any group to articulate its own political agenda as it would involve no economic cost to the group. This is how fractionalization has intensified in the region with definitely deleterious implications for both region and nation.[19] Since no common economic framework has emerged, the dichotomy between the hill economy and the economy of the plains has intensified. Examining the road infrastructure situation of

Manipur, an international team of experts, which included the present author, observed in 1999: One can easily deduce from the district-wise road-density figures the kind of transport bottlenecks being faced in the hilly areas superimpose this on the difficult terrain of the hills and the problem is really enormous. This makes the hill economy a much more costly as compared to the valley economy, and, in turn, serves as a double constraint on development. Firstly, because of the low level of economic activity in the hills, real wages are law there, and secondly, due to higher transport costs, prices are higher in the hills.[20] What is most unfortunate for all of us is that such problems do not get highlighted or articulated by any group. This scenario is to be appreciated from various angles. First, there is the divergence of ethnic groups in the region, and this internally homogeneous and heterogeneous[21] with each other population is settled in more or less spatially contiguous and homogeneous areas. Secondly, not only is there non-emergence of a common economic frame and interdependent growth, but also there is the issue of growth slow down in the region during the 1970s and 1980s;

As a result all the social organizations in the region are now involved in political competition and political up-manship rather than articulating the developmental needs of the general population. This has had the even more unfortunate effect of politicizing the all-important event of decennial census. The trend now is each ethnic group (majority of the many groups) trying to over enumerate its own population in the census as a means to get more out of any intervention. This is seen more among smaller ethnic groups in their efforts to establish a politically equal playing capacity vis-à-vis larger ethnic groups. Such a trend has emerged because a feature of deciding on economic matters on the basis of political weight age rather than economic compulsions has been made inherent in most of our significant development interventions. This has had second round impact of each group articulating, as no economic cost is involved, to have a separate and autonomous administrative unit as that is seen as the only means for any advancement whatsoever. In other words, the dominant articulations in the region are now particular community-centric or specific area-centric. The casualties naturally have been the articulation of an economic agenda, and the building up of a region-wide and across-the-communities articulation for development.

The concept of nation is highly contested in the NER. In fact, it is as if the nation-building process has yet to be initiated micro and macro-wise.

Notes

1. Government of India (1997), *Transforming the Northeast: Tackling Backlog in Basic Minimum Services and Infrastructural Needs,* Planning Commission, pp. 2-3.
2. Whereas the Manipurs merger with India in 1949 was expected to establish and strengthen the foundations for development in the province, it has not even been able to sustain the bases created by the British, and capitalize on the massive social capital mobilized during 1950s to mid-1960s. Cf. D. Acemoglu, 5. Johnson and 3. A. Robinson (2001), "The colonial origins of comparative development: an empirical Investigation", *American Economic Review,* Vol. 91, pp. 1369 - 1402.
3. This dividing line of 1991 is used for practically the very issue of regional balance has been taken out of the agenda with the adoption of structural adjustment programs in this year whereby planning has been put to the backburner, and privatization and liberalization are now the guiding principles of any economic policy.
4. Gunnar Myrdal, (1973): *Economic Theory and Underdeveloped Regions,* Vora, Bombay Chapter 3; Hirschman, Albert O., (1958), *The Strategy of Economic Development,* Yale University Press, New Haven/London, Chapter 10; Williamson, Jeffrey G., (1965), "Regional inequality and the process of national development: a description of the patterns," *Economic Development and Cultural Change,* Vol. 13, pp. 3-45.
5. This attempt to address the adverse partition effects was confined to those felt in the northwestern and eastern parts of the country, but the absolutely deleterious economic impact on the NER went unnoticed.
6. Government of India, (1952), The *First Five Year-Plan,* Planning Commission, p. 44.

7. Ibid., p. 442.
8. This list is so detailed as to cover the entire gamut of industries. Nonetheless, Section 25 of the Act provides for the delegation of power to the State Government or other bodies by a notified order of the Central Government.
9. Government of India, (1956), Second Five Year Plan, Planning Commission, p. 25.
10. Ibid.
11. Government of India, (1961), Third Five Year Plan, Planning Commission, p. 143.
12. Ibid., p. 149.
13. K.V. Sundaram, (1978): "Some recent trends in regional development planning in India", in R. P. Misra, D.V. Urs, (eds.), *Regional Planning and National Development*, Vikas, New Delhi, p. 78.
14. Government of India, (1970), Fourth Five Year Plan, Planning Commission, p. 11.
15. This is the most significant occasion in India's balanced regional development planning attempts for the fallouts of the reports of these two groups shaped the politicking for funds in the subsequent periods.
16. Political competition I have in mind is not the one of competition through the electoral process which can be good both for democracy and development. What I have in mind is the articulation of every issue on political grounds for political reasons and without in any case reflecting the economic situation of the places and people. Cf. Besley, Timothy, Torsten Person and Daniel Sturm, (2005), *Political Competition and Economic Performance: Theory and Evidence from the United States*, Working Paper 11484, NBER.
17. Amar Yumnam, (2004): Regional Cooperation and Development. Strategy for Development in a Conflict Zone, Paper read at the National Seminar on Towards a New Asia. Transnationalism and Northeast India, organized by the Centre for Northeast India, South and Southeast Asia Studies, OKD Institute of Social Change and Development, Guwahati, 10-11 September. See also Atul Sarma, (2005a), "Why the northeastern states continue to decelerate", *Man and Society*, Spring, pp. 1-20; Atul Sarma, (2005b), "Northeast as Gateway to Southeast Asia: Big Dream and Home Truths," Presidential Address, Seventh Annual Conference of North Eastern Economic Association, Itanagar, October 21.

18. See references in note 20.
19. The literature on fractionalization is by now fairly rich. See, for instance, Robert H. Bates, (1999), *Ethnicity, Capital Formation and Conflict*, CID Working Paper 27, Harvard University, and Tan, Chi h Ming, (2005), *No One True Path: Uncovering the Interplay between Geography*, Institutions and Fractionalization in Economic Development, Mimeo., Tufts University.
20. Government of Manipur, Public Works Department, (1999), Strategic Options Study, Project Coordinating Consultancy Services, World Bank Study, pp. 3-27.
21. Cf. Pons-Vignon, Nicolas and Henri-Bernard Solignac Lecomte, (2004), *Land, Violent Conflict and Development*, Working Paper No. 233, OECD Development Centre.

23

ENGLISH, A COLONIAL LANGUAGE
Its Impact and Impression on North Eastern States

Achla Sonker & Shubhra Rajput

The North East in India is a region as interesting and varied as India itself. It comprises of the eight states of Assam, Arunachal Pradesh, Manipur, Meghalaya, Mizoram, Nagaland, Sikkim and Tripura. These states are not only diverse and varied with respect to their resources, level of industrialization as well as infrastructural facility but also this diversity can be seen in their social stratification in terms of cultural and traditional faith. Most accounts and discussion about northeast point out its diversity in people, flora-fauna, vibrant culture, rich natural resources, especially water and forests. Given this richness and vibrancy there is a feeling that the region could potentially be one of the wealthiest regions of India. Yet several indicators reveal not so rosy a picture.

The north eastern region of India is one of the least developed and most problematic. The colonial rulers have paid little attention to the development these regions and their colonial policies has sown the seeds of separatism in the region by their "Line Regulation of 1874" were the tribal population were administered under a succession of extraordinary provisions that segregated them in categories called "non regulated" or "excluded area,"[1] to these areas outsiders were prohibited except for those who obtained special permission. Thus north eastern regions have remained separated and segregated from the other parts of India and this can be one of the causes for the backwardness in these regions. The industrial sector here has mainly grown around tea, timber in Assam and mining, saw mills and plywood factories in other regions, the economy of these regions is still primarily agrarian and its full potential is yet to be exploited. Since agriculture and industry has not really taken off in spite of the potential in the form of vast unexploited resource base available in the region could be said to be the main cause of economic underdevelopment and unemployment in these region. In spite of some progress in a few of northeastern states overall growth rates over the past years have remained low, poverty incidence is high, and there are still a number of areas subject to continued violence. "Several reports document natural resource degradation, depleting the very assets that are usually highlighted as offering the greatest potential for growth and development in the region. Thus in recent years, the region has missed out on the economic growth acceleration witnessed in much of India."[2]

Even the social structure of North East is many folds, there are more than 75 major population groups and subgroups, "speaking more than 500 languages and dialects of which there are about 168 in Arunachal Pradesh, 95 in Nagaland, 87 in Manipur, 100 in Tripura, 200 in Assam, Meghalaya and Mizoram."[3] Thus one can say that northeast agitation also has roots in linguistic sentiments. The north east represents a unique fusion of different racial and linguistic elements. The ethnic groups are demanding autonomy for protecting their land, culture, conserving their language, customs and traditions. North East India which consists of different nationalities has their own history, language and ancestral culture and these factors distinguish them from mainstream. With backwardness, deprivation, exploitation and lack of economic development, the region has become a breeding ground for protests, which has led to insurgencies. Practically every state in the entire North East is not without an insurgent group fighting for the establishment of varied goals ranging from creation of homeland within the Indian union to outright secession.

In a multi structured societies such as it exist in northeast, ethnic assertions in the form of socio-political tensions, autonomy movements and the struggle for a separate political entity have become a widespread phenomenon and have posed a serious challenge to the state. British imperialistic thought of a unique way to rule over these regions by insulating the area and kept it more or less as a pocket of exotic tribal culture. The territory has remained cut off from the main current of socio-economic and political changes in the country not only during the British regime but also after independent India for many years. Referring to the British administration in the region it may be noted that some of the British policies also caused adverse effect on the social life in the region. However British rulers made concessions to the Christian missionaries to develop their base in these regions which brought a breath of relief to the north eastern states as they not only spread Christian faith among these people but also helped in the spread of education and gave them one language, English as a tool to communicate among themselves. English is their main link language largely as a result of British commercial, colonial and educational influence.

During the British rule the administration of the area was mainly involved in the maintenance of law and order and any kind of development in these regions has to face intense social obstacles due to the people's initial indifference to any kind of advancement, lack of technical education and primitive method of production. Even the administrative and political seclusion of the state by the British imperialist resulted in a feeling of alienation and wounded the sentiments of northeasters badly. North East states are poor and underdeveloped and among the various factors the main reason for their underdevelopment is the lack of good roads and developed system of communications; compelling the tribes to live in splendid isolation resulting in the rise to economic difficulties due to the dearth of capital, lack of infrastructure facilities and limited potentialities of the area. Since the territory is devoid of any major mineral resources hence whatever the progress was achieved has not been substantial.

In pre British period north east provinces as they were so called had neither systematic political intuition nor explicit judicial system. Thus it appears from the history of British expedition to north east provinces and their subsequent administrative control over these provinces, that their main aim in the beginning was to maintain peace, law and order. And in this attempt imperialists brought in Inner Line Regulation in order to cut off their link between the hills of northeast regions and other parts of the country. Even then there were revolts and clashes of the hill tribes in the regulated areas. Consequently the British rulers gave up the idea of complete subjugation however on the other hand; they followed more subtle but aggressive policy. "The British rulers in these areas superimposed the capitalist civilization on the tribal people who began to feel the impact of the new material and mental needs. As a result, demand for the goods and the ideas of the new world arose."[4] Imperialist rulers in an effort to satiate the new develop interest of the people of these regions not only educated them but also opened the world of new religion and language to the tribes.

Northeastern region was mostly a home of tribes which were like other primitive people believed in spirits who has to be pleased through various sacrifices and offerings in order to have good health, good harvest and general well-being. However all these primitive religious practices have since been discarded and forgotten as these people found in Christianity a new religion and embraced it with "so much dedication and submission that their entire social life and thought process have altogether transformed to an extent which is amazing."[5] The colonist allowed foreign Christian missionaries to enter the remotest hill areas under the protection of guns. Patronized by the rulers these missionaries with the sole motive started to win over the simple tribesmen by means of seeking their religious conversions. These missionaries also laid the foundation of road building, religion and educational development. And slowly in course of a few decades, a vocal middle class came up in each tribe which became the prop and support of British rule.

In the beginning, people of various northeastern states were hostile to the Christian missionaries. They reacted sharply and thought of missionaries a destructing force of their individuality and identity but very soon, they responded and the message of Christianity started spreading. Christianity has made tremendous advancement in north eastern society they gave them freedom from the heavy burden of costly sacrifices and feasts. The new converts not only felt themselves free from yoke but nothing happened to them when they broke the laws of spirits. This created a solid base for these missionaries converting people of these regions in large folds and it soon became a fashion to be a Christian. In addition, "freedom from the fear of evils, hour able position in the society and good qualification for getting employment, all these things made conversion to Christianity attractive."[6] Today, however, north east frontiers traditional religion or belief is of academic interest.

The spread of Christianity in north east province started almost at the same point, according to the arrangement made by the colonist different areas were parceled out among different missions. "The first Christian missionary Rev. William Williams of Welsh-Calvinistic church stationed in Khasi hills visited Mizoram in 1891 and communicated to the Mizos about Christian God." It was in 1893-94 that Rev. F.W. Savidge and J.H. Lorrian came, toured the district and worked hard to learn and reduce the language to writing, using Roman script. "They translated the gospels and also wrote a grammar and dictionary containing seven thousand words, which was published by the Government in 1898,"[7] almost similar work of this capacity and dedication as being done by the Christian missionaries in the entire north east province which laid the foundation of all educational work. Thus they gave the supreme gift of "language and literature," to the people of north east and prevented

Bengali from becoming the trade and court language.

Once these missionaries have established themselves in the good faith among the north east people by giving them language, literature and a new faith the missionaries had taken steps to establish church which should be self supporting, self governing, and self propagating so that it belonged in the fullest sense to the north east people. The money received was used for education, medical work and the production of literature so that people might be trained to take full responsibility in every field of church's life in the shortest possible time. This was done with a purpose as to have a stronghold over the individual's mind and his daily life at all levels and of age-group. Christian missionaries by involving themselves into social, evangelical work, educational work and medical relief work not only won the faith but also the hearts of these people, in them they found their new ally the impact of which was to stay in the years to come.

Colonist has taken education to be an important tool of conversion for in these regions people had been speaking different languages which proved as a hurdle for people to unify. British rulers and missionaries established Lower Primary, Upper Primary, Middle and High Schools through which they used to do spiritual and educational work for the people who in turn helped the spread of British views as well as Christian faith. McCall recorded that it was "chiefly due to missionary effort, the rate of literacy in Lushai Hills reached 12.9 per cent in 1931 to 19.3 per cent in 1941."[8] They imparted general education, discipline, cleanliness, Christian love, service for others and sharing of gospels. Colonist and their missionaries were also the pioneers in literature work which always accompanied the educational work. These missionaries brought with them the printing press and set up the teaching institutions with a view to getting Christian literature, scriptures, hymn books, school text books and other useful literatures printed. These printed literatures were distributed among the locals and they were encouraged to read. Thus educational progress made by the Missions with their own funds as gauged from all India census report is remarkable.

It will certainly not be out of place to mention here that while in plains, Christian missionaries were mainly engaged in evangelical works, in tribal areas, some of them engaged in politics. As Pandit Jawaharlal Nehru observed in Kohima, on March 30, 1953, "The works of the Missionaries were not clean of politics."[9] They worked on the three fold method in order to achieve their aim: by isolating the district, British colonial regime also protected and helped these missionaries and lastly a sympathetic attitude backed by the acts of practical piety like providing medical facilities and opening schools. Besides educational work, the missionaries were engaged in medical and philanthropic works like caring for orphans and opening of Mission Hospitals. Help, in the beginning, given to the villagers, in the form of medicines was greatly appreciated and it went a long way towards winning their confidence. With the coming of Christianity, ancient feuds ceased to exist and the clans, even the tribes merged and inter married, while retaining the clan names.

Thus Church became a centre of power and patronage which has helped eradicate many evil practices and customs and replaced them with modern intellectual pursuits like the spread of western education, literacy and improved ways of living. They were not only the religious and cultural agency but also an employment of the educated youth who took to teaching and preaching as a black coated occupation, as McCall wrote, "Local educational practice soon gave rise to the belief that education and Christianity were the passport to the salaried job, relief from wearisome toil of cultivating a hard land."[10] However one cannot deny the fact that in spite of their benevolent and humane works these missionaries never tried to help the native people to stand on their own feet neither they established any new industries nor introduced the improved agricultural methods they were functioning for the consolidation of the British rule which resulted in the social imbalance which aggravated with times even after independence.

But at the same time, facts should not be forgotten that it was because of these missionaries, their colonial language and education which brought in the lives of the north east people a new unexplored world. And as the years rolled on, the light of Christianity radiated to the distant corners of the north east frontiers they were the first to establish and acquiring a due sense of unity, centering round a common religion and by the common faith. Today however on e finds a situation quite contrary socio cultural diversity is leading to the emergence the problem of assimilation due to the rise of insurgent groups even then over the past decades, after independence economic development, population growth, growing educational opportunities, commercialization of live hoods, and increasing interaction between the northeastern people, peninsular India, and the south eastern neighbors have started to change the region's social and economic fabric and the outlook on the development challenges. These states has been infused with a new sense of urgency into road building programs, modern methods of production permanent and terrace cultivation show the light of progressive change in the attitude of the north east people. Economic development along with government sponsored urbanization has brought about significant changes in the structure of the economy yet a planned effort is never then less needed to circumvent bottle necks and develop the area.

Development in the region have herald a down of new era in the region with so far deprived of individuality and equality. A silent revolution is been undertaken to illuminate these regions both the centre and the states need to engage themselves on this serious issues if the desired result are to be obtained. But what one can't deny is the role of colonist and their language to have initially started a thought process towards the development and awareness of the new society that benefited northeast people to embark on the path of success with confidence in the age of globalization.

Notes

1. Archana Upadhaya, "Terrisom in North East: Linkage and

implication," *Economic and Political Weekly*. New Delhi, p. 34.
2. *Yojana*, Dec. 2008, Vol. 52, S.B. Sharan (ed.), p. 3.
3. Data from North East Council, 2004.
4. R.N. Prasad, (1987): *Government and Politics in Mizoram*, Northern Book Centre, New Delhi, p. 64-65.
5. Ibid., p. 64.
6. Ibid., p. 66.
7. Ibid., p. 64.
8. Major A.G. McCal, (1949): *Lushai Crysalis*, Londen, p. 208.
9. A.K. Bhattarcharjee, (1987): *Political Evolution of Nagaland*, The Book Trust, Calcutta, p. 39.
10. Major A.G. McCal, (1949): *op. cit.*, p. 205.

24

MAJULI: THE HERITAGE RIVER ISLAND, ASSAM

Dileep Medhi

Introduction

Majuli (26° 45′-27°12′ N & 93°39′-94°35′ E) is vast fresh water River Island of the World. It is the largest *Vaishnavite* cultural centre of Assam Region, which drew attention of entire India in the fifties of Last Century when great Saint Sankardeva propagated the *Neo-Vaishnavite* religion in Indian Subcontinent. The Island stands at 84.5 m AMSL in the upper reaches of River Brahmaputra and harbours 1.6 Lakhs of tribal and non-tribal population who has a much wealthy culture heritage. An earthquake of 1950 did severe damage to the Island and since then Majuli wasted almost 1/3rd of its existence till to date and thus jeopardize the entire landmass and its rich heritage culture. It is continuously shrinking now since the time of 1972 when severe erosion hit the Island after 1950.

Background

Majuli in the midst of River Brahmaputra is famous for its agrarian life ways and grows well almost all kinds of cereals, particularly rice in its annually accumulated fertile alluvia. It is popularly called the 'bowl of rice.' Further Majuli holds an important status in regards to the *Vaishnavite* religion and its institutions, which is unique all over the World and, which provides privilege to the devotees to directly pray to the Almighty. That is why Majuli attracted the common people engaged in farming and cattle grazing and brought them close to the great Saint Shri Shri Sankardeva and his followers since the decade of fifties and also the ancient rulers of India in the past. Enjoyable, charismatic and serene environment and most importantly its accessibility by river transport gave Majuli an important position in ancient Assam. Ancient records as par the *Jogini Tantra,* a Tantric literature in Sanskrit of 16th Century AD, King Dharmapal, a Khetriya King from the mainland India, initially established a kingdom in Assam with its capital west to Guwahati. Later on his successors made their capital at Ratanpur in Majuli. Dharmapal brought a section of Brahmins and nobles from northern part of mainland India. *Kendu Kulai,* a sage of eminence of that time lived in his kingdom. Padma Narayan, Chandra Narayan and others including Ram Chandra (Mayamatta) ruled from Ratanpur, which finally became the capital of a number of Kings. Kusaranya, son of Harabinda, which *Dipika Chand* mentioned, successfully ruled over Gaur, Kamrupa and Jaintia from the capital township of Ratanpur. However owing to a change in the course of River Brahmaputra, the well-reputed Ratanpur was eroded away (Gait, 1905).

Ratnadhvaj, a Chutiya King along with his successors Mayamatta and Arimatta (Mayamatta's son), continued to rule from Ratanpur. Subsequently Samudra, a minister of prominence in the court of Arimatta did throw away the rule of Arimatta and drove out Arimatta's son, Ratna Singh from the Kingdom. Manohar, the son of Samudra succeeded his father. Manohar's had a daughter and she gave birth to two sons- Santanu and Gamanta. At that time Assam was considered as a land of the Mlechhas with a dominating religion of *Saktaism;* however the *Vaishnavism,* the other form of religion made a gradual but significant appearance in the Assam Region. Prevalence of *Shaktism* enabled the people to sacrifice animals and also the human being to a considerable extent and emergence of Vaishnavism began to give new knowledge to the humanity over the Assam about the effects of such kind of cruelty of sacrifice and gradually made people to give up the tradition of sacrificing animals and humans. Santanu became loyal to *Vaishnavism* and Gamanta continued with the fold of *Saktaism;* consequently there was a split between the two brothers. Santanu and his son decided to shift to Rampur in Nagaon, while Samanta stayed back at Lakhimpur. Santanu and his son successfully ruled, and maintained distance from the Kachari Kingdom of Central Assam and the Chutiya Kingdom of Sadiya. The great Ahoms subjugated the Kacharis and the Chutiyas later. Meanwhile Rajdhar, an informidable descendant in the line of the Santanu and who were identified as the great Bhuyan family of Assam, settled at Bardowa in Nagaon.

Without mentioning the famous name of great Saint Shri Shri Sankardeva and his religion, any reference to Majuli River Island can never be complete, and therefore this write-up had to travel a long to finally arrive at Bardowa on the southern bank of River Brahmaputra near Nagaon, a domain of the Bhuyan chiefdom. Kusumbar was the grandson of Santanu and was the proud father of *Jagat* Guru Shri Shri Sankardeva of 15th Century AD.

Ratanpur in Majuli continued to remain the capital till 1189 Century AD and Gauri Narayan with his popular name as Ratnadhvaj Pal of Boro community ruled from here. In fact Ratanpur changed its name to Majuli in course of time because of its location in between the River Kherkatia *Suti,* a tributary south to River Brahmaputra and the Brahmaputra itself. River Brahmaputra embraced the course of Kherkatia Suti afterward and began to flow around Ratanpur. Earlier *Mājāli* (a landmass in midst that resembles a road) was the initial name of Majuli, which represents Ratanpur, the former capital of Assam. *Charit Puthi* or the chronicles/histories of the great *Vaishnavas* and *Mahapurusahas* (the great human beings) of 15th and 16th Centuries AD give the reference of Majuli as *Mājāli.*

In course of time Ahom began to subjugate the small Kings

and Chiefs those were ruling at different parts of Assam and dominated the entire region from its capital towns of Gargaon and Sibsagar. Ahom rulers mostly believed in sacrifice of animals including man in their animistic religious traditions although there were a section of people in their Kingdom, who avoided doing this kind of heinous practices. Sankardeva after he was born in 1949 began to preach a religion of *Neo-Vaishnavism* and was engaged in the research and development to his religious ideals from two places in Majuli-Dhuyanhat and Belguri. Around 1510 Century AD Ahom rule prominently figured in the history of Assam. Majuli River Island was relatively outside the influence of the Ahom's animistic religion, which was having a strong bias of Mlecha tradition already existed in the region, and therefore Saint Shri Shri Sankardeva preferred to live in the peaceful environment of Majuli. During the period of his stay at Majuli Saint Sankardeva did develop number of novel thoughts and ideas that helped him in creating and composing a good number of drama, stimulating dance and engrossing music those very well bear a resemblance to the Classical dance and particularly the music of mainland India. Another but strikingly most significant development was Sankardeva's coming together with Madhabdeva in 1523 Century AD and latter became the greatest disciple to the Saint for his life time and later. Madhabdeva who was originally a believer of *Saktaism* that prescribes the sacrifice of living organisms mentioned earlier, could understand the great person and the religion of Saint Sankardeva to believing in one God, the almighty Krishna that preaches no harm or violence to to any living creatures including bringing a reform amongst the people and societies of that time. This great union of Saint Sankardeva with Madhabdeva in the Island of Majuli is termed as *Mani-Kanchan Sanjoga or Joga* meaning a union of 'beads to gold' in the history of *Neo-Vaishnavism*. The Brahmins who were much close to the Ahom rulers could not tolerate Saint Sankardeva and his new religion and began to lodge irrelevant complaints to the Ahom ruler to bullying him. Initially Saint Shri Shri Sankardeva left Gangmow owing to such kind of harassment and finally left Majuli to Barpeta in Lower Assam.

At that point of time, Naranarayana ruled Lower Assam and he was good Sanskrit scholar and could very well understand the new religion of Saint Shri Shri Sanakardeva.

Madhabdeva was a versatile scholar and mastered the Sanskrit and other ancient Assamese languages, and composed Namghosa with all the essence from Shrimad Bhagabata and other Sanskrit literatures on Hindu mythology. Saint Sankardeva made him the torchbearer of the Neo-Vaishnavite religion after his death. But this irritated the prominent Brahmin devotees of Sankardeva and brought a division between his Brahmana and the Non-Brahmana devotees. They however did not reject the great ideas of Sankardeva to establishing the s and allied religious complex with a Namghar, surrounded by the residential hamlets of the devotees. The Brahmana devotees those include Damodar deva and Hari deva reintroduced the system of worshipping Lord Krishna via the assistance of a priest inside the *manikut* or *sanctum sanctorium* although the *Charit puthis* (Chronicle) never confirm this kind of change in the attitude of these two disciples of Saint Snkardeva but this approach appears to be an open challenge was later introduced by the Brahmin communities who were always at daggers drawn with Saint Sankardeva and his religious faiths; however the tradition of mass prayer called *Nam-Prasanga* remained to the confine of the main Namghar. Sattras like Auniati, Dakkshipat and Garmur continued to follow the Brahmana gurus and dhikars (custodians) of Brahmin caste group. Uttar Kamalabari, Natun Kamalabari, Chamoguri and Bhogpur preserved the statuesque of the great guru Sankardeva. Altogether 22 s were established in the Majuli River Island in the past, and River Brahmaputra eroded away many of them.

The Environment and the Geographical Features

The Island has been formed with change of course of the river Brahmaputra as well as the tributaries from time to time. Some more references on the Majuli Islands are found in the text of the "Third Division of Assam, Majuli or the Great Island," in the book, *An account of Assam* by Dr. John Peter Wade, 1972-93. "Majuli then was constituted with 13 (thirteen) *Chaparis* or small Islands intersected by channels of communication by boat between the Dihing and Lohit, which in reality, it concerts into a cluster of Islands and in addition to these, numerous smaller Island range the whole length, formed by various branches of the principal streams. Some of these were always overflowed in the season of inundation, others occasionally only; all possess a stratum of rich soil above a deeper layer of sand or soil clay."

The geographical feature of Majuli was entirely different when it was visited by Saint Shri Shri Sankardeva. 'From mouth (out fall of the river Subansiri up to Kherkotia Suti the river Island which stretches along was "Majali" or "Majuli" in between the Lohitya (Lohit) and the Dihing river. At that time Lohitya (Lohit) was flowing parallel to the Dihing from Kherkatia suti and fell into Mahuramukh. From Mahuramukh, the upper part of it was known as the Dihing. The Dikhow, Desang, Disai and Dhansiri were tributaries of the River Dihing.

According to Gait Edward at that time (1822 A.D.) the Brahmaputra was flowing along the present channel of Brahmaputra to the south of the Island. After receiving Desang and Dikhow, Dihing had its confluence with the Brahmaputra at the western extreme of the island. Still at an earlier period, Dihing is believed to flow to the Brahmaputra further eastward than the Burhi-Dihing does now. River Dikhow had an independent course further down at far as Kajalimukh, part of which still survive in the Majuli as the Tuni river, and part in Nagaon, as the Kalang."

In 1671, the Dihing changed its course to have its confluence into the upper Lohit. According to Mr. Gait and Captain Billock, River Dihing with a feral flood of great intensity divested the entire area in 1735 when the Brahmaputra after abandoning its course followed the deserted channel of Dihing.

According to the census of 1971, the geographical area of the island (including some *Chars* or *Chapari* area) was 924.60 sq.kms but the actual spread over of the island with smaller islets, as per record of Revenue was 1246 sq.kms. The island is located to the north of the Jorhat Sub-Division and is now a Civil Sub-Division with Headquarters at Garmur since 25th January, 1978. Currently its jurisdiction is bordered by the river

Brahmaputra on the South, the river Subansiri (Lohit) on the North-West and Kherkotia on North East and it extends up to the confluence of Rivers Brahmaputra and Subansiri.

Culture

Assam is a land of river and swamps. Almost all the rivers are navigable and people had to travel via river routes to different destinations of the region in the past. Country boats were used for sailing in addition to temporarily built rafts of bamboo and plantain plants. Rivers from the north and the south had confluences with the River Brahmaputra and therefore the River Brahmaputra was largely used for human transportation and also for shipping of all kinds of commodities to distant localities for marketing as well as for human consumption. Merchants and traders undoubtedly discovered Majuli in course of their business and social activities. Majuli later on with its enormous potentials brought a number of rulers to her territory as mentioned previously. Finally the island received a large Miri population, now popularly called the Mishing from former NEFA, now Arunachal Pradesh. However in depicting the heritage culture of Majuli, popular stories of Mahabharata are largely referred to. Lord Krishna visited Sonitpur, Bhismak Nagar, Ashwakranta in addition to Majuli of Assam on different occasions. Majuli is considered as a recreational ground of Lord Krishna who visited the Island on the days of Ras Purnima (Full Moon day) in the month of Kartika (October/November) to engage in recreation with his beloved *gopinis*. People largely believe in this story, and therefore Ras festival is celebrated in the different s and other places of Majuli with a 3-day cultural programme. People perform music, dance, drama (bhaona) and other programmes of merriment of Neo-Vaishnavite origin. Large numbers of visitors come to Majuli at this time. Further it is also believed that a language called *Brajavali* (a language that is spoken at Mathura and Brindavan of mainland India) was in use at Majuli in the past. Ras festival falls in the winter and visitors could see during these days huge flocks of migratory birds in the swamps of Majuli. With an enchanting beauty of world class, Majuli can equally give the visitors a broad spectrum of a unpolluted environment in the Brahmaputra valley.

Having mentioned this, it must be put on record that it is the great Saint Shri Shri Sankardeva who in fact, brought Majuli into the limelight to the people of Assam in particular and to the people of mainland India in general when he inducted all the cultural traits of *Neo-Vaishnavism* in the 15th Century AD. Saint Shri Shri Sankardeva could make a huge research and development programmes at Majuli with the able cooperation of the people over there. He established the s or the monasteries with a traditional temple called Namghar at the centre of the complex surrounded by four different lanes of resident devotees recruited from amongst the common masses. Apart from the religious performances, the devotees get training in different art and craft making like fan-making from bamboo, cane and betel nut stalk, wooden plate with stand, basketry, canoe building and mask-making. Devotees are also acquainted with knowledge of paper making from the skin of Sachi plant, cotton and bamboo leaves. Scholars in the past wrote all kinds of books-much particularly the religious ones in such papers. Further more every village women-folk irrespective of tribal and non-tribal origin have excellent expertise of handloom textile including spinning. They can produce yarn of cotton, silk and endi cocoons and produce magnificent textile products that include *gamocha, miri-jim, mekhela-chaddar* of cotton and silk with beautiful floral designs and *eri chaddar*.

Mishing, a tribal community with a former name, the Miri live in the platform houses made of bamboo, reeds and cane having a gabbled roof with a hay/thatch topping. They are basically farmers and have an excellent food habit; their menu comprises boiled rice, meat, fish and plenty of vegetables-wild and domestic supplemented by two varieties of local wines-one from boiled rice and another from ashes of paddy straws. Non-tribal population lives in similarly constructed houses but very precisely their houses are constructed on ground plinth and floor. They normally do not prepare any kind of rice wines but love to share the rice wines of the Mishing. Their food habit however differs little and they love to have curry of different lentils, which they either cultivate or purchase from market and use mustard oil as medium of cooking while the Mishing take mostly boiled foods.

Majuli has an ancient tradition of pottery making by hand. The Kumar Kalita of Majuli make varieties of earthenware, much particularly large and small variety of pitchers from finest clay that they dig out from around 20 m deep at the bed of the River Brahmaputra. Similar to the handmade potteries produced in other parts of Assam, the womenfolk of the Kumar Kalita are engaged in this pottery-making tradition. Majuli wares have a good demand and it is either exchanged or traded with a number of communities on both the banks of the River Brahmaputra extending to the territories of Arunachal Pradesh. The male folks and also traders from different localities use country boats for this purpose. Nowadays mechanized country boats are used.

The heritage Island is a well-known territory of fête and carnivals those are organized in different Sattras established since the time of 15th Century AD. Ras, *Palnam* and different *Kirttans* together with staging of Hindu mythological drama—the *Bhaona* are the regular festivals and celebrations, which attract large number of visitors both domestic and international annually. *Bhaonas* are indigenous creation of Saint Shri Shri Sankardeva. Further the Mishing communities celebrate the *Ali-ya-ligang* after harvest of new crop with great enthusiasm.

Majuli Island prior to 1950 earthquake had an area of approximately 1250 sq kms. However, after the great earthquake, erosion of the River Brahmaputra in this reach became highly active and a part of the southwestern side of the Island was washed away. This further threatened the Island and its enormously rich natural and cultural heritage as well. One third of the Sattras of the Island had to be abandoned and was shifted to the north and south banks of the Brahmaputra. Such an impact naturally distributed the cultural heritage of the Island elsewhere and proliferated in those places.

Modern lifestyle of the Island begins to affect physically with the introduction of modern building materials that replace the naturally available reeds, thatching grass, bamboo and wood; today handloom textile competes with modern ones. Original costumes of dances and drama are equally affected. However, cultural heritage of the Sattras has not been influenced by modernity, and the Sattradhikars of every Sattras are successfully safeguarding their original style, composition and content as was set up during 15th Century AD by the founder of the unique heritage Sattra organization of former Assam after *Jagat* Guru Saint Shri Shri Sankardeva.

References

Chatterjii, S.K., (1970): *The Place of Assam in the History and Civilization of India* (2nd Print), Guwahati, Gauhati University.

Dimbeswar, Neog, (1963): *Jagat-Guru Sankardev*, Nagaon, Assam, India: Sreemant Sankar Mission.

Gait, Sir Edward, (1905): *A History of Assam* (Indian Reprint), Guwahati: ABH Publisher.

Maheswar, Neog, (1967): *Sankardeva*, New Delhi: National Book Trust.

25

THE ENCHANTING HERITAGE OF CULTURE
North East India

Alka Chadha

The North East India enfolds in its arms places like Arunachal Pradesh, Assam, Meghalaya, Mizoram, Nagaland and Tripura, which presents the vibrant picture of the panorama of rich and enchanting art, craft and culture. Whether it's the architecture of the regions, the engravings, the jewellery, the musical instruments, the silk weaving, the bamboo bridges (Urokthong), the crafts like the basket-making, the umbrellas (Yenpak), the toys or the effigies and images, all are the reflection of the talent or the artistry that engulfs the area. From a small thing to a big thing, one can see the 'hand-made' impression.

"North East India (erstwhile greater Assam) remained peripheral in horizon of Sanskritization that brought in social and cultural changes within broad outline of the Indian civilization."[1] The excavations have brought up stupa-like stone edifices, along with rock cut relief images of many Hindu deities. The oldest pious structure, Tawang monastery of Mahayana-Vajrayana is located in Western Kamang district and Hinayana

Buddhist complex in Tirap district of Arunachal Pradesh. Umachal rock-cut inscriptions, coins and copper plate inscriptions by Hindu and Ahom kings introduced as a part of writing tradition, terracotta plaques or bricks and bark or leaf manuscripts, present a big vision of the angles which gave birth to an intriguing culture. Besides the common craft of cane and bamboo in all regions, Arunachal Pradesh has to its credit crafts like things made out of goat's hair, ivory, boar's tusks, brass, wood carving, carpet making, masks, hand-made pottery and even weaving. The tag of manuscripts made on Agaru tree bark or Sanchi Pat and later on, on Tula Pat—a kind of hand-made paper adds more to the embellishment of the zone. Many Buddhist monasteries here like in Dirang, Jang, Shangti, Shergaon and in Assam are treasuries of the manuscripts. Tai manuscripts have been found in Hinayana monasteries or Bapusang located in Lohit District. Most of the Mahayana manuscripts, reflecting Buddhist philosophy and related themes, found in Arunachal Pradesh are scripted and written in Tibetan language. "Regional office of Archaeological Survey of India in Guwahati had registered about 250 manuscripts in North East India as antiquities...110 manuscripts are in collection of Department of Antiquarian and Historical Studies, Assam, including 157 illustrated manuscripts. Kamarupa Anusandhan Samity, Guwahati is another institution having large collection of manuscripts...600 or so in Vaishnava monasteries (Satra) and many in Namghars (prayer halls)."[2] The most famous illustrated manuscripts from Brahmaputra valley are Bhagawat, Kirtan, Usha Haran, Shailya Parba and Hastividyarnava (illustrated treatise on study of elephants).

Meghalaya is known for the artistic endi silk weaving and the unique craft of pineapple leaves' fibre articles like nets, bags and purses. Dances like Nohkjot, Mastieh, Shad wait and Shadynti bring more vibrancy to the culture. Handloom weaving trend of endi, muga and mulberry silk also prevails in Assam. Sholapith, fibre craft, ivory, brass and bell metal works are also part of the culture. Basketry, shell and beads articles, bird's wings and flowers products, daily-use utensils, earthen pot making without the use of wheel and wood carvings linked with religious aspects add colour to the culture of Nagaland. Tripura is famous for its bamboo screens, lamps, mats and handloom with its vertical and horizontal striped weaving and dispersed colourful embroidery.

This zone has always been distinct for its architecture. Though there are new developments and changes, still one can see the traditional forms of *Hoomdaang* or lower roof support and *U-ra* or upper roof support houses with thatched roof. Wooden pillars have taken the place of bamboo pillars but the south-western corner or worshipping space of *Sanamahi (Meitei-household diety)* still has the conventional setup. The specialty of the typical Meitei house is the construction without the use of the nails to secure or link the beams with each other. The holes are drilled on the bamboo and then cane and bamboo splits called *Punjeis* are driven into the holes to lock the parts together. *Kangthak-haaba* or pile-dwelling style with bamboo-mat walls and extended verandah of bamboo was the style used by Chin-Kuki groups to build their houses. In Jiribam, just like thatch, the roof is made by cut and smashed pieces of bamboo by laying them one upon another. At many places like Tamenlong, Naga groups arrange vertically split bamboo poles by alternatively putting them up and down. The traditional Hindu architectural styles and high influence of the buildings of Bengal grant richness to the architecture of Manipur. They are mostly constructed with bamboos and the layout of the temples traces the traditional style of construction of North Eastern state in India. Parabolic contours are found almost in all Manipuri temples. Mahabali, Tangal and Govindajee temple commonly share a structural design with hut shape and parabolic contours. Kakching Narsingh Thakur, Krishna Chandra temple at Kakhing bazaar, Krishna temple at Krishnampat are the perfect examples of Shikhara style. And the blend of these two styles of shikhara and pagoda is Kamakhya temple in Hiyangthang Lairenbi. The Brahamanical rule of Vastushastra is mostly found in all temples and buildings in Manipur. "The main structure has a square piece of land in middle, which signifies Panchratna plan with Brahma in centre and other gods on all sides...Every temple has a Mandapa. The most creative part of Mandapa is the paintings that depict the love story of Khamba Thoibi."[3]

Many engravings on rocks at Tharon, Khonpum and Salunghat also contribute to the enrichment of art of Manipur. One can see a perfect blend of Typography, inhabitation and fauna in the simple and indicative drawings. In some, heads of buffalo are shown with mithun figure and at some places human forms are drawn with round heads, biconcave geometric body and semi-circular legs. Animals like pig and horse, weapons like spears and swords also adorn the rocks. At a place in Khonpum, "there is also a design of female genital organ. This must be because of the tantric influence."[4]

Hand woven and embroidered textiles—shawls, blankets, bedcovers; cushions and mats made out of water reed *(Kounaphak)*; double weave mat *(Phak)*, block printed towels or cloth or *Khamen Chatpa*—used to present to honour someone and in religious ceremonies too, all add to the charm of handicrafts and textile weaving, regionally known as *Laichamphi*. This Society which comprises of Meities—the industrious, the Bamons or Brahmins, the Pangans or Muslims and lower caste Lois, celebrates festivals and fairs like Yaoshang, Dol yatra, Rath yatra, Durga puja; Kut and Ningol Chakuba. The feet tapping rhythmic dance of tribal men—*Thabal Chongba* and tribal women, adorned in attractive traditional dresses and elaborate jewellery and their enchanting musical forms like Lai Haroba Ishei and Pena Ishei weave another intricate pattern in the culture of the North East. Even the impression of artistry is visible in bamboo-made flute-like musical instrument called *Puleh, Toutri* or *Theibe* by different tribes. The Lambang tribals play *Relru*—a one metre long hollow bamboo tube with attached projection in middle through which one blows to give birth to musical notes. *Paya* is another instrument made up of configured fine bamboo splits.

The use of dyed bamboo can be seen in beautifully created baskets too, which are used for numerous purposes like to measure rice *(Miruk)*, for washing winnowed rice *(Cheng Chamuk)*, for picking out rice chaffs, weeds, pebbles, steamed rice *(Irang)*, for marriage and some religious occasions *(Lukmai)*, fish basket *(Kaijara)*, elongated-necked and narrow-mouthed basket for not letting the fish jump out (Shou), ones with domed lid *(Chengbon)* and conical ones for carrying things with straps to be balanced on head. Besides all this, the baskets are also used in making effigies and images. Woven basket effigies are utilized to inaugurate a new house, to drive evil spirits away and even for death rituals in memory of forefathers. At the time of festivals like Umunglai Haroaba of Sylvan deities, masks made up of brass are placed inside the baskets woven of bamboo splits by the Meitei priest *(Maiba)* and the priestess *(Maibi)*, which is the symbolic representation of the deity. For creating the image, the cloth is then draped around the basket to depict the body or form of the deity. On the completion of the festivities, the mask and clothes are removed and the basket is treasured and preserved in the temple for use at the next Haroaba.

Myriad kinds of umbrellas are very unique as per their function for different motives. There are ones to be worn over head *(Yenkhrung)* while working in fields or on move to protect from the scorching sun and the rain. Another kind is for protecting things from rain *(Salaitep)* while carrying conical baskets and *Yengoi* is used at the times of a person's death for the goodbye ritual. *Totems* are the huge umbrellas made of circular bamboo rings used for honouring deities, sacred events, in temples and even in death ceremonies.

Another major place which holds a great place in reflecting the craft and culture of North East is Nagaland. It's an area with no caste system despite many tribes, dialects, languages and other cultural traits. Here, all tribes have a few common traditions like bidding dead off on a raised platform, a very contradictory custom of common sleeping house for unmarried men which are a taboo to women on one hand and on the other hand, a live-in relation before marriage between a couple. This land has many sites worth seeing and known for their importance for something or another like Kohima (state capital famous for war cemetery for soldiers who sacrificed their lives during World War II), Khonoma village for its valour for fighting battle against British in 1879 and Shangnyu village for its wooden monument which is believed to have been made by heavenly angels. Many places are now open to international visitors also, like Dimapur, Wokha, Mokochung, Japfu peak, Mt. Saramati and Mt. Tempu.

Wood carving in Nagaland has its own uniqueness for not only cultural but religious grounds also. The tribes like Wanchos, Konyaks and Phom are known for their expertise in wood carving. The purposes for carving are to cut out images of a deceased or funerary image or of some important person, decoration of Morungs or men's communal houses and head-hunting. Wanchos have a tradition of making the young man search for the hidden wooden dummy from fields of enemy or rival, kill it, be victorious and then only marry. Head of the human figure is carved out in low relief, very realistic and with great care. Tattoos, jewellery and hair are intricately designed. Morungs are made attractive by adornments on pillars by high relief carvings of human figures, animals and other rhythmic patterns. Every animal represents the symbolic nature of the boy, for instance, tiger makes nature ferocious, elephant reflects strength and hornbill is aiming at fertility. The Wooden gates or *Kharu* are also engraved with motives.

Wherever the eye roams, the essence of rich cultural heritage is ubiquitous, whether its intriguing social customs, awesome architecture, captivating dance or colourful attire and festivals. The chain diversifies and moves on an on like an incantation.

Notes

1. www.indiadivine.org/articles/918/1/Textual-Tradition-of-North East-India-Antiquity-and-continuity
2. Ibid.
3. www.mapofindia.com / Manipur /society-and-culture
4. www.webindia123.com /Manipur /art /art.htm
5. http:// ignca.nic.in/craft153.htm

26

CULTURAL TRANSFORMATION OF TAI AHOMS OF NORTH EAST INDIA

Manjari Mehrotra

Assam : The Citadel of Ethno-centrism

An area of upper Assam, locally referred to as the 'Ujjani Aham', evokes a plethora of symbols, expressions and emotions which are linked together by the Lohit River. Here a community of people is coming together under a banner called the Tai-Ahom to form an identity which is separate from the Indian national identity. The term Tai-Ahom is very recent in Assam but no one knows what does Tai-Ahom actually means.

Assam is very often called an 'anthropologer's paradise' and a museum of nationalities for sheltering numerous population, and segments of diverse ethnic affiliations, a variety of social structures and plethora of cultural heritages. The tribes and communities inhabiting this part of the country have spanned composite socio-cultural entities and ethnic patterns by exchanging both their cultural and biological traits. But much of the traditions and customs, habits and manners of the various people of this part of the world have escaped the gaze of the world outside.[1] The Ahoms form such a community who entered Assam in the 13th century.

Assam through the Prism of History

A large number of works based on the historiography of the Ahoms are available but studies concerning other aspects are lacking. Infact, in the present globalized world, cross national identities of people and the formation of multi-ethnic societies, shaped through migrations and commerce are important issues. While regional politics have created national borders, cultural processes and encounters transcend such political boundaries. In a dynamic world changes are inevitable. Under changed social conditions, social relations among the people as well as groups are liable to be affected. This is also true of the Ahoms of the Brahmaputra valley. The Tais are a group who are spread across South and Southeast Asia and China. The paper endeavours to focus on the changed social aspects of this community and purports to show their cultural ties with the indigenous people who were ultimately brought into the Hindu cultural fold by the process of acculturation.

Human identity is inextricably woven through the process of culture. So it becomes very important to map a cultural construction in working out relations between ethnic minorities and the nation states in which they are located.[2] Identity is bound to be ambivalence, being constantly reshaped through negotiations and coercion at different levels- local, national and transnational. Analysing the historical process and phases that constructed a new Tai Ahom identity one can explore how the Tai Ahom is a term claimed and presented as being partly Assamese, Indian and Thai but it does not fully approximates any one of them. Identity as a 'thing' can be lost and found through ethnic mobilization or national imagination.[3] It becomes very important to note that culture is a process, which is achieved through negotiations between the symbolic cultures and historical circumstances. Thus culture of an ethnic community is constructed by a discourse on identity within a historical process. In this process the study of past becomes decisive. The role of language and religion and related customs in defining a culture is also meaningful.[4]

The complex and intricate relationship pattern between history, memory and identity are well evident in the contemporary Tai-Ahom identity movement, which took place in Assam. This is basically constructed contemporaneously through a process of appropriation and contestation to create a Tai Ahom identity and to differentiate it from the regional and Indian national identity.

The Coming of Ahoms

The Ahoms ruled over Assam for nearly 600 years 1225-1826 A.D. and they had a separate entity of their own based on their ethnicity, culture and belief-system. At present they form a distinctive and dominant segment of the population of Assam. It may be stated here that migration of the Ahoms continued even after 1826 A.D., the fateful year in which the colonial rulers demarcated the Indo-Burmese boundary through the Treaty of Yandaboo and there were several streams of Tai migration from Myanmar to India. To begin with the number of migrants was little, but soon thereafter this trickle became a torrent, a tidal wave that swamped the entire northeastern region. After the British occupation of Assam in 1826, the Tai Ahoms lost their distinctiveness and iconic status in the Brahmaputra valley and they became confined to the districts of Sibsagar and Lakhimpur in eastern Assam.

In the realms of economics their influence covers a sizeable portion of the plains which covers the peasantry of Upper Assam. In their social and cultural life one can still find the prevalence of many traditional features together with elements that have been incorporated from other sources, primarily from Hindu socio-cultural system. In a way, it can be stated that the Ahoms as a whole represent a population that have undergone varoius social changes taking place over the years. It may be noted that not every Ahom peasant group reflects the same degree of persistence of old forms. Some have been fully incorporated into the Hindu social fold while others are traditional in their practices and structures. These people have retained their traditional forms which imparts them their distinctive identity and at the same time it has also incorporated certain new features.

Cultural Renaissance and Literary Incandescence

The Ahoms were the first to introduce their literature called the buranjis that contain a very good historical account of the Ahoms, and many of the buranjis have been translated into Assamese and English by various writers. One may mention the names of certain eminent historians such as Dr. S.K. Bhuiyan, G.C. Barua, Dr. Padmeswar Gogoi, K.L. Barua, B.K. Barua, P.C. Choudhury and N. K. Basu. The Tai Historical and Cultural Society of Assam has also contributed its share in throwing light on some historical and cultural information found in certain original Tai manuscripts.

The Ahoms, who belong to the Tai or Shan group of the Mongoloid race, entered Assam from Upper Burma by the North Eastern route and established their kingdom in Upper Assam and extended their territory down to the banks of Brahmaputra. Gradually, under the impact of Hindu Brahmanical orthodoxy, they were Hinduised and adopted the local Assamese language by the 17th century. They inhabit India's northeast, several regions of Burma, Thailand, Laos, Northern Vietnam and in the provinces of China- and are known differently having a variety of names and appellations. They are known as the Ahoms, Ajtons, Khamtis, Khamyangs, Phakes, Turungs in Northeast India; the Shans, Khuns, Laems, Khamtis in Burma; the Thais, Lao-Tais, Saeks in Laos, the Tai-Dams, Tai Khaos, Tai-Dengs, Nangs and the Lis in Southern China.

The Ahoms call themselves as 'Tai' in their language and this has appeared in all their works including some of the major writings of Tai-Ahom language. The word Ahom appears to be a phonetic variation of *'Asam'* or *'Asama'* which itself is a Sanskritised distortion of *Asam*, a form of Bodo origin. When the Tai or Sams conquered the upper part of the Brahmaputra valley in *Assam* and established their kingdom in it, the Bodo people called the area A-Sam or the kingdom of the Sams. The words *Asam*, *Acam* were further distorted during the British period into *Aham* and finally into Ahom. But the Ahoms have never referred to themselves as Sams or by any of its Assamese variants including Ahom in their own literature, the *'buranjis'* that was written in Tai. More importantly, in due course, the Ahoms had even identified themselves with the Assamese as they made formidable contribution in the consolidation of composite Assamese culture and society and were virtually absorbed into the Hindu social structure.

Linguistic Pluralism and Historiographies

Language is an expression of shared ideas, thoughts and a determining factor in the identity formation of a particular group of people. The Ahoms were conscious of the importance of historical records and wanted to incorporate every detail of their rule in the *'Buranjis.'* They began compiling their historical accounts since the year 568 A.D., prior to their migration to Assam. 'But it is not until Sukhapa became king in 1228 A.D. that they can be treated as historical records and it is since then that they became trustworthy.'[5]

The Tais had settled in widely varying geographical tracts owing to political constraints, so much so that various Tai groups lost contact with each other. Earlier their chief language was Tai but gradually it became Ahom. The Tai language traced its origin and linkage to the Siamese Chinese family of the Indo-Chinese form of speech. The different Tai groups speak different language in different places may be because of diverse acculturation and assimilation with different local groups. It is an accepted fact that the Tai Ahoms were the speakers of an Indo-Chinese form of speech, who migrated from the same racial group whose parental home was in China.[6] But this change of Tai-Ahom into Assamese can also be traced from historical records. During the early period of Ahom rule in Assam their original language was their mother tongue. But gradually when they got mixed up with the local people they relegated to the background of their own language in favour of the dominant Assamese language. Also because of inter-marriage, they began to abandon their own language. Sukhapa, who was the founder, himself, married the daughter of a Borahi king.[7] He also encouraged inter-marriages between the Ahoms and Morans and Borahis. In course of time the Ahom kingdom also got involved in wars, which largely affected the Tai language and its development and continuity. The Deodhai pandits of the royal courts, who were responsible to keep the Ahom language alive, gradually lost their powers and their language suffered.[8]

With the passage of time, more and more Assamese words came to be used alongside the Ahom language. During the British rule, Hinduism played a major role in the decline of the use of the Ahom language. There was no recognized school to learn the language. They started learning Hindi, Assamese and English. Now days the Ahoms make use of the Assamese language more than their own language. They leaned at first more towards Hinduism and later on towards Buddhism. It can be noted here that initially after the Ahoms had settled in the Brahmaputra valley there was no major change in their language but with gradual mixing up with the local people changes started taking place. With independence the migration of the Tais was totally stopped and these people lost contacts with their counterparts in Burma, Thailand & elsewhere and gradually their culture too underwent change. Presently the Ban Ok Publik Muang Tai is involved in keeping the Tai language alive among the present day Ahoms. They are trying to restore the old Ahom language so that they can hold on to their old language and literature.

Religion, Traditions and Rituals

Religion has become an important tool to assess the cultural extent of a community. According to historians like Phya Anuman Rajadhon, H.G. Quaritch Wales, the Ahoms were initially animists.[9] They had their own traditional ideas, beliefs and practices. When the Ahoms had come down in the 13th century Hindu culture was already established. Initially they followed their own traditions but gradually as a result of the steady contact they were much influenced by Hinduism. But according to historians like Romesh Buragohain such leaning towards Hinduism was not basically because of any religious zeal but due to some historical reasons.[10] They did not altogether abandon their traditional cults.

The Hindu influence first entered the Ahom court during the rule of the King Sudangpha, who was the ruler in 1397 and was brought up by a Brahmin family in his childhood. After he ascended the throne, he brought an idol of *Lakhsmi Narain*, which found a special niche in the royal household. He also took the title of Swarga Narayan, a Hindu appellation. So it can be noted that the Hindu tradition was getting hold of the Ahom kings. Later on this title with its different variants came to be used by the Ahom kings in their official documents.[11]

Even before the advent of the Ahoms the, Tantric cults had prevailed in Assam and the ancestors of Sankardeva, the chief Vaishnav preacher in Assam, worshipped *'shakti'* with animal sacrifices. It was believed that power in the universe came from the women goddess like Kali and Parvati. Also one finds that another important ruler, Cu-Hum Mung (1497-1539) made some dents along with Brahmin influence. Also, the 20th Ahom ruler, Chao- Hpa-Hso-Tam- La (1648-1663) had accepted the Hindu religion and assumed the new name Jayadvaj Singha. He was the first in the dynasty to receive initiation from a Vaishnav abbot named Niranjan Bappu in A.D. 1654. He was the first abbot of the Vaishnav monastery in the Majuli in the Sibsagar district and Jayadvaj Singha made a land grant for the maintenance of the Satra (monastery). This was the beginning of the Hindu period of Ahom rule in Assam and since then every Ahom king officially assumed a Hindu name in addition to his Tai-Ahom name on the accession to the throne. The coronation ceremony was also held both according to the Ahom as well as the Hindu traditions.[12] It suggests that at first the rulers came under Hindu influence and then the masses.

Gadadhar Singha (1681) was a follower of Sakta Hinduism and he took many steps to check the growing influence of the Vaishnava leaders. Also in the beginning of the 18th century the Ahom king Rudra Singha brought a very famous Brahmin Sakta priest, Krishnaram Bhattacharya, from Santipur of Nadia district in Bengal and established him at Kamakhya on the Nilachal hills. It can also be cited here that one Ahom king Siu

Sheng Pa, who bore the name Pratap Singha, was under some evil spirit and he got rid of it by performing some Brahmanical rites and therefore he patronized the Brahmins.[13]

The Ahom priests were patronized and allowed to perform all their socio-religious rites. Till the end of the Ahom rule the royal functions were carried out in the traditional way by the Deodhais, which were the priestly sections.[14]

Thus the Ahom rulers followed all the three beliefs- Sakta faith, Vaishnavism, and traditional Ahom rituals. The accidental situations helped them for assimilating Hindu traditions within their cultural fold. The Ahom priestly section, the Mohans and Deodhais continued to perform the traditional ceremonies and have still stuck to their original religious ceremonies. Towards the close of the Ahom rule, the Ahoms came under the Hindu influence. They also got divided into Saktas and Vaishnavas sects. Only the priestly class followed the old traditions. Of course there was change in certain areas because they had accepted different traditions at different period of time. Even today along with the priestly class many Ahoms strictly adhere to their traditional Tai-culture, which is almost similar to those of the Tais of Southeast Asian countries. Since the early seventies, there has been awareness among the Ahoms to revitalize their traditional language and culture. Nevertheless, it is interesting to note that amongst the traditional Ahoms, particularly those who lived in relatively isolated villages, there the old cultural practices representing the Tai-culture still survived.

Summing-up

From the above account it becomes clear that there are certain facts relating to the Tai Ahom identity that can be explained in the context to their cross border migration. A question that arises is why do some people in Assam want to be recognized as Tai-Ahom. It becomes clear that initially they did not totally abandon their language and religion. As they settled in the valley they were assimilated in the local culture, which was very necessary at that point of time. Much interaction took place among the Ahoms and the local population and finally there was an extensive process of Hinduization. It was not a forceful process but a process of cultural assimilation. It should be remembered that Indian rural societies present a varying degree of change from state to state and region to region besides providing great variation within a single state due to cultural, geographical, economic and other peculiarities. Both the endogamous and exogamous factors have contributed in bringing about a change in the Ahom traditional society. At present the attempts by the Tai-Ahoms to create a separate identity of their own has forced them to associate themselves with something called Tai. This makes them as non-Hindu and therefore outside India. Maybe they are neither orderly nor homogenous and they view it as a political and professional necessity for empowerment and economic improvement. The deodhais may be viewing it as a process to come to power once again for religious and social leadership. But it should be kept in mind that geographically Tai-Ahom is located in Ujjani Assam (Upper Assam), which is deemed to be located in the heartland of Assam. They continue to struggle for their recognition and to have an economic and a political voice in Assam. The Ahoms have adopted new ways and bought them under their own moral umbrella by usage and recommended them to the younger generation. They now present a shared cultural heritage which has emanated from the interplay of two different cultural traits.

Notes

1. Indira Barua, (1978): *Social Relations in an Ahom Village,* New Delhi: Sterling Publishers Pvt. Ltd.
2. Lipi Ghosh, (2007): "Tai- Cultural Matrix in Indian History: A Study of Tai-Ahom Heritage in Northeast India," in *Prachya: A Journal on Asia Past and Present,* No. 2, Dept. of South and Southeast Asian Studies, University of Calcutta, Calcutta, pp. 32-33.
3. Sayeeda Saikia Yasmin, (1999): *A Name without a People: Searching to be Tai-Ahom in Modern India;* UMI Dissertation Services, Michigan, p.vi

4. Lipi Ghosh, *op. cit.*, pp. 32-33.
5. E.A. Gait, (1965): *A History of Assam*, Calcutta, 3rd reprint, p.xiii
6. G.A. Grierson, (1904): *Linguistic Survey of India*, Vol. 2, p. 59, 1904 as quoted in Indira Barua.
7. Indira Barua, *op. cit.*, p. 14.
8. Lipi Ghosh, *op. cit.*, pp. 39-40.
9. See detail H.G. Quaritch Wales, (1987): *Siamese State Ceremonies*, B. Quaritch Ltd. London, 1931 and Phya Anuman Rajadhon, *Essays on Thai Folklore*, Bangkok.
10. Romesh Buragohain, (1994): *The Lost Trails*, Vol. 1, Ban Ok Publik, Dhemaji, p. 62.
11. E.A. Gait, *op. cit.*, p. 87.
12. Padmeswar Gogoi, (1976): *Tai-Ahom Religions and Customs*, Assam, Gauhati: Publication Board, p. 17.
13. See cited in Lipi Ghosh, *op. cit.*, p. 43.
14. Indira Barua, *op. cit.*, pp. 16-17.

27

A GLIMPSE OF TRADITIONAL NAGA SOCIETY & CULTURE

Shilpi Singh

Nagas are the indigenous group of people belonging to the Indo-Mongoliad stock and inhabiting the area between the Brahmaputra valley of Assam in the west, the lower Himalayas in the north, the Chindwin river of Myanmar in the east and Imphal valley of Manipur in south. Neivetso Venuh has described Nagas as a "generic term referring to a group of tribes, who inhabit the hills on both sides of the international border between India and Myanmar." [1]

The name 'Naga' is derived from the Burmese word 'Naka' meaning 'people with perforated ears.' Another derivation is from the Sanskrit word "Nanga' or "Naaga" meaning "naked" or "mountain" respectively as the nagas are hillman and also have history of being semi naked.

It is estimated that there are at least 45 Naga tribes living in the four states – Nagaland, Assam, Manipur and Arunachal Pradesh of North East India and also in East Myanmar. All the tribes of the Nagas have their own distinct name and are remarkably different from one another in terms of language, dress and customs. In Nagaland the 17 Nagas tribes are Anagami, Ao, Chakhersang, Chang, Chirr, Khiemnungan, Konyak, Lotha, Makhori, Phom, Rengna, Sangtaim, Sena, Tikhir, Yinchunger, Zeliang and Pochur. In Manipur the Naga tribes are Anal, Thangal, Thangkul, Mao, Poumai, Kabui and Zeliangrong. In Arunachal Pradesh the Naga Tribes are Tangsas, Wanches and the Noctes. Some of the Zeliangrong Nagas fall under the administration of North Cachar Hill district of Assam.[2]

Traditionally Nagas are tribally organized people with strong warrior traditions. They are self respecting with high morals, honesty, sincerity and truthfulness. In describing the qualities of the Nagas, J.H. Hutton writes (quoted by N. Toshi Ao)

> "Nagas are honest and truthful people. Stealing is not known or common... and has respect for the elders... Nagas are generous and begging is an abomination ....they are healthy, active, vigorous and brave people."[3]

Each Naga tribe has a unique political organization of their own. In the words of an eminent Naga historian Gangmumei Kabui " all types of political systems are found among the Nagas, ranging from the pure democracy of the Anagami to, the autocratic rule of the Angs of the Konyaks, from the gerontocracy (Tatar) of the Aos to the Semi Republics of the Zeliagrongs."[4]

Naga society was basically a close rural society, which remained isolated, thus keeping its culture intact until the arrival of the British and Christianity in the 19th Century. Today also, a majority of Naga population lives in small isolated villages. Built on the most prominent points along the ridges of the hills, these villages were once stockade with massive wooden gates called 'kharun', approached by narrow sunken paths, the village are usually divided into 'khels', or quarters each with its own headmen and administration.

In earlier days, inter village feuds between tribes were the order of the day. So, the villages were mostly sited on hilltops and were strongly fortified and well guarded against any attack. Naga villages were self-sufficient units. They were the axis of life for the Naga people. In these villages, the village council looked after individual needs, which were common to entire community and for the satisfaction of such need, the entire village was responsible.

The Nagas are mainly agriculturists. There are two methods of cultivation mainly wet terraced cultivation and jhumming. Anagami, Zeliang, Chakhesang, Thangkul practice both terraced cultivation and jhumming, whereas Ao, Sema, Lotha, Rengma, Konyak, Sangtham, Phom, Chang etc. practice only jhum cultivation.[5] The main crop production is rice and it is the staple food. The Nagas are generally non-vegetarians for ecological and cultural reasons. Chilly is integral ingredient of curry and bamboo shoots of different kinds are very popular. Rice beer called 'zu' was at one time an inseparable asset of the Nagas, which was considered something more than the usual item that was taken as a nutritious food. It was also an important component of their culture itself. With the coming of Christianity, such consumptions of wine have become a thing of the past for the majority of Nagas.

Animals such as pigs, buffaloes, cows and mithuns have a great socio-religious significance in the Naga tradition and culture. These animals were domesticated for both food and economic purposes. Earlier many of these were also used as item of exchange among the Naga tribes.

Nagas in the beginning were animist by faith. The word "animism" is derived from Latin word "anima" literally meaning "breath", hence carrying the idea of soul and spirit. Animism thus can be defined as a belief that objects and natural phenomena are inhabited by souls or spiritual beings.[6] They believed in the existence of a Supreme Being, in angels and also in life after death.

In the 19th Century with the advent of British rule, Christianity was introduced and Baptist missionaries became especially active in the regime. As a result, the population now is predominantly Christian.

The ancient Naga society was classless and casteless.

Equality was the base of social relations.[7] Some kind of communism was prevalent in the society which makes some people feel that the Nagas had a proto mode of socialism. Nagas have both village or commercial (clan wise) and private (individual) land holding systems. The ancient Naga's wants were limited and they were self-satisfied with what they used to each by their manual labour. The concepts like exploitation, social dignities at the cost of others etc were not known to the early people. There were no slavery system, robbery, theft, stealing etc. in the society.

The "Morung" used to be an essential part of the Naga life. It was the pivot around which the social, religious, educational and cultural life of the young people revolved. The Morung (bachelor's dormitory) and ladies dormitory are therefore rightly called the Naga schools.[8] They were constructed at the village entrance or a spot from where the village can be guarded effectively. The Anagamis called them Kichuki, Aos- Arijiu, Lothas- Champo, Thangkhuls- Longshum, Semas- Apuki/ Illuki and Chang- Hakuh.[9] On attaining the age of puberty young boys and girls were admitted to their respective dormitories. The Naga culture, customs and tradition which were transmitted from generation to generation through folk music and dance, folk tales and oral traditions, wood carving and weaving were conveyed to the young in the Morungs. Announcement of meetings, death of village, warning of impeding danger etc. were made from morungs with the beating of xylophones or log drums. Sadly, the institution of morung disappeared after the arrival of modernity.

One of the striking social characteristics of the Nagas was the practice of Headhunting. A.C. Bowers described the Naga Hills as the 'paradise of headhunters.'[10] The headhunting had both political and social importance as it involved both power and status over the people. A man was not considered a full-fledged member of the community until he had brought home a human head. The warrior who hunted a head was entitled to wear special kinds of dresses and ornaments. A person who did not have a single head to his credit had difficulty in getting a bride and became an object of ridicule with girls.[11]

The practice of headhunting was also ritualistic and associated with belief of getting good yield and harvest. It also ensured fertility in women, good luck and prosperity for the people. A village drum cannot be beaten unless a human head has been taken and placed on it. The Nagas also had ceremonies (gennas) attached to the headhunting. The disposal of the head taken varied from tribe to tribe. Some tribes exposed the head in front of the Morungs, the other hung it on head tree. The Anagamis buried even the head of their enemies.[12] Providentially with the arrival of the British and Christian missionaries the practice of head hunting gradually ceased.

The "Feast of merit" was another customary practice of the Nagas, which was the hall made social distinctions for a Naga villager. This feast was mostly performed by the rich with splendor of color and extravagance, ceremonies and killing animals for sacrifice and feasts for the whole village. However, the purpose and celebration of feasts varied from tribe to tribe. For the Semas the feast signified friendship with one another, whereas for the Aos it was an expression of thanks giving to God for the gift of wealth and blessing.

The practice of the Nagas of having "collective communal provisions" or "paddy store house" (maazum) of paddy for the poor and needy, the village guests and visitors has been a unique culture indeed. The poor and the needy would be provided paddy according to their needs. Such human practice could be one reason for non-existence of beggars in the Naga society.

Naga society both in past and today is patrilineal, patrilocal and patriarchal in structure. Naga women unlike other tribal women have a high place in society, work and agricultural activities. Furer Haimendr of writes:

"Many women in more civilized parts of India may well envy the women of the Naga Hills, their high status and their free and happy life and if you measure the cultural level of the people by the social position and personal freedom of its women you will think twice before looking down on the Nagas as savages."[13]

The Naga tribes follow the exogamous principle in

marriage. Persons of the same clan do not intermarry and commissions of such crime resulted in banishment from the village with a huge fine. Monogamy was normally practiced except for a few rich powerful headmen who practiced polygamy. The girls were free to choose the husbands of their choice. For many tribes the payment of bride price as a custom was not essential, unlike the Lothas and the Semas. Divorce was easy in all tribes and the person who was widowed or divorced were free to remarry. Although a married woman has no right in the property of her father, the unmarried daughter has a right to a share of property of her parents. Women also inherit rare ornaments, expensive wares and dresses from their mothers, sisters and aunts.

The Nagas were distinguished by an impressive bearing and splendid dress. The most prominent item of Naga dress was shawl. It was different for every tribe. The most prominent ones are Aviki- iphi (Semas), Tsungkotepsu (Aos), Kasksi nei (Chang) and Lohe (Anagamis). The most popular decoration for male dresses was ivory armlet, leggings, headdress, earnings, ornamented belts and embroidered cross straps. Women wear shawl skirts and knitted sleeves of shawls, necklaces and brass earnings. Tattooing was the form of decorating body parts like thigh, breast and face. Among the Konyaks, Changs and Phoms, both men and women were tattooed whereas among the Aos and Sangtams only women were tattooed. In earlier days they could do so usually after they had taken a head, but this restriction does not apply any longer.[14]

Music and folktales were essential ingredients of the traditional Naga culture. The oral tradition was kept alive through media of folktales and songs. Naga folk songs were both romantic and historical, narrating entire stories of famous ancestors and incidents. There were also seasonal songs, which describe various activities done in a particular agricultural season. The early western missionaries opposed use of folk songs by Naga Christians, as they are perceived to be associated with spirit worship, war and immortality. As a result versions of western rhyme were introduced leading to the slow disappearance of indigenous music from the Naga Hills.

The Nagas were expert craft men. The important handicrafts of Nagas were woodcarving, bamboo work, pottery and black smithy. They were known for making wonderful woolen clothes and utilitarian items. Nowadays also, the Naga shawl is justly reputed all over India. Naga furniture made of bamboo and cane are also famous for the intricate craftsmanship.

Life of Nagas was replete with festivals throughout the year as all the tribes had their own festivals, which they gently cherish. They regarded their festivals sacrosanct and participation in them was compulsory. They celebrated their distinct seasonal festivals with pageantry, color, music and fanfare. Most of these festivals revolved around agriculture where people predominantly offered prayer to the Supreme Being. Some of the important festivals of the Naga tribe can be listed below: Anagami (Sekernyi - February), Chakesang (Tsukhen –iyie – March or April), Konyak (Aoling- April), Ao (Moatsu- May), Sema (Tuluni- July) and Lotha (Tokhu- Emong- November).

A study of the Nagas past life, their social behavior and cultural values brings the fact to the light that the early Nagas lived in rigid physical isolation and seclusion. The whole fabric of the ancient Naga society was woven in social and religious customs and traditions. It was these customs and traditions that bonded the Naga family, clan, the village and the tribe.

The beginning of the 19th century initiated the process of change and transformation among the Naga people. The change in the Naga society was largely due to the influence of the British rule. The certain natural by products of the British rule—development of road communication, changes in agricultural methods and promotion of public health- had significant transforming impact on the Nagas. From that time the Naga society is undergoing through the phase of transition. Although, the advent of modernization has tremendously changed the tribal Naga society and its complexion and character but those who are living in the remote areas in the opaque jungle have still maintained their identity, culture and traditions.

Notes

1. Venuh Neivetso, (2005): *British Colonization and Restructuring of Naga Polity*, Delhi: Mittal Publication, p 7.
2. U.A. Shimray, (2002): "Equality as a tradition- Women's role in Naga Society," *Economic and Political Weekly*, Vol. 37, No. 5, 2. Feb. 8 Feb. 08, p. 375.
3. Ao N. Toshi, (1995): *Mission to the Nagas: A tryst with the Ao*, Radha Publishers, p. 6.
4. Vahum Reisang, (2005): *Naga's Right to self Determination*, Delhi: Mittal Publication, p. 22.
5. Venuh Neivetso, *op. cit.*, p. 6.
6. Shikhu Inato Yekheto, (2007): *A Rediscovery and Rebuilding of Naga Cultural Values: An Analytical Approach with Reference to Maori as a colonized and minority group of people in New Zealand*, Delhi: Daya Books, p. 12.
7. Chandrika Singh, (2004): *Naga Politics—A Critical Account*, Delhi: Mittal Publication, p. 3.
8. R.R. Shimray, (1985): *Origin and Culture of Nagas*, New Delhi: Pamleiphi Shimray, p. 193.
9. Shikhu Inato Yekheto, *op. cit.*, p. 21.
10. A.C. Bowers, (1929): *Under Headhunter's Eyes*, Philadelphia: Judon Press, p. 195.
11. G.K. Bhargava and S.C. Bhatt, (2006): *Land and People of Indian States & Union Territories*, Vol. 20, Nagaland, Delhi: Gyan Publishing House, p. 41.
12. B.B. Kumar, (2005): *Naga Identity*, Delhi: Concept Publishing Company, p. 97-98.
13. Von C. Furer Haimendrof, (1993): *The Naked Nagas*, Calcutta: Thacker Spink & Co., p. 96.
14. T. Ratan, (2006): *History, Culture and Tradition of Northeast India*, Delhi: Gyan Books, p. 236.

28

DEVELOPMENT OF TEA INDUSTRY IN COLONIAL ASSAM

Sakshi Roy

With the coming of the British in India and the introduction of cash crops by them had its own motive. The guiding principal was that all the raw material for their industries could be provided by their colonies. One such effort was in Assam when the plantation of tea industry was started there. Assam at that time comprised of the valleys of Brahmaputra, Barak together with the intervening hill treks.[1].

During the British period for their own interest, some areas of Assam were formed into non-regulatory areas.[2] The provinces and the entire administration was placed under the charge of a Chief Commissioner who was immediately under the order of Governor General-in-Council.[3]

Indian spices which were the attraction for traders held their charm for the British also and it was the real cause behind the development of the tea industry in Assam. Robert Bruce an English man was first to discover the existence of tea in Assam.[4]

In 1823 he visited Brahmaputra valley for trading purposes and identified a wild plant as tea. This region at that time was under the dominance of Burma.[5] But war with Burma shortly broke out. C.A. Bruce brother of Robert Bruce volunteered for service. It was during this war that he obtained some tea plants and sent it to Botanical Garden at Calcutta[6] for examination. But nothing much was known till 1832. Governor General Lord William Bentinck started the official proceedings about tea production. He deputed Capt. Jenkins to report on special resources available at Assam and tea plants prevalent in Assam were brought to notice.[7] A tea committee was formed consisting of seven civilians, three Calcutta merchants, two native gentlemen and Dr. Walliach of Botanical Gardens. Secretary Gorden was sent to China to procure plant seeds and persons skilled in tea manufacture.[8] By this time Capt. Jenkins submitted the tea committee report and the government made fresh inquiries and was at last convinced about the identity of Assam tea plant.

The first official tea plantation was located at the sand bank near the confluence of Brahmaputra and Kundil River. In 1835 the first tea garden was opened at Lakhimpur.[9] in 1838 the first twelve chests of tea from Assam were received in England. They had been damaged to some extent through the passage. But the report of the sample was highly favorable. But the government had no intention to carry on the tea trade. It was given to private enterprises as soon as it became clear that the cultivation could be successfully done in Assam. Thus began the planting and manufacturing of tea in this Northeastern state of Assam. And in 1840, Assam tea Company was established on an experimental basis.[10] In the initial years the output was not encouraging but after 1852 the prospects began to improve. In 1859, it had 4000 acres under cultivation and an overturn of 760,000 pounds of tea. By 1853 nine other tea gardens were started and soon after they spread to Cachar and Sylhet and in 1855 a huge tea garden in Cachar district was opened.[11]

In the next few years industry made rapid strides. The success of Assam and Jorhat companies, the later which was formed in 1858 gave a Philip to prospects of tea cultivation and a period of wild excitement and speculation supervened. Now government officials for example three Deputy Commissioners, four Assistant Commissioners and several police official threw up their appointments to engage in tea planting. As a result decisions were taken in haste and irrespective of suitability or availability of labor tea was planted with insufficient number of tea bushes. As a consequence there was a general collapse. Most of the companies had to wind up and those which remained were either suffering from one problem or the other or by serious depreciation.[12] By 1969, the picture began to change. Tea plantation was now established on a sound basis and was making progress year by year. In 1872, the area of land taken up for the tea plantations was 27,000 acres in the Brahmaputra valley, 23,000 in Cachar and 1,000 in Sylhet. The outturn in these tree tracts was respectively six million, five million and three million pounds.[13] In 1901, it was close to 134 million pounds that reached to an output of 234 million pounds.[14]

The production in tea industry was on the brighter side but the cause of concern was that it was mostly owned by British capitalists who were attracted towards this industry by prospects of high profit. In 1914, the total capital invested in producing tea amounted to Rs 30.3 million only about Rs 43.1 million were accounted by companies registered in India and rest were companies registered in England.[15] This foreign owned industry was hardly of any advantage to Indian people. The profits went out of the country. A large part of the salary was spent on highly paid foreign staff. They purchased most of their equipments abroad. Most of their products were sold in foreign market resulting in the foreign exchange which was utilized by Britain. Overall the profit of tea industry was with the British and was not coming to India.

Another feature of tea industry was related to laborers working in tea gardens popularly called as coolies. The scarcity of laborers in Assam valley had developed an important system of coolie immigration. During 1871, the average monthly number of laborers employed on the tea gardens of Assam was 54,326 of whom 38,000 were imported under Labor Transport Acts chiefly from the western districts of lower Bengal.[16]

Of all the sectors tea plantation of Assam is perhaps most

oppressed in the case of working class. Low wages, poor housing and lack of avenues for social mobility has been recurring theme in these enterprises. The legal provisions were aided by acts such as Worksman' Breach of Contract Act X, XII, XII of 1859 and its amended act of 1865 where workers could be punished for striking and were held as slaves for minimum wages.[17] However government passed a series of enactments from 1863-1901 with the twofold object of ensuring to the employer the services of labor imported by him for a period sufficiently long to enable him to recoup the cost of recruiting and bringing them to the garden. On one hand and on the other of protecting the laborers against fragmental recruitment providing for them a proper and sanitary system and transportation facility, and securing their good treatment and adequate remuneration during the term of their labor contract. Out of 210 reported cases of conflict between the planters and workers from 1904-05 and 1920-21 as many as 141 were cases of rioting, unlawful assembly arising from the issue of inadequate remuneration and poor economic condition. A plantation worker who was arrested during riot said that he justified his actions because he was not given his due.[18] These instances show that steps taken by the government for the well being of the plantation workers were half done. The tea industry which developed in the second half of the 19th century with its centre in Assam was an integral part of economic British India. The benefits from this industry were all directed towards the British. The only advantage that Indians got out of this industry was creation of unskilled jobs. The province became materially prosperous but the real beneficiaries were Britain and British companies. One important factor of industrial development was that it did not help in the development of the region. This unequal regional economic development not only led to wide region disparities in income but also affected the level of national integration.

Notes

1. *Imperial Gazetteer of India,* Vol. 1, p. 238.
2. Henry Yule and A. C. Burnell, Hobson-Jobson, (eds.), Wilhem Crook (1903, (reprint ed.) Delhi: Munshiram Manoharlal 1968).
3. *Imperial Gazetteer of India,* Vol. 1, p. 238.
4. Ibid., p. 504.
5. *Parliamentary Papers,* 1 February 1835, No. 90.
6. Sir Adward Gait, *A History of Assam,* Chapter 23, p. 404.
7. *Imperial Gazetteer of India,* Vol. 1, pp. 249-250.
8. *Imperial Gazetteer of India,* Vol. VI, Chapter 17, pp. 504-507.
9. *Imperial Gazetteer of India,* Vol. 1, pp. 249-250.
10. Sir Robert Guit, *A History of Assam,* Chapter 23, p. 407.
11. Ibid.
12. P. Griffins, *The History of Indian Tea Industry,* p. 192.
13. *Imperial Gazetteer of India,* Vol. 1, p. 250.
14. Ibid.
15. Sanjay Barbora, *Struggles in the Tea Plantations of Assam: Then and Now,* p. 01 (Quoted from the report of the Indian Tea Association Report).
16. *Imperial Gazetteer of India,* Vol. 1, p. 250.
17. N.C. Bardoloi, *Condition of the Laborers in the Tea Garden of Assam* Calcutta.
18. A. Guha, *From Planter Raj to Swaraj,* (Quoted from the *Assam Labor Enquiry Report,* 1921-22).

29

ANGAMI: NAGA'S AND THEIR FESTIVALS

Pankaj Sharma and Rashmi Nirwal

India has always been characterized as an amazing mosaic of human affairs. The tribal India, too exhibits the same amount of diversities in term of racial/ethnic, linguistic, religious, ecological features.

The Nagas are a group of tribal people inhabiting the Indian State of Nagaland, parts of Maniapur,, Assam and Arunachal Pradesh and the Northwestern hill tracks of Myanmar such as the Sagaing Division. They bear the Mangolian features and cultural traits. They have their distinctive tribal names with a number of sub-names, about fifty, of which better known are Angams, Chakhesang, Ao, Sema, Dengama, Lotha and others. They are a fine, stalwart, cheerful, humorous and devout people.[1] The Nagas love dance, music and songs and celebrate many festivals.

The festivals of the Angamis are very ancient which play an important role in the political, social and economic life of the people. Some of their festivals are participated and celebrated by the whole village, but there are certain rituals and rites performed by an individual or by a family. There are six major festivals involving different complicated rituals and rites, which are celebrated on village level but not the same time by all villagers. They are considered major festivals because the whole villages are involved. Each village is unique in its own way. They fix the time and date of the festivals according to their agricultural works and at their convenience.[2]

Following are the six major festivals of Angami Nagas.

Sekrenyi

Sekrenyi falls on the second day after the full moon of the month of kent or of the month of Kezi.[3] The Sekrenyi is the beginning of Angami month, falls in the month of Feb. The Angami calendar and the rituals involved in this festival amounted to New Year celebration. It falls in the month of February and lasted for 10-15 days, it is held before the beginning of the agricultural season[4]. The ceremony is to ensure the health of the community during the coming year. This festival begins with some rituals, among them invocation of the ancestors and recollection of the past been important. Another part of the Sekrenyi festival is the Thekrahie (boys and girls) or the dancing and singing by the adolescents to understand each other and marriage often resulted from such understanding. The main purpose of the Sekrenyi is to purify the people physically and mentally before the agricultural activities would start. The rituals also aim at good health for the entire village community in the coming year and to dispel sickness.[5]

Gnonyi

This festivals falls on the third day after the full moon of the month of kera or April and continues for a period of 4-5 days. This celebration marks the completion of the sowing of jhum land.[6] Besides the rituals, the actual beginning of agricultural activity is done by the oldest male member in the village. He later on collects contribution from each house after the harvest.[7]

Kerunyi

Kerunyi festival falls on the day of the full moon of the month Chachu or June and lasts for 4 days.[8] The beginning of wet cultivation is marked by this festival kerunyi. An interesting feature of this festival is that every one in the village would participate by treating themselves with the best food they could afford to nourish their body for the hard work.[9]

Chadanyi

This very festival is celebrated in the month of August and it lasts for 4 days. Chadanyi festival is known as 'Path Clearing.'[10] The village roads and graves are cleared and no one is allowed to speak to anyone of another village.[11] In fact during this celebration, people understand community works and indirectly the nursing of the paddy fields.

Khoupfunyi

The beginning of the harvest season is again marked by another festival called Khoupfunyi, which lasts for 4 to 5 consecutive days. But the festivities as such continues for the entire harvest period which continue from September to November. The end of the harvest season will be marked by a one day celebration of Kevakete ritual which is known as thanks giving and all the female members of the village will participate in the ritual. The Kevakete ritual marks the end of the Khoupfunyi festival.[12]

Terhuonyi

Terhuonyi is the concluding festival in the series. Terhuonyi, 'a feast of merit', falls in the month of December. It last for about 10 to 15 days. This festival is an exclusive one usually been given by the new emerging wealthy person. The people to be invited for the feast was at the discretion of the host. The first two feasts of merits are followed by the construction of special type of house known as Nyieso and Pfuge. The third feast is marked by the dragging of a wooden carved piece. The fourth and fifth feasts are marked by stone pulling. This stone is a commemorative symbol of the feast. The last or the sixth feast is marked by the digging of a lake in honour of the performer. During these feasts of merits, a rich person who aspires to alleviate his social status would share his wealth to the prosperous members of the community by providing enjoyment and food in abundance. In these big feasts people would indulge in singing, dancing and merry-making.

It is found that most of the people no longer conform to the rituals prescribed for an Angami by the traditional beliefs and practices, although they have not altogether change their belief. One reason is that they have no one within the family to perform the rituals from work to work as a result of Christian conversion. After the Angamis embraced Christianity, there was very few left with the traditional beliefs, which became practically impossible for them to carry out the entire rites and rituals prescribed.[13]

Notes

1. Yonuo Asoso, *The Rising Nagas*, pp. 6-7.
2. P.D. Sorhie, (1985): *The History of the Angamis as Reflected in Festivals*, M.Phil Thesis, NEHU, 1985, p. 45.
3. J.H. Hutton, *The Angami Nagas*, p. 197.
4. P.D. Sorhie, *op. cit.*, p. 132.
5. Ibid., p. 133.
6. J.H. Hutton, *op. cit.*, p. 198.
7. P.D. Sorhie, *op. cit.*, p. 134.
8. J.H. Hutton, p. 198.
9. P.D. Sorhie, *op. cit.*, p. 134.
10. Ibid, p. 134.
11. J.H. Hutton, *op. cit.*, p. 198.
12. P.D. Sorhie, *op. cit.*, p. 135.
13. Ibid., pp. 136-137.

30

GAROS: A STUDY OF STRUGGLE AND ACCOMPLISHMENTS

Madhu Rajput

Tribes are natural, spontaneous and simple for their sense of values, feelings and believes are reflective of what they think and various institutions they have built as part of their social structure. The Garos of Meghalaya have distinct rich culture which has over the years seen change with inroads of modernization and technology. In this paper I have made an attempt to understand the traditional and developing society of the Garos. Garo Hills, the main homeland of the Garos, is the south-western district of Assam. It was formed into a district in 1866 with Captain W. J. Williamson as its first Deputy Commissioner, and is one of the major constituent units of the state of Meghalaya. The area lies between 25° 57′ 18″ and 25° 9′20″ North latitude and 91°0′0″ and 90°0′10″ East longitude, having a total area of 8164 Sq Km and is bounded on the north and west by the district of Goalpara of Assam, on the east by west Khasi Hills district of Meghalaya and on the south by the Mymesingh district of Bangladesh.[1]

The Garo Hills is a transition between the civilization of Indian subcontinent and south-east Asia. Its eco system is rich in flora and fauna. Agriculture is governed by tropical monsoon climate of moderate to high rainfall, warm summers and mild winters, wet tropical forests, fertile loamy soil in hills and alluvium in narrow flat valleys. Other resources are coal, limestone, white clay, kaolin, glass sand, iron ore, gypsum, quartz, feldspar, phosphate and sillimanite.[2]

Even today in many parts of the district the forests are being uprooted for the purpose of cultivation. The local primitive people, since time immemorial have depended on Jhum cultivation. All the vegetation is cut in winters, dried for sometime and set on fire during dry months (March/April). The Jhummia families change their cultivation land every year. The denudation and degeneration of the forest cover of the district has already led to serious problem of soil erosion all over the hilly area. The Department of Soil Conservation has responded to the alarming situation and is aiming at controlling soil erosion. The shift from Jhuming to settled cultivation is resulting in the emergence of individual land holding in place of community ownership. The area by itself may not mean much, but social change caused by these economic innovations is significant. The erosion control works result in the creation of new economic assets like dams, embankments and irrigation channels retaining walls.[3]

The main ridge lies east and west near about the south attaining highest elevation at the Norker peak of the Tura range. Norker peak is 1,457 meters high and is the highest peak among Garo Hills and second highest in the Meghalaya state. The hills and ranges include steep ridges separated by valleys which are now utilized as rice fields, government establishments and plantations.

The largest river is Semsang which the non Garo call Someswari after Someswari goddess and falls into Kangra River in Mymenseng district of Bangladesh. Other big rivers on the south flowing towards Bangladesh are the Moheskheli, Dareng and Bugi, while on the north and the west are the Iidek, Manda, Didram, Didak, Jimjiram, Rongai, Galwang, Ganol and Rongkai.

The district is also gifted with beautiful waterfalls, plateau and landscapes connected with traditional folk lore sand and religious beliefs but today Garo Hills present a grim picture due to commercial exploration by Jhummer's unscrupulous administrators and businessmen.

The Garo Hills are famous for its beautiful wild elephants. It is also a good ground for Bisons, wild buffaloes, tigers, leopards, bears, boars and antelopes of different kinds and also for game birds.[4]

The Inhabitants

The physical features of the Garos indicate their Mongolian origin. They are of medium height with small eyes, high cheek bones and are dark brown in complexion. Majority of the population of the district are the Garos. Other indigenous inhabitants are the Hajongs, Rabhas, Koches, Rajbansis, Meches, Kacharis and the Dalus. Other inhabitants are the Bengalis, Muslims, Marwaris, Biharis and few others from north India and the Nepalese who apart from Garos are dispersed throughout the districts. They maintain herds of cattle and sell milk or manufacture ghee.[5] It can also be added according to Sinha (1966) that they are bold, frank and simple as well as their kind hospitality when they become friendly, deserve s special mention. They are humble yet proud, submissive but dignified and honest and good natured people.

History

Col. Dallon, in his "Descriptive Ethnology of Bengal", mentions about the Garos as one of "the Mechkachari" or "the Bodo nations." Traditions indicate that they came from Tibet and settled down in Cooch Behar for about 400 years. Then they shifted to Rangamati, present day Bangladesh. From there they had to move out due to the king's wrath to Dhebri where they stayed for a while, subsequently moving to right bank of the Brahmaputra and finally reaching the Manas River.

As the song goes, the local king of the region was captivated by the beauty of Garo maiden Jugi Silche and tried to carry her off. To defeat his plans Garos hid her in a cave at a place called Jugighopa (Jugi – Girl's name, Ghopa means to bury) and hence the name of the present Jogighopa. Garos crossed Brahmaputra and reached Kamakhya where they were persecuted at the hands of the king named Litasing. Arambit the neighboring chief fell in love with Garo maiden, married her and allowed Garos to settle in his kingdom. But with time Arambit began to enslave them. This forced Garos to move to Baghmela Pahar, a hill about eight km east of Boko. But the fear of wild animals drove them westwards and it was here that the tribe broke into various directions. The hills they entered now were called Garo hills.[6]

Though one does not come across the names of king Lilasing and Arambit in Assam history, there are certain names like Koch Behar, Rangamati, Jogighopa, Garomari and they are still in existence today.

Garos conducted raids at plains and had internal warfare among them. After the attack the head of the victim was brought as a trophy. On two occasions Garos took part in contests for mastery of Assam, one was during the Moghul campaigns between 1608-1624 when Mirza Nathan recruited about 4000 Garos to attack a fortress of Rongjuli in the Goalpara district of Assam, the other was in 1671 when the Garos along with the Raja and Rani helped the Ahoms to escape Mohammedan invasion led by Raja Ramsingh.

On August 12, 1765 Bengal was brought under the defacto authority of the East India Company. As a natural consequence they came in contact with independent and semi- independent tribes in North East frontiers, Renghta the Garo chief became subject to Zamindar of Karaibari. The raids on the plains continued. To have peace on the frontiers, Thomas Sisson, the joint magistrate of Rangpur, in his report on 15 February 1815, recommended appointment of native agents and a local corps and deputation of an experienced officer. David Scott, the magistrate of Rangpur was chosen for this task. On his suggestion the Regulation X of 1822 was passed by the government. Accordingly the Garos were separated from the control of the Zamindars and brought under government management. A new form of administration emerged known as Non- Regulation system where all forms of administration of civil and criminal justice and collection of revenues rested in an officer appointed by Governor General in Council, named Civil Commissioner of North Eastern parts of Rangpur.[7]

David Scott was the first civil commissioner for North Eastern parts of Rangpur in December 1821. He entered into an agreement with independent Garo chief on 03 December 1824, who promised to acknowledge the British authority, pay tributes, report criminal cases to police and help to suppress the murder of human beings for their skulls. Scott could not complete his work as he was appointed Governor General's Agent for North Eastern frontier on November 20, 1823. After him a policy of non-interference was followed which encouraged raids and murders.[8]

The Garo chiefs continued to evade payment in 1834-35. Lieutenant Brodie was sent to inquire into the causes of non payment of dues. This time the Garo chiefs came and settled the matter. From 1835 to 1852 fresh disturbances in the Garo hills followed.

Between 1857 and 1859, there were nine raids on the Goalpara side. In 1859, the commissioner of Assam reported that raids were on increase and closure of markets was of no use in stopping the raids. So an expedition was sent again under Beckett in 1860 but returned due to shortage of food.

In March 1860, murders and outrages continued. To counter it Colonel Jenkins, commissioner of Assam, proposed to take the control of Garo hills from Zamindars, construct roads all along the frontier and appoint a Sub Assistant for special charge of the Garo hills. No action was taken on the proposal while expeditions under Captain Morton and Lieutenant Chambers, brought only temporary respite. Due to incessant heinous crimes Lieutenant Governor proposed to detach the Garo hills and Goalpara from the control of the Assam commissioner and place it under commissioner of Cooch Behar. The idea was implemented with Lieutenant W. J. Williamson joining as Deputy Commissioner of Garo hills in December 1867.

The Act XXII of 1869 outlined the administrative system to be introduced in Garo Hills District. However in 1872-73

Garos were finally defeated by the British and the hills were annexed. The inner line regulation was passed for the Garo Hills in 1876 which was extended till 1882, to be implemented by Deputy Commissioner from 1899 to 1946. Political demands of the region included abolition of forced labor and prohibition of conversion of Garo lands into Reserve forests by the British specially the Habraghat Pargana in the Goalpara district. There was no political party in Garo Hills, although in the first general elections of India in 1937, two Garo leaders, namely Jobey. D. Marak and Benjamin Ch. Momin were elected to Assam Legislative Assembly and Benjamin Momin was appointed as the parliamentary secretary. In 1942 during Quit India movement, Phukan Sangma started the movement in Garo Hills for which he was jailed.

At present Indian National Congress and Garo National Council are the main political parties.[9]

Social and religious institutions

Human society has developed a religious and social system which serves as a bond of union. So far as the individuals are concerned, Garos have great faith in anything and everything around them. They are shy about everything new but possess a keen inquisitiveness about the new objects. There are five clans or exogamous sects called Ehatchi among the Garos, with a number of sub clans called Machong. Originally there were only two clans i.e. Sangma and Marak. Later on Momin, Areng and Shira have evolved. Garos call themselves Hachiks or the hill people.

The social structure of the Garos depends upon the matriarchal form of inheritance where usually the youngest daughter inherits the property from the mother. If the mother desires she may select the youngest or any one of her daughters to be the Nokna, i.e. the future heiress of her property. The Nokna stays in the family even after marriage. The wife is practically the owner of all the inherited properties from her mother and she has absolute authority over its use, care and disposal. Maternal uncle has a voice over the sisters, nephews and nieces in the case of a dispute arising out of property.

Husband is given paternal authority in his new house. If the husband is a Nokkrom (husband of the heiress), he is placed next to his father-in-law, whose place he takes after his death. He is given all the responsibilities; the wife is subordinate to him despite the uxorial residence. According to the Garo customs he is served first, he can beat his wife if she acts unreasonably but wife can not beat her husband. Husband can have more than one wife with the consent of the first wife but polyandry is never permitted. But one can notice slight change due to cultural contact. Garos in the plains are trying to adopt patriarchal system. Grown up males, now Christians have developed the tendency to demand authority of spending the money they earn by themselves.

The family dwelling houses are known as Nok. There is another type of house used as bachelor's dormitory known as Nokpanthe. It is a strongly built house in the village and is usually a very big one.[10]

There are different forms of marriages in a Garo society; the main system is to marry a father's sister's son by negotiation. Consent of the girl is necessary. If the boy refuses and the girl insists then physical force is used. In another form of marriage if the girl offers food to any young man particularly one of her mother's brother's sons who may perchance come to the village and stay in the Nokpanthe. If the boy eats the food offered to him, the marriage is accepted. The third form of marriage is a matter of secret arrangement between the girl and the boy whereby the latter comes to stay with the girl in her house in the night. In morning formal marriage takes place.

The marriage ceremony is a simple affair. Both the bride and bridegroom sit on the floor on the bride's house and the Khamal i.e. the priest utters some of his exorcism and finally Dodokka i.e. killing fowls ceremony is performed by killing two fowls one cock and one hen by striking with a wooden rod.

Among the three main clans viz Marak, Sangma and Momin the Garos usually observe exogamy. They do not marry into the same clan. Marriage with girls of other societies is rare and a Garo woman does not usually take to a man of any other society as her husband.

On the birth of a child, Darichik and Saljong (deities) are worshipped and offerings are made to them. The people of the house drink liquor to solemnize the occasion. The Khamal usually gives a name to the child after birth. No other ceremony is observed for the naming.[11]

In earlier times Garos were scantily dressed, the principal garment of the men are strip of woven cloth about six inches wide and six feet long. No shirt is used to cover their body. Both males and females wear turbans, which are dark or blue cotton, while some are white. Chiefs on important occasion wear turban of red Assamese silk with an ornamented fringe. With time this has also witnessed change.

Women wear a cloth about 18 inches long and 14 inches broad. It is tied at the waist and remains open on the thighs. In winters they wear shawl. On festive occasion they wear a dress which is dyed Assamese silk.

Death disturbs Garos more. Rituals and other formal observances, therefore, are more numerous in connection with death than with any other event in life. Although there is a difference in observances connected with death among different clans. Those living in the plains of Mymensingh observe distinctly different rituals from those living in the interior of the hills. The dead body can not be cremated before the relatives assemble. The relatives carry their own rations and some liquor and an ox or a pig or a fowl to contribute to the ceremony. The body is either cremated or buried. The Delangsua ceremony i.e. the burning of the Mimang's (spirit of the dead) house is performed. An ox is also killed during the cremation.

Among the Garos there is a saying which runs as follows:

> MANDE SIANA MACHUU DENNA
> Which in English means, "Bull is to be slaughtered when a human being dies"

Mette is the word Garos use for a deity having some of the characters of a spirit. It is considered immortal.[12] The chief Mette is called Thatt Hara Rabuga. Marang is used for sinful or unlawful. The Garos do not go out in the field on the day when a child is born in nearby villages. It is Marang to violate this rule and whoever does so his crops will be cursed and hence spoilt. It is a Marang to kill a man. In earlier times Garos used to perform a ceremony named Marang Harikkha on their return from war to ward off the evil of the bloodspots on their body during the war.

The Garos believe in the existence of Supreme Being and the spirits. These good and evil spirits are everywhere. Some are attributed to the creation of the world; others control the destiny of man from birth to death. Men are governed by host of spirits whose anger must be appeased by sacrificing. The principal spirits are:

(1) Talara- Rabuga at whose command the world was made by lesser spirits, Nastu- Nopantu and Machi.

(2) Saljong- one of the greatest gods and a giver of all things to man.

They also believe that the constellation of stars has power and they represent the spirits therefore, animals must be sacrificed to them. They also believe in the existence of spirits in men which after death goes to the abode of spirits. Napak village and Balpakram plateau are believed to be places where the spirit of the dead person goes and these spirits dwell for a period of time before reincarnation.[13]

However, these believe and worship gave way to the doctrine of Christian thoughts by foreign missionaries, who not only preached to the people but also were responsible for the spread of education, development of Garo literature and health care. David Scott took the first step in this direction. He opened a school for 40 Garo boys at Simgimari which ran from 1826-29. The American Baptist mission was first to establish their mission in the Garo Hills. It was Omed Momin and Ramke Momin who first became Christians and were baptized at Gauhati on Feb. 8, 1863. In 1864, they came back to Garo Hills. Ramke opened a school at Damra and preached while Omed went to his village and preached. With their efforts they were able to convince 37 Garos to convert to Christianity.

Between 1867 and 1877, missionaries worked on the northern side of Garo Hills, with Goalpara as the mission station. In 1877 Rev E. G. Philips went to live at Turafor first time leaving Rev M. C. Mason at Goalpara. Now American missionaries work was extended to whole of Garo Hills. Roman Catholic came in 1933 and in 1954. Seventh Day Adrentist established their mission station at Raja Simla in 1954. As a result 60 % of the Garos have become Christians.

There have been many unconscious motive factors which have shaped socio-economic transformation of the Garo tribe. Like other tribes are impervious to change, even Garos are, for the tribe man live not only for himself alone he is also integral part of the community to which he belongs.[14]

Margaret Mead has said that it is a society in which the flow of learning is predominantly from older generations to the younger ones. Education is vital to ensure development from grass root level. World's poorest people being illiterates and their children not attending school, live in rural areas. A study of Meghalaya state by A. G. Khan and J. V. Madhusudan puts these factors as high illiteracy rate. Large number of villages in this region is yet to be provided schooling facilities. Majority of the teachers in this region is untrained that shows lack of efficiency and concern from the administration.[15]

Although Garos have now become accustomed to modern formal education system, in earlier times they had a system called "Nokpanthe" means bachelor's dormitory. No females were allowed to enter this house. Here the bachelors slept at night and learnt disciplines pertaining to agriculture, hunting, wood carving, songs, music, musical instruments, dances, arts and crafts. They were taught all the arts which are necessary for their future life. Change is evident as in Pirgacha more than 98 percent of the Garo population is literate, many of them with higher education. The mission runs 24 primary schools educating 1,700 children with 50 qualified teachers, most of whom are female. The high school in Pirgacha has 12 teachers and 550 students, who are introduced to computer education in class 9.

Due to the efforts of the church and a host of famous national and international NGOs, including World Vision, CARE, CARITAS, Bangladesh Rural Advancement Committee

(BRAC) and the United States Peace Corps in development programs, a sea change has been witnessed in Garo households in all the 32 villages that now represents a model way of living. Each household has an efficient sanitary system that has over the years almost totally wiped out attacks of diseases caused by worms. Every family has a tube well system that ensures pure drinking water. Hygiene in the traditional tin-roofed, earthen houses is rigorously maintained. The small open space in front of each house is adorned with flower plants. Animal breeding is very common with villagers rearing poultry, pigs, goats and even turtles. The transportation system too, is efficient enough to allow bananas and pineapples, the two principal produces of the area, to be carried to the market place.

One of the most remarkable things in the Garo community is the level of empowerment of women. The Garo tribe gives all rights of property to the women. It is the groom who moves into the bride's house and lives with her and only with the permission of the wife can he act as a mere administrator of the real estate. All real property and possessions automatically belong to the woman. Garo law does not allow men to own property and so they cannot sell anything without the permission of the wife's family. According to US-born Reverend Eugene E Homerich of the Pirgacha church, who has been officially adopted in the Mandi tribe for his 50 years of services, "This is an avuncular society where the mother's brother has more power over the child than the father. The British, Pakistani and now the Bangladeshi governments have recognized the customary law in case of Garos."

Conflict within

But this is just one side of the story. The Mandis have their own problems. Although for centuries the tribe, originating from Southwest China and Tibet, has lived in the 'Sal' forest with their own religion, culture and way of life, their right to land till date remains uncertain. The first onslaught on the Garo tribe probably came when the British Colonial Government of India granted the entire Madhupur Tract to the Raja of Natore in 1927. The Raja dedicated the forest to the god Govinda under the title "Debittor" or "a gift to the gods." The Garos were allowed to live on homestead plots paying a yearly tax. Garo women tenants were also granted permission to register low-lying land in their names. The registration started from 1892 and incorporated again in the Cadastral Survey of 1914-1918. By an exception of the law, certain Aboriginal Tribes enumerated in the Bengal Tenancy Act were exempted from the Succession Act of 1865. This exemption recognizes the Garo Law of Succession and Inheritance. Again, by an Act of Law in 1972, Bangladesh recognized all previous laws. This established the registration of land under the Bengal Tenancy Act.

In 1984 when the government in a gazette notification placed much of the Modhupur tract under the category of the Government Forest Land it was not welcomed by Garos. The whole procedure was completed without any notification to the. When the government move was challenged in the court of justice and in the land settlement office, the authorities allegedly refused to give any opportunity to the Garos to produce their documents. The government then refused to recognize the tenancy rights and barred Garos from paying any land tax, terming their land documents as "bogus."

The events of 1984 sealed the fate of the famous Madhupur Tract and made the Garos defenseless against reckless government decisions of indiscriminate Asian Development Bank-funded tree plantation projects. Successive governments have served eviction notices to the Garos, while depleting the local Sal forests and sometimes replacing them with totally unknown species of imported trees, highly detrimental to environment and local inhabitants. Interestingly, once the Bangladesh Tea Board proposed to remove the entire Garo population to the tea gardens elsewhere, under a scheme of 'creating job opportunities' for the tribal population to work as coolies. The government failed to sell the scheme.

In October 1996, the government tried a new idea about Madhupur Tract, and this time it was the World Bank providing the funds. The scheme envisaged creating 13 national parks and deporting the 16,000 Garos into cluster villages. A high official of the World Bank, Emilio Rozario flew in from the

Philippines to launch the project through the Forest Department under the Ministry of Environment and Forest. An outcry from the public representatives and the public put a stop to the planning.

Most recently the Forest Department started enacting a wall around 3,000 acres of Madhupur forest insisting that they were trying to create an eco-park for safeguard of tree species and wildlife. The move to encircle the forest at a cost of 9.7 crore and with a 10-foot-high wall outraged both the tribal and non-tribal residents of the area. On January 3, 2004, 22-year-old Piren Snal was killed and over 25 others were injured when forest guards opened fire on the demonstrators. Ajoy Amree, Convener of the Committee for Indigenous People's Land Rights and Environment Preservation, says that the whole government scheme is not only destroying the Garo culture but also threatening their livelihood. "We have appealed to the Prime Minister to create a permanent settlement for us and to abandon the scheme for a national park," Amree added that the committee was also demanding the withdrawal of false cases lodged by the forest department and its contractors.

Sources say that more than 3,000 cases have been lodged with the Madhupur police station under the Revised Forest Act in which hundreds of Garo men and women have been implicated. Most of those accused now live under constant fear of persecution. Nere Dalgot, a former teacher is implicated in eight cases, which he described as "totally false and fabricated." He says he has just served 45 days in prison. "There are Garo people against whom the forest department and its contractors have lodged more than 50 cases and I can tell you all these are totally fabricated cases," says Dalgot.[16]

Efforts for Transformation

Development programs have made positive impact in the region transforming people socially, physically and mentally. Apart from the five year plans, South Garo Hills Livelihood Improvement Project for the Himalayas (LIPH) is being implemented since 2006 under the joint aegis of Government of India and International Fund for Agriculture Development

(IFAD). The objective is to improve the livelihood of the vulnerable groups of people in a sustainable manner through improvement management of their resources while protecting and restoring the environment, empowering marginal farmers of the state for sustainable livelihood while ensuring optimized community resource management and enterprise development.[17]

The system of village administration is simple. The whole Garo hills were owned by a large number of A'King Nokmas or the clan chiefs. Each of these A'King lands were owned by a clan chief called A'King Nokma and was administered by the chief and his council of elders. Instead of Panchayatraj each village had a council headed by the Mukhiya called "Nokma" who usually perform the inaugural rituals of cultivation by cutting in the field. Following this if Nokma sees a bad dream it means leave the current field and search for new fields for cultivation.

Festivities are of course linked with farming operations. Wangala is a festivity of thanks giving after harvesting. During the festival, people worship the Saljong, the deity who supplies to the human society with Nature's amplitudes and assures their prosperity. The Wangala festival is celebrated in the month of October. Preparations are done beforehand and "Nokma of the village" supervises the whole arrangement done by the villagers. Feasting is an integral part and a huge quantity of food and rice-beer are being made well ahead. The culmination of the celebration approaches when the colorful Wangala dance is performed.

Village Development Councils (VDC) and Self Help Groups (SHG) carry out project activities. The Gasuapara Development Block is one of the four Development Blocks of South Garo Hills with an approximate population of 21,094 (Male 13,425, Female 11,545). The area stands at an average height of 600m characterized by rugged hilly terrain and is surrounded by the three rivers viz., Bogai, Dareng, and Rompa rivers, and the main hills are Nokrek, Kondok and Dura Asakgre ranges. The mean temperature is 27.5°C in summer and 17.5°C in winter. It receives an annual rainfall of about 1500-4000 mm.

Remote sensing data reveals that the region has good forest cover occupying 43·32 per cent of total geographical area. Shifting cultivation is extensively practiced in this part of the region occupying 38.69 per cent with a meager wet cultivation of 6.96 per cent. Grazing land occupies a negligible 0.34 per cent with the wastelands of 1.67 per cent. This region is suitable for various horticultural and plantation crops like areca nut, cashew nut and rubber. The villages under this Development Block are inhabited by Garo tribe with diverse cultural heritage and dialects. The Garos had a matrilineal system of inheritance and women enjoy greater equality than their counterparts in non-tribal society. Socially, the communities lag behind in critical areas such as literacy, healthcare and other basic minimum needs. On the economic front, major part of the labor is invested in agriculture particularly Jhum cultivation. Out of 167 villages, 4,309 households and 21,094 people, 38 villages were selected for the first phase of the project interventions covering 723 households and 4068 people. The project started operating in this Block in 2006. At present, the Block has divided into four clusters, viz., Rongchong, Wagebok, Ruga and Dasin.

With the background realities of the communities, the project strategy offered livelihood improvement activities for the communities as efficient incentives to mobilize the groups in the villages. The process started as an awareness campaign on the project concept and philosophy for the villagers with the principle of Self Help Group. The SHGs were offered an opportunity to enter the project by signing a social agreement with District Management Unit (DMU). In terms of reference, the Nokma (village chief and custodian of the land) signs a written provision declaring no objection to the program, and then only the project implementation process continues further. The efficient communication through participatory mode of action offered the communities an appropriate opportunity to improve and strengthen the sources of livelihood and skills up-gradation. The principles of savings and thrifts and at the same time capacity building trainings imparted were the dream schemes for the communities and the participatory approach adopted by the project was a new introduction for them.[18]

The constitution of India has made provisions for the upliftment of tribes throughout the country. 'Social order justice-social, economic and political: the weaker sections' these words occur in Part IV of the constitution under Directive Principles of the state policy specially Article 46 under 'Promotion of Education and Economic interests of Scheduled Casts and Scheduled Tribes' and other weaker sections. Social justice was seen as an instrument to transform our society into an egalitarian one. For without understanding the deeper underlying psychological factors it is not possible to help in an honest growth. Social reforms thrust on people without having a clear understanding of their psychic characteristic saps their vitality, thus the need is to focus scientific reform measures and education to help build individual who are responsive, self confident individuals who will contribute for the progress of community, nation and world. A clear understanding of pshyche of Garos has to be developed otherwise their case will not be different from those tribes which have perished or those which are on the verge of extinction. Progress in real terms can only be achieved by translating their dreams and aspirations into reality.

Notes

1. Tarunchandra Sinha, (1966): *Anthropological Survey of India*, Calcutta, pp. 1-2.
2. B.B. Dutta, (1984): "Modernization of a Tradition the Garo Dimension," in 222, L.S. Gassah, (ed.), Garo Hills Land & the People New Delhi: Omsons Publication.
3. Ibid.
4. Tarunchandra Sinha, (1966): *Anthropological Survey of India*, Calcutta, pp. 2-3.
5. History and Culture of the Garos, Milton Sangma, pp. 3-4.
6. B.B. Dutta, (1984): *Modernization of a Tradition the Garo Dimension*, in p. 222, L.S. Gassah, (ed.), *op.cit.*, Omsons Publications.
7. Ibid., p. 125.
8. Ibid., p. 126.
9. Ibid., p. 127.

10. Tarunchandra Sinha, (1966): *op. cit.*, p. 131.
11. Ibid., p. 26.
12. Ibid., p. 28.
13. Ibid., pp. 31-32.
14. Khan Ali Morshed, (2004): "Cheated out of their Own Land," *The Daily Star.net*.
15. Jhum A.G. Khan and J.V. Madhusudan, *Cultivation and Societal Status: An Enquiry of Garo Tribe Women in Meghalaya.*
16. Khan Ali Morshed, (2004): "Cheated out of their Own Land," *The Daily Star.net*.
17. A.C. Mehta, (undated, untitled paper on Educational development in North Eastern states of India).
18. *Overview—Livelihood Improvement Programs in South Garo Hills*, published on April 17, 2009, http:/google.com.

INDEX